CW00521954

VTune™ Performance Analyzer Essentials

Measurement and Tuning Techniques for Software Developers

James Reinders

**INTEL
PRESS**

Publisher: Richard Bowles
Editors: Phyllis Moore, David Clark
Managing Editor: David B. Spencer
Content Architect: Stuart Goldstein
Text Design & Composition: Wasser Studios, Inc.
Graphic Art: Wasser Studios, Inc. (illustrations), Ted Cyrek (cover)

Library of Congress Cataloging in Publication Data:

Printed in the United States of America

    10 9 8 7 6 5 4 3 2

First printing, March 2005

Contents

Chapter 6   Hotspot Hunting 103: Counter Monitor   173

Chapter 7   Automatic Hotspot Analysis   201

Preface

The Intel® VTune™ Performance Analyzer has become a favorite of software developers because of the insights they gain using this tool. Many developers cannot imagine going back to the days of stumbling in the dark without the data that the VTune analyzer can provide.

I have had the pleasure of visiting many VTune analyzer users over the years. Their feedback has pushed and inspired us at Intel to greater heights. For instance, we expanded the product to include Call Graph capabilities because we learned, along with our users, just how powerful Sampling and Call Graph can be together.

We are grateful for the feedback from our customers. They have shared how they think and have shown us what interfaces are the most intuitive. This advice has helped fuel a fundamental shift in the interface design to improve the ease of use of the VTune analyzer.

This book exists because users have asked me over and over for a book about the VTune analyzer. We frequently teach classes on how to use the tool, and after teaching these courses we get a great deal of encouragement to write a book covering what we have shared during the class and more. It took some time for me to realize that I would be the one to step forward and write the book.

It is not that the VTune analyzer is too hard to use. The book is needed because the VTune analyzer simply has so many features that users sometimes have difficulty deciding where to begin. In this book, I walk you through the many features of the VTune analyzer and share insights into why they are useful. Part I covers reasons for using the VTune analyzer, the basics of computer architecture, and key VTune analyzer concepts like projects and activities. These chapters prepare you for the rest of the book, and you can easily skim through them if the concepts are already familiar to you. Part II explains each of the four basic analysis methods employed by the VTune analyzer. Parts III and IV show ways to use or combine the four analysis methods for more advanced or specific needs.

Writing the book was made much easier because of the wealth of input we were able to obtain from the VTune analyzer documentation team. The built-in Help for the VTune analyzer is incredibly good, and represents an enormous body of information with details beyond the scope of this book. Also, the Intel Software College team contributed training material and experiences based on many years of VTune analyzer classroom instruction. I have many people to thank in the acknowledgements.

I have made every effort to produce a book useful for multiple VTune analyzer versions and releases. The actual VTune Performance Analyzer screenshots used in the book were taken using Version 7.1 for Windows[†], Version 2.0 for Linux[†], and the beta release of Version 3.0 for Linux in the Eclipse[†] Integrated Development Environment. New features in later versions of the analyzer make a compelling case to upgrade if you have not already done so. Once you register, Intel makes free downloadable updates available to you for a year after your purchase. For the very latest information on VTune products, visit Intel's Web site at http://www.intel.com/software/products.

It is my sincere hope that this book opens doors for you, and that you come to rely on the VTune analyzer as a valuable tool.

James Reinders
Product Evangelist and Director of Business Development
Software Products Division
Intel Corporation
January 2005

Acknowledgements

Many people deserve acknowledgement for their help and encouragement during the effort involved in putting this book together.

Everyone in the award-winning VTune™ analyzer documentation team is to be commended for the wonderful material they have created and graciously encouraged me to adopt for use as the basis of many parts of this book. Padma Neppalli helped me with information and sage advice on how to construct this book. Vanitha Shedden and Mohamad Ridha helped me to access and download the large quantities of material.

Many people on the VTune analyzer engineering, marketing, training, and support teams were very supportive with input, help, advice, and review. Reviewers of the book encouraged me to do more, in some cases making me wish that I had more pages to work with so that I could write on and on. I want to especially mention a few who went out of their way an extra amount: Paul Parenteau, Jack Donnell, Dave Anderson, Birju Shah, Israel Hirsh, Aaron Levinson, Eric Moore, Osnat Levi, Paul Cohen, and Robert Mueller. I appreciated input from James Rose for his advice on how to tune for the Pentium® M processor with the VTune analyzer. My deep appreciation for extra help from Gary Carleton along the way, and for many years before the book even started. And a special thank you to James Piechota of Alias, Daniel Staheli of Roxio, Ik S. Yoo of Morgan Stanley, and Malik S. Maxutov of Moscow State Geological Prospecting University for their thoughtful review and comments. They each had an effect on the book through their encouragements, which really make a difference.

I want to thank Bruce Bartlett who was the first one to basically drill into my head that, "It's all about the source code view, stupid." Bruce constructed the very first internal training class for the VTune analyzer, which really addressed the needs of new users in a comprehensive manner.

The folks at Intel Press have been most helpful; a special thanks to Stuart Goldstein and David Spencer for their support, encouragement and patience. I know that the many deadlines I bent or bruised, as I avoided writing in favor of flying to see customers, gave them reason for considerable doubt. They were nothing if not supportive and patient, with an underlying encouragement you just do not want to let down.

Most important has been the help of Phyllis Moore in adapting materials from many sources and providing constant review and feedback on my writing as well. Her talents have spelled the difference between merely having an idea for a book and having a book that actually exists.

Part I
Getting Started

Chapter 1

Fishing for Things to Tune

Give a man a fish and he will eat for a day.
Teach a man to fish and he will eat for a lifetime.

—Chinese Proverb

A user of the Intel® VTune™ Performance Analyzer once summed up the situation by telling me that the VTune analyzer "finds things in unexpected places." Many users have expressed this sentiment in various forms. Frequently they say, "I was sure that the VTune analyzer was wrong. I was going to send in a problem report, and then I realized the VTune analyzer was right—much to my surprise."

Users of the VTune analyzer are enthusiastic about this tool largely because of this remarkable capability. As complex as computer systems are today, with their vast array of applications and system software, it is no surprise when things happen that you cannot easily anticipate. When you seek to refine your computer system, the best place to start is with a tool that can find these hidden problems by giving you a comprehensive performance exam.

Measurements are the key to refinement. Put a different way, "Knowledge is power." The Intel VTune Performance Analyzer is a tool to make measurements. It also has wonderful features to help you understand those measurements, and it even advises you on what exceptional values may mean and what you can do about them. When you hear the word "VTune," think "measurements."

Typographical Conventions

When describing step-by-step procedures, this book displays commands, options, and icons in a distinguishing font (for example: **File → Open**) to guide the reader. New terms and events are indicated with italics (for example: *Clockticks*).

All Roads Lead to the Source

All roads lead to the source is the key concept I teach about the analyzer. No matter which analysis you perform, you will end up with data that lead you to source code.[1] This is the first thing you need to know about the analyzer.

The VTune analyzer offers several ways to analyze and summarize the activity of your system. As Figure 1.1 illustrates, you can choose any of a number of analysis methods. Whether you use Sampling, Call Graph, Counter Monitor, or Tuning Assistant, each method is a pathway. As you *drill down*, progressing through layers looking for an area of interest, you eventually arrive at the source code. The area of interest is usually a potential performance bottleneck that you want to examine.

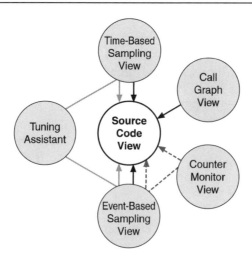

Figure 1.1   Each Form of Analysis Leads to Source Code View

---

[1] Of course, to show the source code, you need to have it on hand; otherwise, the analyzer displays assembly language, which it creates by disassembling the binary code you are analyzing.

When to Use the VTune™ Performance Analyzer

Some developers have the VTune analyzer in front of them every day, others pull it off the shelf when they feel a need.

A Development Cycle Approach

During the development cycle, you will find many opportunities to take advantage of the VTune analyzer's strengths. Use the analyzer:

- *For Big Changes.* When changing a program or system significantly such as during a major revision, or when porting an application to another platform, the VTune analyzer is your best ally.

- *Nightly.* Routinely throughout development, nightly runs of the VTune analyzer can help you track performance and identify any major changes.

- *For Tune-ups.* After writing the initial code, use the analyzer to gain more performance for an application or system.

A Performance-centric Approach

To take a performance-centric approach, use the analyzer when:

- *You must have more performance.* When your application or system is not meeting a performance goal, the VTune analyzer can give you much-needed information about where to prioritize your investigations in seeking a remedy.

- *You would like more performance.* Use the analyzer to examine your application or system from a performance perspective, so you can get a sense of whether "low-hanging fruit" can improve the performance of your product.

- *You do not want to lose performance.* As part of regular performance tracking of a project, the VTune analyzer can help you detect and correct regressions soon after they degrade the performance of your project. It is increasingly important to consider having performance tests as part of your nightly testing, instead of simply testing for correctness issues.

Some Case Histories

Here are a few cases where customers have shared their experiences with me about how they use the VTune analyzer.

An unexpected culprit. With interactive game speed less than desired, a game development team decided to run the VTune analyzer before cutting back the budgeted animation time to reduce CPU usage. The analyzer revealed that the bottleneck was not in the game application at all. Instead, it was lurking in a key graphics driver thought to be highly tuned. A trivial coding error was causing the graphics driver to consume 15 percent of the system time when it was expected to take less than 3 percent. After the customer fixed the graphics driver, the application ran as expected without the need to reduce the animation.

A weekly incentive. During development, one project team used the VTune analyzer to create weekly reports covering all the modules in an application and export them to a spreadsheet. The project leader then highlighted the most time-consuming module in a weekly e-mail message to the team. The prompt encouraged the lead engineer for that module to improve its performance during that week.

Analyzing a specific time period. An interactive program exhibited annoying delays during screen updates and in response to keyboard and mouse inputs. Using the VTune analyzer's Pause and Resume API feature to analyze only the time periods of poor updates, the developer found that some unnecessary operations were occurring during these critical times. After the developer made some slight adjustments, the program stopped its undesirable behavior.

Nightly regression testing. After careful tuning, a program development team was able to meet specific performance targets for operations. In order to avoid performance regressions, the nightly build included some automated runs of the VTune analyzer to collect key performance data. If certain performance measurements fell out of specification, the nightly testing marked that test as failing. This procedure allowed the team to address performance regressions within a day of the changes that caused them, just as many development teams try to catch any correctness regressions.

Optimizing a port. After porting a program from Microsoft Windows to the Linux operating system, a development team compared performance measurements to see differences in the behavior of the program. The analysis traced several big differences to questionable operating system calls under Linux. After incorporating better code specifically for Linux, the team achieved better performance.

Calling a better routine. The VTune analyzer revealed that a key byte-copy routine was consuming a large amount of time. The customer greatly improved performance by changing the code to call an optimized routine from the Intel Integrated Performance Primitives (Intel IPP).

Finding an I/O bottleneck. Tuning routine after routine for better performance did not seem to matter. After using the VTune analyzer's Counter Monitor to examine CPU utilization, the customer realized that the program was I/O-bound and that, even if the CPU were infinitely fast, key points in the program would stall waiting for I/O. Modifying the program to reduce I/O and do some threading greatly improved performance.[2]

Focusing on the right routines. A number of routines originally hand-tuned for use with the Intel 8088 processor seemed ready for rewriting 12 years later. Using the VTune analyzer revealed that only two routines really mattered to the performance of the program. As a result, the customer saved time and money by focusing the effort on just these two routines, instead of rewriting all of them.

Tracking misaligned data. One of the application's routines was taking an unreasonable amount of time, but it was not clear why. Additional investigation revealed that the routine was sometimes being called with misaligned data, which greatly slowed those particular calls. Using Call Graph analysis, the user found where the misaligned data were being created. A simple change improved performance in every area of the program that was using this data.

---

[2] See the section of this chapter "Learning to Fish: A Tuning Methodology" for suggestions on how to avoid tuning out of order, which can lead to this sort of problem.

How to Find Bottlenecks

You may ask, "How should I use the VTune analyzer to find performance opportunities?" Here is the short answer:

1. Come up with a goal, such as: "I want this program to run 20 percent faster," or "I want to eliminate the occasional annoying delays the user experiences in the user interface."

2. Observe what you can without the VTune analyzer.

3. Observe what you can with the VTune analyzer, using any of the analysis methods.

4. Think about what your observations mean. In other words, form a hypothesis.

5. Imagine a test for your hypothesis, especially a test whose results will guide you to make changes to reach your goal.

6. Conduct your test with Steps 2 and 3 in mind; observe what you can with and without the VTune analyzer.

7. Repeat as needed until you reach your performance goal.

Finding bottlenecks is just that simple. You fish for interesting observations that steer your opinion on what changes are required for progress. Without these observations, you could still make guesses and try them out. Using the VTune analyzer, however, greatly increases your odds of making the right guesses by improving what you can see and how well you can see it.

The VTune analyzer expands your observations *and* what you are able to test. The tool incorporates sophisticated features to help you complete your analysis: features like timing, call graphs created dynamically during your testing, measurements from internal counters built into Intel processors, extensive documentation, and built-in expert advice.

What Expertise Is Required?

Naturally, your knowledge of computer systems and applications affects what you can do with the VTune analyzer. Novices and experts alike, however, regularly use the analyzer effectively. No matter what your expertise, the analyzer can steer you to focus your time on those areas most likely to be of benefit.

The Intel VTune Performance Analyzer is a tool that makes inquiries possible, and inquiry is always the first and most important step. You simply cannot make good decisions based on bad data. The VTune analyzer gives you good data; you only need to ask. To a lesser extent, the analyzer tries to tell you what your observations mean and what you may want to do about them.

When analyzing a system and the programs that run on it, learn to rely on *observations*, *expertise*, and *specifications*. Keep these points in mind:

■ Increase what you can *observe* and your confidence in those observations by using the VTune analyzer.

■ Your *expertise* in tuning grows with experience. Use the VTune analyzer's advice, documentation, and this book to help grow your experiences.

■ Know your *specifications*. What do you expect from the system you are tuning? What is realistic? What is required? Conduct experiments aimed at changing the performance to meet your goals knowing the before-and-after measurements.

Without observations, you are simply tuning in the dark. You can see only so much yourself. The VTune analyzer serves as a flashlight to help light your path. You can point the flashlight where you want, and your decisions on where to shine it will shape what you observe—as Figure 1.2 illustrates.

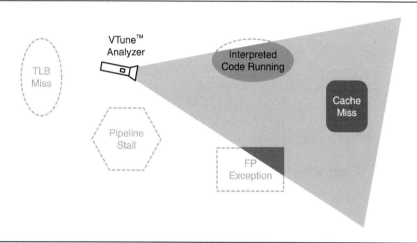

Figure 1.2   Avoiding the Perils of Tuning in the Dark

Chapter 2 reviews some basic computer architecture to give you all the expertise you really need to use the analyzer effectively. But first, here are a few vital points about methodology.

Learning to Fish: A Tuning Methodology

Learning to fish means discovering the basics about how to choose the right equipment and bait, how to cast, and some likely places where fish tend to hang out. Learning to tune a program is similar; you start with the basics.

A few early readers of this book, like many who take our classes, have made remarks like "a methodology is fine for others, but I can skip ahead." With all due respect, I would encourage everyone to take a complete approach to tuning. It is the unexpected find that usually yields a disproportionately big boost with a small effort. You will not find where you do not hunt. Recall that the highest praise for the VTune analyzer is that it finds things in unexpected places.

Different Fishing Rods and Bait

The VTune analyzer includes four basic views, each of which builds on different technologies. The chapters in Part II of this book cover each type of analysis in detail, with examples and other information. They are: Sampling, Call Graph analysis, Counter Monitors, and Tuning Assistant. After you become familiar with each, you can formulate your own ideas about when to use them.

Users of the VTune analyzer are no different from anglers who espouse a favorite fishing method. Some believe you should always fish with Sampling first; others are much more comfortable with Call Graph analysis. Still others decide that you should always start with the Tuning Assistant, letting the computer do the work for you. Whatever method you choose first to analyze the code that runs on your system, you are on your way to finding the critical parts that you need to study. When in doubt, try one out and see what you can catch.

No Matter What Gear You Choose, You Need a Method

Part II of this book walks you through the VTune analyzer's particular analysis techniques. Before jumping into that type of detail, you may wish to consider an overall tuning methodology that can help you to formulate an approach. This methodology urges you to begin at the system level and work down to the computer architecture level. You can use the VTune Performance Analyzer to implement this tuning methodology, which usually realizes the fastest speedup in the shortest amount of time for your target platform. Keep in mind that, regardless of your specific tuning goals, you should conduct analysis level-by-level, from high to low level, in the following order:

1. System-level tuning
2. Application-level tuning
3. Computer architecture-level tuning

Fishing Lesson #1: Conduct Your Analysis in Top-to-Bottom Order

Start tuning at the system level to ensure you have no system-level bottlenecks. If you were to start with computer architecture tuning, but the processor was only in use 10 percent of the time because of system-level bottlenecks, a 50-percent speedup at the computer architecture level would only achieve a 5-percent workload speedup, since the processor would only be in use 10 percent of the time during the workload. Starting your tuning at the highest level ensures that you tune efficiently.

Once you ensure that the processor is being used efficiently, focus on application bottlenecks, followed by computer architecture bottlenecks. System tuning generally yields greater speedups than application tuning, which in turn usually yields greater speedups than computer architecture tuning.

Fishing Lesson #2: Higher Levels Yield Greater Speedups

As a general rule, given the same time investment, you achieve greater speedups at a higher level than a lower level. Performance analysts at Intel have tuned hundreds of applications. Their experience indicates that speedups are very common in the:

■ 3× range when performing system-level tuning;

■ 2× range when performing application-level tuning;

■ 1.1 to 1.5× ranges when performing computer architecture-level tuning.

Though system-level tuning achieves the greatest speedup, most application developers mistakenly believe they have little control over system bottlenecks. It turns out that several kinds of system-level optimizations usually improve overall application performance. For example:

■ You might be overusing partial writes on the system bus, causing a system bus bottleneck that, in turn, starves the processor.

■ Your application might be reading memory in bytes instead of double or quad words that yield faster reads.

Table 1.1 shows some goals and areas to investigate at each level of tuning.

Table 1.1   Tuning Goals and Areas to Investigate

Order	Tuning Level	Goals	Key Areas to Investigate	Estimated Potential Speedup
1	High: System level	Speed up the application by improving how it interacts with the system	Network Problems Disk Performance Memory Usage	3×
2	Medium: Application level	Speed up the application by improving its algorithms	Locks Heap contention Threading Algorithm API Usage	2×
3	Low: Computer architecture level	Speed up the application by improving how it runs on the processor	Architecture Coding Pitfalls Data/Code Locality (Cache) Data Alignment	1.1–1.5×

Decide What to Catch: Your Tuning Goals

Deciding on your goals is the starting point for any tuning or fishing expedition, as shown in Figure 1.3. Once your goals are clear, you can follow the methodologies provided here to achieve the best speedup in the shortest amount of time on your targeted Intel processor(s).

Fishing Lesson #3: Set Some Goals

When you are fishing, your goal might be to catch a 6-pound bass on Lake Fork, or to catch a 20-pound salmon from the Columbia River. When you are tuning software, your goals should be equally specific. Decide on your goals, including your target processors. For example, if your goal is to tune your application for the Intel Pentium® 4 processor, with and without Hyper-Threading Technology, knowing which target configuration to tune for first matters greatly and can make a significant difference in how quickly you achieve your speedup goals.

If you are aware of the latest trends in processor technologies and prepare your code for potential future innovations, you can reduce the time needed for making additional architecture changes to your software to take advantage of these new technologies. For instance, the latest Hyper-Threading Technology appears to be paving the way for a future where desktop processors support multitasking and multithreaded applications. You should consider this trend to get the most out of your next generation of software products.

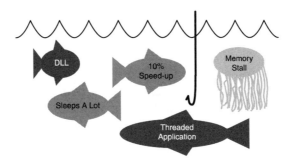

Figure 1.3   Do You Know What You Want to Catch or Are You Just Fishing?

Many new users of the VTune analyzer mistakenly use the tool before creating a good *benchmark*. A benchmark gives you a way to measure the performance of the code you are trying to optimize. If you do not have such a benchmark, the data you collect with the VTune analyzer will not be very useful for performance tuning.

Fishing Lesson #4: Create a Good Benchmark

Before you even run the VTune analyzer, create and run a good benchmark. A good benchmark is measurable, repeatable, and should model a common-use case for the software you are optimizing. Some examples of metrics that you can use to characterize software performance are execution time, frames per second, or transactions per second. A good benchmark is specific. For example, the benchmark for an application might be the amount of time that it takes to calculate a 4096×4096 pixel image, which initially takes 19.95 milliseconds on this particular system.

After creating a benchmark, run it to measure the performance of your software. This will be your program's *baseline performance*. Then use the VTune analyzer to identify performance bottlenecks. Once you have identified a bottleneck, make a code change, and then rerun the benchmark to see if the performance of your software has improved. Keep repeating this process until you reach your performance goals. Knowing where you start and where you hope to go will allow you to judge the value of your work.

System-level Tuning

The goal of system-level tuning is to optimize system resource utilization and to speed up your application by improving how it interacts with the system. System-level tuning usually gives the greatest speedup with the least amount of effort, making it the right place to start. It is especially relevant for I/O-intensive applications such as those that are disk-intensive or network-intensive. However, if you know that your application is very processor-intensive (and not I/O-intensive), you may want to skip system-level tuning and move directly to application-level tuning.

Checking Your Application's Processor Usage

On Windows 2000 or Windows XP systems, you can use the operating system's built-in Performance Monitoring capability (**Task Manager →** **Performance** Tab) to gain a high-level look at processor usage, as shown on the left side of Figure 1.4. On Linux systems, the KDE System Guard's System Load Tab provides much the same functionality in a graphical form as well, as shown on the right side of Figure 1.4. Many Linux users prefer the pure text top command, which achieves the same purpose in a more linear fashion.

The VTune analyzer can show you this information as well. While your application is running, you can use the VTune analyzer's Counter Monitor data collector to check the processor object's *% Processor Time* counter (see Chapter 6). Figure 1.5 shows a Counter Monitor graph where processor and disk usage are synchronous, so that when one increases dramatically, the other takes a dive.

Regardless of the tool you use, you want to know if your CPU is maxed out with work or just sitting around waiting for something to do.

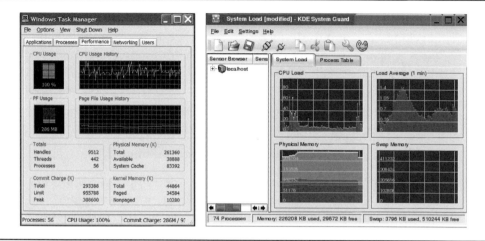

Figure 1.4 Monitoring CPU Usage on Windows and Linux Systems

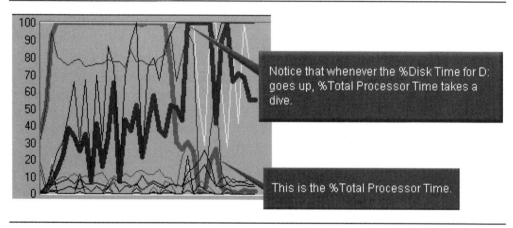

Figure 1.5 A Counter Monitor Graph Showing Processor Usage

Fishing Lesson #5: Check Processor Usage

Checking your application's processor usage helps you understand how much speedup to expect from application or computer architecture-level tuning. This can help determine whether your application is processor-intensive, I/O-intensive, or somewhere in-between. If processor usage is:

■ *Low*, then your application has many system bottlenecks (network, disk, memory usage, and so on).

■ *High*, then your application is processor-intensive.

System- and application-level tuning can specd up your application by balancing I/O and computation, thus raising processor usage. Application- and computer architecture-level tuning can speed up your application by allowing it to accomplish the same amount of useful work using less or more efficient computation, thus lowering processor usage.

After some amount of system- or application-level tuning increases processor usage, you may find your application is ready for computer architecture-level tuning. Conversely, after some amount of application- or computer architecture-level tuning decreases processor usage, you may find you are ready for more system-level tuning.

If processor usage is high, computer architecture-level tuning has the potential for a 1.1 to 1.5× application speedup. Lower levels of processor utilization indicate a lower level of potential speedup through computer architecture-level tuning.

Using the Counter Monitor

Here are some suggested steps for performing system-level tuning using the Counter Monitor:

1. Use the Counter Monitor wizard to create an activity with the Counter Monitor data collector as described in Chapter 6. The Counter Monitor tracks a default set of OS counters over a period of time. These counters provide insights into the overall performance of your system, help you determine system resource usage, and help you identify system-level bottlenecks.

2. Interpret the counter data using Counter Monitor views to locate system-level performance bottlenecks and opportunities for improving the way your application interacts with the system.

3. On supported systems,[3] zoom in to the time range of interest, then use the Intel Tuning Assistant feature as described in Chapter 7 to obtain relevant insights and advice related to system-level tuning.

Note	Counter Monitor data and its associated Tuning Assistant advice can vary depending on the system configuration of the test system. Be careful not to optimize your application for a particular system configuration that does not represent the system that will be used by the majority of your end-users.

Types of System-Level Optimizations

You can perform system-level optimization in two ways:

- Changing the application so that it matches the system better

- Changing the system configuration so that the system matches the application better

If you have complete control over the configuration of the target system on which your application will run, both optimization types are equally relevant. If you have less control over the end user's system configuration, choose test system configurations that represent the range of systems on which your application will run, and then focus more on optimizations that affect your application and less on optimizations that affect system configurations.

Once you have resolved system-level performance issues or have determined that no significant ones exist, move on to the next tuning level: application-level tuning.

Application-level Tuning

The goal of application-level tuning is to speed up the application by improving its algorithms, threading implementation, and/or use of APIs or primitives. You can identify code regions that have a high impact on application performance using the Sampling and/or the Call Graph data collectors.

You always want to perform this level of tuning, if you can, before diving into computer architecture tuning. However, certain microarchitectural concerns have a huge impact on application-level tuning. This

---

[3] The Tuning Assistant supports advice for Counter Monitor data only on Windows NT[†] 4.0, Windows 2000, and Windows XP systems.

book assumes you understand these concerns and "do the right thing" at this level. In reality, none of us gets this right the first time every time. Try to be aware of what you do and do not know about your algorithm's effect on microarchitectural issues. For example:

- Use regular strides through memory instead of random walks through memory as much as possible in any memory-intensive algorithm.

- Design your application to consume memory in whole blocks, instead of grouping both used and unused items together in memory.

Using Sampling

Here are some suggested steps for performing application-level tuning using Sampling:

1. Use the Quick Performance Analysis wizard to create an activity with the Sampling data collector as described in Chapter 4. For application-level tuning, generally you only need to monitor the *Clockticks* event.

2. After sampling, start at a high level by selecting all processes and/or modules that you are interested in tuning.

3. Use the VTune analyzer's Tuning Assistant feature to obtain tuning advice. The Tuning Assistant can automatically help you find high-impact code regions. Code regions appearing towards the top of the report are more heavily used. Focus on these regions for application-level tuning, even if the listing shows few problems.

   In each code region, the Tuning Assistant lists the computer architecture problems it found. These problems often suggest application-level changes because of issues such as "branchy" code or data structures that are too large to fit into cache. You might, for example, need to modify data structures or algorithms to make them more efficient.

Using the Call Graph

Here are some suggested steps for performing application-level tuning using the Call Graph:

1. Use the Quick Performance Analysis wizard to create an activity with the Call Graph data collector as described in Chapter 5.

2. Analyze data in the Call Graph view to determine your program flow and identify the most time-consuming function calls and call-sequences.

3. Select high-impact code regions identified in the Call Graph views. Double-click to see the Source view for those regions and look for algorithmic improvements that could speed up your application.

Once you have resolved application-level performance issues or have determined that no significant ones exist, move on to the next tuning level: computer architecture-level tuning.

Computer Architecture-level Tuning

The goal of computer architecture-level tuning is to speed up performance by improving how the application runs on the processor. This type of tuning is especially relevant for processor-intensive applications. If you know that your application is very I/O-intensive (for example, disk-intensive or network-intensive) and not very processor-intensive, be especially sure you have used system-level and application-level tuning to improve processor usage before trying computer architecture-level tuning.

Computer architecture-level tuning follows this general methodology:

1. Find the most time-consuming code regions that have a high impact on application performance.

2. Analyze the execution of those code regions on the target Intel architecture.

3. Identify computer architecture-level performance problems.

4. Determine how to avoid them to improve performance.

Recap

Here are the major points covered in this chapter:

- Use the VTune analyzer to improve your observations—a critical aspect of fishing for tuning opportunities.

- VTune offers four primary analysis methods and views: Sampling, Call Graph, Counter Monitor, and Tuning Assistant; all four lead you to the source code to examine it for possible improvement.

- A methodology for tuning that has proven very useful can be summed up in five fishing lessons:

  - Fishing Lesson 1: Conduct your analysis in top-to-bottom order. Start tuning at the system level to ensure you have no system-level bottlenecks.

  - Fishing Lesson 2: As a general rule, for the same time investment, you achieve greater speedups at a higher level than a lower level.

  - Fishing Lesson 3: Decide on your goals, including your target processors. Unless you know what you want to catch, you are just "fishing."

  - Fishing Lesson 4: Before you tune, create and run a good benchmark. This will represent your program's baseline performance.

  - Fishing Lesson 5: Check processor usage. This can help you determine whether your application is currently processor-intensive, I/O-intensive, or somewhere in between.

Chapter 2

Computer and Application Architecture Basics

No architecture is so haughty as that which is simple.

—John Ruskin

Successful application tuning requires a fundamental understanding of computer architecture. Much as mechanics need to know something about an engine's working principles even if they never design an engine, users of the VTune™ Performance Analyzer should understand the working principles of a computer.

This chapter is a whirlwind tour of key concepts in computer architecture as they pertain to application tuning. It also touches on the related concepts of threading and parallelism, because these concepts are so tightly linked with computer architecture.

Users of the VTune analyzer need not have a comprehensive education in computer architecture; however, a working knowledge of the high-level structure of a computer is valuable. As computers become more and more complex, their basic structure remains quite simple at a high level. This chapter only addresses the high level. Many books about the inner workings of the computer are available should you want to learn more.

If you are well versed in computer architecture and related concepts of parallelism and threading, I highly recommend that you skip this chapter and jump to Chapter 3.

Computer Architecture in a Nutshell

Computers are pretty simple, although they look more and more complex over time because of the many enhancements here and there aimed at improving them. Figure 2.1 illustrates a typical computer in its simplest form.

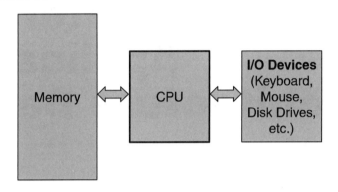

Figure 2.1   Computer Architecture

At the heart of a computer is a *central processing unit (CPU)*. The CPU communicates with the rest of the universe via *input and output (I/O)*. What a CPU can communicate with is limited only by your imagination. One of the most important things with which a CPU can communicate is a scratch pad known as *memory* or the *memory subsystem*. Memory is such an important I/O device that today's computer architects seldom speak about memory as I/O. Memory is "special" because a typical CPU spends most of its time shuffling numbers in and out of this area. Consequently, memory I/O is a realm where a great deal of performance tuning can take place, by limiting the amount of shuffling that occurs.

The Clock

To maintain order inside a computer, a *clock* is used as the basis for synchronizing activity timing. Think of the clock as a "drum beat" for the operation of the computer. On a given "drum beat," a CPU performs some operations, and reads in and writes out data for consumption by the *I/O systems*—meaning mostly the memory subsystem. Thinking of everything inside a computer as happening on a clocked basis is a fundamental concept in computer design known as *synchronous design*.

Among the most common things examined with the VTune analyzer are *clockticks,* sometimes called *clocks* for short, which are little more than a way of thinking about the passage of time.

Caches

The internals of the CPU and of the memory subsystem are important to understand for detailed tuning. The connection between the CPU and memory can be direct, but seldom is, because of the larger discrepancy between the speed of a CPU and the speed of memory. Making all of memory as fast as a CPU would simply prove too expensive for computers to be affordable for most uses. Instead, designers make small amounts of memory, known as *caches*, as fast as the processor, while the main memory is of the more affordable and slower variety. Information is moved in and out of caches as needed, thereby adding to the number of places where data are shuffled on the journey between memory and the CPU.

Modern CPUs are so hungry for data that they often want several items at the same time. Solving this need requires the caches to have multiple paths in and out to access data. Such a cache design is called *multiported*. In the earliest days, CPUs read or wrote only one location in memory at a time. Modern CPUs are ready to read and write multiple locations at the exact same time. Modern cache architecture allows for this by complex designs that deal with all the implications of such *parallelism*. More than anything, this extra complexity, rather than a simple need for speed, makes caches far more expensive than main memory. Simply wiring a multiported cache together with the CPU is a challenge because of the large amount of data consumed at one time. The amount of data that can be moved at one time is referred to as a measurement of *bandwidth*.

Virtually all computers use caches only for a temporary copy of data that should eventually reside in memory. Therefore, the function of a memory subsystem is to move data needed as input by the CPU to caches near to that CPU, and to move data produced by the CPU out to the memory. CPUs are designed to read and write data to their closest cache. The closest cache to the CPU is known as *level-one cache* and is designated *L1 cache*. Following outward from the processor, most computers have *L2 cache*, and *L3 caches* are very common as well.

The number of caches is likely to increase as the increase in processor performance continues to grow faster than memory performance. This growth is because caches are critical in helping with the mismatch in memory versus processor speed. Figure 2.2 illustrates a simple computer expanded with L1, L2, and L3 caches. Notice that the design splits the flow of instructions and data when it arrives at the level-one caches. Since CPUs usually request instructions and data differently, the computer designer finds that *split caches* offer opportunities for specialized optimization in the design. CPUs typically request some instructions in virtually every clock, and data in most clocks as well. Separating the caching of instructions and data simply reduces the peak bandwidth demand on each cache.

The design illustrated here leaves the level-two caches as combined caches, meaning that instructions and data compete for the same limited cache space. This is a common design, which can be summed up by saying that design incorporates separate *instruction* and *data L1 caches* and a *unified L2 cache*.

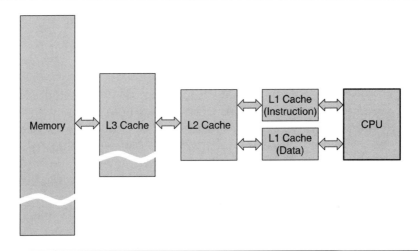

Figure 2.2   Modern Computer Memory and Cache Hierarchy.

Caches have been an intense area of focus for computer architects for many years. Consequently, many techniques have evolved and caches have a terminology of their own. To conclude our overview of the CPU-memory connection, here is a glossary of additional concepts that you will encounter when discussing caches.

Cache Coherency

Since caches are used to hold a local copy of data, the memory often does not have the current data that belong there, because the cache may have a newer value that has yet to make it back to memory. As a result, the computer must satisfy any request for the data with the value from the cache rather than with the stale version in memory. This process becomes particularly complex on systems with multiple CPUs, where each CPU makes requests to main memory. Today, almost everyone can simply take *cache coherency* for granted, and expect that the computer designers make it all work like magic.

Cache Line

Data move between memory and caches in *cache lines*, which are larger than any of the fundamental data types such as bits, bytes, integers, and floating-point numbers. Computer architects know that when the CPU accesses data, it is highly likely to request the data next in memory within a short period of time. This is especially true for instructions that make up a program, but is also highly likely for data as well. Because computer architects design the memories and caches to move more data than the CPU requested, the system is often preloading the cache with data that has yet to be requested. This increases the number of cache hits.

Having data that are not aligned to natural boundaries, such as a 32-bit integer with an address of 0x01000005 that is not divisible by 4, leads to delays for multiple reasons. One of the worst delays occurs frequently when the data span more than a cache line, and therefore requires two fetches from memory/cache, whereas one fetch always suffices for a well-aligned data item. The analyzer offers several counters to help find misaligned data accesses that affect the performance of your system or application.

Cache Hit or Miss

When a CPU requests memory from the L1 cache and the L1 cache has that data in cache, the L1 cache returns it immediately for the CPU to use. This is known as a *cache hit*, since the requested data were found immediately. Likewise, an *L2 cache hit* refers to a request from the L1 cache that is satisfied by data in the L2 cache. When data are not available in the cache for immediate return, a *cache miss* takes place. Cache misses are inevitable but undesirable, because enough of them will slow or stall the ability of the CPU to get work done. At one time, developers considered every cache miss as bad when tuning, because the CPU stalled or waited for every cache miss. Modern CPUs have so much work to perform that cache misses can be tolerated in moderate quantities without significant performance penalties. This seeming contradiction just makes the job of performance tuning a little more exciting. Unfortunately, most current performance issues are like that. Even though the VTune analyzer helps you find out that a cache miss is happening, you still need to figure out if it matters. Most tuning is done on the assumption that it does matter, and this tactic is usually successful.

When a cache miss happens, the CPU generally consults the next level of cache for the data. Since each level of cache is larger, each level helps avoid the long time delay involved for the data request to go all the way to memory.

Dirty Cache

Writing data to memory starts with dumping data to the first level of cache. Once the CPU writes into a cache line, that line is said to be *dirty*. Dirty cache lines need to be maintained until the data make it out to the next level of cache, and then eventually to main memory. This scenario is in contrast to data that are not dirty and can be replaced in the cache with more urgently needed data, without any need to copy it back to memory.

When writing data to a cache, if the computer has no room to write that is not already dirty, the equivalent of a cache miss occurs, because the write cannot complete until some data are moved out to make room.

Multi-Way Caches Such As 8-Way Cache

Because computers use caches to hold a local copy of data, the problem of where to put data in the cache arises, since caches are smaller than memory. This notion involves the concept of *mapping* from memory to any given level of caching. *Fully associative caches* allow any given item from memory to go anywhere in the cache desired. This flexibility is wonderful, because it allows maximum use of the cache. This flexibility is also terrible, because when you want a certain piece of data, you have to check every spot in the cache. This flexibility is terrible, too, because it adds considerably to the complexity of a multiported cache.

The opposite of a fully associative cache is a *direct-mapped cache*, which maps any given location in memory to exactly one location in cache. This kind of cache is the simplest to implement, and therefore easiest to design as a fast solution. Unfortunately, this approach leads to the nasty possibility of *cache collision*, where two urgently needed items of data are both mapped to one location in cache. What happens in such a case is known as *cache thrashing* because of the senseless shuffling of data to and from memory, since the cache cannot hold both items at the same time on account of the cache policies.

The solution to these two extremes is a compromise known as *partially associative caches*, which are neither fully associative nor direct-mapped. Computer architects measure the compromise in terms of how many spots in cache exist for any single memory location. Direct-mapped caches are really just 1-way *set associative caches*, because every memory location has only one spot allowed for it in the cache. Most caches are 2-way or 4-way, although newer designs use 8-way and 16-way caches for L1 caches. As caches increase in size, the level of *set-associativity* must also increase to prevent underutilization of the caches.

Replacement Policies Such As LRU

For anything other than direct-mapped caches, when a computer loads new data into a cache, it must choose what data to replace. The best method would be to replace the data not needed for the longest time. Since this method is not possible, most designers settle for a method known as *least recently used (LRU)*. This solution is an approximation based on the common temporal properties of data usage.

Implementing LRU for a 2-way cache was a simple matter. Most caches with more than two sets implement an approximation to LRU.

Virtually all performance tuning assumes that caches replace data using LRU, and any deviation from this policy is a detail of interest only to computer architects.

Memory Management, Addressing, and TLBs

Coding a program to run in just one place in memory is undesirable and unnecessary. The solution to this problem occurs in a part of a computer's design called *memory management*, through the concept of *virtual addresses* and *physical addresses*. Programs work in terms of virtual addresses; this simplifies memory management but also allows the *operating system* to be in full control of what physical memory each application can access. Without memory management, every program could access the memory of every other program. The problems with such access would range from annoying computer crashes to the ability of one user's program to steal information from another's. With issues this great, virtually every computer has some form of memory management.

The hardware maps virtual addresses into the physical addresses necessary to access memory. This process of mapping relies on operating system information stored in *page tables*. Since page tables reside in memory, they have their own simple caching system for the information needed to translate virtual memory addresses into physical memory addresses. These caches are so small they are called *buffers*. The full name for these buffers is *translation look-aside buffers*, or TLB for short.

For programs that use large amounts of memory, minimizing the thrash in the TLB is important. This issue is enough of a bother that CPU designers have worked to make TLBs larger and larger to avoid having this kind of thrash become a common problem. Despite these efforts, tuning memory-intensive programs can still involve measuring *TLB misses* and working to reduce them.

Inside the CPU

The *central processing unit* is responsible for manipulating data. To do so, a CPU consists of several parts that perform the functions needed by a processor. Figure 2.3 illustrates the various processing components of a simple computer, including caches and memory. All these components can exist on a single piece of silicon known as a *die*, or coexist broken up into many discrete parts. When processors were made up of many chips, engineers could analyze the behavior of individual parts, such as a *multiplier unit*, by attaching an oscilloscope. Today many special devices have come along to analyze the *bus traffic* going from the processor to caches or memory. The trend to put more and more elements on a single die makes the oscilloscope route impractical if not plain impossible in many cases. The VTune analyzer is the modern answer to the oscilloscope, for levels of analysis needed by today's programmers.

In computer design, the *control unit* is responsible for orchestrating the many activities of the processor, from fetching memory to multiplying numbers. Other individual units such as *memory read/write* and *arithmetic units* perform their specialized functions when the control unit requests them. A *register file* is a high-speed multiport temporary storage place for intermediate values. The control unit derives its actions from a stream of *instructions*, and directs other units to operate on data from the register files and memory via the caches.

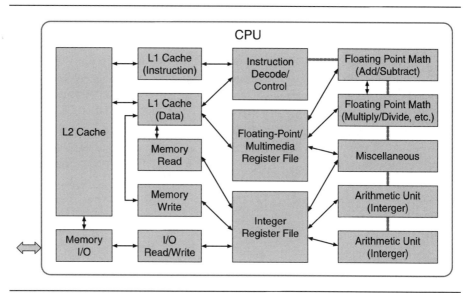

Figure 2.3   A Simplified Look Inside a Modern Computer

Any computer design has bottlenecks. Running into such bottlenecks generally has a negative performance impact; not running into any bottlenecks can indicate underutilization of your system's full power. Either way, studying system usage and points of bottleneck can give you insights into ways to improve your program.

Processor Differences That Matter

Processors from Intel cover a wide spectrum of uses, from battery-powered devices such as cell phones and PDAs, all the way up to clusters of high-powered server processors. Intel offers five major families of processors, with many variations within each. Intel calls them Intel® Personal Internet Client Architecture (Intel® PCA), Celeron®, Pentium®, Intel Xeon™, and Itanium® processor families. Architecturally, these five families have their origins in four architectures: Intel XScale® microarchitecture, P6 microarchitecture, Intel NetBurst® microarchitecture, and Explicitly Parallel Instruction Computing (EPIC) architecture. The biggest differences by far are between architectures, with only minor variations for processors based on the same architecture. Even with these differences, most concepts such as cache misses, cycles executed, memory accesses, and so forth are roughly the same across all architectures.

Intel XScale® Technology

Intel processors such as PXA255, PXA263, and IXP425 with Intel XScale technology are low-powered processors for embedded devices like cell phones, handheld computers, and storage controllers. These processors have the simplest control units of all Intel's architectures and therefore the fewest performance counters. The processors are very similar as a whole but vary in their microarchitecture. For instance, newer processors feature Intel Wireless MMX™ technology, and some have a signal-processing component. To eliminate CPU bottlenecks on this platform, try using Intel Wireless MMX technology and Intel compilers. For help with memory bottlenecks, try using Intel compilers or reorganizing your program.

P6 Microarchitecture

Introduced in 1995, P6 is Intel's oldest microarchitecture still in production. It is also the architecture with the largest installed base (Pentium Pro, Pentium II, Pentium III, some Celeron versions, and Pentium III Xeon processors), making it a very important target to consider for your software. The CPU has a very complex control unit that specializes in reordering incoming instructions to maximize processor utilization, using a feature called *dynamic execution*. All processors built on this architecture support MMX technology, and later versions support Streaming SIMD Extensions (SSE). For CPU bottlenecks, try using the Intel compilers, and if you can, modify your program to use MMX technology and SSE instructions. For memory bottlenecks, try using Intel compilers or reorganizing your program.

Intel NetBurst® Microarchitecture

This Intel replacement for P6 microarchitecture debuted with the Pentium 4 processor. All processors based on Netburst architecture include support for Streaming SIMD Extensions 2 (SSE2). Later versions of the Celeron, Pentium M, and Intel Xeon processors also use this architecture. Key features added in later versions of processors with Intel NetBurst microarchitecture include Hyper-Threading Technology (HT Technology) and Intel Extended Memory 64 Technology (Intel EM64T). The Intel Xeon processor features very large caches, often including up to three levels of caches in the processor. In general, you should not consider the Celeron processor, which is more affordable but encounters more bottlenecks, as a distinct target for performance optimizations. Optimizing for the Pentium 4 processor is the best approach, since this target is close enough technically and systems with Celeron processors are not the first choice of performance-oriented buyers. For CPU bottlenecks, try using the Intel compilers, and if you can, modify your program to use MMX technology and SSE/SSE2 instructions. For CPU bottlenecks, coding for HT Technology can be very effective. For memory bottlenecks, try using Intel compilers or reorganizing the program.

EPIC Technology

Intel has released two microarchitectures based on EPIC technology: the Itanium and Itanium 2 processor microarchitectures. You can think of EPIC technology as an architecture in itself. EPIC is radically different from any other architectural design, in that Intel specifically designed it for programming by highly sophisticated compilers. Even with such a major shift in emphasis, the basic Itanium and Itanium 2 processor structure, from a performance-tuning standpoint, remains the same. Most fundamental to this processor is the notion that the actual program code, as produced by the compiler, explicitly uses parallelism and speculation. Because they make better use of compilers, Itanium processors have been *in-order* machines. (They have no dynamic execution.) However, since these processors do not rearrange instructions while executing them, the compiler does so extensively. Consequently, performance tuning on such a machine becomes an easier task at the instruction level, but understanding the instructions laid out by the compiler can be more challenging. For CPU bottlenecks, try Intel compilers. For memory bottlenecks, try Intel compilers or reorganizing the program.

Recurring Themes When Tuning Software

Even though the specifics of the processor architecture may vary, the VTune analyzer lets you think of them in similar fashion. In Chapter 4 on Sampling, you will see screens with various event registers that differ based on the processor being used for your tuning work. When tuning, you should first consider the highest-level issues, such as cache activity and CPU utilization, which affect all processors. Later, your tuning may lead you into dealing with other elements unique to a particular processor, such as stalls and others ways to look at bottlenecks.

Characteristics not mentioned here, such as cache line size, latency-to-memory, and the penalties for misaligned data, differ from processor to processor. Instead of trying to enumerate these differences and consider them for tuning, you should sample various events with the VTune analyzer, paying attention to those that also correlate with the passage of time in *clockticks*.

Threading and Hyper-Threading Technology (HT Technology)

If one processor is good, two must be better. Once you have more than one processor, you can either run different applications at the same time, or run one application on multiple processors. Running an application on multiple processors requires multiple *threads* of execution. In a sense, your application goes from stepping through instructions based on a single pointer, to stepping though one instruction based on more than one pointer at the same time.

This concept is easy to imagine when you have multiple processors, because each processor is doing its own work, stepping through instructions—in other words, running applications. Such *thread-level parallelism in a multiprocessor configuration* allows operations to truly happen in parallel, thereby giving a performance boost. However, a single processor can also execute multiple threads by having an operating system frequently switch between executing threads. Most operating systems support such multitasking. The *thread-level parallelism in a single processor multitasking configuration* does not allow operations to truly happen in parallel; therefore, performance gains are limited. Nevertheless, this limited form of parallelism yields some benefit by doing useful work in one application while another is stalled, perhaps, waiting on an I/O operation such as writing to a disk.

In between the idea of multiple processors and the concept of multitasking on a single processor lies an Intel hardware solution called *Hyper-Threading Technology*. This technology enables multithreaded applications to execute threads in parallel on a single processor. Since a processor with Hyper-Threading Technology appears to the operating system and applications as multiple processors, Intel refers to this arrangement as multiple *logical processors* on a single *physical processor*. Multiple threads truly execute in parallel, yet they share the power of a single processor such as the one illustrated in Figure 2.3. Thus, Hyper-Threading Technology provides thread-level parallelism on each processor, resulting in increased use of processor execution resources, and giving greater performance on a single processor than multitasking would yield. Each processor on a multiprocessor system can and frequently does have Hyper-Threading Technology.[1]

The VTune analyzer can help you look at the combined or separate thread activities in an application or on the system as a whole.

Dynamic Libraries

Applications are commonly not monolithic executable images. Instead, they make use of common libraries, often created by other developers frequently from outside the company writing the application. As such, source code is not always available, making it impossible in many cases to measure the performance tradeoffs involved in different approaches to library usage.

The VTune analyzer can analyze a program, even if you do not have the source code. Call Graph and Sampling still work in such scenarios. The amount of information about the original source, such as symbol names, is limited, depending on what data the supplier left behind in the binaries. In cases where no high-level source code is available, the VTune analyzer's source code views display disassembled machine code instead.

What Lies Ahead

In the future, computer systems will emerge with faster processors, larger caches, more memory, more chip-level parallelism through additional functional units, and more processors. More processors can come in the form of logical processors, such as with Hyper-Threading Technology, as well as in the form of more physical processors. You can expect much variation in this area.

Also, computers in embedded and low-power situations will grow by leaps and bounds. The demands of such environments will add new twists to tuning, including concerns about battery life.

Developers will continue to build applications more and more from building blocks of software, whether they take the form of libraries or *managed code.*

---

[1] To learn more about this topic, read *Programming with Hyper-Threading Technology* from Intel Press.

The complexities of these hardware and software environments will only increase the need for a tool to observe behaviors on working systems, instead of relying on developers to have knowledge of the whole system themselves. In the years to come, these issues will make the VTune analyzer an important tool for more and more developers.

Recap

Here are the major points covered in this chapter:

- Computer systems are similar in that they contain one or more processors hooked to *I/O devices* (input/output devices).

- The most used I/O device is *memory*, which is important because it is so heavily used.

- *Caches* intervene between processors and memory to buffer instructions and data to improve performance; best use of caches is important for performance.

- While interesting to know, this book does not describe the many differences in details between Intel microprocessors, although they are available elsewhere. As far as the VTune analyzer is concerned, the key is to watch what events correlate with time and *then* study those events to understand what you can do about them. The VTune analyzer's built-in help makes this straightforward to do.

- *Threading* is a way to increase performance by doing more than one thing at a time; true *parallelism* happens through hardware support in the form of multiple physical or logical processors.

Chapter **3**

Projects, Activities, GUI, and Command Line

Any activity becomes creative when the doer cares about doing it right, or doing it better.

—John Updike

Ｔhis chapter introduces some fundamentals at the core of the Intel® VTune™ Performance Analyzer; namely, the *interfaces* through which you can interact with the program and the *containers* for collecting tuning data about your application. If you have never used the VTune analyzer before, the information presented here should help familiarize you with basic program usage; however, it is not intended to be comprehensive nor meant to replace the extensive Help information that accompanies the program. For other useful introductory information, spend an hour or two with the *Getting Started Tutorial*, available on Intel's VTune Performance Analyzer Web site.

A Quick Overview

Before actually fishing, every angler must learn how to use a rod and reel, and gain some practice in casting a line and reeling it back in. No fishing lessons would be complete without learning about the various tools in the tackle box and getting some hands-on experience in using them.

Similarly, before you cast your net upon the waters of performance analysis, it might help to learn about the tools of the trade and the rudiments of using them. The following sections present some terms and concepts and familiarize you with the look-and-feel of the tuning environment.

GUI and Command Line Interface

You can control the VTune Performance Analyzer in two ways: either by using its *graphical user interface (GUI)* or its *command line interface (CLI)*. The information gathered through either interface is compatible with the other. In general, you can get started easier and accomplish more by using the GUI shown in Figure 3.1 and Figure 3.2[1]—with its drop-down menus, multiple windows, and color graphics—than by using the command line, which can only display results in tables.

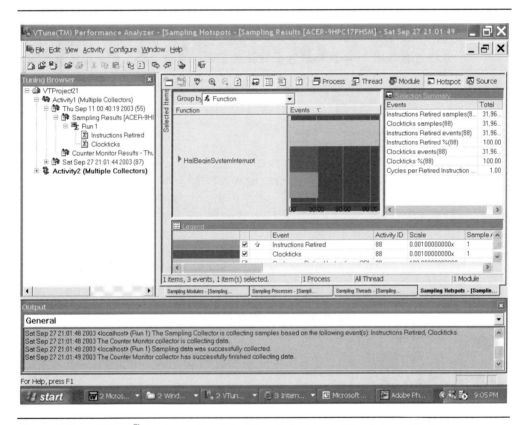

Figure 3.1   VTune™ Analyzer Graphical User Interface in Standalone Mode on Windows

---

[1] On systems running Version 3.0 of the VTune analyzer under Linux, the GUI is integrated into the Eclipse Interactive Development Environment (IDE), as shown in Figure 3.2.

The GUI running on Windows can be installed to stand alone, apart from other GUIs, or as a GUI integrated into Visual Studio .NET. This is an installation time decision. Most users still choose the standalone option because it has been with us for years, but users of Microsoft Visual Studio .NET will find the integration to be a welcome addition and should choose this option.

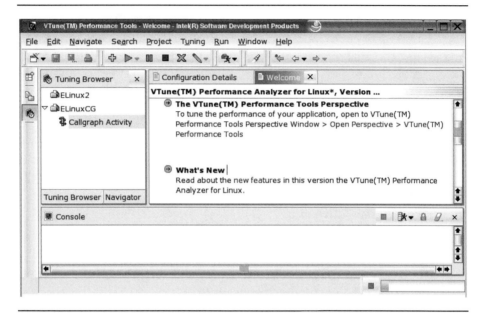

Figure 3.2   VTune™ Analyzer Graphical User Interface Integrated into Eclipse on Linux

The GUI running on Linux is a recent addition for the VTune analyzer. Intel has implemented a new perspective inside Eclipse called the VTune Performance Tools perspective. You can navigate to different perspectives under Eclipse using the **Window → Open Perspective** option on the Eclipse Toolbar.

On the other hand, the Windows DOS or Linux shell command line is essential for performing repetitive tasks, especially those you want to repeat in the future using a batch file or script. Because the command line is more limited in its ability to display information compared to the GUI, programmers often use the command line to gather information and do preliminary analysis, and then switch to the GUI to dive deeper into the data gathered.

The GUI and command line versions of the VTune analyzer coexist on your system, and you can choose either one every time you need to use the analyzer. Developers most often use the GUI for interactive exploration of performance and use the command line for tasks that can be scripted and need to be done repeatedly.

You can access the Windows command line in a variety of ways, depending on the software installed on your computer. I most often just use a DOS command window (from Windows XP, click **Start** → **Run** and type cmd). Linux users find command lines using any of the many shells available such as "Konsole."

Projects and Activities

Common to both types of interface is the notion of *projects* and *activities* within those projects. A *project*, stored with a .vpj filename extension, contains and organizes the activities and activity results used to improve the performance of your applications.

Activities control data collection. The data collectors included in an activity collect performance data, with different data collectors amassing different types of data. Within an activity, you specify the types of data you wish to collect and configure the appropriate data collector for each type. Each time an activity runs, the analyzer launches that activity's data collectors and generates an *activity result* for each data collector.

Tuning Environments

The environment in which the standalone analyzer runs is known as the *VTune Performance Environment*. This environment:

- ■ Lets you add one or more activities to a project and specify the types of performance data you want to collect using different analysis techniques. The analyzer offers multiple analysis techniques to help you understand your software's performance, as you will see in subsequent *Hotspot Hunting* chapters.

- ■ Provides wizards to help you create and configure activities and data collectors. You can either add an activity to a project or reconfigure an existing activity.

- ■ Displays the activity results at the end of data collection.

When you install the VTune Performance Analyzer on a system that also has Microsoft Visual Studio .NET, you have the option of creating and tuning your application in a single integrated environment. For more about using this feature, see *Creating Projects in the Visual Studio .NET Environment*.

Creating Projects

Creating a project is the first thing you do when using the VTune Performance Environment. The project you create contains all the activities and activity results related to the project.

The easiest way to create a project is via the Easy Start screen that appears when you launch the VTune Performance Environment. You can also create a new project from within the VTune Performance Analyzer graphical user interface. To create a new project from within the user interface:

1. Click the **Create New Project** icon from the toolbar:

    The New Project dialog box opens.

2. Select a wizard from the list of available wizards.

   On the Windows-based version, a short description of the wizard appears on the right side of the dialog box, as shown in Figure 3.3. The Linux-based Eclipse interface is currently a little simpler, as shown in Figure 3.4.

3. Either type the name and desired location of the project file (.vpj file) or use the default name and location. Each project should be in a different location.

4. Click **OK** to launch the selected wizard.

   The wizard prompts you for the required information and guides you through the process of configuring your activity.

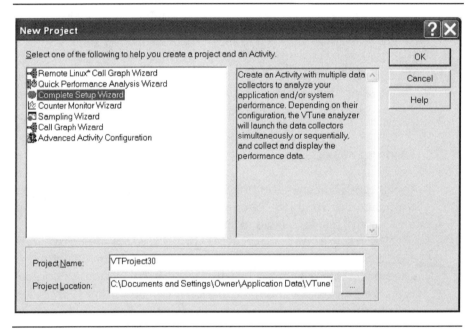

Figure 3.3   Available Wizards in the New Project Dialog Box
(Windows Version)

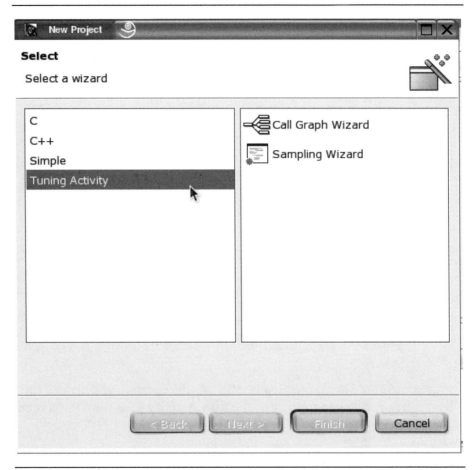

Figure 3.4   Available Wizards in the New Project Dialog Box (Linux Version)

Note

Most wizards walk you through the creation of an activity but are limited in what they can create. For more flexibility, select the **Advanced Activity Configuration** option from the list of wizards. This dialog box, shown in Figure 3.5, lets you manually configure all aspects of an activity. Later, after you have already created an activity, you can also reach this screen by selecting **Activity → Modify *activity-name...*,** or by double-clicking an activity in the Tuning Browser.

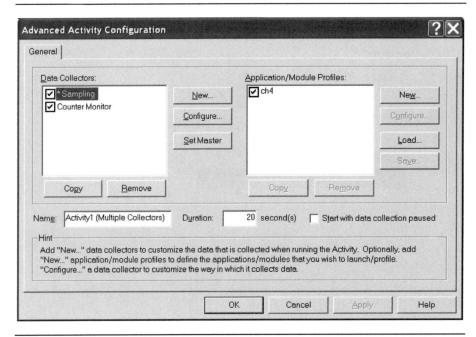

Figure 3.5   The Advanced Activity Configuration Dialog Box (Windows)

5. If necessary, select the newly created activity in the **Tuning Browser** and click the **Run Activity** icon from the toolbar

to start data collection and generate the activity results.

6. If you want to open the results later on a different machine, select **Pack and Go** from the **File** menu to save the contents of the project along with any associated files in a single file (.vxp file). Chapter 8 explains more about this feature.

Graphical User Interface (GUI)

The Graphical User Interface includes three major window components:

■ Tuning Browser

■ Data views

■ Output window

The Tuning Browser

Once you create an activity, it appears in the Tuning Browser along with an entry for the activity results. The Tuning Browser (Figure 3.6), formerly called the Project Navigator window, displays a hierarchical list of the contents of a project. This window lets you view and use all the project's activities and activity results.

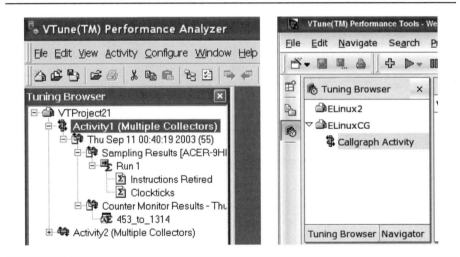

Figure 3.6   The Tuning Browser in Windows (Left) and Linux (Right)

To display the Tuning Browser:

■ In the VTune Performance Environment, select **View** → **Tuning Browser** or click the **Tuning Browser** icon in the toolbar:

■ In the integrated Microsoft Visual Studio .NET environment, from the **Tuning** menu, select **Tuning Browser**.

The currently selected activity appears highlighted in the Tuning Browser window with bold text. Its name also displays in the toolbar, as shown in Figure 3.7.

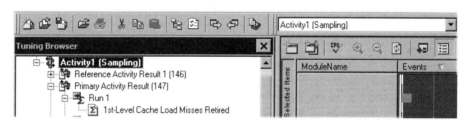

Figure 3.7   The Current Activity Appears in the Tuning Browser and Toolbar

If you do not see any icons below the menus or if the activity name is missing from the toolbar, select **Configure** → **Options...**, choose **Toolbars** under **Environment**, and make sure **Standard** and **Activity** are both checked.

Table 3.1 summarizes the kinds of icons that appear as graphical *nodes* in the Tuning Browser. Depending on which data collector you use—Sampling, Call Graph, or Counter Monitor—different icons appear for activity results and sub-results, as shown in Figure 3.8, Figure 3.9, and Figure 3.10.

Table 3.1   Icons in the Tuning Browser

Node Name	Icon	Description
Project		Name of the project in which the activity you created resides. Contains one or more activities, activity results and/or folders.
Folder		Enables adding another level of organization into your projects. You can place activities, activity results or other folders inside a folder.
Activity		Name of the activity you configured with a data collector. Used to collect data for later use in analysis and tuning. Contains one or more data collectors, each of which collects a specific type of data.
Activity Results		Name of the result that appears after running an activity configured for the Sampling and/or Counter Monitor data collector(s).
Runs		Each Sampling run saved in an `.sdb` file. The number of runs depends on the number of times you initiate Sampling data collection for a configured activity. See Figure 3.8.
Events		Each event for which data were collected in a particular Sampling run. Time-based Sampling runs list the timer event, indicating use of the OS timer interrupt to collect data. See Figure 3.8.
Activity Results		Name of the Call Graph result that appears after running an activity configured for the Call Graph data collector.
Sub-Results		Timing and function call information collected during a Call Graph activity run. See Figure 3.9.
Sub-Results		Sampling data for the time range selected in the Counter Monitor's Logged Data view. These results are available only if you select the **Collect sampling data to correlate counter data to application source** option in the Counter Monitor Configuration Wizard (Step 3 of 3). See Figure 3.10.

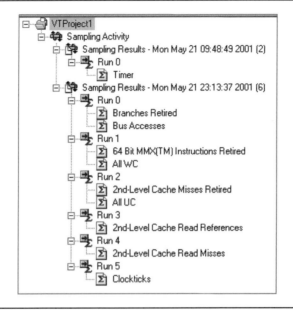

Figure 3.8 Sampling Results in the Tuning Browser with Event Information

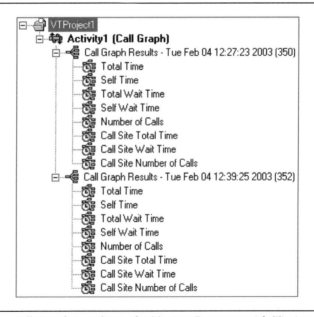

Figure 3.9 Call Graph Results in the Tuning Browser with Timing and Function Call Information

Figure 3.10   Counter Monitor Results in the Tuning Browser with Performance
                   Counter Information

Sampling Data Views

The VTune analyzer saves activity results as nodes in the Tuning Browser
window so you can view the results again later without having to rerun
the activity. To view Sampling activity results:

1. Double-click a Sampling results node in the Tuning Browser.

    A related *data view* opens to the right of the Tuning Browser, as
    shown in Figure 3.11.

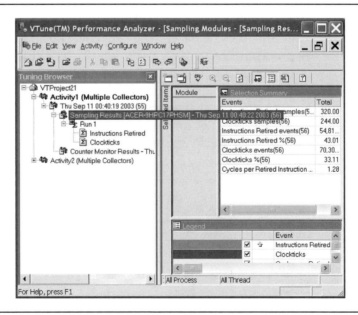

Figure 3.11   Double-clicking an Activity Opens a Related View

Parts of the data view shown in Figure 3.12 typically include a *chart* or *table* on the left, a *Selection Summary* on the right that summarizes the data collected, and a *Legend* at the bottom that provides details about the results on display.

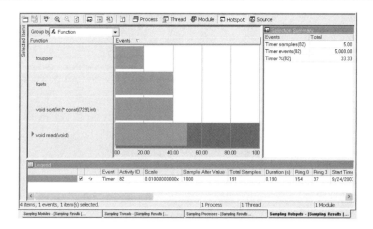

Figure 3.12   Chart, Selection Summary, and Legend Panes in Hotspot View

2. From the data view, you can filter the view more by *drilling down* to see more details or a particular section of your code, if you are tuning a specific application.

    Thus, if you use the Sampling data collector to sample events from all processes, you can choose to see all the threads for one process; from all threads you can choose a single thread, from that thread you can choose a single module, in that module you can choose a hotspot, and in that hotspot you can take a look at the source code. The diagram in Figure 3.13 shows the drill-down order for viewing increasingly greater detail about Sampling results.

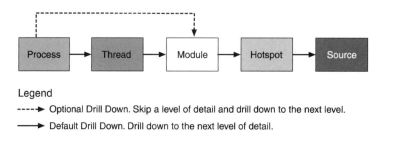

Legend

----▶ Optional Drill Down. Skip a level of detail and drill down to the next level.

——▶ Default Drill Down. Drill down to the next level of detail.

Figure 3.13   Drill-Down Order for Viewing More Detail in Sampling Results

3. In Sampling mode, the VTune analyzer creates a tab for each view you open. You can go back and forth between views by clicking the tabs at the bottom of the view pane as shown in Figure 3.14.

Figure 3.14   Click Tabs to Switch Between Open Views

4. Activity results enable you to compare performance before and after modifying an application. For example, you can generate activity results for one version of the executable file, revise the code, generate a new executable file, run the same activity, and generate new activity results. You can then select **Cascade** or **Tile Horizontally** from the **Windows** menu to compare the two sets of activity results to see if the performance has changed. Figure 3.15 shows two activity results in cascaded and horizontally tiled windows. Chapter 8, "Comparing Multiple Activities," explains more about making comparisons.

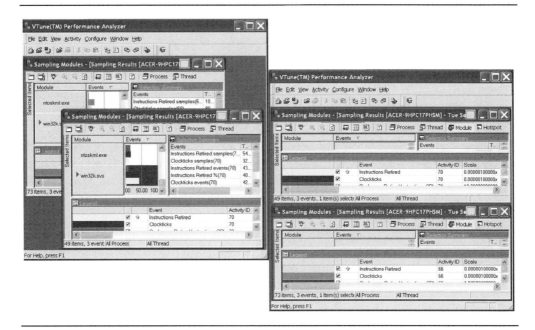

Figure 3.15   Two Activity Results in Cascaded and Horizontally Tiled Windows

Working with Processes

A *process* is the object created when a program is run. Processes are executing applications with specific virtual addresses. Every process is an intrinsic combination of code, data, and several operating system resources.

The VTune analyzer's Process view displays a system-wide view of all the processes that were running on your system when Sampling occurred. From this view, you can select the process(es) with the most samples and drill down to Thread view to see a breakdown for these processes by thread. From Process view, you can also drill down to Module view.

To drill down to the Thread or Module view,

■ Double-click the selected process, or

■ Select one or more process(es) and click **Thread** or **Module** in the Sampling toolbar.

Note
> Drill-down order goes from Process to Thread to Module to Hotspot to Source views. Drill-down is easy with a simple double-click of your mouse. Of course, you can manually switch between the views in any order you want.

Working with Threads

A *thread* is the object that executes instructions. It is a set of instructions that either executes simultaneously with the rest of the program because of multiprocessing, or appears to do so because of operating system capabilities. Another way of looking at a thread is simply as a basic unit of CPU utilization.

To run a process efficiently, the CPU assigns several threads to each process or task. Even though only one thread at a time is active, multithreading is still efficient because threads share operating systems resources and code and data sections. This makes CPU switching among threads inexpensive.

The VTune analyzer's Thread view displays all threads that run within the selected process(es). Threads are not shared across processes but threads from different processes can run a common module. The diagram in Figure 3.16 helps to clarify the relationship between process, thread, and module.

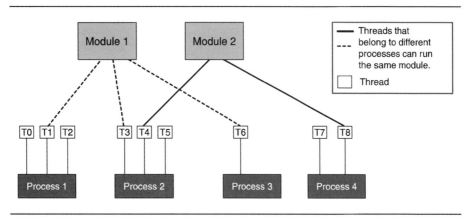

Figure 3.16   The Relationship Between Process, Thread, and Module

In Thread view and in other data views, you have a choice of viewing the data as a table as in Figure 3.17 or as a horizontal bar chart as in Figure 3.18. To choose a view format, right-click on the view and select **View As → Table** or **View As → Horizontal Chart**.

By default, threads are named `Thread0`, `Thread1` and so on. To distinguish threads better while analyzing data, you can assign them more meaningful names. To rename a thread in table format, click a row to select a thread and type a new name.

Thread	Process	Clockticks samples (70)	Instructions Retired samples (70)	Clockticks % (70)
thread19	VTuneEnv.exe	101	104	97.12
thread6	VTuneEnv.exe	3	2	2.88
thread23	VTuneEnv.exe	0	1	0.00

Figure 3.17   Thread View Displayed as a Table

When viewing the Horizontal Bar Chart, right-click and select **Fit in view** to display all the items at one time in the view pane.

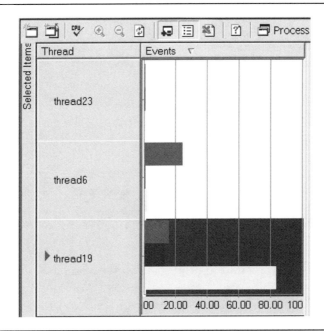

Figure 3.18   Thread View Displayed as a Horizontal Bar Chart

From Thread view, you can drill down to Module view:

■ Double-click the selected thread.

or

■ Select one or more threads and click Module in the Sampling toolbar.

Working with Modules

Modules are executable binary image files. Examples of modules are .exe, .dll, .ocx, and .jit files. Module view displays all the modules in the selected thread (s) that were running during the period of Sampling. Modules called frequently during Sampling data collection show the highest number of events or the most CPU time. You can use the information from Module view to drill down to hotspots and to gauge the performance of your module in relation to others.

As with other data views, you can display modules as a horizontal chart or in a table. Module views displayed in table format have a + sign before each module name. Click the + as shown in Figure 3.19 to display the list of processes calling this module and the corresponding number of samples collected for each instance of the module. You can use this feature to pinpoint which process called the module with the highest number of samples or events.

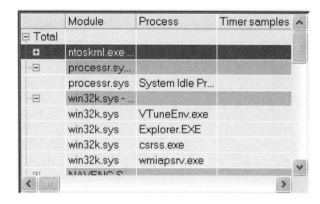

Figure 3.19   Click the + Sign in Module View to See Calling Processes

Once you identify the critical module or modules, you can drill down to see more detail in Hotspot view using one of the following:

■ Double-click a single module.

■ Select several modules and click Hotspot in the Sampling toolbar.

Figure 3.20 shows Module view before drilling down, and Figure 3.21 shows Hotspot view after drilling down.

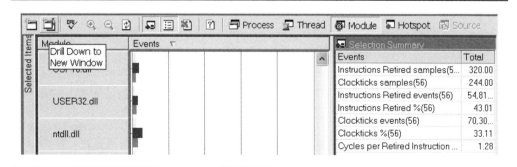

Figure 3.20   Module View Before Drill-Down to Hotspot View

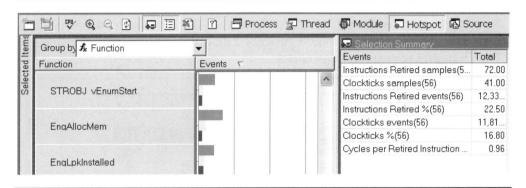

Figure 3.21 Hotspot View After Drill-Down from Module View

Note If the VTune Performance Analyzer cannot locate the symbol files for the selected modules, it prompts you for them. You can also right-click on the Sampling results in the Tuning Browser and select **Module Associations** to provide the location of the binary and symbol files for the selected modules. Without symbol information, function names do not appear correctly in Hotspot view. For more about symbol files, see *Appendix A: Types of Line Number and Symbol File Information*.

Working with Hotspots

A *hotspot* indicates a section of code within a module that took a long time to execute, resulting in many samples. The Hotspot view can display individual hotspots as they appear in memory, hotspots of active functions, or hotspots of active source files, depending on the option you select.

The Hotspot view displays function names associated with selected modules that have symbol information available. If only the executable file is available, either the nearest available external function name or the module name and offset appear. If executable and debug information are not available, Hotspot view displays only the *relative virtual address (RVA)* information. You can use the **Group by** pull-down menu to group hotspots by Function, RVA (Location), Source Files, or Class. From the Hotspot view, you can drill down to Source view in either of the following ways:

■ Double-click a single hotspot item, such as a function or class.

■ Select a hotspot item and click **Source** in the Sampling toolbar.

Working with Source Code

Source view helps you pinpoint problem areas in your code. In this view you see the high-level-language source code and/or assembler-language-level disassembly code of one source file in the monitored module. The VTune analyzer displays source code for any program compiled with debugging turned on, or for which you specify symbol files. If this symbol and line number information is not available, the program prompts you for the missing files. If you cannot provide them, only the disassembly view appears.

Typically, you drill down to Source view after performing an initial analysis such as static module analysis, sampling, or call graph profiling. To go back to the Call Graph or Sampling view from which you came, right-click and choose **Go To → Sampling** or **Go To → Call Graph**.

In Source view, the upper *Source pane* contains the code and related information about each code line. The lower *Summary pane* contains information about the functions in the monitored source file and the selected range(s). Figure 3.22 shows both of the Source view panes.

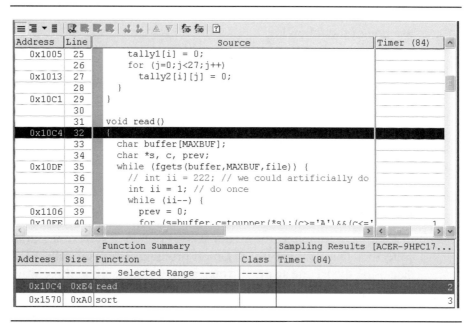

Figure 3.22   Source and Summary Panes in Source View

Since the Source and Summary panes are synchronized, you can navigate to the beginning of a function in the Source pane by double-clicking its name in the Summary pane.

If you hover your mouse over column heads, summary information about Sampling results appears, as shown in Figure 3.23.

```
Timer (84)
Sampling Results [ACER-9HPC17PHSM] - Thu Sep 25 23:12:33 2003
Started at: Thu Sep 25 23:12:32 2003
Finished at: Thu Sep 25 23:12:33 2003
Duration: 1 second
```

Figure 3.23   Summary Information When You Hover Over Column Heads

After viewing the data in Source view, you can select a code line or range of code lines and obtain targeted performance tuning advice from the Intel Tuning Assistant. Chapter 7, "Automatic Hotspot Analysis," describes the use of this helpful tool. To invoke the Intel Tuning Assistant use one of the following:

■ Double-click a line of code.

■ Select a block of code and then right-click and select **Get Tuning Advice**.

■ Click the **Get Advice Using the Intel Tuning Assistant** icon in the main toolbar:

Call Graph Data Views

In addition to Sampling, the VTune analyzer offers several other kinds of data collectors. One of these is Call Graph profiling. After you collect Call Graph data using the VTune analyzer, you can view the results in three ways:

■ A *Function Summary* in the upper section of the Call Graph window provides full information on all the application functions in table format, as shown in Figure 3.24. This view is synchronized with the Graph so that the currently selected function in this table is highlighted in the Graph.

Module (94)	Function (94)	Class (94)	Calls (94)	Self Time (94)	Total Time
⊟ Total			102	124	
⊟ KERNEL32.DL...			53	25	
KERNEL32.DLL	ExitProcess		1	0	
KERNEL32.DLL	FreeEnvironmentStringsW		1	0	
KERNEL32.DLL	GetACP		1	0	
KERNEL32.DLL	GetCommandLineA		1	0	
KERNEL32.DLL	GetCPInfo		2	0	

Figure 3.24   Function Summary in Call Graph Window

■ A *Graph* in the lower section of the Call Graph window visually depicts the structure of application execution including the critical path through the currently selected function's parents (callers) and child functions (callees), as well as timing information. Hovering your mouse over any node in the graph reveals more information about that function, as shown in Figure 3.25.

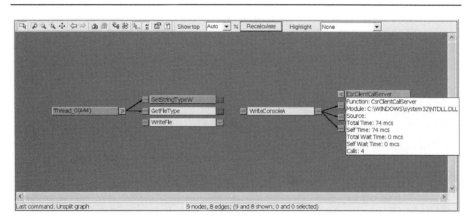

Figure 3.25   Graph in Call Graph Window

■ A *Call List*, in the lower section of the Call Graph window on another tab, provides timing and call information including callers and callees for the *focus function* selected in the Function Summary or Graph, as Figure 3.26 illustrates. To access this view, click the **Call List** tab.

Focus function					
NTDLL.DLL	CsrClientCallServer			4	74

Caller Function	Contributi... ▾	Edge Time	Edge Calls	
WriteConsoleA	66.2%	49		1
VerifyConsoleIoHandle	33.8%	25		3

Callee Function	Contributi... ▾	Edge Time	Edge Calls

Figure 3.26   Call List for the Focus Function in the Call Graph Window

Counter Monitor Data Views

Counter Monitor is the third data collector offered by the VTune analyzer. This method is powerful but much less used than Sampling or Call Graph, and is not available for all machines and operating systems. The Counter Monitor collects data from the performance counters you select. You can view the results in three ways:

■ A *Runtime Data* view, similar to *Logged Data* view, permits you to watch data collection in real-time mode.

■ A *Logged Data* view displays a graph of the performance monitor data after it has been collected, as Figure 3.27 illustrates, along with a *Legend* that describes the counter information, as shown in Figure 3.28.

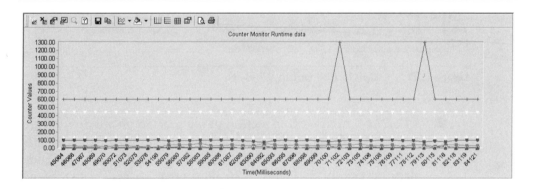

Figure 3.27   Logged Data View of Counter Monitor Data

Legend				
Counter Name	Graph Scale	Average	Min	M
System : Processor Queue Length	10.0	3.447	1.000	6.0
System : Context Switches/sec	0.01	933.113	710.999	2366.5
Memory : Available Bytes	0.000001	137458724.141	133496832.000	139685888.0
Processor (0) : % Processor Time	1.0	5.668	0.000	61.7
Processor (0) : % User Time	1.0	2.266	0.000	17.6
Processor (0) : % Privileged Time	1.0	3.343	0.000	44.1
Processor (0) : Interrupts/sec	0.01	139.183	106.847	283.6
Processor (0) : % Interrupt Time	1.0	0.070	0.000	1.0
Processor (0) : % Idle Time	1.0	94.391	38.235	105.0
Processor (_Total) : % Processor Time	1.0	5.668	0.000	61.7
Processor (_Total) : % User Time	1.0	2.266	0.000	17.6
Processor (_Total) : % Privileged Time	1.0	3.343	0.000	44.1
Processor (_Total) : Interrupts/sec	0.01	139.183	106.847	283.6
Processor (_Total) : % Interrupt Time	1.0	0.070	0.000	1.0
Processor (_Total) : % Idle Time	1.0	94.391	38.235	105.0
Redirector : Network Errors/sec	1.0	0.000	0.000	0.0

Figure 3.28   Legend Accompanying Counter Monitor Data

■   A *Summary Data* view presents a bar graph as Figure 3.29 illustrates, with summary information for each counter you selected for display in the *Logged Data* view. To access this view, toggle the **Display Logged Data or Summary View** icon on the Counter Monitor toolbar:

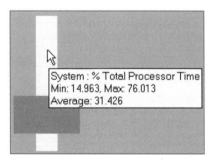

Figure 3.29   Summary Data View of Counter Monitor Data

Static Module Analysis View

Without gathering any dynamic performance data, you can still analyze an executable module and view a summary of the functions and classes in the module. This analysis shows the functions along with their source file paths, classes, starting point, and size, arranged in groups by source files and classes.

To view Static Module Analysis information:

1. Click the **Open static module viewer** icon in the toolbar:

   If you do not see any this icon below the menus, select **Configure** → **Options...**, choose **Toolbars** under **Environment**, and make sure **Open Static Module Viewer** is checked.

   The Open dialog box appears with executable files selected as the **Files of type:** option.

2. Browse to the correct file location, select an executable file, and click **Open**.

   The VTune analyzer analyzes the executable file statically and displays the Static Module Analysis view shown in Figure 3.30.

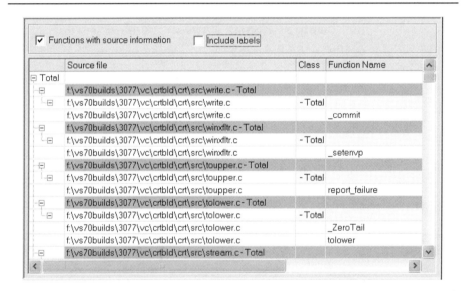

Figure 3.30   Static Module Data View

This view presents a list of function names and classes if symbol information is available. If symbol information is not available, a list of unique symbol names appears, with a summary of static analysis information per *basic block* of consecutive instructions with one entry point and one exit.

Output Window

In addition to the Tuning Browser and the data view window, the VTune analyzer's GUI includes an Output window that displays messages during data collection and analysis. To open this window in the VTune Performance Environment, select **View** → **Output**. The Output window shown in Figure 3.31 appears at the bottom of your screen.

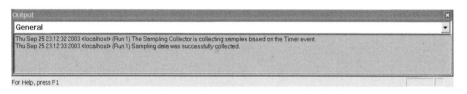

Figure 3.31   Output Window with Messages from Data Collection and Analysis

VTune™ Analyzer's Command Line

In addition to using the VTune analyzer's GUI, you can invoke the VTune Performance Analyzer from the Microsoft Windows operating system command line. The command line interface (CLI) of the VTune analyzer (vtl) lets you collect data about application and system performance and view it in table form. It provides a quick way to configure a single activity with a collector and a single optional application, and then run the activity and collect results.

The vtl program stores the results in a persistent default project. To view the results, you can specify viewer filter parameters as command arguments to the vtl executable. When the executable runs in view mode, it reads from the default project, displays the results, and then terminates. To view the results with different filters, use repeated invocations.

To invoke the command line interface and obtain help with using it:

1. Type **vtl** at the command line prompt to launch vtl.

   The command line interface executes by repeatedly invoking the vtl executable on a single project.

2. Type **vtl -help** to see the VTune analyzer command line help.

Figure 3.32 shows a portion of the summary of vtl options and commands that appears on the command line.

```
C:>vtl -help
VTune(TM) Performance Analyzer 7.1
Copyright (C) 2000-2003 Intel Corporation. All rights
reserved.

Usage:
vtl [options(s)] [command(s)]

Options:
.
. (shown here)
.
Commands:
.
. (shown here)
.
See the online help for complete documentation.
```

Figure 3.32　Subset of vtl Command Line Help Summary

To see the online HTML version of help for the command line:

■ From the table of contents of the VTune help system, select **Launch Help for Command Line Support**

or

■ At the command line, type:

VTune-analyzer-installation-path/Help/WindowsCLI.chm

The Command Line Interface Help file appears, as shown in Figure 3.33.

You can use vtl in standalone mode or together with the GUI. For example, you might collect data in command line mode and then export it to the GUI version of the VTune analyzer. You can also save the whole project and load it into the GUI version.

The current VTune analyzer command line version supports Sampling data collection only. You can collect and view system-wide data by setting Sampling configuration and view options.

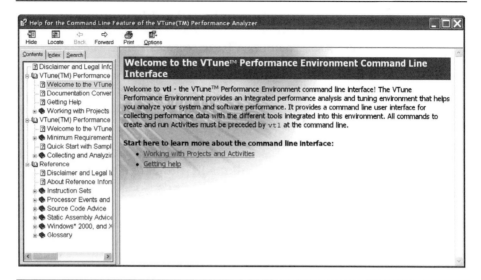

Figure 3.33   Command Line Interface Help File

Creating Projects in the Visual Studio .NET Environment

When you install the VTune Performance Analyzer on a system that also has Microsoft Visual Studio .NET, you have the option of incorporating the VTune tool into the *Integrated Visual Studio .NET Environment*, so that you can create and tune your application in a single integrated environment. In this environment, the Visual Studio .NET user interface incorporates these special windows, menus, and toolbars:

- ■ *Tuning Browser.* The Tuning Browser is tabbed to the Solution Explorer window but can be docked anywhere on the screen. The Tuning Browser displays all the activities and results for the selected Visual Studio .NET project.

- ■ *Output Window.* To open this window from the **View** menu, select **Other Windows → Output**.

- ■ *Tuning Menu.* A Tuning menu appears in the Visual Studio .NET menu bar. This menu contains commands for accessing all commonly used VTune analyzer features—including items for accessing the Tuning Browser; creating, running, and stopping an activity; merging activity results; and accessing the Tuning Assistant.

■ *Options dialog box.* Selecting **Options...** from the **Tools** menu opens the Options dialog box. All categories related to VTune tools are listed under **VTune Performance Tools**.

■ *Toolbar for VTune Performance Tools.* An additional VTune Performance Tools toolbar appears when you open a tuning project. This toolbar contains an icon for creating an activity and other icons to access key features.

In the integrated Visual Studio .NET Environment, you add tuning activities to an existing Visual Studio .NET project. When you add an activity for the first time, the VTune Performance Tools automatically creates a tuning file (.vpj file) entry under the .NET project in the Solutions Explorer. When you add more activities to the same project, they are saved in the originally created .vpj file. In the example shown in Figure 3.34, VTuneDemo is the .NET project file and VTuneDemo.vpj is the tuning file.

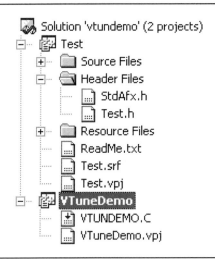

Figure 3.34 A Tuning File Saved Under a .NET Project File in the Solution Explorer

A .vpj tuning file entry in the Solution Explorer in the Visual Studio .NET Environment is equivalent to a *project* in the VTune Performance Environment. You can add multiple activities to the .NET project in order to analyze the performance of your application. However, the added activities appear under the respective tuning project in the Tuning Browser as shown in Figure 3.35, not under the .NET project in the Solution Explorer window.

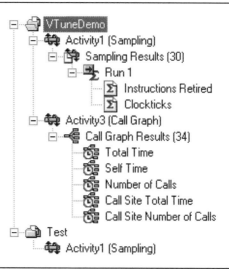

Figure 3.35   Multiple Activities in the Tuning Browser in the Integrated .NET Environment

All Visual Studio .NET projects in a solution appear as tuning projects in the Tuning Browser. Unlike the standalone VTune Performance Environment, more than one tuning project at a time can appear in the Tuning Browser in the integrated .NET environment.

To create an activity in the Visual Studio .NET environment:

1. Select the .NET project in the Solution Explorer window.

2. Select **Add → Add New Item...**

   The Add New Item – *project-name* dialog box opens.

3. From **Categories**, select from the list of VTune tools.

4. From **Templates**, select a wizard.

   The Templates panel displays the corresponding wizards to help you create an activity.

Recap

Here are some main points in this chapter:

- The VTune analyzer offers two kinds of interfaces:
  - The *graphical user interface* displays more information and is easier to use with its drop-down menus, multiple windows, and color graphics.
  - The *command line interface* can only display text and tables but is good for performing repetitive tasks, especially those you want to repeat in the future using a batch file or script.

- A *project* contains and organizes activities and activity results.

- *Activities* control data collection.

- The three data collection tools are *Sampling*, *Call Graph*, and *Counter Monitor*.

- The three parts of the VTune analyzer's GUI are the *Tuning Browser*, *Data Views,* and the *Output Window*. This layout is true in standalone mode on Windows, as well as when integrated into Visual Studio .NET on Windows or into the Eclipse IDE on Linux.

- Sampling allows you to see increasingly greater detail by moving from *Process view* to *Thread view* to *Module view* to *Hotspot view* to *Source Code view*.

- If you are using Microsoft Visual Studio .NET on Windows or the Eclipse IDE on Linux, you can create and tune your application in a single, integrated environment.

Part II
Examining Your System and Applications

Chapter **4**

Hotspot Hunting 101: Sampling

The proof of the pudding is in the eating.
By a small sample we may judge of the whole piece.
—Miguel de Cervantes

The first and most important step in tuning is to find out what is happening with the software as a whole. One technique you can use to gain this kind of insight is *sampling*. The Intel® VTune™ Performance Analyzer actually started out as a tool that used the sampling capabilities of Intel microprocessors to gather data and relate the results to the source code and processor instructions. Only in later versions did the VTune analyzers include Call Graphs and Counter Monitors, other tuning techniques to be explored in later chapters.

Table 4.1 gives a quick overview of the Sampling feature, including software and hardware specifics for using this analysis technique. Note that the GUI examples and illustrations in this chapter all use the Windows version of the VTune analyzer. Users on Linux-based systems can use the Linux GUI to follow the examples, after entering the Performance Tools Perspective (by selecting **Window → Open Perspective → VTune Performance Tools**) and selecting the **New Activity...** option as shown in Figure 4.1. The concepts, terminology, and basic display layouts are the same in any version of the VTune analyzer. The Linux GUI, in its first release with version 3.0 for Linux, is not yet as refined as the Windows version 7.2, which has had more than 10 releases to fine-tune its GUI. The Linux illustrations in the book are subject to change in future releases.

Figure 4.1 Creating a New Activity Using VTune™ Analyzer for Linux

Table 4.1 Sampling at a Glance

Feature:	Sampling, Time-based and Event-based
Benefit at a glance:	System-wide non-intrusive determination of *hotspots*. Offers the best evidence of places for effective tuning. All done without source code changes and without binary instrumentation.
	Viewing *Over Time* lets you see the samples collected for a single event chronologically. Helps you identify which threads are consuming the most time and see when threads are running serially or in parallel.
Versions:	All versions of the VTune™ analyzer. The Over Time view requires at least version 7.1 on Windows[†], or version 3.0 on Linux[†].
OS:	Windows and Linux operating systems.
Collectors:	Remote and local data collection. The Over Time view not available in Hotspot or Source View.
Languages:	All languages. Display of source code for compiled code requires symbol information in the executable. Java source code display requires use of JITs with support for Java[†] performance tuning, based on Java SDK 1.3 or later.
Processors:	Pentium® processors, Itanium® processors, and Intel® processors with Intel XScale® technology. Platforms must have ACPI interrupts enabled. To save power, some older (Pentium III processor-based) notebook designs disabled this capability with no ability to reactivate, thereby eliminating the VTune analyzer's ability to do Sampling.
	Event-based sampling requires updates to the VTune analyzer for each major new processor, and is limited to Intel processors. Intel provides such updates at no extra charge during the support period for the product (currently one year from the date of purchase).
	Time-based sampling, by its nature, is not always tied to highly specific processor event registers, and therefore often works on some non-Intel processors.
	The Over Time view is not available for data collected on systems with Intel XScale technology, because the sampling files are compressed to save space and needed information is lost in the process.

Ideally, when you run a program, you would know everything that is happening as it runs. You could do this hypothetically by watching a system and continuously noting everything that occurred. Unfortunately, such an approach would intrude on the performance of the very system you want to examine. At a minimum, this approach would create unacceptable delays and, most likely, would distort system performance so much that the resulting information would be useless.

The VTune analyzer solves this problem by interrupting normal system execution only occasionally to take a sample. This kind of interruption is so slight that it is almost always completely unintrusive. Such a sampling method is called *statistical sampling*.

The analyzer implements sampling in such a way as to require no source code modification and no instrumentation of the compiled code. This approach allows system-wide sampling regardless of what application or part of the system code may be of interest, and can even examine code that runs in Ring 0, such as device drivers.

Users of tools such as `prof` and `gprof` know that time-based sampling of just one application leaves a great deal unknown about system performance, especially since the key bottleneck in a system may not even occur in the application you are examining. By taking a system-wide perspective, the VTune analyzer Sampling feature avoids these pitfalls associated with more limited solutions that only give you part of the picture.

To recap, sampling with the VTune analyzer has these advantages:

■ It requires no code modifications.

■ It requires no instrumentation.

■ Low overhead means minimal intrusion.

■ Sampling is system-wide.

■ It can even sample in Ring 0 (for example, device drivers).

What Is a Hotspot?

A *hotspot* is a point of interest in a program where something happens more often than it happens elsewhere. If that thing is *time*, then a hotspot is a place where your program spends more time than other parts of your code.

The VTune analyzer adds interest by allowing the thing identified as happening more often than it happens elsewhere to be events rather than time. Examples include cache misses, floating-point multiples, pipeline stalls, and unaligned memory accesses. Although you may not expect your program to do any of these things, the ability to highlight unexpected or undesirable activities is a big part of what locating hotspots is all about.

In addition to sampling an application or *module of interest*, the Sampling data collector tracks and records processor time spent on modules running as part of your operating system. In fact, while sampling, the VTune Performance Analyzer monitors all the software executing on your system—including your application, the operating system, JIT-compiled Java class files, 16-bit applications, 32-bit applications, 64-bit applications, VxDs, and DOS device drivers. As mentioned earlier, since the VTune analyzer conducts sampling non-intrusively and does not modify any binary files, it has no impact on your application's performance.

After analyzing all the code associated with the collected samples, the VTune analyzer summarizes the hotspots or bottlenecks in Hotspot view, as shown in Figure 4.2. Whereas hotspots are locations of significant activity, *bottlenecks* are areas of significant performance constraint. Finding software hotspots is one way the analyzer can help you identify bottlenecks.

Figure 4.2   Hotspot View Icon on the VTune™ Analyzer Toolbar (Windows)

Once you find a hotspot, the VTune analyzer makes it easy to move from Hotspot view to the source or assembly code. This is called *drilling down* in the documentation. Once you view the source causing the hotspots, you can consider how to modify your code to remove the bottlenecks and improve the performance of your application. It is mostly up to you to decide what to do about the identified pieces of code. Chapter 7, "Automatic Hotspot Analysis," describes how the VTune analyzer can analyze and offer advice automatically.

■ Before You Begin Sampling

You can use the VTune Performance Analyzer while building release or debug versions of your application, with or without compiler optimization. Normally, however, your goal is to tune the fully optimized, release version of your application—and this is exactly what you should do. While the analyzer will work correctly with release builds, you do need to know that the VTune Performance Analyzer requires *line number information* and *symbol information,* also referred to as *debug information*, in order to display the function names in Sampling, Call Graph, and Static Module Analysis views. It also uses this information to display the source code view.

Depending on how you configure settings, your compiler generates line number and symbol information either in a separate file or as part of the binary file. See Appendix A, "Types of Line Information and Symbol Files," for more details about how to generate this information using several popular compilers.

The VTune analyzer recognizes many types of line information/symbol files, and tries to obtain this information in this manner:

1. It searches for symbol information in the binary it launches, such as an `.exe`, `.obj`, `.ocx`, `.dll`, or `.VxD` file.

2. If it doesn't find the information, the VTune analyzer prompts you to specify a file that contains the symbols, such as a file in `.pdb`, `.dbg`, or `.sym` format.

3. If you can't supply this information, the VTune analyzer resorts to showing you virtual addresses in hexadecimal and assembly code instead of your source code.

Don't worry about overhead in your target code. Generating line number and symbol information properly during compilation does not modify any existing optimizations in your application, and the generated code remains the same.

Types of Sampling

Sampling comes in two flavors: *time-based* and *event-based*. Both types collect samples of active instruction addresses, but:

■ Time-based sampling (TBS) collects the samples at regular time-based intervals and is 1 millisecond by default.

■ Event-based sampling (EBS) collects the samples after a certain number of processor events.

In either case, the sampling results show you where your program is busy doing something. When this something happens more in one place than another, it is considered a hotspot. In the case of time-based sampling, the thing being counted is *spending time*. You can think of time-based sampling as simply a special form of event-based sampling, where the event just happens to be the tick of a clock. Increasingly, VTune™ analyzer users accomplish time-based sampling by running event-based sampling on the *clockticks* event. However, two reasons exist for making the distinction:

■ Many programmers are familiar with time-based sampling because of tools like `prof` and `gprof`.

■ Time-based sampling can be implemented without using an event register in the processor (since time-based interrupts are available separately on many processors). This means that you may be able to use time-based sampling with processors not specifically supported by the VTune Performance Analyzer.

Time-Based Sampling

To get a feel for time-based sampling, you can start by doing some basic profiling. If you want to learn how to use the graphical user interface (GUI) as well as the command line interface, work both Example 4.1 and Example 4.2. Otherwise, you can learn the basic concepts about time sampling by working either example.

Using the Program Example

To help you learn about time sampling, a small program called `prog0401` that I wrote as an example is available on the book's companion Web site. Information about the Web site is located on the inside back cover of this book. I purposely made the program very simple, and I encourage you to modify it and then use the analyzer to explore and investigate the effects of your modifications. If you want to use this program to work the examples, download `examples.zip` and expand it somewhere on your disk. The `prog0401` file is in the `examples\ch4` folder; the coding examples in this chapter assume that you placed them in the `C:\examples\ch4` folder. Each indicated operating system and/or system type has its own subfolder under `\ch4` on the Web site, each containing the appropriate compiled source code and corresponding projects already created. To get started, simply choose the appropriate subfolder for your system and operating system.

Using Your Own or Another Program

If you have your own application, feel free to use that instead of the one provided. To use your own application, be sure to:

- Compile/link with symbols and line numbers.
- Make *release* builds with optimizations.

If you don't do this, the VTune analyzer will probably display assembly language code instead of source code. See detailed instructions for various environments in the previous section entitled "Before You Begin Sampling" and in Appendix A.

If you have neither the sample nor your own application, simply pick an application on your system such as `C:\WINNT\system32\notepad.exe`.

Example 4.1: Time-Based Sampling Using the Graphical Interface

Follow these steps to perform time-based sampling from the graphical interface.

Step-by-Step Procedure

1. Double-click the **VTune Performance Analyzer** icon to start the analyzer.
2. Click the **Create New Project** icon.
3. Click **Sampling Wizard** and select **OK**.
4. Select **Windows/Windows CE/Linux Profiling** and click **Next**.

5. In the **Application To Launch** text box, type the path:

    ```
    C:\examples\ch4\windows\prog0401.exe
    (Linux users: examples/ch4/linux/prog0401)
    ```

    or whatever executable file you want to sample, possibly:
    ```
    C:\WINNT\system32\notepad.exe or /bin/ls
    ```

6. In the **Command Line Arguments** text box, type:

    ```
    input0402.txt 1000
    ```

    for `prog0401`. For other applications, either type the options you want or leave it blank if you're not sure.

7. Select the **Modify default configuration when done with wizard** checkbox and click **Finish**.

    The Advanced Activity Configuration dialog box appears.

8. Click **Configure...** in the middle of the screen for the Data Collector called `Sampling`, which is already selected.

    The Configure Sampling window appears.

9. Select **Time-based sampling (TBS)** and click **OK** to return to the Advanced Activity Configuration dialog box.

10. Click **OK**.

    Once `prog0401` finishes executing, the VTune analyzer displays a screen showing the applications detected as running while Sampling took place. If you are running your own application or Notepad, you are probably running with a time limit, because this is the default setting. If so, either close that program or click the **Stop Activity** icon on the toolbar (Figure 4.3) in order to see the Sampling results screen.

Figure 4.3   The Stop Activity Icon on the Toolbar

Table 4.2 shows some important toolbar icons for navigating among Sampling data views.

Table 4.2   Important Icons for Navigating Sampling Views (Windows)

Name	Icon	Description
Tabs	See description.	Click tabs (usually positioned at the bottom of the screen) to switch between open data views: Sampling Hotspots - [Samplin...] Sampling Processes - [Sampli...] **Sampling Threads - [Sampling...]**
Previous (Standard Toolbar)		Displays the previous open data view window. For example, if you drilled down from Module to Hotspot view, clicking **Previous** would take you back to Module view, much like the **Back** button in an Internet browser.
Next (Standard Toolbar)		Displays the next open data view window. For example, if three views are open: Sampling Hotspots - [Samplin...] Sampling Processes - [Sampli...] **Sampling Threads - [Sampling...]** clicking **Next** would take you to the next view in the series, much like the **Forward** button in an Internet browser.
Drill Down		Drills down to a lower level in the data view hierarchy by opening the selected item (such as a process, thread, module, or function) in a new window.
Processes	Process	Displays all the processes that ran on your system when Sampling data collection took place.
Threads	Thread	Displays the threads for the selected process(es).[1]
Modules	Module	Displays the modules for the selected thread(s).[1]
Hotspots	HotSpot	Displays the hotspots for the selected module(s) grouped by function, relative virtual address, source file, or class.[1]
Source	Source	Displays the source code for the selected hotspot(s).[1]

Which Application Took the Most Time?

Looking at Figure 4.4, which application took the most time? Notice that it was not prog0401, at least not on the system used to prepare this example.

---

[1] Hold down the Ctrl or Shift key to make multiple selections.

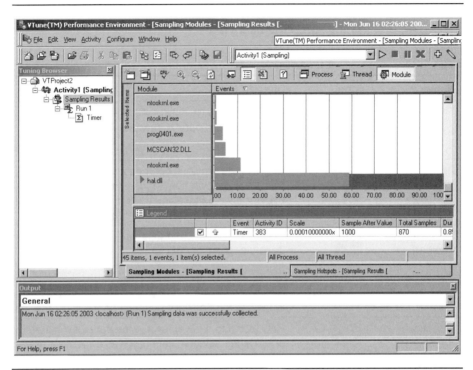

Figure 4.4   Sampling Results for `prog0401` with Virus Protection Software

Instead, the OS (`hal.dll` and `ntoskrnl`) plus the virus protection software (`MCSCAN32.DLL`) appear to be the culprit. Linux users, you will see shortly, have a similar issue with Java on their system. This may seem frustrating for the purposes of this example, but it illustrates the power of the VTune analyzer. The analyzer is telling you that, if you must make this particular system run faster, the biggest problems with this particular example are the OS and the virus protection software (or perhaps Java on Linux) that analyzes `prog0401.exe` before it ever runs.

If you can eliminate that software, you can speed up system execution more than if you worked on `prog0401` all day long. Take a look at the results of running the `prog0401` program again after disabling the virus protection software; in other words, rerun Example 4.1. The screen shown in Figure 4.5 tells the tale; `MCSCAN32.DLL` has disappeared, `hal.dll` is now taking less than half the execution time, and `ntoskrnl` is taking almost no time.

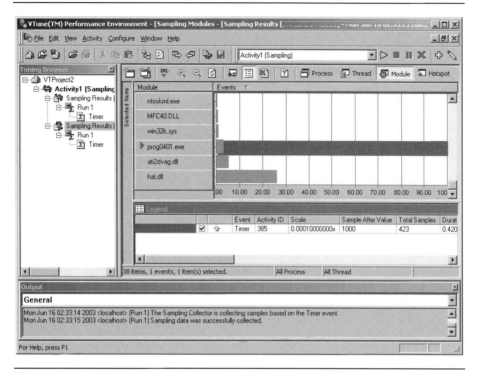

Figure 1.5 Sampling Results for `prog0401` Without Virus Protection
Software

You can drill down to the function level next to see which functions
in `prog0401` took the longest to run. To do this, simply double-click on
the dark horizontal bar to the right of the filename `prog0401.exe`. Before you click, while your mouse is pointing at the dark bar, you might
notice that the analyzer displays a small box with the information `Timer
32,000`. The VTune analyzer is showing you the number of timer inter-
rupts that occurred while `prog0401` was the active process.

After drilling down you see the view shown in Figure 4.6, which
clearly shows that the top three functions in terms of time spent are
`fgets and toupper` (parts of the C library), plus `sort` and `read`, which
are in the `prog0401` code. By mousing over the dark bar for the `read`
function, you can see the message `Timer 10,000`. This means that
`prog0401` spent about 31 percent of its run time in the `read` function
(10,000/32,000).

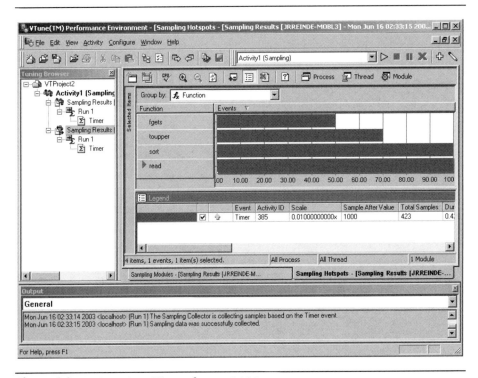

Figure 4.6   Functions View of `prog0401`

Linux users may not have virus protection software running, but they will see that Java is consuming a lot of resources. The Eclipse user interface uses Java, so it is running on the system even though the example program itself has no Java code. The resulting analysis shown in Figure 4.7 has the example program not even ranking in the first screenfull as it was too trivial a task on the system. The VTune analyzer is offering its analysis as to what is really happening on the computer; it is up to you to use or ignore the wealth of information as it suits your purposes.

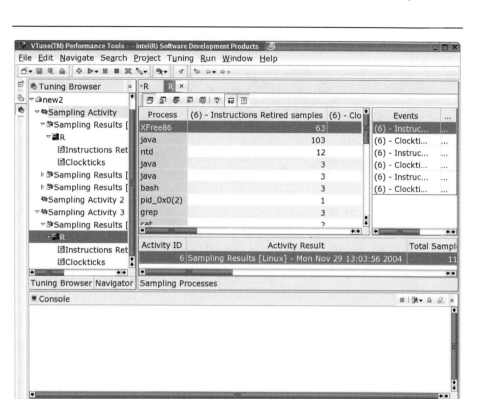

Figure 4.7   Sampling Results for `prog0401` on Linux with Java Dominating

Drilling Down to the Source

You can take your analysis of the prog0401 program one step further by drilling down to the source code to look for hotspots at the individual-line level. Simply double-click on any horizontal bar next to the read function and the analyzer displays the source code. If a dialog box pops up telling you that source code is not available, you have the option of looking at assembly language, telling VTune analyzer the directory with the source code in case it is located in an unusual place, or revisiting the instructions in the earlier section entitled "Before You Begin Sampling," that explain how to compile your program so you can view the source code.

Figure 4.8 shows the Source Code view of the `prog0401` program. Mouse over the column heading for *Timer*. Notice that the analyzer shows information about this column. Right-click on the column heading and take note of the many options. Selecting the **What's This Column?** option is a very powerful way to see the VTune analyzer's built-in documentation on this event. Another important option is **View Events As**, which controls the numbers shown in the column; the default view is **Sample Counts**. Since VTune analyzer Sampling works by interrupting your program occasionally, this option shows you how many actual interrupts occurred. In the `prog0401` example, the Timer occurred 10 times (7+3) in the `for` loop in the `read` routine. Seven of these happened to land on line 37 of the program, and three on line 45 (not shown). You can choose to change the column to display **% of Module**, which is often more meaningful for users who prefer to look at performance data in terms of percentages, rather than sample counts.

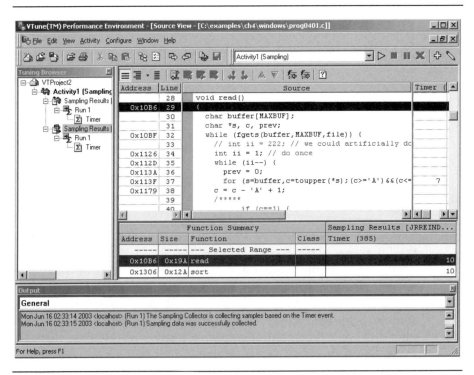

Figure 4.8   Source Code View of `prog0401`

Each line of compiled C code resolves to many assembly instructions, which you can view by clicking on the **Mixed by Execution** icon, the second icon just above the Address column in the Source Display window. Figure 4.9 shows the mixed assembly and C source code view. Each C source line shows the total count of assembly instructions associated with it. For instance, line 45 (`tally2[prev][c]++`) has 21 assembly instructions, three of which were interrupted at once by time-based sampling. The C source line gets credit for all three interrupts; the assembly language code shows exactly which machine instructions were interrupted.

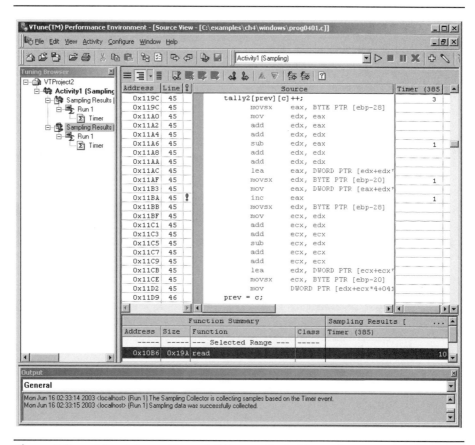

Figure 4.9   Mixed Assembly and C Source Code View of `prog0401`

Figure 4.10 shows the Disassembly View, which is used when source code is not available because you do not have the source code, because you may need to compile differently, or because you may need to tell the VTune analyzer more information so that it can find the source code to display. This view can occur on any version of the VTune analyzer. The illustration is from the Linux version.

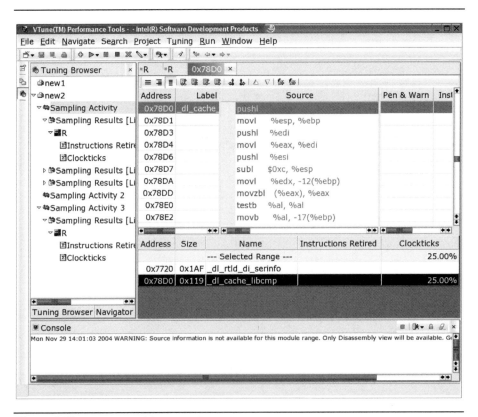

Figure 4.10 Disassembly View (Linux)

Example 4.2: Time-Based Sampling Using the Command Line

As mentioned in Chapter 3, you can use the VTune Performance Analyzer's command line to collect data about your application and system performance, and view the results in table form. This capability opens up many possibilities for automating performance collection, tabulation, and some types of analysis.

Like Example 4.1, this exercise uses the sample application (`prog0401`) from the companion Web site. If you have your own application, feel free to use it instead. If you have neither, just pick an application on your system such as `C:\WINNT\system32\notepad.exe` or `/bin/ls`.

Using the command line for Sampling involves repeated single invocations of the `vtl` command on a single project. Using these and other commands, you:

■ Configure a single activity with a collector and an application.

■ Run the activity and collect results.

■ Store the results in a persistent default project so that you can use the view mode to display results in your final commands. Of course, you can also use the VTune analyzer's graphical interface to view the data collected in the project, as shown in Example 4.1.

Note

Save projects (with a `.vpj` file extension) containing all activities, results, and associated files to the *home directory*.

For Windows, the `VTUNE_USER_DIR` environment variable specifies the home directory (this defaults to the `VTune` directory under the directory specified by the environment variable `APPDATA`).

For Linux, the `VTUNEHOME` environment variable determines the home directory (this defaults to `$HOME/.VTune`).

Step-by-Step Procedure

Follow these steps to perform the VTune analyzer's time-based Sampling from the command line, either by typing commands directly at the prompt >, or by placing them in a Windows-based batch file (.bat) or Linux-based script file that runs them all at once:

1. To ensure you know where the data are stored, start by setting the home directory:

    Windows commands (cmd):

    ```
    mkdir c:\tmpvtune
    set VTUNE_USER_DIR=C:\tmpvtune
    ```

    Linux commands (sh/ksh):

    ```
    mkdir c:/tmp/vtune
    set VTUNEHOME=/tmp/vtune
    export VTUNEHOME
    ```

    Linux commands (csh):

    ```
    mkdir c:/tmp/vtune
    setenv VTUNEHOME=/tmp/vtune
    ```

2. Write the test results to a batch file so it can be viewed later:

    Windows command (cmd):

    ```
    echo c:\examples\ch4\windows\prog0401.exe
        input0402.txt 1000 > prog0401.bat
    ```

    Linux command:

    ```
    echo '~/examples/ch4/linux/prog0401.exe
        input0402.txt 1000' > prog0401.bat
    ```

3. Configure an activity with a collector and an application:

    Windows command (cmd):

    ```
    vtl activity -d 0 -c sampling -o "-sm tbs"
        -app c:\examples\ch4\windows\prog0401.bat
        -moi c:\examples\ch4\windows\prog0401.exe
    ```

    Linux command:

    ```
    vtl activity -d 0 -c sampling -o "-sm tbs"
        -app ~/examples/ch4/linux/prog0401.bat
        -moi ~/examples/ch4/linux/prog0401.exe
    ```

4. Run the activity:

    ```
    vtl run
    ```

5. Display the results:

    ```
    vtl show
    ```

6. View the results:

    ```
    vtl view a1::r1 -sort
    ```

Note The `a1::r1` parameter is not really necessary; `vtl view -sort` will do what you need here.

Figure 4.11 illustrates the first few lines of output from using the VTune analyzer in command line mode on a system running Windows. (Due to space considerations, full paths are not shown in Figure 4.11 although they are displayed onscreen by the VTune analyzer).

```
vtl view a1::r1 -sort

VTune(TM) Performance Analyzer 7.1
Copyright (C) 2000-2003 Intel Corporation. All rights reserved.

Module        Process            Timer   Process Process Original
                                 samples Path    ID      Module
                                                         Path
hal.dll       System Idle Process 472            0x0     ...\System32\hal.dll
ntoskrnl.exe  System Idle Process 444            0x0     ...\System32\ntoskrnl.exe
prog0401.exe  prog0401.exe        30     ...\    0x6b0   ...\windows\prog0401.exe
```

Figure 4.11   Time Sampling Results for `prog0401` in Command Line

After the `vtl a1::r1 view -sort` command executed, notice that System Idle Process, specifically the Window's Hardware Abstraction Layer (`HAL`) and the NT-OS kernel (`ntoskrnl`), actually ran more than the `prog0401` program that the VTune analyzer was sampling. After the system idle, the output shows that `prog0401.exe` ran long enough for 30 timer samples to be taken while it was active. Unlike the GUI version of the VTune analyzer, the time spent setting up the program to run is part of the Sampling run, hence the large amount of time shown for the Idle process.

Drilling Down

The command line supports *drill down* capabilities beyond the module level, but currently stops at the function name. If you want more information than that, you can obtain it in one of these ways:

■ *Pack* the project you created using the command line, move the packed file to any machine you want, and then open, unpack, and study it using the graphical interface built into the VTune analyzer. See Chapter 8 for more about opening a packed project.

■ Use the *remote capabilities* of the VTune analyzer's GUI to control data collection on a remote Linux machine. See Chapter 10 for more about remote analysis.

■ Use the text-based source viewer supplied with the VTune analyzer.

Use these Windows-based commands to drill down to the function and source-file level, respectively:

```
vtl view -hf -mn prog0401.exe -sort
vtl view -hs -mn prog0401.exe -sort
```

Figure 4.12 shows the results of using the first `vtl view` command, which produces the function-level (`-hf`) information regarding the time spent in `prog0401.exe`. (Due to space considerations, the full path of the Source File column has been removed and the Resolved Module column has been omitted, although they are displayed onscreen by the VTune analyzer.) The function-level output reveals that `prog0401.exe` spent the most time executing the `read` function. Thirteen samples were gathered while `read` was executing, nine while `sort` was active, six during `fgets` (a C I/O library), and one while in `_isatty`, another C I/O library routine.

```
vtl view -hf -mn prog0401.exe -sort

VTune(TM) Performance Analyzer 7.1
Copyright (C) 2000-2003 Intel Corporation. All rights reserved.

Function Module       Timer    Segment Offset Address Size  Class Full    Source …
                      samples                                     Name
read     prog0401.exe 13       0x1     0xb6   0x10b6  0x19a       read    …\prog0401.c
sort     prog0401.exe 9        0x1     0x306  0x1306  0x12a       sort    …\prog0401.c
fgets    prog0401.exe 6        0x1     0x9a2  0x19a2  0x57        fgets   …\fgets.c
_isatty  prog0401.exe 1        0x1     0x5c12 0x6c12  0x27        _isatty …\isatty.c
```

Figure 4.12   Drill-down Time Sampling Function Results for `prog0401` in Command Line

Figure 4.13 shows the results of using the second `vtl view` command, which produces the source file (`-hs`) information regarding the time spent in `prog0401.exe`. The source-file information for `fgets` and `_isatty` shows the path information used when Microsoft built the library files `fgets.c` and `isatty.c`. (Due to space considerations, the full paths are not shown in Figure 4.12.) Twenty-two samples occurred inside the `prog0401.c` code; thirteen in `read` and nine in `sort`.

Inside the VTune™ Analyzer: Time-Based Sampling

If you're wondering exactly how the VTune analyzer performs time-based Sampling, here's how the program works. The analyzer uses a timer to generate sampling interrupts. When you run an activity configured for time-based sampling, the VTune analyzer:

1. Executes the application that you told it to launch.

2. Waits until the Delay Sampling time elapses, then interrupts the processor at the Sampling Interval and collects samples of the instruction addresses. By default, the analyzer interrupts after every 1 millisecond of the operating system timer and collects one 32-byte sample per interrupt.

3. Stores the samples in a buffer. When the buffer gets full, the analyzer suspends sampling, writes the samples to disk, and again resumes sampling.

4. Continues to sample until the application terminates or until the Sampling Duration ends.

At the end of sampling data collection, the VTune analyzer:

1. Analyzes the data.

2. Creates an activity result in the Tuning Browser window.

3. Displays the total samples collected for each module.

```
vtl view -hs -mn prog0401.exe -sort

VTune(TM) Performance Analyzer 7.1
Copyright (C) 2000-2003 Intel Corporation. All rights reserved.
```

Source File	Module	Timer samples	Resolved Module Path
prog0401.c	prog0401.exe	22	c:\...\prog0401.exe
...\fgets.c	prog0401.exe	6	c:\...\prog0401.exe
...\isatty.c	prog0401.exe	1	c:\...\prog0401.exe

Figure 4.13 Drill-down Time Sampling Source Results for prog0401 in Command Line

Event-Based Sampling

The VTune analyzer extends the concept of time-based sampling by allowing the counting of *events* other than time. Examples include cache misses, floating-point multiplies, pipeline stalls, and unaligned memory accesses. If you know your program is memory-bound, focus on memory-related events.

Based on the same `prog0401` program example as before, Example 4.3 explores event-based sampling by adding a third parameter to the command line arguments. This parameter causes the program to slow down when it has certain values. Be sure to type the command line arguments as shown in Step 6.

Example 4.3: Event-Based Sampling Using the Graphical Interface

Follow these steps to perform event-based Sampling from the VTune analyzer's graphical interface.

Step-by-Step Procedure

1. Double-click the **VTune Performance Analyzer** icon to start the program.
2. Click the **Create New Project** icon.
3. Click **Sampling Wizard** and select **OK**.
4. Select **Windows/Windows CE/Linux Profiling** and click **Next**.
5. In the **Application To Launch** text box, type the path:

   ```
   C:\examples\ch4\windows\prog0401.exe
   ```

6. In the **Command Line Arguments** text box, type:

   ```
   input0402.txt 1000 3
   ```

7. Select the **Modify default configuration when done with wizard** checkbox.
8. Click **Finish**.

   The Advanced Activity Configuration dialog box appears.

9. Click **Configure...** in the middle of the screen (for the **Sampling** data collector, which is already selected).

   The Configure Sampling window appears.

10. Select **Event-based sampling (EBS)** and make sure the **Calibrate Sample After value** checkbox is checked (do *not* clear it).

11. Click the **Events** tab.

12. Select **All events** from the Event Groups pull-down menu.

13. If you have a Pentium® 4 processor, highlight **Split Stores Retired (TI-E)** and **Split Loads Retired (TI-E)** from the Available Events scroll-down list and click the **>>** button to select these events for Sampling.

Note

> These two memory conditions are caused when memory loads and stores are not aligned to natural boundaries. In the `prog0401` program example, integers are not aligned on 4-byte boundaries. This creates a problem on Pentium® 4 processor-based systems, because the loads and stores sometimes have to involve two cache lines.
>
> On other processors, you might find one or more event(s) that measure a similar memory condition caused by alignment problems. You can click the **Explain...** button to see explanations of highlighted events

Figure 4.14 shows how the Sampling configuration looks after selecting events targeted to the Pentium 4 processor.

14. Notice that the VTune analyzer has scheduled three sampling runs and three Calibration runs to take place. With these particular four events selected for Sampling, the VTune analyzer requires that a program run three times in order to gather all the requested samples. Different processors and different events take differing amount of runs to complete.

15. Click **OK** after making your selections to return to the Advanced Activity Configuration dialog box.

16. Click **OK**.

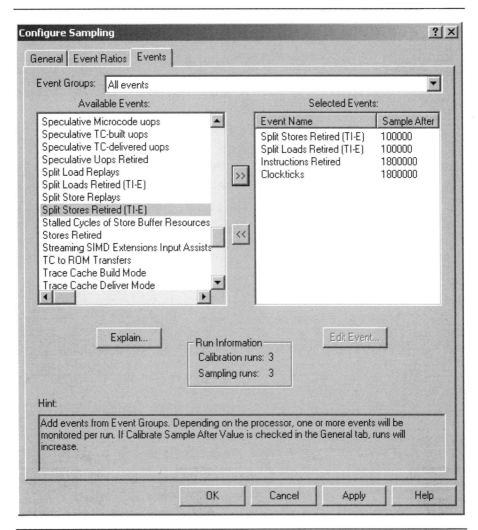

Figure 4.14 Event Sampling Configuration for a Pentium® 4 Processor-based System (Windows)

Once the `prog0401` program finishes executing, the VTune analyzer displays a screen showing the applications detected as running while Sampling took place. Figure 4.15 shows the resulting view. This time, the screen displays three more horizontal bars than appeared after time-based sampling alone. The four new bars represent information about the two events added to the list of events to sample.

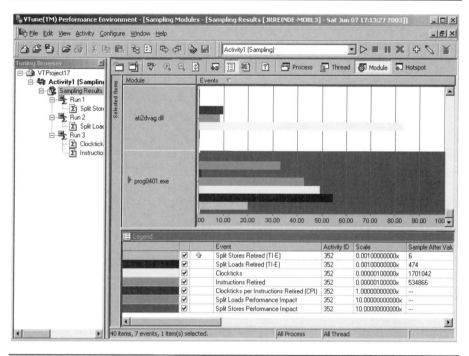

Figure 4.15 *Split Loads* and *Split Stores* on a Pentium® 4 Processor-based System (Windows)

How Often Did the *Split Loads* and *Split Stores* Occur?

Here, the Legend information has become much more interesting than in the previous time-based Sampling example. The *Sample After Values* column shows that the program had so few *Split Stores* that the VTune analyzer's Calibration run set the Sample After Value for *Split Stores* to 6. This change means that the processor was set to interrupt every six *Split Stores*, a value small enough to enable the VTune analyzer to interrupt about 1,000 times a second for that event. The *Split Loads*, on the other hand, happened more often, so the VTune analyzer set the Sample After Value for that event to 474, creating less frequent interrupts than for the *Split Stores*. The other Sample After Values are much higher. The *Clockticks* event is set to about 1.7 million, which is also designed to interrupt a little more than 1,000 times per second, since the test system had a 1.8 GHz processor.

In the default event-based Sampling runs, the VTune analyzer computes and displays *Clocks Per Instructions Retired* (CPI) in addition to the *Clockticks* event, which is measured directly. Now, with these new *Split Loads* and *Split Stores* events added to the Sampling, the VTune analyzer performs similar kinds of computations. It computes and displays the *Split Load Performance Impact* and *Split Store Performance Impact* in addition to the actual measured *Split Loads Retired* and *Split Stores Retired* events.

Drilling Down to the Source

By double-clicking on any horizontal bar for prog0401 or by simply clicking the **HotSpot** button, you arrive at the HotSpot view, as shown in Figure 4.16, which reveals that the read function has the majority of the *Split Loads* and *Split Stores* in it.

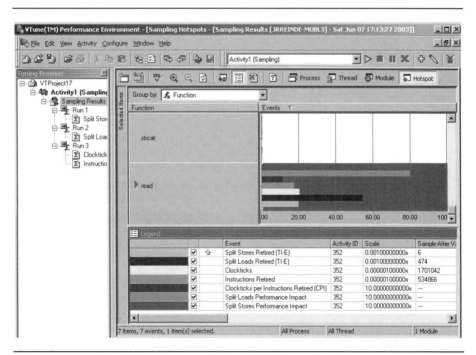

Figure 4.16   Hotspot (Function) View of *Split Loads* and *Split Stores* Events

Double-clicking on any horizontal bar for the `read` function leads to the VTune analyzer's Source view shown in Figure 4.17. If a dialog box pops up telling you that the source code is not available, either look at the assembly language instead or revisit the instructions in the earlier section of this chapter entitled "Before You Begin Sampling." These instructions explain how to compile your program so that you can view the C source code in the VTune analyzer.

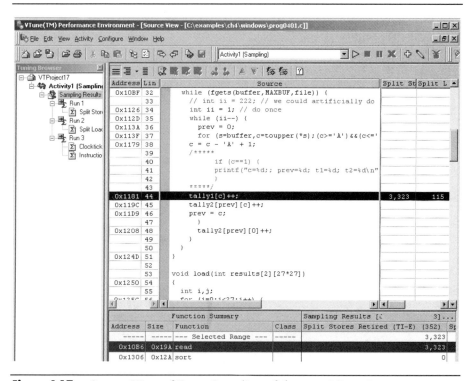

Figure 4.17　Source View of Event Sampling of the `read` Function

Mouse over the column heading for Split Stores Retired. Note that in Figure 4.17 you see only the abbreviated heading *Split St*. The VTune analyzer shows information about this column. Right-click while mousing over the column heading and take note of the many options. As noted earlier, clicking the **What's This Column?** option is a powerful way to see the VTune analyzer's built-in documentation on this event. Another important option is **View Events As**, which controls the numbers shown in the column; the default view is of **Sample Counts**. Since the VTune analyzer Sampling works by interrupting your program occasionally, this option shows you how many actual interrupts occurred. Chapter 7 addresses another option: **Get Tuning Advice**. If you want to try it quickly, select **Get Tuning Advice** and **For Current Selection**, and then click **OK** on the dialog box that opens.

My computer showed the following advice/information:

Significant coding pitfalls

⊞ Cache line splits due to loads:
0.00091 sec processor time

⊞ Cache line splits due to stores:
0.00055 sec processor time

Chapter 7 explores how to dig into this automated advice more.

Press the **Mixed by Execution** button above the Address column to see assembly language mixed in with the source code. Figure 4.18 shows the mixed assembly and C source code view.

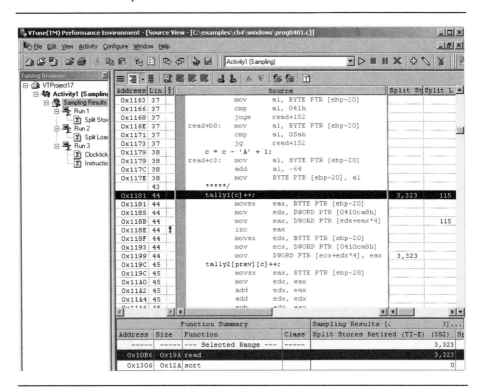

Figure 4.18   Source View of Event Sampling of the `read` Function, Assembly Language Mixed View

The C source lines show the total count of assembly instructions associated with each source line. For instance, notice the seven assembly language instructions just below the C code source line 44 (`tally1[c]++`). Two of these instructions are causing split cache line accesses. A load into `eax` from `[edx+eax*4]` is causing *Split Loads*. A store from `eax` to `[ecx+edx*4]` is causing the *Split Stores*.

These events are what Intel calls *precise events* because they are associated with the correct instructions. In general, events that include the word *Retired* in them tend to be *precise*. The VTune analyzer documentation for each event will tell you for sure.

If you sample using an event that is not precise, expect the exact lines of assembly or even source code to be off by a few lines. This is because interrupts frequently occur a few instructions beyond the instruction that caused the interrupt. In such a case, you may see a store event attributed to a non-store instruction that falls a few instructions beyond the actual store instruction. In VTune analyzer terminology, this is known as *event skid*. Skid is something users say they get used to after a while because the VTune analyzer puts you within a few instructions of the problem—you don't have to hunt around much to figure the rest out. Nevertheless, newer Intel processors support many exact, precise events that are not subject to skid.

Events associated with branches, including `call` and `return` instructions, can be much more troublesome. In such cases, you will not easily see the instruction that caused the problem. Fortunately, you have plenty of retired events to choose from, where you do not have to bother with this issue.

After finding the problem with split memory accesses, you would typically fix it by correcting the source code and then rerun Sampling by following these steps:

1. Double-click the **activity** in the **Tuning Browser**, decide whether to modify the activity or a copy of it, and click **OK**.

   The Advanced Activity Configuration dialog box appears.

2. Select the `prog0401` application in the **Application/Module Profiles** and click **Configure...** on the far right side of the screen.

   The Application/Module Profile Configuration window appears.

3. Change the **Command line arguments** to:

    ```
    input0402.txt 1000 0
    ```

4. Click **OK** to return to the Advanced Activity Configuration dialog box.

5. Click **OK**.

6. Click the **Run Activity** icon—a green right-pointing triangle shaped like a Play button—on the VTune analyzer's toolbar or select **Run** from the **Activity** menu.

The Sampling results that appear are very different from when `prog0401` generated multiple splits memory accesses in the `read` function. This time the number of *Split Stores* and *Split Loads* is virtually zero.

Example 4.4: Event-Based Sampling Using the Command Line

As you did for time-based sampling, you can use the VTune Performance Analyzer's command line interface to collect event-based data about your application and system performance and view the results in table form.

As in Example 4.2, this exercise uses the sample application (`prog0401`) from the companion Web site. Follow these steps to perform event-based sampling from the command line.

Step-by-Step Procedure

1. To ensure you know where the data are stored, start by setting the home directory:

    Windows commands (`cmd`):

    ```
    mkdir c:\tmpvtune
    set VTUNE_USER_DIR=C:\tmpvtune
    ```

    Linux commands (`sh/ksh`):

    ```
    mkdir c:/tmp/vtune
    set VTUNEHOME=/tmp/vtune
    export VTUNEHOME
    ```

    Linux commands (`csh`):

    ```
    mkdir c:/tmp/vtune
    setenv VTUNEHOME=/tmp/vtune
    ```

2. Write the test results to a batch file so it can be viewed later:

Windows command (cmd):

```
echo c:\examples\ch4\windows\prog0401.exe
    input0402.txt 1000 3 > prog0401.bat
```

Linux command:

```
echo '~/examples/ch4/linux/prog0401.exe
    input0402.txt 1000 3' > prog0401.bat
```

3. Configure an activity with a collector and an application:

Windows command (cmd):

```
vtl activity -d 7 -c sampling
    -o "-ec en='Split Loads Retired (TI-E)'
    en='Split Stores Retired (TI-E)'
    -calibration yes"
    -app c:\examples\ch4\windows\prog0402.bat
    -moi c:\examples\ch4\windows\prog0401.exe
```

Linux command:

```
vtl activity -d 7 -c sampling
    -o "-ec en='Split Loads Retired (TI-E)'
    en='Split Stores Retired (TI-E)'
    -calibration yes"
    -app ~/examples/ch4/linux/prog0401.bat
    -moi ~/examples/ch4/linux/prog0401.exe
```

4. Run the activity:

```
vtl run
```

5. Display the results:

```
vtl show
```

6. View the results:

```
vtl view a1::r1 -sort
```

Figure 4.19 illustrates the output from using the VTune analyzer's command line mode on a computer running Windows. After the `vtl a1::r1 view -sort` command executes, the results reveal that `prog0401` has 985 *Split Loads Retired* and 1018 *Split Stores Retired*. Note that only the first line of output is shown. (Due to space considerations, the full process and original module paths are not shown in Figure 4.19.)

```
vtl view a1::r1 -sort

VTune(TM) Performance Analyzer 7.1
Copyright (C) 2000-2003 Intel Corporation. All rights reserved.

Module      Process      Split   Split   Process Process Original
                         Loads   Stores  Path    ID      Module
                         Retired Retired                 Path
                         (TI-E)  (TI-E)
                         samples samples
prog0401.exe prog0401.exe 985    1018    ...\    0xab4   ...\prog0401.exe
```

Figure 4.19   Event Sampling Results for `prog0401` in Command Line

Drilling Down

Currently only the Windows version of the command line supports drill-down capabilities beyond the module level, and even then only to the function name. If you want more information than that, you can obtain it in one of the three ways described earlier in the "Drilling Down" section of Example 4.2. Use these Windows-based commands to drill down to the function and source-file level, respectively:

```
vtl view -hf -mn prog0401.exe -sort
vtl view -hs -mn prog0401.exe -sort
```

Figure 4.20 shows the results of using the first `vtl view` command to produce function-level (`-hf`) information regarding event times in `prog0401.exe`. (Due to space considerations, full path names are not shown.) The function-level output reveals that `prog0401.exe` experienced the most *Split Loads* (981) and *Split Stores* (1015) while executing the `read` function.

Figure 4.21 shows the results of using the second `vtl view` command to produce the source file (`-hs`) information regarding event times in `prog0401.exe`. (Due to space considerations, full path names are not shown.) The source-file information confirms that 981 *Split Loads* and 1,015 *Split Stores* occurred inside the `prog0401.c` code.

```
vtl view -hf -mn prog0401.exe -sort

VTune(TM) Performance Analyzer 7.1
Copyright (C) 2000-2003 Intel Corporation. All rights reserved.
```

Function	Module	Split Loads Retired (TI-E) samples	Split Stores Retired (TI-E) samples	Segment	Offset	Address	Size	Class	Full Name	Source File	Resolved Module Path
read	prog0401.exe	981	1015	0x1	0xb6	0x10b6	0x19a	read		prog0401.c	prog0401.exe
strcat	prog0401.exe	3		0x1	0x5790	0x6790	0xe8	strcat		strcat.asm	prog0401.exe
_output	prog0401.exe	4		0x1	0x1dd7	0x2dd7	0x7fa	_output		output.c	prog0401.exe

Figure 4.20   Drill-down Event Sampling Function Results for prog0401 in Command Line (Windows only)

```
vtl view -hs -mn prog0401.exe -sort

VTune(TM) Performance Analyzer 7.1
Copyright (C) 2000-2003 Intel Corporation. All rights reserved.
```

Source File	Module	Split Loads Retired (TI-E) samples	Split Stores Retired (TI-E) samples	Resolved Module Path
prog0401.c	prog0401.exe	981	1015	...\prog0401.exe
...\strcat.asm	prog0401.exe		3	...\prog0401.exe
...\output.c	prog0401.exe	4		...\prog0401.exe

Figure 4.21   Drill-down Event Sampling Source Results for prog0401 in Command Line (Windows only)

Inside the VTune™ Analyzer: How Sampling Analysis Works

The VTune analyzer implements sampling by interrupting the system periodically and keeping a record of where the interrupt occurred. The analyzer records the active thread, module, time, and location in the module. Time-based sampling (TBS) collects the samples at regular time-based intervals, which are 1 millisecond by default. The manner of accomplishing this varies on different processor and operating system combinations. Event-based sampling (EBS) collects the samples after a certain number of processor events, using model-specific registers on the processor. Intel calls these registers *model-specific* because they vary from processor to processor.

Regardless of the type of register, it is programmed to count some event on the processor; an interrupt is generated when this count overflows. The VTune analyzer programs the counter to overflow after a certain number of events by preloading the event-counting register with the appropriate value. By calibrating the values used to interrupt about 1,000 times per second, the VTune analyzer achieves a balance between interrupting too often and thereby disturbing the results, and interrupting too little and losing the required visibility to have faith in the results.

Sampling Rates

The number of events required to trigger an interrupt to take a sample of the execution context is called the *Sample After Value*. At one time, the VTune analyzer could not calibrate Sample After settings itself. Intel's support team would spend significant time explaining how to set these values correctly and then see users frustrated when they got them wrong.

In the event-based Sampling exercise described in Example 4.3 and Example 4.4, if you do not leave the default checkbox checked for **Calibrate Sample After value** in the GUI or use the -calibration yes option in the command-line version, you will find out that the VTune analyzer collects no samples for *Split Loads* or *Split Stores*. This is because the default Sample After Value for those events is set to 100,000 (refer back to Figure 4.14), and the sample program as run did not have that many *Split Loads* or *Split Stores* (about 55,000 *Split Loads* and 20,000 *Split Stores*). The prog0401 program was a "toy" example on purpose, but even so, it would be frustrating to get no samples taken at all.

To inspect the Sample After values that were automatically calibrated for events in Example 4.3 and Example 4.4:

1. In the VTune analyzer's GUI, double-click the activity name in the Tuning Browser (or select **Modify Activity Collector** from the **Configure** menu) to pull up the Advanced Activity Configuration dialog box.

2. Click the **Configure** button in the middle of the screen for the Sampling data collector to bring up the Configure Sampling options.

   Figure 4.22 shows the Configure Sampling event options after the prog0401 program ran.

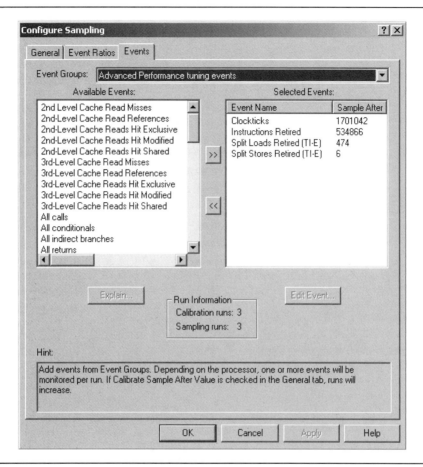

Figure 4.22   Configure Sampling Event Options After a Program Run

The Sample After Values used, 474 and 6, were considerably less than the default 100,000. By double-clicking on a Sample After Value, you can also manually change the value to any number you like. If you set it too large, you will not get enough samples taken to do your tuning properly. If you set it too small, the program may be interrupted too often and Sampling will become intrusive. The rule of thumb that the VTune analyzer uses is to generate 1,000 interrupts per second on average over the life of the program. If your program runs a long time, but the events are all piled up in one place, this could be too often. There may be cases where you want a little more sampling. For the prog0401 example, you can pick values that are half of those used by the VTune analyzer automatically and have no problem at all.

Similarly, the command-line version of the VTune analyzer allows a modifier (sa) on the activity command to specify a Sample After Value. The following command, for example, would set up the activity to sample after each 200 *Split Loads* and after each 10 *Split Stores*:

Windows command (cmd):

```
vtl activity -d 7 -c sampling
    -o "-ec en='Split Loads Retired (TI-E)':sa=200
    en='Split Stores Retired (TI-E)':sa=10
    -calibration no"
    -app c:\examples\ch4\windows\prog0402.bat
    -moi c:\examples\ch4\windows\prog0401.exe
```

Linux command:

```
vtl activity -d 7 -c sampling
    -o "-ec en='Split Loads Retired (TI-E)':sa=200
    en='Split Stores Retired (TI-E)':sa=10
    -calibration no"
    -app ~/examples/ch4/linux/prog0401.bat
    -moi ~/examples/ch4/linux/prog0401.exe
```

Event Ratios

An *event ratio* is a dynamically calculated value based on the events that make up the formula. The VTune analyzer includes a rich collection of commonly-used predefined event ratios for your convenience. The program allows you to use these predefined event ratios or to define your own new ratios in terms of predefined events.

Event ratios provide information based on processor performance-related events or Call Graph events. These event ratios can be monitored and sampled during event-based Sampling or used during a Call Graph analysis. By default, the VTune analyzer selects the *Cycles Per Instruction (CPI)* event ratio for event-based Sampling, consisting of the ratio of *Instructions Retired* and *Clockticks* events.

Event ratios can help you understand and compare results across several runs of an activity. Consider an activity in which one run operates for 50,000 *Clockticks* with 25,000 *Instructions Retired*, while another run operates for 20,000 *Clockticks* with 22,000 *Instructions Retired*. In this example, the difference between the two runs is much clearer when you compare the ratio of *Instructions Retired/Clockticks* known as CPI. Using CPI, the analyzer displays 0.5 CPI for the first run and 1.1 CPI for the second.

When looking at events alone in these two runs, you would need to check all four results in order to understand the difference between them. If, however, you have event ratios displayed in addition to the events themselves, the difference in the data becomes clearly visible. Differences in the performance of your application would not be as apparent if you did not have event ratio data displayed alongside the event data.

When configuring the Sampling collector, if you select events that make up a predefined ratio, the data for that event ratio automatically appear in your Sampling view as well. This occurs even though you may not have selected the event ratio itself in the configuration options.

More About Sampling Events and Event Ratios

Many events are available on Intel processors, and therefore the VTune analyzer offers numerous event counter options that correspond to these events. The particular event counters offered depend on the processor on which Sampling is being run. The counters for various Pentium 4 processors differ some from each other, but even larger differences exist between Itanium processors and Pentium 4 processors. These differences make sense, given their very different architectures.

In addition to event counter options, the analyzer also provides easy-to-use event ratios. These ratios consist of nothing more than taking two or more counters, doing a little math for you, and then displaying the result as though it were an actual counter that was read.

Fortunately, the Help system built into the VTune analyzer is very good at explaining each event counter and event ratio one by one. This book could not come close to matching the breadth of that documentation in the space of these pages. Nevertheless, you might want to flip through Appendix B, which contains some very useful summaries of event counters and ratios in an easy-to-browse book format. While the Reference section of the VTune analyzer online Help provides even more information, it is not as easy to browse because it is designed to answer specific questions and to pop up summary information a single counter at a time.

Appendix B has additional details on the event counter and can serve as a reference to help with the wealth of counters available within the VTune analyzer. The analyzer remains the single most complete source of details, but is less useful as a reference.

Sampling Usage Tips

When you start out with Sampling, you are likely to be hunting hotspots in your program or system. At this point, using the defaults in the Sampling wizard will work for you quite well. Once you find a hotspot, it may provide inspiration about the cause. For example, you might find out that the cause of the bottleneck has something to do with handling denormalized floating-point numbers. Finding this out would motivate you to learn about event counters related to this type of issue. Similarly, if the cause had something to do with 64K-aliasing issues, you would be motivated to learn about event counters that monitor those issues.

Going beyond this simple usage, this using of default settings to look for time hotspots, generally involves special insights that come from experience. User studies have shown this lack of experience to be a major barrier to using more of the many events available for analyzing programs. These studies led to the introduction of an automated set of steps for Automatic Hotspot analysis, covered in Chapter 7.

For speed issues caused by data, the solution is often to track down the routine that created the data. This is one motivation for complementing Sampling analysis with the addition of Call Graph analysis, covered in Chapter 6.

Always start with the methodology discussed in Chapter 1, "Learning to Fish: A Tuning Methodology." If you do not start with this methodology, you may spend unproductive time tuning small issues while missing the big picture.

Sampling Over Time View

The Sampling Over Time view provides a whole new dimension to sampling data. Using this feature, introduced in version 7.1, you can see how your application's performance changes over time, and easily visualize thread execution patterns. You can also use this view to identify processor resource contention issues on multiprocessors or microprocessors with Hyper-Threading Technology (HT Technology), as illustrated in the two analysis examples in this section.

Regular sampling views group-sampled data by process, thread, module, function, and line of code. While these views are useful for identifying hotspots, they do not give you any insight into the temporal behavior of your program. Sampling Over Time views show how performance characteristics of your software vary over time, and let you zero in on active sections of your program.

While regular sampling views show which threads ran during data collection, Sampling Over Time views can tell you whether the threads ran serially or in parallel. Using the Sampling Over Time thread view, you can see when a particular thread is executing, and how it is interacting with other threads in the application or the entire system. This visibility can help you find problems in thread synchronization or resource sharing.

The Sampling Over Time view is easy to use. Just collect sampling data, select the items such as modules, processes, or threads you are interested in, and then click the **Display Over Time View** icon. The icon looks like an hourglass:

Sampling Over Time views display the samples collected chronologically during a data collection run. As illustrated in the Over Time view shown in Figure 4.23, the VTune analyzer divides the selected time range equally in seconds. The x-axis represents time and the y-axis can represent threads, processes, or modules. Each box represents a time slice and is a color continuum that goes from green to red.

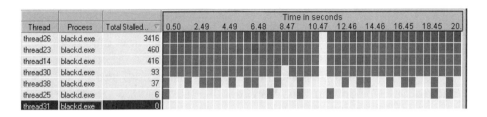

Figure 4.23 Example of a Sampling Over Time View

The legend for Over Time views, shown in Figure 4.24, provides a general idea of the number of samples collected for a square, based on its color. Green means fewer samples and red means more. If no samples exist for that item in that particular time slice, the box is light gray.

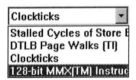

Figure 4.24 Example of the Legend for Sampling Over Time

In Sampling Over Time view, you can only view one event at a time. If you collected multiple types of events and want to look at another event, select that event from the pull-down list and update the view with the distribution over time for that event. You can only view events that were collected in the same run.

```
Clockticks                    ▼
Stalled Cycles of Store E
DTLB Page Walks [TI]
Clockticks
128-bit MMX[TM] Instruc
```

You can zoom in the view by holding down the left mouse button and dragging the mouse over the time range you are interested in. Then click the **Zoom In** icon:

If you want to see the regular Sampling view for this time range, click the **Display regular sampling view for selected time-range** icon:

This is useful for identifying hotspots in a particular time range. You can also zoom out to your previous view by clicking the **Zoom Out** icon:

If you want to see what was executing on the different logical or physical CPUs in your system, click the CPU icon:

All these icons appear in the Sampling toolbar at the top of Figure 4.25.

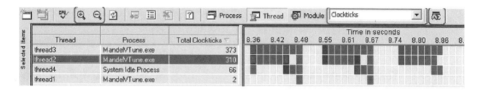

Figure 4.25   Sampling Over Time User Interface

Example 4.5 Over Time Analysis of Dual Processors

The Sampling Over Time feature can help you investigate multithreaded and multitasking applications to answer questions such as these:

- ■ Is the application's threading model operating as intended?

- ■ Which threads are running serially or in parallel?

- ■ When are threads competing for limited resources?

Using the answers to these questions, you can answer other performance questions such as:

- ■ Which processors are idle at a specific time?

- ■ Are events distributed evenly over time or grouped in temporal hotspots?

Configuring Sampling Over Time

By default, Sampling Over Time is turned on during Sampling, causing the VTune analyzer to save the sample time when recording a sampled event. To verify that Sampling Over Time will be activated during Sampling data collection:

1. From Step 4 of the Sampling Wizard, select the **Modify default configuration when done with wizard** checkbox.

2. Click **Finish**.

   The Advanced Activity Configuration dialog box appears.

3. Click **Configure...** in the middle of the screen (for the **Sampling** data collector, which is already selected).

   The Configure Sampling window appears.

4. Select **General** and make sure the **Display sampling results over time** checkbox is checked (do *not* clear) as shown at the bottom of Figure 4.26.

5. Click **Ok**.

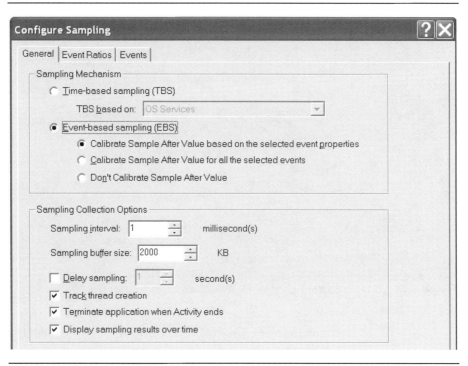

Figure 4.26 Activating Sampling Over Time

Generating Over Time Views

From the Process, Thread, and Module views, you can invoke the Over Time view. To generate an Over Time view after collecting Sampling results:

1. Select the items of interest in a regular Sampling view:

   ■ To select a single item, left-click that item.

   ■ To select multiple items, hold down **Ctrl** and left-click the items.

   ■ To select all the items, hold down **Ctrl** and press **A** (**Ctrl-A**).

   Figure 4.27 shows Module view with two modules selected as items of interest: processr.sys and Transitions.exe.

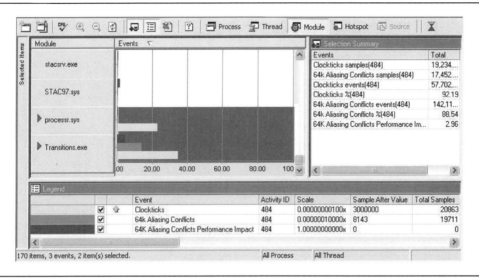

Figure 4.27   Two Items Selected in Module View

2. Click the **Display Over Time View** icon (note that if the analyzer window is too small, the icon may not be visible):

The Modules Over Time view appears, as shown in Figure 4.28.

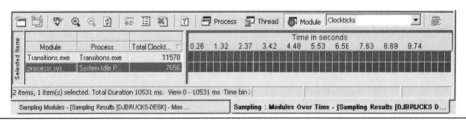

Figure 4.28   Over Time View for Two Modules

The initial view displays the data for the entire run over the selected items. The Time in seconds panel uses color to display the sample density. In Figure 4.28, red represents the highest sample density and green represents the lowest. This example uses the percentage of *Clockticks* for `processr.sys` (the idle process) to evaluate parallel processing.

On a dual-processor system, 50-percent idle time indicates no parallel processing, while less than 50-percent idle time indicates some degree of parallel processing. In this example, the idle process has less than half the *Clockticks*, indicating that some parallel processing is occurring. Because the number of *Clockticks* in the idle process is significantly above zero, there may be room to improve the parallel processing of the `Transitions.exe` process. To investigate this further, it could help to view sampling data for the application's threads.

3. Select **Process** view and then select the process of interest.

4. Choose **Thread** view and select the threads of interest.

   Figure 4.29 shows the `Transitions.exe` process with two threads selected.

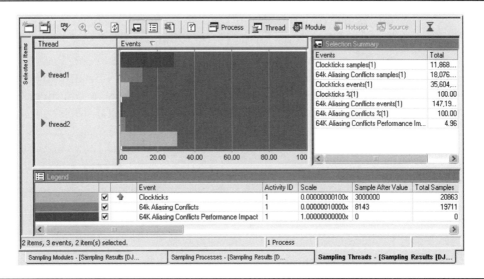

Figure 4.29 Thread View of `Transitions.exe` Process, Two Threads Selected

5.   Click the **Display Over Time View** icon.

Figure 4.30 shows the resulting Threads Over Time view.

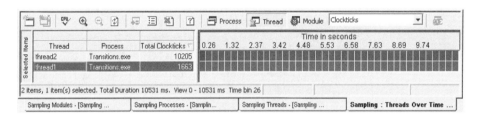

Figure 4.30   Over Time View of Clockticks for Two Threads

The colors indicate that these threads are not balanced—
`thread2` had many more *Clockticks* samples. (This program used
functional decomposition to divide the work between threads.
The two threads perform different functions.)

When sampling results include more than one event, you can use
the Event pull-down list to select the event to be displayed over
time. In the example shown in Figure 4.31, you can switch between displaying *Clockticks* and *64k Aliasing Conflicts*.

Figure 4.31   Use the Event Pull-down List to Select the Event

Figure 4.31 shows that `thread2` has more *Clockticks* data,
while Figure 4.32 shows that `thread1` has more *64k Aliasing
Conflicts* data.

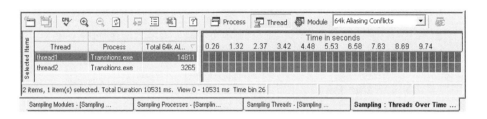

Figure 4.32   Over Time View of *64k Aliasing Conflicts* for Two Threads

This data suggest that fixing 64k aliasing problems in this program will have more effect on the performance of `thread1`, which was underperforming in Figure 4.30. The data appear in sorted order.

6. To change the order of the sort, click on the event column heading in the Selected Items pane—*64k Aliasing Conflicts* in this case—as shown in Figure 4.33.

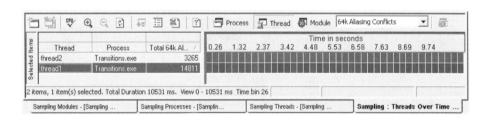

Figure 4.33   Click on the Event Column Heading to Change the Sorted Order

You can also open Over Time view from Process view. To do so, choose the **Process** icon, select the processes of interest, and then click the **Display Over Time View** icon.

Using Zoom

You can zoom in and out and switch back and forth between the Sampling Over Time view and the regular Sampling view. To zoom in on any Over Time view:

1. Click and drag a portion of the time data displayed on the colored portion of the Time in seconds panel (left-click and hold down the mouse button while dragging to complete the selection).

   The Zoom slider highlights the selected range. Figure 4.34 shows a selection highlighted from the start of execution to just beyond 1.32 seconds of run time.

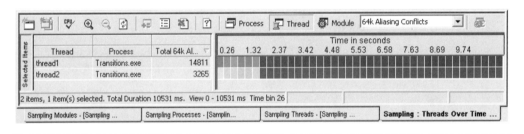

Figure 4.34 Selected Region from 0 to 1.32 Seconds of Run Time

2. Click the **Zoom-In** icon:

   to expand the selection for this event—in this case, *64k Aliasing Conflicts*.

Figure 4.35 shows the new Threads Over Time view after zooming in.

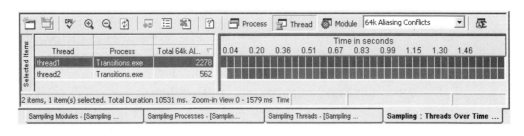

Figure 4.35   Threads Over Time View After Zooming in Once

You can zoom in repeatedly up to the limit of half a millisecond granularity. Figure 4.36 shows the Threads Over Time view for *Clockticks* after zooming in twice—first to 0 to 1.32 and then again to 0 to 0.36.

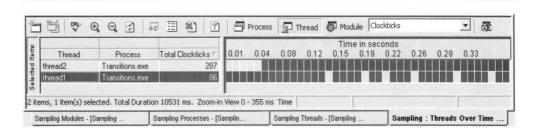

Figure 4.36   Threads Over Time View Zoomed in Twice

Figure 4.36 clearly shows when `thread2` was created and also gives a hint regarding the imbalances when `thread1` is idle waiting for `thread2`; the uncolored or light gray sections indicate no activity. In this program, `thread1` creates `thread2` and waits for `thread2` to alpha blend two images. The program then renders the alpha-blended frame and waits for the next image. Some parallel activity occurs because, while `thread1` is rendering, `thread2` alpha blends the next image. The alpha-blend task requires more CPU cycles than the render task, and `thread1` is often waiting for `thread2`.

Saving a Zoomed-in Time Range

After you have zoomed into a time period, you can save that view as a regular Sampling view. Doing so allows you to focus your investigation on a portion of an activity, such as startup time. Depending on the view, you can see exactly which processes, threads, or modules executed during the selected time period.

To save a time period as a regular Sampling view:

1. Zoom into a given time period, as described earlier.

2. Click the **Display regular sampling view for selected time-range** icon:

   This icon is only enabled after zooming in, because it creates a new view just for the zoomed-in data. Figure 4.37 shows a new regular Sampling Process view. To show the Duration(s) column for the new view, scroll the Legend pane to the right as indicated in the figure.

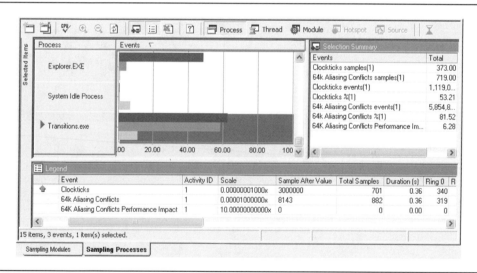

Figure 4.37   New View Created from a Sampling Over Time Drilldown

Every time you click the **Display regular sampling view for se-lected time-range** icon, the VTune analyzer generates an .sdb file and creates a new node for the project in the Tuning Browser window. The letters SOT indicating Sampling Over Time, precede the name of the node. Figure 4.38 shows the corresponding Tuning Browser window for this example. The new node name, SOT Drilldown 0.00 sec to 0.35 sec, includes the drilldown time.

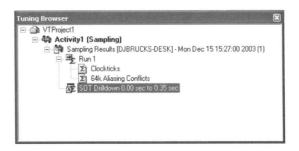

Figure 4.38   A New SOT Node Is Added to the Project

Although you zoomed in on the Transitions.exe process, all processes with samples captured during the selected time period also appear in this new view. Even though the new view is a regular view, it cannot be used to create an Over Time view; Over Time views are created from original Sampling results only.

3. To return to the regular Sampling view for the entire Activity run, you can do any one of the following:

■ From the Windows menu, select the view you wish to go back to.

■ Click the tab at the bottom of the Sampling view.

■ Use the navigation icons on the main toolbar to go back to a specific view.

Example 4.6 Over Time Analysis of Hyper-Threading Technology

Have a look at another analysis example involving Sampling Over Time. Figure 4.39 shows the threads of the MandelVTune.exe application and the System Idle Process, running on a Pentium 4 processor-based system with Hyper-Threading Technology.

Thread	Process	Total Clockticks	Time in seconds
			0.50 2.49 4.48 6.47 8.46 10.45 12.44 14.43 16.42 18.41
thread3	MandelVTune.exe	8471	
thread2	MandelVTune.exe	8417	
thread1	MandelVTune.exe	168	
thread5	System Idle Process	8916	

Figure 4.39   Threads Over Time View of `MandelVTune.exe` Application

This Java application, which also appears in Example 9.1 in Chapter 9, calculates a Mandelbrot image using two worker threads. `Thread1` is the master thread and `Thread2` and `Thread3` are the worker threads. `Thread2` calculates the top half of the image and `Thread3` calculates the bottom half. `Thread5` is the System Idle Process thread. The benchmark for this application is the amount of time that it takes to calculate a 4096×4096 pixel image. Benchmark execution initially takes 19.95 seconds on this system.

If both logical processors were fully utilized, there would be little to no samples in the System Idle Process. In this case, however, almost 30 percent of the samples are in the System Idle Process. The presence of red squares in the System Idle Process row in Figure 4.39 indicates that most of the samples in the System Idle Process occur at the beginning and end of program execution. The presence of green squares at the beginning of the `Thread2` row and at the end of the `Thread3` row explains why. The idle process runs at the beginning because `Thread2` is not fully utilizing one of the logical processors. It runs at the end because `Thread3` is not fully utilizing one of the logical processors.

Figure 4.40, Figure 4.41, and Figure 4.42 are zoomed-in views of the beginning, middle, and end of the Sampling run, respectively. At the beginning, `Thread2` runs for very short periods of time and then goes to sleep. At the end, `Thread3` displays the same behavior. In the middle, both threads execute simultaneously and then go to sleep for short periods of time.

Thread	Process	Total Clockticks	Time in seconds
			1.54 1.74 1.94 2.14 2.34 2.54 2.74 2.94 3.13 3.33
thread3	MandelVTune.exe	1419	
thread2	MandelVTune.exe	139	
thread1	MandelVTune.exe	5	
thread5	System Idle Process	1277	

Figure 4.40   Zoomed-in View of the Beginning of the Sampling Session

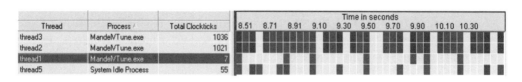

Thread	Process	Total Clockticks	Time in seconds
thread3	MandelVTune.exe	1036	
thread2	MandelVTune.exe	1021	
thread1	MandelVTune.exe	7	
thread5	System Idle Process	55	

Figure 4.41 Zoomed-in View of the Middle of the Sampling Session

Thread	Process	Total Clockticks	Time in seconds
thread3	MandelVTune.exe	225	
thread2	MandelVTune.exe	1386	
thread1	MandelVTune.exe	8	
thread5	System Idle Process	1161	

Figure 4.42 Zoomed-in View of the End of the Sampling Session

The main loop of each of the worker threads calculates a few rows of pixels of the Mandelbrot image and then updates a status bar that shows the progress of each of the worker threads. Figure 4.43 shows this portion of the code.

```
for (y=pParms->y; y<pParms->height; y++) {
    pBitmap = (DWORD *)pParms->pBitmap + y *
        pParms->pitch/4;
    for (x=pParms->x; x<pParms->x + pParms->width; x++)
    {
        c.real = REAL_MIN + ((float)x*SCALE_REAL);
        c.imag = IMAG_MIN + ((float)y*SCALE_IMAG);
        DWORD color = cal_pixel(c);
        pBitmap[x] = (color << 16) + (color << 8) +
            ((color & 0x0F) << 4);
    }
    if ((++UpdateBars) == UPDATE_STATUS_BARS_LINES) {
        UpdateBars = 0;
        SendMessage(pParms->hWndProgress, PBM_STEPIT,
            0, 0);
    }
}
```

Figure 4.43 MandelVTune.exe Main Loop

However, this analysis does not explain why the system is idle for about 30 percent of the execution time. Upon closer inspection of the main loop, the only function call that could potentially block is the `SendMessage` Win32 API call at line 12. The API's definition specifies that it will call the window procedure for the specified window and not return until the procedure has processed the message. If you change the `SendMessage` call to `PostMessage`, you should see less time in the idle process, since `PostMessage` posts the message to the thread that created the Window's message queue and then immediately returns.

This change does indeed speed up the application. The benchmark execution time after the code change takes only 10.02 seconds—almost a 2× speedup. Figure 4.44 shows the Sampling Over Time thread view after the call to `SendMessage` is changed to `PostMessage`. As you can see, very few samples appear in the System Idle Process now.

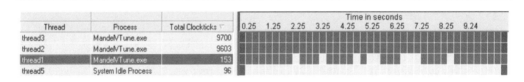

Figure 4.44   `MandelVTune.exe` using `PostMessage`

Sampling Usage Tips

Sampling is best used when there is a particularly dominant hotspot that the user wants to analyze in more detail, or when the user wants to tune the application more precisely for the CPU architecture, such as looking at cache misses to tune cache blocking algorithms or prefetching. Call Graph analysis, by contrast, is used to get an algorithmic or high level look at the program. Call Graph analysis can often be useful when the Sampling profile is "flat"—when there isn't one dominant hotspot. Call Graph analysis is covered in the next chapter.

In general, you should run Sampling first and see if a dominant hotspot is found. If so, drill down to source to analyze it in more detail. If not, it is time for Call Graph analysis.

For some users, Call Graph analysis remains their dominant methodology for measuring performance, with occasional use of sampling to make sure that new "low-hanging fruit" has not emerged. Often applications that are characterized by data processing, as opposed to loop-based calculation type programs, are better suited for Call Graph analysis, since it is less likely that they will have a only small number of significant hotspots. After exhausting tuning based on sampling of such applications, users generally rely on Call Graph analysis for their primary tuning methodology.

If you are working in an environment that includes Java or C#, be sure to tell the analyzer that you are working with managed code as you set up the session. The VTune analyzer can show managed code alongside unmanaged code, but to do so the analyzer has to listen differently, so to speak, when dealing with unmanaged code in the mix. Enable this capability with a single click on the data collector setup if you're using the GUI; if you're using the command line, you may use one of these options: Java, applet, or jitprofiling. Chapter 9 contains more information on this method.

Going beyond a simple usage of "doing the default look for time hotspots" has generally involved special insights that come from experience. User studies have shown this to be a major barrier to using more of the many events available for analyzing programs. This led to the introducion of an automated set of steps for Automatic Hotspot analysis. Automatic Hotspot analysis is covered in Chapter 7.

For speed issues that are caused by data, the solution is often to track down the routine that creates the data. This is one of the motivations for adding Call Graph analysis to complement Sampling. This is covered in the next chapter.

Always start with the methodology discussed in Chapter 1, "Learning to Fish: A Tuning Methodology." If you do not start with the big picture, you may spend unproductive time tuning small issues while missing the big picture.

How Sampling Analysis Works

The VTune analyzer implements sampling so that the system is interrupted periodically, and a record is kept of the location the system was interrupted. The active thread, module, time and location in the module are recorded. Time-based sampling (TBS) collects the samples at regular time-based intervals (1 millisecond by default). How this is accomplished varies on different processor and operating system combinations. Event-based sampling (EBS) collects the samples after a certain number of processor events. This is implemented using model specific registers on the processor. Intel calls these registers *model specific* because they vary from processor to processor. What they share in common is that the registers are programmed to count an event on the processor, and an interrupt is generated when the counts overflows. The VTune analyzer programs the counter to overflow after a certain number of events by pre-loading the event counting register with the appropriate value. By calibrating the values used to interrupt about a thousand times per second, a balance is accomplished between interrupting too often and thereby disturbing the results and interrupting too little and losing the require visibility to have faith in the results.

Recap

Here are some key points in this chapter:

- A *hotspot* is a point of interest in a program where "something" happens more often than it happens elsewhere.

- Sampling offers a number of benefits for hotspot hunting:
    - It is system-wide so you can find out what is happening with the software as a whole, and even sample code running in Ring 0, such as device drivers.
    - It requires no code modifications or instrumentation.
    - Low overhead means minimal intrusion.

- The VTune analyzer requires line number and symbol (debug) information from your compiler so it can display function names in various views and display your source code.
    - Generating this information does not require you to disable any existing optimizations in the monitored application. In fact, you want to analyze optimized code.
    - Your compiler can generate this information in various formats, but try to avoid using the .map file format, since it provides less complete information and functionality.

■ You can use the VTune analyzer's GUI or command line interface to run Sampling and view the results.

   – The VTune analyzer's GUI offers multiple ways to view Sampling results in graphical form, identify hotspots, and drill down to the source level to find the root cause.

   – The Mixed by Execution button lets you view assembly language code mixed with your compiler's source code.

   – The VTune analyzer's command line interface involves using the `vtl` command with various options and switches.

■ Options like the **Explain...** button and **What's This Column?** are powerful tools for locating topics in the VTune analyzer's Help documentation.

■ Events that include the word *Retired* tend to be *precise*, meaning that they are always associated with the correct instruction. Events that are not precise tend to be associated with a later instruction because of *event skid*.

■ If you check the Calibrate Sample After Value checkbox when configuring an event-based Sampling activity or use the `-calibration yes` option with the `vtl` command, the VTune analyzer automatically sets the sampling rate by calculating the Sample After value for you.

■ Appendix B provides an easy-to-browse overview of the event counters and event ratios of several Intel microprocessors. The online Help built into the VTune analyzer is always being updated and is much more detailed and complete, but is not as convenient to browse through for overview purposes.

■ Sampling Over Time allows you to see how your application's performance changes over time, and easily visualize thread execution patterns.

■ Sampling Over Time views are particularly useful for identifying processor resource contention issues on multiprocessors or microprocessors with Hyper-Threading Technology.

■ In Sampling Over Time view, you can only view one event at a time. You can zoom in the view for a particular time range one or more times, and then save that view as a node in the Tuning Browser. Color-coding reveals the number of samples for each time slice, with red indicating more, green less, and light gray indicating the absence of samples.

Chapter 5

Hotspot Hunting 102: Call Graph

If you don't know where you are going, you will probably end up somewhere else.

—Laurence J. Peter

Nothing tops a picture for conveying meaning quickly. When you want a quick look at what is happening in your application, a pictorial view of its program flow can help you isolate critical functions and calling sequences. *Call Graph profiling*, the second of three analysis methods offered by the VTune™ analyzer, provides this picture. In all VTune analyzer versions, you use a graphical viewer to inspect the calling patterns and timing of each function in your program. Unlike some call-profiling tools, you do not need a special compiler or special API calls in your code; you only need to build your application so that it generates debug information and is linked to allow base relocations. Table 5.1 summarizes the Call Graph feature, including software and hardware specifics for using this analysis technique.

Table 5.1   Call Graph at a Glance

Feature:	Call Graph Profiling
Benefit at a glance:	Allows you to see the calling patterns of each function in your program. Helps you understand your program's architecture and figure out where its routines are being called from.
Versions:	The VTune™ analyzer supports Call Graph analysis on Windows and Linux for Pentium® and Itanium® processors.
OS/Environments:	Windows and Linux operating systems. Supported applications: Win32/Win64, stand-alone Win32/Win64 DLLs, stand-alone COM+ DLLs, Java, .NET, ASP.NET.
Collectors:	Pentium and Itanium processors, Windows and Linux. Not yet supported on collectors for processors with Intel XScale® technology.
Languages:	All languages. Display of source code for compiled code, such as C++ and Fortran, requires symbol information in the executable. The VTune analyzer supports profiling Java2 applications via the Java Virtual Machine Profiling Interface (JVMPI) using the –Xrunjavaperf option if running manually, or via Microsoft-specific API's for Jview. Java source code display requires use of JITs. with support for Java performance tuning, based on Java SDK 1.3 or later. ASP.NET data collection start/stop requires the VTune analyzer to set/unset certain environment variables; the IIS and IIS-related web services are restarted as well.
Processors:	Pentium and Itanium processors.

Call Graph Overview

Call Graph presents a high-level control flow diagram of your program as it actually ran on your system. Using this analysis method you can understand your program's architecture, gain insights into how to adjust its flow, and answer questions like "Which function has the longest execution time and what functions are calling it?"

You can also figure out where a particular routine in your application is called from, and answer questions such as "Which execution path in my code takes the most time?" and "Which functions in my program are getting called?" This area is where the VTune analyzer shines. Analyzing an application frequently leads to a need to know which functions call the "hot" routine in your program so that you can make adjustments for better performance. Like all the VTune analyzer techniques, Call Graph analysis supports this goal.

To Sample or Not to Sample

For compiled code such as that written in C, C++, or Fortran, Call Graph analysis is typically much more useful after you have already obtained Sampling information. This approach is common but not at all necessary. Users with a history of using other tools before the VTune analyzer often perform Call Graph analysis first, because they previously had no tool that offered Sampling. The VTune analyzer design lets you start with either and then expand your thinking to include both, with the goal of finding and analyzing program hotspots regardless of how you started.

For developers of applications written in Java, C#, and Visual BASIC, Call Graph collecting and analysis is the most useful and popular VTune analyzer feature. Sampling holds limited value for these types of interpreted or "just in time" (JIT) compiled programs. While Sampling analysis can isolate bottlenecks and relate them to processor features, developers who write code in these languages generally feel they have too little control over the actual interpreted or JIT-generated code to need much more information than simply the amount of time spent in a routine. Exceptions exist, but, for the most part, starting with Call Graph analysis works very well in these circumstances, because it presents time summaries for functions. If function-level timing yields insufficient data, such users may be able to obtain more information from time-based Sampling, depending on their exact environment.

In What Environments Does Call Graph Work?

Unlike Sampling, Call Graph is not system-wide and can only profile code running in the least privileged protection ring (Ring 3). Therefore, the Call Graph trace does not extend into most system code including device drivers, nor does it work with `setuid` images on Linux.

Call Graph is available in those environments where Intel has implemented instrumentation code. As of version 7.1, this feature works with Win32/Win64 applications, stand-alone Win32/Win64 DLLs, stand-alone COM+ DLLs, Java applications, .NET applications, ASP.NET applications, and Linux applications.

What About Managed Code?

With the advent of the Microsoft .NET environment, a number of new buzzwords have emerged. One of these is *managed code.* A program written with managed code can operate with the .NET Framework *common language runtime*, which supports common services such as memory management, cross-language integration, code access security, and automatic lifetime control of objects.

By extending C++, Managed Extensions for Visual C++ make it easy to add support for the .NET Framework. Using the /clr compiler option, by selecting **Properties** → **General** → **Use Managed Extensions** → **Yes** in the Microsoft Visual C++ .NET Environment, enables Managed Extensions for C++ and creates an output file that runs using the .NET Framework common language runtime.

Fortunately, Call Graph provides performance data for both managed and unmanaged code in .NET and Java applications. Because Call Graph uses a managed-code profiling API with binary instrumentation, it can offer insight into how managed code calls translate into Win32 calls.

When tuning mixed mode code (managed and unmanaged code), it is interesting to highlight .NET or Java methods so you can see which functions are native and which are not. This highlighting is often useful for pure managed code because you often have unmanaged code in the runtime or other library functions.

Inside the VTune™ Analyzer: Call Graph Data Collection

What really happens when you activate the Call Graph data collection feature? After you finish walking through the steps of a Call Graph wizard, or manually run an activity configured for Call Graph data collection, the VTune analyzer:

1. Instruments the application and/or module of interest.

2. Launches and profiles the instrumented program until it either terminates or you manually stop running it.

3. Keeps track of the program exit and entry points.

4. Records the number of times each function in the program was called.

5. Establishes a relationship between each caller (parent) and callee (child) function.

6. Stores all this data.

At the end of Call Graph data collection, the VTune analyzer:

1. Analyses the profile data.

2. Generates a new activity result in the Tuning Browser.

3. Displays the Call Graph results data in tabular and graph view.

Before You Begin Profiling

As with Sampling, be sure to compile and link with symbols and line numbers so that you will be able to view the source code in Source view. See Appendix A, "Types of Line Number and Symbol File Information," for details about how to generate this information using several popular compilers. With Call Graph, you must consider two additional items as well: generating base relocations and making the source code for relevant functions available.

Generating Base Relocations

Before you start up the Call Graph Wizard, double check to make sure you have compiled your application using the right switches; otherwise, Call Graph cannot instrument your code correctly. When developing for Microsoft Windows, you must set the linking options to enable base relocations for Call Graph analysis.[1] If necessary, relink your program with the /FIXED:NO option and rebuild your application. On Linux, use binaries that have not been stripped; specifically, do not use the --strip-unneeded option to build your application.

Note

> The /FIXED option tells the Windows operating system to load the program only at its preferred base address and not to generate base relocation information. By default, Microsoft Visual C++ generates base relocation information for .dll files but not for .exe files. To generate a base relocation section in your program, specify /FIXED:NO.

C++ in Visual Studio .NET Environment

If you are compiling Visual C++ code from within the Visual Studio .NET environment:

1. In the Solution Explorer window, right-click the Project and select **Properties**.
2. Click the **C++** tab.
3. Click the **Linker** tab.
4. Select **Command Line**.
5. Add **/fixed:no** to **Additional Options** as shown in Figure 5.1 to enable base relocations for Call Graph profiling.

---

[1] This requirement applies only when you are using the All Functions instrumentation level. For Export and Minimal instrumentation levels, base relocation is not necessary.

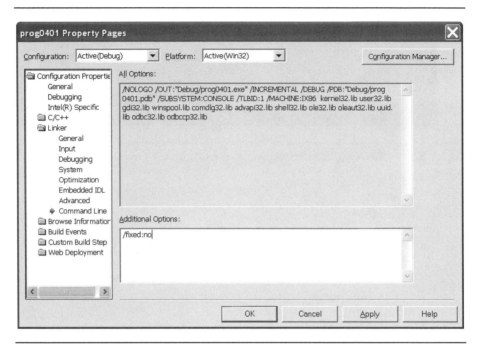

Figure 5.1   Enabling Base Relocation in Visual Studio .NET

C++ in Visual Studio 6.0 Environment

If you are compiling C++ code from within the Visual Studio 6.0 environment:

1. Select **Project** → **Settings**.

2. On the **Link** tab, add /fixed:no to the switches listed in the **Project Options** box.

C++ Using Command Line Interface

If you are compiling C++ code using the command line interface, do *one* of the following:

■ Add the -link -fixed:no switches to the **cl** (Microsoft C++ compiler) or **icl** (Intel® C++ Compiler) command as shown in Figure 5.2

  or

■ Add the -fixed:no switch to the link command if using separate compile and link commands.

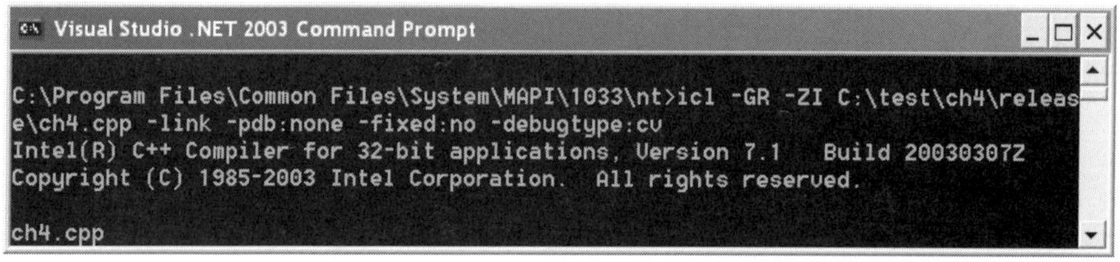

Figure 5.2   Enabling Base Relocation in the Command Line

Visual Basic 6.0

To generate base relocations for an application developed in Microsoft Visual Basic 6.0:

■ Define the environment variable LINK=/fixed:no before building the application.

or

■ Perform SET LINK=/fixed:no in a DOS Command Line window and run Visual Basic from this window.

or

■ Set a global environment variable:

– In Windows NT, add the global environment variable to **Control Panel → System → Environment**

– In Windows 2000 and Windows XP, add the global environment variable to **Control Panel → System → Advanced → Environment Variables**.

Enabling Source Code View

If you plan to view the code for individual program functions in Source view, Call Graph must be able to find the source code for those functions. Make sure the location where you have stored the source code is available in the VTune analyzer's Source File search path (**Configure → Options → Directories → File Associations**), or be prepared to browse to the correct location when prompted.

Configuring for Call Graph Data Collection

Using the Call Graph Wizard

The steps of the Call Graph Wizard are similar to those of the Sampling Wizard; in many cases, selections are identical. To start up the wizard:

1. Select **File → New Project...** or right-click the existing project and select **New Activity...**
2. Select the **Call Graph Wizard** and click **OK**.
3. Select **Windows*/Linux* Profiling** and click **Next**.

Aside from the usual path through the steps, here are some tips for handling some special cases involving specific types of application files.

Analyzing Scripts or Automated Testing Programs

To analyze an application launched by a script, batch file, or automated testing program:

1. Start up the Call Graph Wizard as described earlier.
2. Select the executable, script, or batch file that launches your application as the **Application to Launch**.
3. Check **Modify default configuration when done with wizard** and click **Next**.
4. Remove the launcher from the **Modules of Interest** list.
5. Add the module(s) to be profiled to the **Modules of Interest** list and click **Finish**.

Follow these steps only if the test script compares the process ID or the handle of the process that the script creates with that of the process being profiled, or if the modules must be located at a specific path:

1. From the Advanced Activity Configuration dialog box, click the **Configure...** button in the middle of the screen.
2. Set the Force Instrumentation column to **Yes** for the modules that require in-place instrumentation and click **OK**.
3. Click **OK**.

Instrumenting a Single DLL

Instrumenting a single DLL can be useful if you are writing a DLL that acts as plug-in to another application for which you lack the source or debug information. Java, .NET, and COM profiling are not supported in this mode. To instrument a single DLL:

1. Start up the Call Graph Wizard as described earlier.

2. Check **No application to launch**.

3. Uncheck **Run Activity when done with wizard** and click **Next**.

4. Add the DLL that you want to profile to the **Modules of Interest** list and click **Finish**.

   The Copy Instrumented Modules dialog box asks if you want to manually copy the files or use a batch file created by the VTune analyzer.

5. Select one of the options (either is fine) and click **Run**.

6. Run the application that uses the DLL.

7. After you finish collecting performance data, click the **Stop** button.

   The VTune analyzer displays the results.

Analyzing COM+ and COM+ .NET DLLs

You can also analyze COM+ and COM+ .NET DLLs with Call Graph. Before you begin, make sure that you have administrative privileges on the computer that you are profiling. Also make sure all COM+ objects that you want to profile are running under the account named Interactive User.

1. Open the **Control Panel**.

2. Double-click **Administrative Tools**.

3. Double-click **Component Services**.

4. Click **Component Services** in the left pane.

5. Double-click **Computers** in the right pane.

6. Double-click **My Computer** in the right pane.

7. Double-click **COM+ Applications** in the right pane.

8. Stop the application that you want to profile by right-clicking it and clicking **Shut down**.

9. Right-click the application you want to profile and click **Properties**.

10. Record the **Application ID**.

11. Start up the Call Graph Wizard in the VTune analyzer as described earlier.

12. Enter `%WINDIR\system32\dllhost.exe` in the **Application to launch** text box.

13. Enter `%WINDIR\system32\` in the **Working directory** text box.

14. Type `/ProcessID:{GUID}` in the **Command line arguments** text box, where *GUID* is the Application ID recorded in step 10.

15. Make sure the COM+ application you want to profile is not running, and click **Finish**.

16. After Call Graph finishes instrumenting all the modules, start your COM+ workload.

17. When the workload is finished, press **Stop**.

Analyzing ISAPI DLLs

Before you begin analyzing an ISAPI DLL, make sure that you have administrative privileges on the computer that you are profiling.

1. Start up the Call Graph Wizard as described earlier.

2. Check **No application to launch**.

3. Uncheck **Run Activity when done with wizard** and click **Next**.

4. Add the DLL(s) that you want to profile to the **Modules of Interest** list and click **Finish**.

    The Copy Instrumented Modules dialog box asks if you want to manually copy the files or use a batch file created by the VTune analyzer.

5. Select one of the options; either is fine.

6. In the command line window, type `iisreset`. This restarts the IIS server and unloads previous instances of your ISAPI extension DLL.

7. Click **Run**.

8. Run your test or workload.

9. After you finish collecting performance data, type `iisreset` in the command line window. This command restarts the IIS server and unloads all instances of your ISAPI extension DLL.

10. Click the **Stop** button.

    The VTune analyzer displays the results.

Advanced Configuration Options

Call Graph has many advanced configuration options. To access these options, use the Advanced Activity Configuration dialog box shown in Figure 5.3. You can access this dialog box in two ways.

■ In Step 2 of the Call Graph Wizard, check **Modify default configuration when done with the wizard**. After you proceed through all the steps of the wizard, click **Finish** to display the Advanced Activity Configuration dialog box.

   or

■ If you have already created an activity and would like to modify its configuration, right-click the activity in the **Tuning Browser** window and select **Modify Activity**. With **Modify the selected Activity** selected, click **OK** to display the Advanced Activity Configuration dialog box.

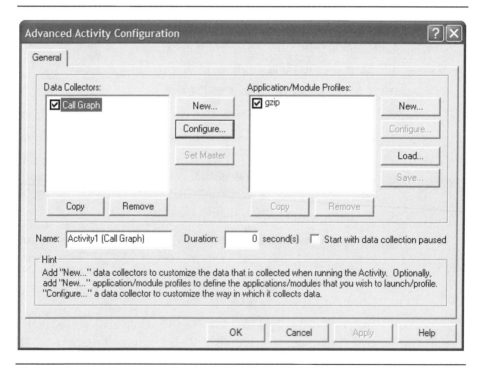

Figure 5.3   Advanced Activity Configuration Dialog Box

In the Advanced Activity Configuration dialog box, make sure that **Call Graph** is highlighted in the Data Collectors list and click the **Configure...** button in the middle of the screen. You should now be at the Configure Call Graph dialog box shown in Figure 5.4.

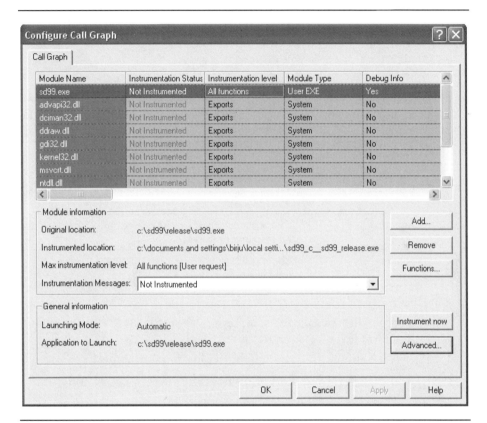

Figure 5.4   Configure Call Graph Dialog Box

This dialog box shows you the instrumentation status of all the modules. You can add and remove modules by clicking the **Add...** and **Remove** buttons respectively.

Controlling Performance Overhead

During the profiling session, Call Graph can result in significant performance degradation in your application. You can reduce this degradation by adjusting the module instrumentation levels. Choose from the four module instrumentation levels shown in Table 5.2. Notice that symbol and line-number debug information is required if you select **All Functions** or **Custom**.

Table 5.2 Instrumentation Levels

Instrumentation Level	Description	Debug Info Required?
All Functions	Every function in the module is instrumented.	Yes
Custom	You can specify which functions are instrumented.	Yes
Export	Every function in the module's export table is instrumented.	No
Minimal	The module is instrumented but no data are collected for it.	No

From the Configure Call Graph dialog box, you can set the instrumentation level for each module:

1. Highlight the module in the instrumented modules list.

2. Click on the module's **Instrumentation Level** column.

3. Select the desired instrumentation level from the drop-down menu.

You can also control the overhead by selecting which functions are instrumented using the Function Selection dialog box. From the Configure Call Graph dialog box:

1. Select the module in the instrumented modules list and click **Functions...**

   The Function Selection dialog box shown in Figure 5.5 appears.

2. Select which functions get instrumented by checking or unchecking them in the Instrument column.

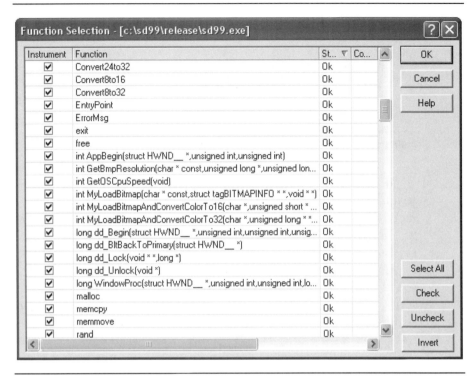

Figure 5.5   Function Selection Dialog Box

If you are still looking for even lower performance overhead, try using the VTune analyzer's Sampling profiler instead; however, you should be aware that Sampling does not provide caller/callee relationship information as Call Graph does.

Forcing In-Place Instrumentation

The Force Instrumentation column shown in Figure 5.6 appears in the Configure Call Graph dialog box if you select **No application to launch** or use an uninstrumented launcher (script) when you configure the Call Graph Wizard.

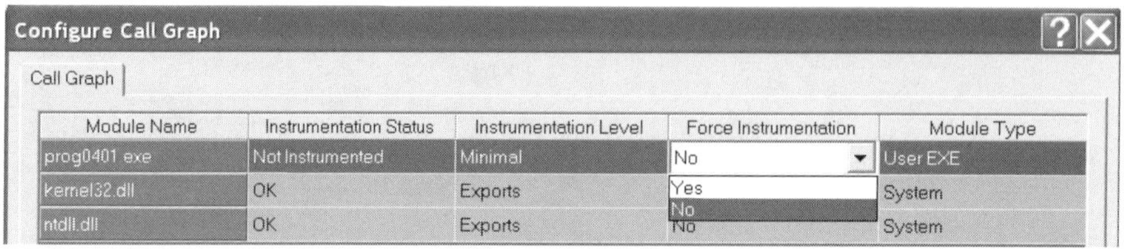

Figure 5.6 Force Instrumentation Column

If you set the Force Instrumentation column to **Yes**, Call Graph instruments the module *in place*. In other words, the VTune analyzer makes a backup copy of the original module and replaces it in its original location with an instrumented version of the module. You can only use in-place instrumentation with `.exe` files.

If you are profiling an application that is launched by a script, and the script compares the process ID or the handle of the process that the script creates with that of the process being profiled, use in-place instrumentation. If you do not use in-place instrumentation, the VTune analyzer replaces the original executable with a stub executable, and backs up the original executable and automatically restores it after the profiling session. The stub executable is used to communicate with the VTune analyzer. In-place instrumentation is also necessary to profile out-of-process COM servers.

When you use in-place instrumentation, the VTune analyzer completely re-instruments the modules for every profiling session. Since this can take a lot of time, do not use in-place instrumentation unless absolutely necessary. You cannot use in-place instrumentation for system DLLs on Windows 2000 and Windows XP operating systems.

Setting Other Advanced Options

From the Configure Call Graph dialog box, click **Advanced** to display the Call Graph Advanced Options dialog box shown in Figure 5.7.

The **Limit collection buffer size** checkbox allows you to control how much memory Call Graph uses to store performance data per thread. Once the buffer(s) are full, Call Graph suspends profiling and writes the data to the hard drive. This feature is useful if you are profiling an application that requires a lot of memory or runs for a long time. If you do not check this option, the buffer can keep growing until the system runs out of memory.

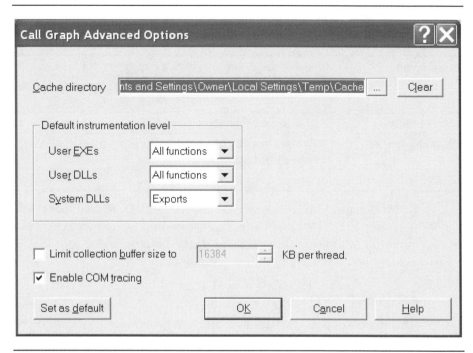

Figure 5.7   Call Graph Advanced Options Dialog Box

The **Enable COM tracing** checkbox allows the VTune analyzer to instrument COM interfaces. This option is checked by default. If you are only interested in profiling the COM interfaces of your application, set the module's Instrumentation Level to **Minimal** on the Configure Call Graph dialog box and leave **Enable COM Tracing** checked here.

Viewing Call Graph Results

The VTune analyzer displays Call Graph results using three different viewpoints: Function Summary, Graph, and Call List. These three views are all synchronized with each other. The Graph depicts your application's call flow as a call tree. The Call List presents caller/callee relationships in a table format. The Function Summary displays a table with complete timing information for every function called by your application. Table 5.3 explains some key timing metrics that Call Graph generates for each instrumented function.

Table 5.3   Some Key Call Graph Performance Metrics

Performance Metric	Description
Total time	Time measured from a function's entry to its exit point
Self time	Total time in a function excluding time spent in its children (includes wait time)
Total wait time	Time spent in a function and its children when the thread is blocked
Wait time	Time spent in a function when the thread is blocked (excludes blocked time in its children)
Calls	Number of times the function is called

If the application is single-threaded, the VTune analyzer does not collect wait time. You can view the source in all views by right-clicking the function of interest and selecting **View Source**. If the source is not available, you can see the function's disassembly code.

Function Summary

The Function Summary lists all the functions your application calls along with the performance data listed in Table 5.3. By default, the list stays grouped by module even if you sort by the other columns. You can break this grouping by right-clicking in the Function Summary and un-checking **Hierarchy**. The hierarchy grouping is checked by default because most developers want to look at the performance of their own modules first.

Graph

The Graph view shows each thread as a separate root. Callers appear on the left and callees on the right. Each node on the tree represents a function. If you mouse over a node, a pop-up window appears displaying that function's performance data. Nodes are also color-coded. A brighter colored node indicates that the function has a longer execution time. Red outlined edges indicate the critical path; that is, the most time-consuming execution path. You can highlight functions in the Graph based on different criteria such as:

- Top 10 self time
- Top 10 total time
- .NET methods
- Java methods
- Recursive functions

If your application has a large, complex call flow, the Graph Navigation window shown in the upper right portion of Figure 5.8 is very helpful. It displays an overview of the entire Call Graph in reduced form. You can use this window to navigate around the larger, standard Graph shown in the lower portion of Figure 5.8.

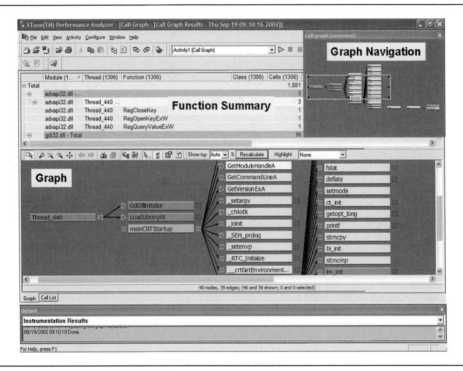

Figure 5.8   Graph Tab with Function Summary and Graph (Windows)

Call List

The Call List tab shown in Figure 5.9 provides performance data for the function highlighted in the Function Summary and Graph. This tab includes the Function Summary at the top as well as three separate lists that make up the Call List: focus function, caller functions, and callee functions. The Focus function is the function highlighted in the Function Summary and Graph. The caller function and callee function lists break down the focus function's time by callers and callees. The Caller functions list breaks down the focus function's time by the functions that called it. The Callee functions list shows how the focus function's time was spent in its callees. It tells you what functions the focus function called and gives timing information for each.

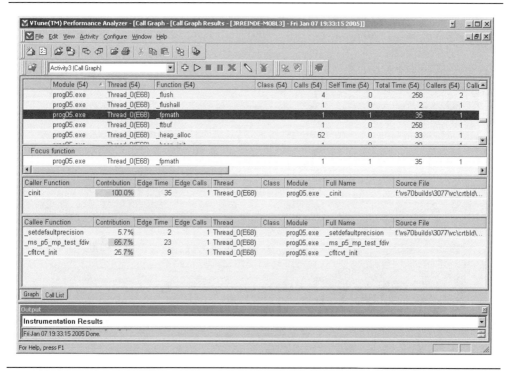

Figure 5.9 Call List Tab with Function Summary and Call Lists

Table 5.4 explains some key terms that appear in columns of the Call List.

Table 5.4 Some Key Terms on the Call List

Column Name	Column Explanation
Self Time	Time spent in the focus function itself, excluding time spent in its children, where:[2] *Self Time = Function Total Time – sum of its Callees' Edge Times*
Total Time	Time spent in the focus function as well as in all the functions it called (callees).
Contribution	Relative contribution to the focus function's Total Time made by this call to or from the focus function.

---

[2] This time includes any wait time during which the function was blocked (suspended).

Table 5.4 Some Key Terms on the Call List *(continued)*

Column Name	Column Explanation
Caller Edge Time	Time elapsed between when this function starts execution and when it terminates. This value is the sum of this function's Self Time and all its callees' times, where:
	Caller Edge Time = Caller Self Time + sum of its Callees' Edge Times
Callee Edge Time	Time contributed by this function to the focus function's Total Time, where:
	Callee Edge Time = Function Total Time – [Function Self Time + Sum of all other Callee Edge Times]
Edge Calls	The number of times the focus function called or was called by this function.

Hands-on Call Graph Profiling

The best way to learn to fish is to take your rod and reel to a pond, river, lake, or ocean and cast your line. The best way to find out how Call Graph works is to experience it firsthand. The VTune analyzer is rich with features to let you explore Call Graph functionality.

Choosing a Program Example

To learn about Call Graph analysis, you can turn again to the small program from the companion Web site called `examples/ch4/windows/prog0401`. This example, shown in sample screens in this chapter, is the same one used in Chapter 4. Later in this chapter, you will explore another example called `examples/ch5/windows/prog05`. These two examples can help you gain confidence in how Call Graph works, and are small enough to allow you to perform quick and easy experiments should you wish to test the VTune analyzer's responses. If you have your own application complete with source code, feel free to use that instead. To use your own application, be sure to:

- ■ Compile/link with symbols and line numbers

- ■ Link with base relocations enabled (using the `/fixed:no` linker switch)

- ■ Make *release* builds with optimizations

Example 5.1: Call Graph Profiling Using the Graphical Interface

The VTune analyzer's Call Graph profiler can help you understand the call flow of your application and find where most of the time is being spent. In this example, you collect Call Graph data for a program and identify the function that takes the most time. Follow these steps to perform Call Graph profiling from VTune analyzer's graphical interface.

Manually Instrumenting and Running a Call Graph Activity

1. Double-click the **VTune Performance Analyzer** icon to start the program.

2. Select **File → New Project** or open an existing project and create a new activity in it by clicking **Activity → New Activity...**.

3. Select **Call Graph Wizard** and click **OK**.

4. Select **Windows*/Linux* Profiling** and click **Next**.

5. In the **Application To Launch** text box, type this path or browse to its location:

   ```
   C:\examples\ch4\windows\prog0401.exe
   ```

   or use whatever executable file you want to profile.

6. In the **Command Line Arguments** text box, type:

   ```
   input0402.txt 1000
   ```

   for `prog0401` (for other applications, either type the options you want or type nothing if you are not sure).

7. Select the **Modify default configuration when done with wizard** checkbox and click **Finish**.

   The Advanced Activity Configuration window appears.

8. Click **Configure...** for the **Call Graph** data collector, which is already selected.

   The Configure Call Graph dialog box appears. You can use this dialog box to fine-tune instrumentation of your application and system DLLs before running the activity. You can even select which functions to instrument, to help control overhead.

9. Highlight your application and select **Functions...**

   The Function Selection dialog box appears as shown in Figure 5.10.

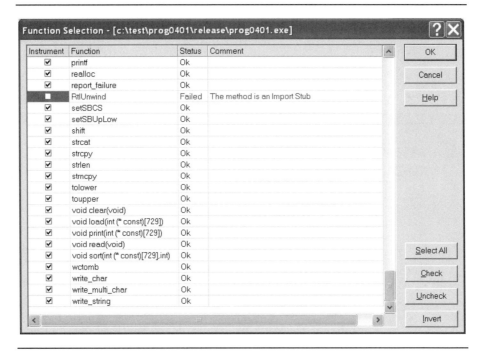

Figure 5.10 Function Selection Dialog Box for `prog0401.exe`

10. To improve the speed of the instrumented application, you can uncheck boxes here if you wish to disable instrumentation for particular functions. Click **OK** or **Cancel** to return to the previous screen.

11. Click **Advanced...**

    The Call Graph Advanced Options dialog box appears. These options control default instrumentation levels and specify where instrumented modules are located. The VTune analyzer keeps instrumented files in the cache directory for use when you run the Call Graph data collection activity.

12. Notice that the default instrumentation level for System DLLs is **Exports**. Click **Cancel** to return to the previous screen.

13. Click the **Instrument Now** button and click **OK** twice to launch instrumentation with the specified setup.

Once `prog0401` finishes executing, the VTune analyzer displays a screen similar to Figure 5.11, which shows the instrumented functions detected as running while Call Graph data collection took place. If you are running your own application, you must first either close that program or click the **Stop Activity** icon on the VTune analyzer toolbar.

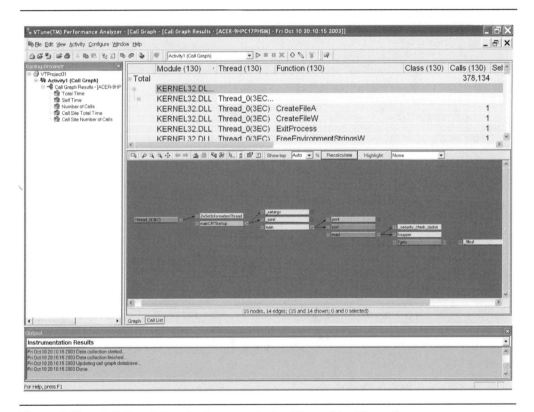

Figure 5.11   Call Graph Results for `prog0401` (Viewed by Thread)

The Graph Tab

The Graph tab shows a Function Summary in the upper pane and a Graph in the lower pane. Bright orange *nodes* in the Graph indicate functions with the highest self-time. The red lines, also called *edges*, show the critical path; that is, the most time-consuming call path based on self-time.

1. Right-click on a gray area of the Graph and uncheck **View by Thread**.

   The Thread column in the Function Summary disappears. Since the prog0401 function is not multithreaded, this column was just taking up space.

2. Drag the **Class** column to the left to reveal the Self Time and Total Time columns.

3. Click the **Self Time** column heading twice to display the Function Summary in descending order based on self-time, as shown in Figure 5.12.

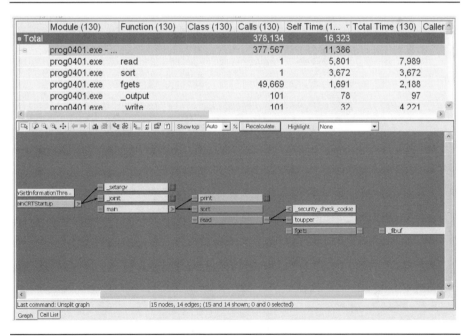

Figure 5.12   Graph Tab with Function Summary in Self-Time Descending Order

4. Notice that the **read** function shows the greatest self-time as 5,801 microseconds.

5. Click the **Graph Navigation Window On/Off** icon on the Button toolbar:

If you do not see any icons above the graph, right-click, select **Properties**, and make sure the **Filter toolbar** and the **Button toolbar** are both checked.

The Graph Navigation window appears superimposed on the Graph tab, as shown in Figure 5.13. This window displays a miniature overview of the entire graph, with a movable rectangle positioned around the functions that appear in the actual Graph in the lower pane. You can move this rectangle around to expose different parts of the Graph.

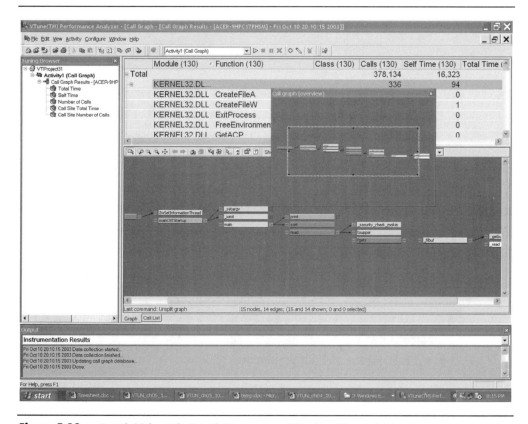

Figure 5.13 Graph Tab with Graph Navigation Window Turned On

The Button toolbar also has other navigation icons that allow you to drag the graph, zoom, zoom in, zoom out, and fit in window.

In the Filter toolbar, the **Auto** value appears by default in the Show Top dropdown menu. In this view, the nodes expand to show a limited number of children/parents in order to fit in the window. The **None** value appears by default in the Highlight field.

6. Select **Top 10 Self-Time** from the Highlight dropdown menu.

Red outlining appears around the 10 functions with the longest self-time, as shown in Figure 5.14.

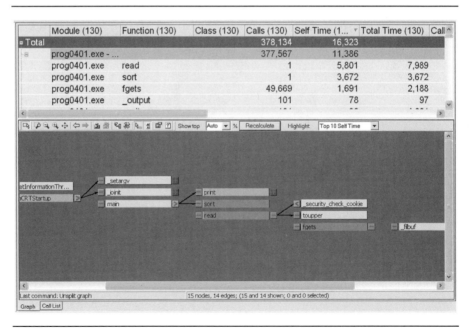

Figure 5.14   Graph Tab with Top 10 Self-Time Functions Highlighted

Clicking the red + sign to the right of a function node in the Graph reveals more children; clicking the green – sign to the left of a function node reveals more parents.

7. Select the `read` function in the diagram.

The function turns blue in the Graph and appears highlighted in the Function Summary.

8. Click the **Call List** tab at the bottom of the window to display a list of all the callers and callees for the selected function.

The Call List appears with `read` as the focus function, as shown in Figure 5.15.

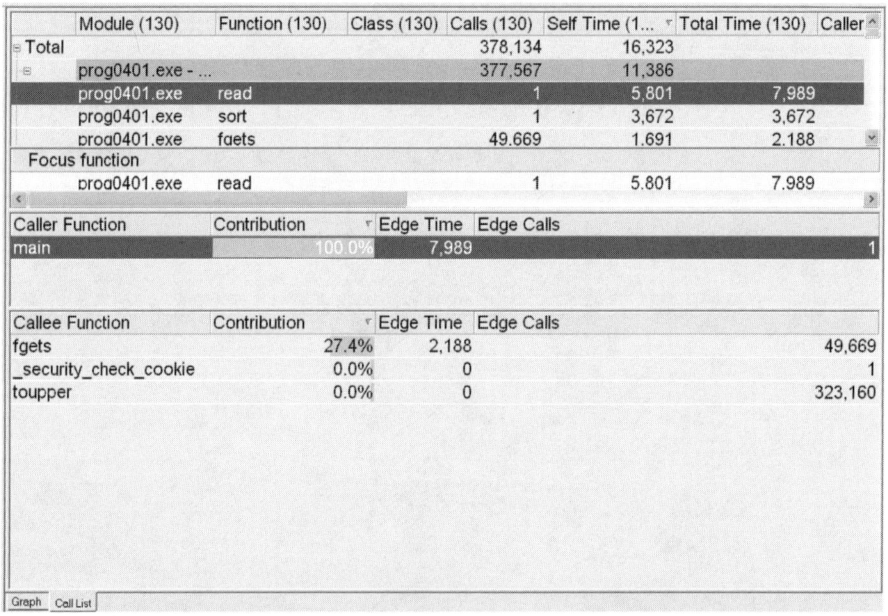

Module (130)	Function (130)	Class (130)	Calls (130)	Self Time (1...	Total Time (130)	Caller
Total				378,134	16,323	
prog0401.exe - ...				377,567	11,386	
prog0401.exe	read		1		5,801	7,989
prog0401.exe	sort		1		3,672	3,672
prog0401.exe	fgets		49,669		1,691	2,188
Focus function						
prog0401.exe	read		1		5,801	7,989

Caller Function	Contribution	Edge Time	Edge Calls	
main	100.0%	7,989		1

Callee Function	Contribution	Edge Time	Edge Calls	
fgets	27.4%	2,188		49,669
_security_check_cookie	0.0%	0		1
toupper	0.0%	0		323,160

Graph   Call List

Figure 5.15   Call List Tab with `read` as the Focus Function

The Call List Tab

The Call List tab displays the same Function Summary that appears on the Graph tab. Below it are three sections:

- A *Focus Function* section lists the name of the currently selected function; in this case, the `read` function.

- A *Caller Function* section lists the focus function's parent functions; in this case, the `Main` function.

- A *Callee Function* section lists the child functions called by the focus function; in this case, the `read` function calls three functions: `fgets`, `_security_check_cookie`, and `toupper`.

Viewing the Source Code

To see the source code associated with a function in Call Graph, select the function anywhere in the Graph tab or Call List tab, right-click and select **View Source** from the pop-up menu. Figure 5.16 shows the source code that displays when you select the `read` function, which had the longest self-time.

Address	Line	Source	Total	Self	Call	Call Site Time	Call Site Calls
	21	void clear()					
0x1000	22	{	2	2	1		
	23	int i, j;					
0x1001	24	for (i=0;i<27;i++) {					
0x1005	25	tally1[i] = 0;					
	26	for (j=0;j<27;j++)					
0x1013	27	tally2[i][j] = 0;					
	28	}					
0x10C1	29	}					
	30						
	31	void read()					
0x10C4	32	{	7,989	5,801	1		
	33	char buffer[MAXBUF];					
	34	char *s, c, prev;					
0x10DF	35	while (fgets(buffer,MAXBUF,file)) {				2,188	49,669
	36	// int ii = 222; // we could artificia					
	37	int ii = 1; // do once					
	38	while (ii--) {					
0x1106	39	prev = 0;					
0x10FE	40	for (s=buffer,c=toupper(*s);(c>='A')					323,160
0x1121	41	c = c - 'A' + 1;					
	42	/*****					

		Function Summary		Call Graph Results - [ACER-9HPC17PHSM] - Fri Oct 10 20:10:1...			
Address	Size	Function	Class	Total Time (130)	Self Time (130)	Calls (130)	Call Site Time
-----	-----	--- Selected Range ---	-----	7,989	5,801	1	
0x1000	0xC4	clear		2	2	1	
0x10C4	0xE4	read		7,989	5,801	1	
0x11A8	0x3C8	load		7	7	1	
0x1570	0xA0	sort		3,672	3,672	1	
0x1610	0xA4	print		4,294	11	1	

Figure 5.16 Source View with the `read` Function Selected

Regardless of whether you select the function in the Function Summary, Graph, focus function, caller, or callee section, the target source line is always the beginning of the function. Notice that many columns in this view correspond to those shown in other Call Graph views. To return to the previous view, click the Previous icon in the Standard toolbar:

Viewing Functions by Thread

When examining Call Graph data, you have the option of viewing functions and their timing and call information by thread. To view a function by thread:

1. Right-click in the Graph or Function Summary.

2. Select **View by thread** from the pop-up menu.

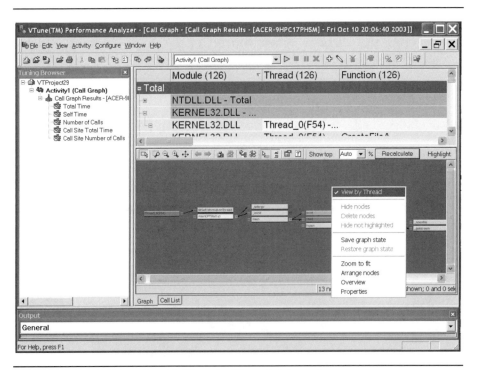

Figure 5.17 Call Graph with View by Thread Selected

The Thread column appears in the Function Summary and other Call List sections, and nodes corresponding to threads appear in the Graph.

The Linux Call Graph Viewer

VTune Performance Analyzer Version 7.1 for Windows and Version 2.0 for Linux support Call Graph from the command line. Version 3.0 offers a Call Graph viewer inside the VTune analyzer perspective within the Eclipse framework, as shown in Figure 5.1. You can invoke it the viewer from the command line with the `vtl view -gui` command.

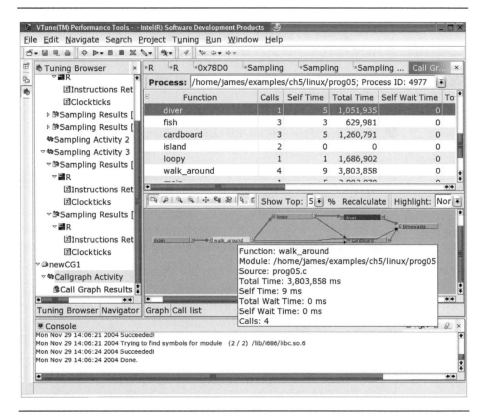

Figure 5.18   Call Graph Viewing from the Linux GUI (Eclipse)

Like all command-line functions, Call Graph analysis is a thin layer on top of the same routines that the GUI uses for the same functionality. Consequently, the data collected from the viewer match the data collected if you were to perform the same analysis from the VTune analyzer's built-in GUI.

Graphical viewing, while not necessary for collecting the data, is very important for Call Graph analysis. Gathering Call Graph data using the command line interface is easy, but viewing the resulting dumps raw is tedious at best. For this reason, Call Graph data were not accessible from earlier versions of the command line. The best approach is to collect the data from the command line and then view the results in one of these ways:

■ Use the Linux Call Graph viewer by typing this command on the command line:

```
vtl view -gui
```

Note | Starting with version 3.0 for Linux, the Call Graph viewer is available inside the Eclipse environment.

■ Read the data with a spreadsheet program such as Excel, using ';' and the Tab character as the two delimiters.

■ Pack the project and then read it using the viewer built into the VTune analyzer GUI.

Example 5.2: Call Graph Analysis Using the Command Line

As mentioned in Chapter 3, you can use the command line to collect data about your application and system performance and then view the results in table form. This capability opens up many possibilities for automating performance collection, tabulation, and some types of analysis.

This exercise uses a different sample application (prog05) from the companion Web site. If you have your own application, feel free to use it instead.

Using the command line for Call Graph involves repeated single invocations of the vtl command on a single project. Using these and other commands, you:

■ Configure a single activity with a collector and an application.

■ Run the activity and collect results.

■ Store the results in a persistent default project so that you can use the view mode to dump the results into a file, or use pack so the project can be viewed using the viewer built into the VTune analyzer GUI.

Note | Save projects (with a `.vpj` file extension) containing all activities, results, and associated files to the *home directory*.

For Windows, the `VTUNE_USER_DIR` environment variable specifies the home directory. By default, it is the `VTune` directory under the directory specified by the environment variable `APPDATA`.

For Linux, the `VTUNEHOME` environment variable determines the home directory. The default is `$HOME/.VTune`.

Create and Run a Call Graph Activity

In the example directories you will find build commands in `make05.bat` and run commands in `callgraph.bat`.

Follow these steps to perform VTune Call Graph profiling from the command line, either by typing commands directly at the prompt, or by placing them in a Windows- or Linux-based batch file (`.bat`) that runs them all at once:

1. To ensure you know where the data are stored, start by setting the home directory:

    Windows commands (`cmd`):

    ```
    mkdir c:\tmpvtune
    set VTUNE_USER_DIR=C:\tmpvtune
    ```

    Linux commands (`sh/ksh`):

    ```
    mkdir c:/tmp/vtune
    set VTUNEHOME=/tmp/vtune
    export VTUNEHOME
    ```

    Linux commands (`csh`):

    ```
    mkdir c:/tmp/vtune
    setenv VTUNEHOME=/tmp/vtune
    ```

2. Write the test results to a batch file so you can view them later:

    Windows command (`cmd`):

    ```
    echo c:\examples\ch5\windows\prog05.exe nothing.txt
        1000 > prog05.bat
    ```

    Linux command:

    ```
    echo '~/examples/ch5/linux/prog05.exe nothing.txt
        1000' > prog05.bat
    ```

3. Configure an activity with a collector and an application:

Windows command (`cmd`):

```
vtl activity -d 7 -c "call graph"
    -app c:\examples\ch5\windows\prog05.bat
    -moi c:\examples\ch5\windows\prog05.exe
```

Linux command:

```
vtl activity -d 7 -c "call graph"
    -app ~/examples/ch5/linux/prog05.bat
    -moi ~/examples/ch5/linux/prog05.exe
```

4. Run the activity:

```
vtl run
```

Once `prog05` finishes executing, you can display the results. If you are running your own application, you must either have the program exit or use the `ActivityController` command in a separate shell to stop the activity.

Display the Call Graph Results

To display the Call Graph results, you can choose from several methods:

◼ To display the results in the command line window, type:

```
vtl show
```

Figure 5.19 illustrates that our project now contains a single activity with Call Graph results. You could add more Sampling or Call Graph activities by invoking the `vtl activity` command more times.

```
vtl show

VTune(TM) Performance Analyzer 7.1
Copyright (C) 2000-2003 Intel Corporation. All rights reserved.

a1__Activity1    r1_____Call Graph Results - [MYCOMPUTER] - Sun Feb 22 08:01:38 2004
```

Figure 5.19   `vtl show` Command Output of Project with `prog05` Activity Results

■ If you installed the Call Graph viewer, you can use that tool to display the results instead by typing:

```
vtl view -gui
```

Note Version 2.0 for Linux included the viewer in a second `tar` file from the CD or web download. On Version 2.0 CDs, the file was named `vtune_cgview_1.0.277.tar`.

Starting with Version 3.0 for Linux, you can view Call Graph results inside the Eclipse environment.

On Linux-based systems, the command line pops up a graphical viewer displaying the current activity. Figure 5.20 shows the Graph tab as seen through this viewer.

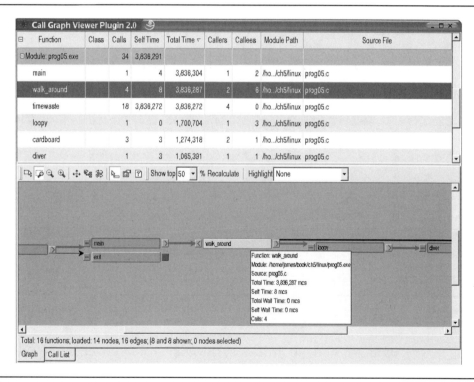

Figure 5.20   Graph of `prog05` Using the Call Graph Viewer on Linux (Not Eclipse)

Figure 5.21 shows the Call List tab as seen through the Call Graph viewer on Linux.

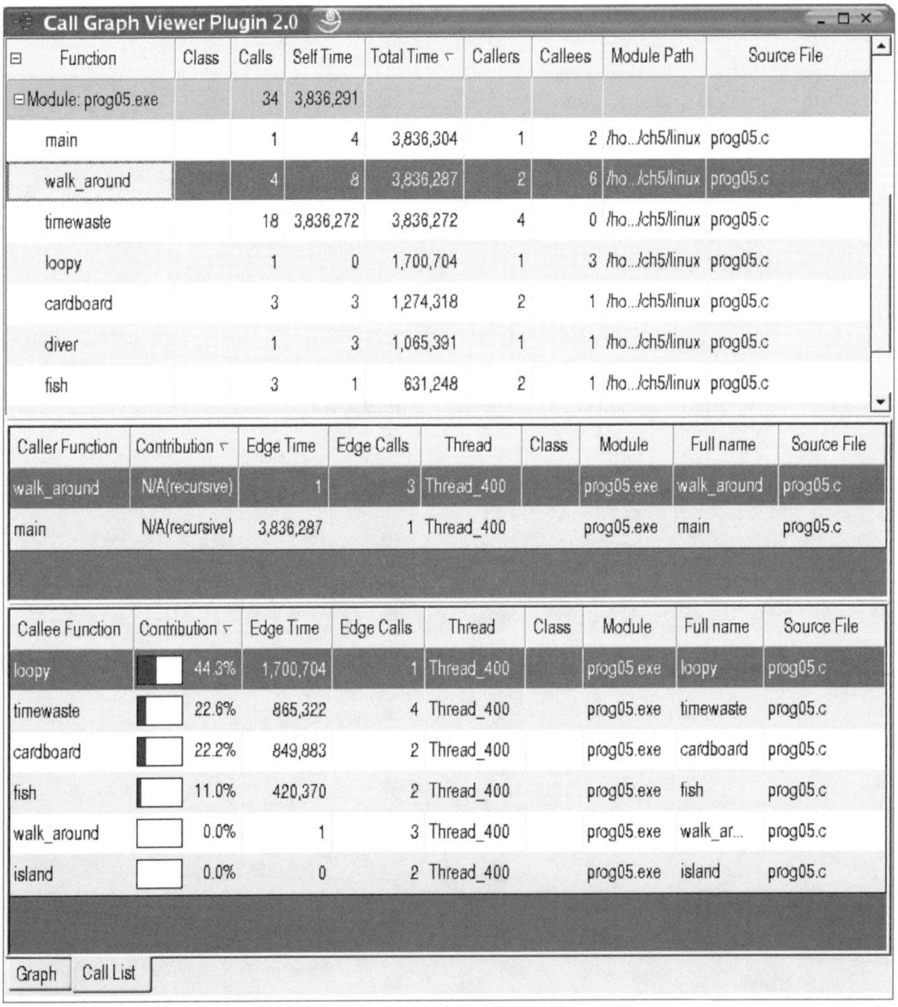

Figure 5.21   Call List of `prog05` Using the Call Graph Viewer on Linux (Not Eclipse)

With Version 3.0 for Linux, the graphical interface in the Eclipse environment supports a slightly different viewer for Call Graphs. All the viewers are similar, with minor variations based on differences in the look-and-feel of the windowing systems.

- Dump the Call Graph results this way if you want to view them with a spreadsheet program such as Microsoft Excel:

```
vtl view -calls > vtlcalls.txt
vtl view -functions > vtlfunctions.txt
```

Figure 5.22 shows Call Graph information imported into a Microsoft Excel spreadsheet from the `vtlcalls.txt` file.

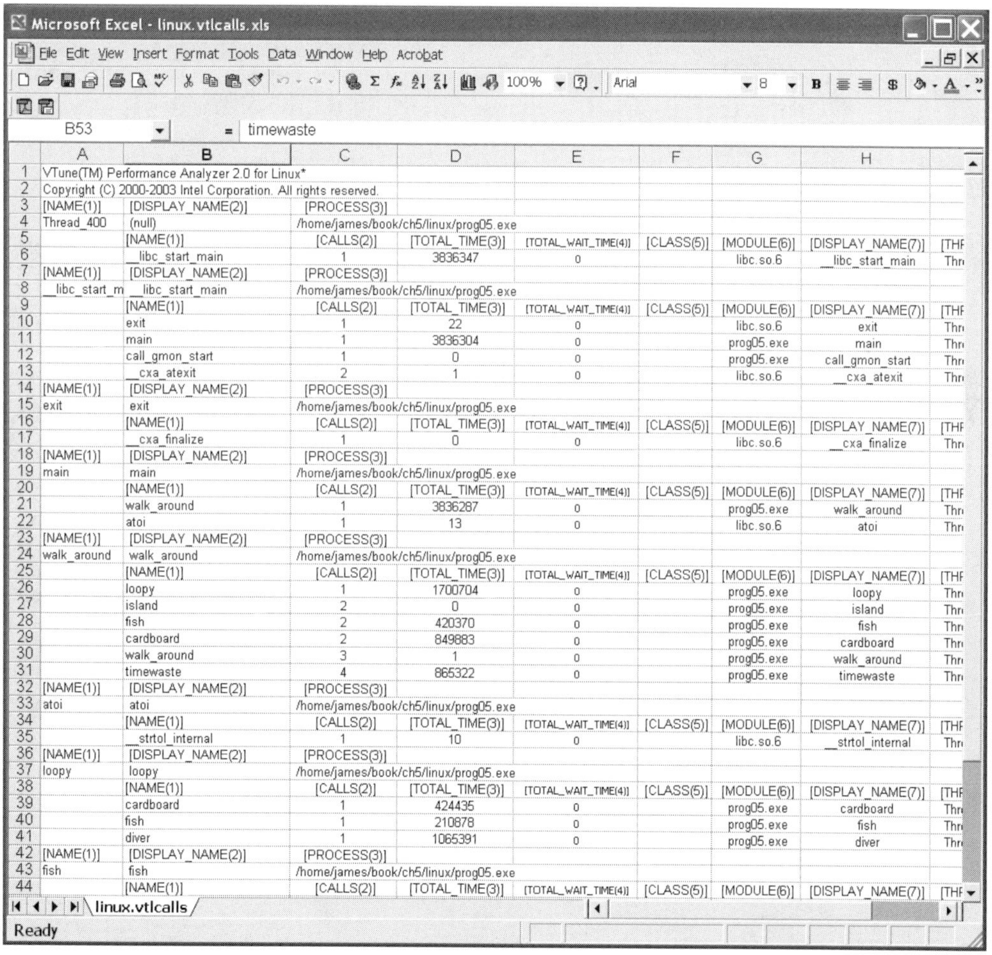

	A	B	C	D	E	F	G	H	
1	VTune(TM) Performance Analyzer 2.0 for Linux*								
2	Copyright (C) 2000-2003 Intel Corporation. All rights reserved.								
3	[NAME(1)]	[DISPLAY_NAME(2)]	[PROCESS(3)]						
4	Thread_400	(null)	/home/james/book/ch5/linux/prog05.exe						
5		[NAME(1)]	[CALLS(2)]	[TOTAL_TIME(3)]	[TOTAL_WAIT_TIME(4)]	[CLASS(5)]	[MODULE(6)]	[DISPLAY_NAME(7)]	[THR
6		__libc_start_main	1	3836347	0		libc.so.6	__libc_start_main	Thr
7	[NAME(1)]	[DISPLAY_NAME(2)]	[PROCESS(3)]						
8	__libc_start_m	__libc_start_main	/home/james/book/ch5/linux/prog05.exe						
9		[NAME(1)]	[CALLS(2)]	[TOTAL_TIME(3)]	[TOTAL_WAIT_TIME(4)]	[CLASS(5)]	[MODULE(6)]	[DISPLAY_NAME(7)]	[THR
10		exit	1	22	0		libc.so.6	exit	Thr
11		main	1	3836304	0		prog05.exe	main	Thr
12		call_gmon_start	1	0	0		prog05.exe	call_gmon_start	Thr
13		__cxa_atexit	2	1	0		libc.so.6	__cxa_atexit	Thr
14	[NAME(1)]	[DISPLAY_NAME(2)]	[PROCESS(3)]						
15	exit	exit	/home/james/book/ch5/linux/prog05.exe						
16		[NAME(1)]	[CALLS(2)]	[TOTAL_TIME(3)]	[TOTAL_WAIT_TIME(4)]	[CLASS(5)]	[MODULE(6)]	[DISPLAY_NAME(7)]	[THR
17		__cxa_finalize	1	0	0		libc.so.6	__cxa_finalize	Thr
18	[NAME(1)]	[DISPLAY_NAME(2)]	[PROCESS(3)]						
19	main	main	/home/james/book/ch5/linux/prog05.exe						
20		[NAME(1)]	[CALLS(2)]	[TOTAL_TIME(3)]	[TOTAL_WAIT_TIME(4)]	[CLASS(5)]	[MODULE(6)]	[DISPLAY_NAME(7)]	[THR
21		walk_around	1	3836287	0		prog05.exe	walk_around	Thr
22		atoi	1	13	0		libc.so.6	atoi	Thr
23	[NAME(1)]	[DISPLAY_NAME(2)]	[PROCESS(3)]						
24	walk_around	walk_around	/home/james/book/ch5/linux/prog05.exe						
25		[NAME(1)]	[CALLS(2)]	[TOTAL_TIME(3)]	[TOTAL_WAIT_TIME(4)]	[CLASS(5)]	[MODULE(6)]	[DISPLAY_NAME(7)]	[THR
26		loopy	1	1700704	0		prog05.exe	loopy	Thr
27		island	2	0	0		prog05.exe	island	Thr
28		fish	2	420370	0		prog05.exe	fish	Thr
29		cardboard	2	849883	0		prog05.exe	cardboard	Thr
30		walk_around	3	1	0		prog05.exe	walk_around	Thr
31		timewaste	4	865322	0		prog05.exe	timewaste	Thr
32	[NAME(1)]	[DISPLAY_NAME(2)]	[PROCESS(3)]						
33	atoi	atoi	/home/james/book/ch5/linux/prog05.exe						
34		[NAME(1)]	[CALLS(2)]	[TOTAL_TIME(3)]	[TOTAL_WAIT_TIME(4)]	[CLASS(5)]	[MODULE(6)]	[DISPLAY_NAME(7)]	[THR
35		__strtol_internal	1	10	0		libc.so.6	__strtol_internal	Thr
36	[NAME(1)]	[DISPLAY_NAME(2)]	[PROCESS(3)]						
37	loopy	loopy	/home/james/book/ch5/linux/prog05.exe						
38		[NAME(1)]	[CALLS(2)]	[TOTAL_TIME(3)]	[TOTAL_WAIT_TIME(4)]	[CLASS(5)]	[MODULE(6)]	[DISPLAY_NAME(7)]	[THR
39		cardboard	1	424435	0		prog05.exe	cardboard	Thr
40		fish	1	210878	0		prog05.exe	fish	Thr
41		diver	1	1065391	0		prog05.exe	diver	Thr
42	[NAME(1)]	[DISPLAY_NAME(2)]	[PROCESS(3)]						
43	fish	fish	/home/james/book/ch5/linux/prog05.exe						
44		[NAME(1)]	[CALLS(2)]	[TOTAL_TIME(3)]	[TOTAL_WAIT_TIME(4)]	[CLASS(5)]	[MODULE(6)]	[DISPLAY_NAME(7)]	[THR

Figure 5.22 Excel Spreadsheet of Project with `prog05` Activity Results

You can import the results stored in the `vtlcalls.txt` file as well as the results stored in the `vtlfunctions.txt` file into spreadsheets. Obviously, results displayed in this way take more time to explore and understand than more graphical representations. If your goal is to explore the data looking for hotspots, you should use the VTune analyzer viewer instead. However, since text information can be gathered in a script and analyzed by programs instead of requiring manual viewing, Call Graph data in this format open up possibilities for automated processing that more graphical formats do not.

■ Pack the results if you want to view them with the viewer built into the VTune analyzer GUI:

```
vtl pack prog05
```

You can load the `prog05.vxp` pack-and-go file with the VTune analyzer and unpack the results so you can view them. Figure 5.23 shows a view of the Call Graph created by this exercise using the VTune analyzer viewer on Windows. This viewer is available on Windows in the VTune analyzer GUI (not from the command line). In this example, the mouse (not visible) was hovering over the edge from `driver` to `timewaste`, causing a pop-up window to appear showing the number of calls from `driver` to `timewaste` and other information related to those calls.

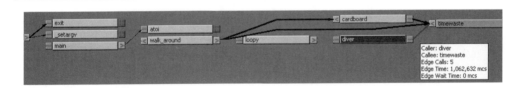

Figure 5.23   Linux Call Graph Results in the VTune Analyzer Viewer on Windows

Blocked Time on a Thread/Function Basis

Of special interest is time spent waiting because a thread is blocked from execution. Call Graph can show this information, which can be quite valuable in fine-tuning an application through better synchronization.

Does My System Show Wait Time?

Certain fields related to Wait Times may always display as zero on your computer, depending on your operating system. Collection of exact Wait Time information is not supported when running on a single processor. This feature is exclusively available on multiprocessors or processors with Hyper-Threading Technology. If your computer does show nonzero Wait Times, be aware that:

- *Self-Time*, the time spent inside a function excluding its children, does include Wait Time during which the thread is blocked (suspended).

- *Self Wait Time* shows time spent inside a function while its thread is blocked.

- *Total Wait Time* shows time spent in a function including its children during which the thread is blocked.

Why Do Sampling and Call Graph Have Different Hotspots?

If you collect the time for a hotspot function using Sampling and then collect the time for that same function using Call Graph, the two times may not match. Sampling, whether event-based or time-based, does not include Wait Time during which the thread is suspended waiting for another thread to complete, whereas function Self-Time in Call Graph does include Wait Time. If you calculate non-blocked Self-Time by subtracting Self Wait Time from Self-Time, the hotspots for both Sampling and Call Graph data collectors should be the same.

Finding High-level Inefficiencies Related to Hotspots

Call Graph can help you understand where and why hotspot functions are being called. Look for redundant (wasted) work. For example, you may find that a hotspot function is being called multiple times to perform the same calculation. In this case, you could modify the code so that the hotspot routine is only called once and the results are stored.

Use Call Graph's list of frequently called functions, and note the number of times functions are called and the amount of time spent in each function. Look for measurements that do not make sense given your understanding of how the application works. When you see these anomalies, track them down to understand what is happening. Often anomalies are caused by undetected bugs that may be decreasing performance.

Call Graph Usage Tips

Call Graph analysis is used to get an algorithmic or high level look at the program, whereas sampling is best used when you want to analyze a particularly dominant hotspot in more detail, or when you want to tune the application more precisely for the CPU architecture. Often Call Graph analysis can be useful when the Sampling profile is "flat," when no single hotspot is dominant. Sampling analysis was covered in Chapter 4.

When initially using the VTune analyzer, you should run Sampling first and see whether a hotspot is dominant. If so, drill down to source to analyze it in more detail. If not, it is time for Call Graph analysis. Often, data-processing applications are better suited for Call Graph analysis than programs that employ loop-based calculation, since it is less likely that the data processing applications are going to have only a small number of significant hotspots. In such cases, after first using VTune analyzer to exhaust tuning based on Sampling analysis, you would generally rely on Call Graph analysis for your primary tuning methodology with occasional use of sampling to make sure that new "low-hanging fruit" has not emerged.

The general usage model for Call Graph analysis starts by gathering the data and sorting the resulting results by Self Time to find the function that took the longest time. Double-click on it to make it the central node of the graph. Looking at the immediate call environment around that function is generally the next useful thing to do, so you should click on the Call List tab in the lower right corner and get the many details on all the callers and callees of that function. You can then double-click on any of the callers and callees in the Call List display and make them the central node (or focus function, as VTune analyzer calls it) and you can navigate up and down the call path for the details of the functions in the immediate vicinity of the function hotspot.

Highlighting is a feature worth exploring. On the right side of the middle icon row, you can choose to highlight certain types of functions. Highlighting Max Path to Function can help in call graphs that are complex. Sometimes it is also interesting to highlight functions with source or recursive functions. It is interesting to highlight .NET or Java methods so you can see which functions are native and which are not. This is often useful even when tuning pure managed code because there is usually unmanaged code in the run time or other library functions.

Windowing in on portions of your program is another feature worth exploring. If you right-click in the display portion of the graph and select Overview, you see the complete call graph with the currently displayed portioned highlighted. You can scroll either one to navigate through the graph.

The overhead of using Call Graph analysis can be a concern for users, especially if a lot of instrumentation is needed for the whole program but you know you do not need a full program analysis. You can go to **Configure → Modify** and select which DLLs/SharedObjects you do or do not want to be instrumented to make the instrumented program run faster. Defaults can be set by clicking on **Advanced**, and you can even select individual functions to be instrumented or not. In this manner, you can control the amount of instrumentation and data results that are generated. This method can be particularly useful for larger applications.

Always start with the methodology discussed in the section "Learning to Fish: A Tuning Methodology" in Chapter 1. If you do not start with the big picture, you may spend unproductive time tuning to address small issues while missing the big picture.

How Call Graph Analysis Works

Call Graph analysis works by gathering performance data for your application using a technique known as *binary instrumentation*, which is the process of injecting code into a copy of each binary module. On Microsoft Windows operating systems, these modules usually have the .exe or .dll filename extension. Instrumentation modifies a compiled program by adding data collection routines. When the modified program executes, the VTune analyzer calls these collection routines at specific execution points to dynamically record run-time performance information such as function timing and function entry and exit points. It uses this data, based on time rather than events, to determine program flow, critical functions, and call sequences.

At run time when performing Call Graph data collection, the VTune analyzer automatically instruments all Ring 3 application-level modules used by your application. As noted earlier, it cannot instrument Ring 0 kernel and driver modules. If your application dynamically loads libraries; that is, if it calls LoadLibrary instead of linking to stub libraries, Call Graph intercepts the module loads and automatically instrument the modules.

Call Graph places all these instrumented modules in a cache directory. When the application runs, its modules load from this directory; however, the application runs in the working directory specified by the user. Call Graph does not modify any of the original modules unless you specifically request this in the advanced configuration options.

For Java and .NET applications, Call Graph profiling uses the Java Virtual Machine Profiling Interface (JVMPI) and the .NET Profiling API, respectively, to collect performance data for managed code. By using instrumentation and the profiling APIs together, Call Graph can provide mixed-mode performance data for both Java and .NET. Mixed-mode profiling allows you to see how your managed code calls result in unmanaged code calls; however, if you are only interested in Java and .NET method calls, you can use pure mode profiling.

Call Graph uses debug and base relocation information to instrument your application's modules. It uses the debug information to locate functions in the modules. Without this information, only the exported symbols are visible and only those visible functions can be instrumented, thus limiting the Call Graph analysis. Call graph uses base relocation information to help understand the relationships between different pieces of code in a module. Under Microsoft Windows, .dll files contain base relocation information by default, but .exe files do not unless you specifically link them with the `fixed:no` option. Under Linux, all executables contain this information unless you explicitly remove it with an option such as `--strip-unneeded`, resulting in what is commonly called a *stripped binary* or image.

Since instrumentation happens automatically, you do not need to recompile before using the Call Graph feature, although you may need to relink as noted earlier. Instrumentation does not change program functionality; however, it does slow down performance since it adds overhead. You can take steps during configuration to minimize this overhead, as you will see.

Recap

Here are the major points covered in this chapter:

- Call Graph profiling:
  - Visually represents the function-level hierarchy of your application including call counts, times, and the critical path.
  - Provides a way to track function entry and exit points of your code at run time.
  - Allows you to see which function is taking the longest to execute.

- When tuning applications written in a compiled language such as C++, Fortran or C, most users start with Sampling analysis and use Call Graph to refine their analysis. Users with a history of using other tools often jump to Call Graph analysis first because they have not had a tool that offered Sampling like the VTune analyzer previously.

- When tuning applications in C#, Java or Visual BASIC, most users start with Call Graph analysis and resort to time-based Sampling to refine their analysis if necessary.

■ Unlike Sampling, Call Graph profiling:

  − Is not system-wide and can only profile code in the least privileged protection ring, or Ring 3.

  − Requires *instrumentation*, which modifies a program by adding data collection routines.

  − Imposes some overhead on the execution of your program, so your program will usually run a bit longer and take additional time to start running when instrumentation has to be done. The VTune analyzer does cache the instrumented copies to speed up repeated runs by eliminating redundant instrumentations.

■ Call Graph usage requires that you build your program using a linker option that generates base relocations.

■ You can move between Graph and Call List views by clicking tabs:

  − The Graph tab shows a hierarchical view of the critical path and calling structure of your application.

  − The Call List tab shows caller and callee data for the focus function selected on the Graph tab.

■ From Call Graph, you can:

  − Drill down to see the source code view of any listed function whose source code is accessible from your computer.

  − Collect data for more than one process with fully automated threading support.

■ The command line (`vtl`) supports Call Graph collecting and dumping. The output is nearly impossible to read on a screen as text. Instead, view it in one of these ways:

  − Use the `vtl view -gui` command under Linux to pop open a graphical viewer.

  − Pack the project and then open, unpack, and view it on another system using the graphical interfaces built into the VTune analyzer.

  − Redirect the output from `vtl view` into text files and pull them into Excel.

Chapter **6**

Hotspot Hunting 103: Counter Monitor

You can observe a lot just by watching.

— Yogi Berra

Counter Monitor is the third of the three methods of analyzing a program using the VTune™ Performance Analyzer. Counter Monitor differs from Sampling by checking performance counters rather than event counters. Unlike event counters, performance counters are hardware- or software-defined counters that provide information about the overall state of the machine. You can use performance counters defined by the operating system, or design your own counters and have your own program increment them.

Unlike Sampling and Call Graph, this analysis method does not associate the collected data with any specific application or code. Because this analysis tracks counter values on a time basis, correlating with the interrupted code to collect the sample has no useful meaning. You can, however, run Sampling concurrently with the Counter Monitor and then correlate the two kinds of information.

The Counter Monitor can help you obtain an overview of overall performance, determine system resource usage, and identify system-level bottlenecks. The monitored performance counters help you understand the cause-and-effect relationship between your computer's subsystems and your application. Tracking these counters is particularly useful in helping identify system and computer architecture-level performance issues, and for monitoring large applications involving servers and the network. Table 6.1 summarizes the features of the Counter Monitor.

Table 6.1 Counter Monitor at a Glance

Feature:	Counter Monitor
Benefit at a glance:	Monitors selected counters in *performance objects*: collections of counters used to count a single event representing the state of a system entity such as an application, OS subsystem, or hardware device.
	Allows you to collect data about different computer subsystems, provides insights into overall system performance, and helps you determine system resource usage and identify system-level bottlenecks.
	You can correlate performance counter data with Sampling. You can even trigger the collection of counter data on events other than a periodic timer.
	You can create your own counters and triggers using the *Performance DLL Software Development Kit (SDK)* included with the VTune™ analyzer.
Versions:	Windows version of VTune analyzer, graphical user interface only (no support in the command line interface).
OS/Environments:	Windows operating systems only, excluding WinCE (Pocket PC, Smartphone).
Collectors:	Windows local data collection only.
Languages:	All languages.
Processors:	Not processor specific but, because of limited OS environments, available only on Pentium® and Itanium® processors.

The Counter Monitor only adds overhead to the counter data of certain subsystems. The runtime display mode produces some processor overhead, and logging mode writes data to disk, which can affect physical disk performance. If you need to collect precise data about either of these subsystems, you can disable the mode that impacts its performance.

Performance Counters, Objects, and Triggers

A *performance counter* is a feature that counts an event (such as *Available Bytes*) representing the state of a particular system entity (such as memory or disk). Performance counters are grouped into collections known as *performance objects*. A software object is a collection of counters that originate from a software component such as an OS subsystem. A hardware object is a collection of counters tracked by counter registers on a hardware device such as the microprocessor.

You can think of performance counters as characteristics of performance objects. Available performance counters and objects vary from one system to another, depending on operating system, processor type, and installed applications. Figure 6.1 shows the performance monitor registers built into the Itanium® processor, for instance.

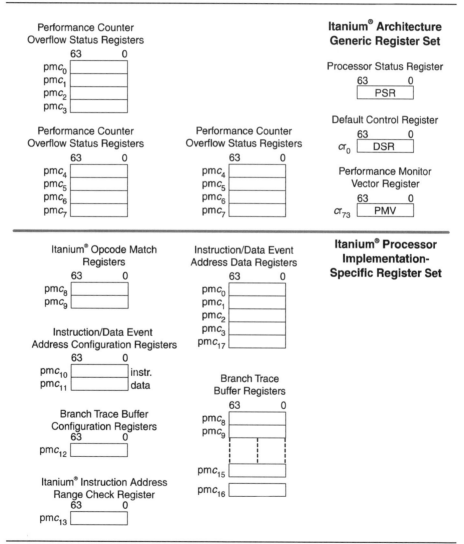

Figure 6.1 Performance Monitor Registers on the Itanium® Processor

If you simply allow the VTune analyzer to use the default set of OS counters, the Counter Monitor tracks the counters shown in Table 6.2, based on your operating system. Performance objects and counters take the form *Object: Counter* in the table.

Table 6.2   Default Objects and Counters by Operating System

Windows 98 / ME	Windows 2000 / XP	Windows NT
Kernel: Processor Usage (%)	System: Processor Queue Length	System: Processor Queue Length
Memory Manager: Unused Physical Memory	System: Context Switches/sec	System: Context Switches/sec
Memory Manager: Page Faults	Memory: Available Bytes	System: %Total Processor Time
Memory Manager: Swapfile in Use	Processor (_Total): Processor Time	System: %Total Privileged Time
Disk Cache: Cache Misses	Processor (_Total): Privileged Time	Memory: Available Bytes
	Redirector: Network Errors/sec	PhysicalDisk (_Total):% Disk Time

Counter Monitor Data Collection

In understanding the behavior of your application, the interaction with the operating system has been indirect. Sampling analysis focuses on the software interaction with the system hardware architecture and specific implementations. The Call Graph analysis focuses on the interaction of an application with itself and with software routines it calls into. Both of these are fairly low-level compared with what Counter Monitor analysis can offer. In general, Counter Monitor analysis shows interaction of your application and high-level hardware or software subsystems. Examples include the operating system or subsystems like memory allocation.

Operating systems are complex and a very important part of computers today. As such, it is entirely logical that they contain internal counters that you can examine and interpret. The VTune analyzer lets you tap into OS-oriented data, such as the amount of available memory, as a function of time, then click and drag to select a portion of the overall run in which the OS counter, or available memory, became unusual, pointing out available memory craters. The analyzer allows you to click and drag to define that time subset and drill down to your source code to see what your application was doing when that counter became alarming.

The first step to using the Counter Monitor is to have a notion of what you want to dive into analyzing. The analyzer groups counters into categories to help you cast a broad net based on the type of application you are analyzing: database, graphic-intensive, or network applications.

Choosing a Program Example

To help you learn about Counter Monitor data collection, turn again to the trusty program from the companion Web site called `prog0401`. This example, shown in this chapter's screens, is the same one used in Chapters 4 and 5. If you have your own application complete with source code, feel free to use that instead. Any example will do; nothing specific about this application makes it more suitable than one of yours, as long as you have the corresponding source code and symbol file.

Example 6.1: Counter Monitor Data Collection Using the Graphical Interface

In this example, you collect performance data for the default set of objects and counters, and also collect event-based Sampling data for the default events and event ratio. Once you have the activity results, you then zoom in to peaks in the Counter Monitor data and drill down to see the Sampling View associated with those peaks. Follow these steps to collect Counter Monitor data using the graphical interface.

Choosing and Using a Wizard

1. Double-click the **VTune Performance Analyzer** icon to start the program.

2. Click the **Create New Project** icon or open an existing project and create a new activity in it by clicking **Activity → New Activity**.

   The New Project window appears with a list of wizards from which to choose.

3. Choose any of the following wizards and select **OK**.

   ■ **Counter Monitor Wizard**.

   ■ **Quick Performance Analysis Wizard** and check **Collect sampling with counter monitor data** on the next screen. This wizard uses default settings for Counter Monitor values.

   ■ **Complete Setup Wizard** and check **Collect sampling with counter monitor data** on the next screen. This wizard lets you enable all three kinds of data collection in a single activity.

   ■ **Advanced Activity Configuration** and manually add new **Counter Monitor** and **Sampling** data collectors on the next screen. This is the most manual method of launching an activity, providing total control over every option.

   The following steps assume that you chose the Counter Monitor Wizard.

4. In the **Application To Launch** text box shown in Step 1 of the wizard screen, type this path or browse to its location

   ```
   C:\examples\ch4\windows\prog0401.exe
   ```

   or whatever executable file you want to run; if none, check **No application to launch**.

5. In the **Command Line Arguments** text box, type

   ```
   input0402.txt 1000
   ```

   for `prog0401` (for other applications, either type the options you want or type nothing if you are not sure).

Note

For Counter Monitor analysis, you may not specify *modules of interest* because counter data collection does not depend on modules. You can, however, specify *an application to launch* if you want a particular application to run when you monitor counters.

6. Select the **Modify default configuration when done with wizard** checkbox and click **Next**.

7. On the Step 2 wizard screen, leave the **Typical application** checked under the *What do you want to analyze?* heading and click **Next**.

   Other options on this screen include **Database**, **Graphic-intensive**, and **Network applications**, each of which has a default set of associated objects and counters. It is possible to check all these options at once if your analysis demands all the data.

8. Check **Collect sampling data to correlate counter data to application source** on the Step 3 wizard screen, as shown in Figure 6.2, and leave the rest as is.

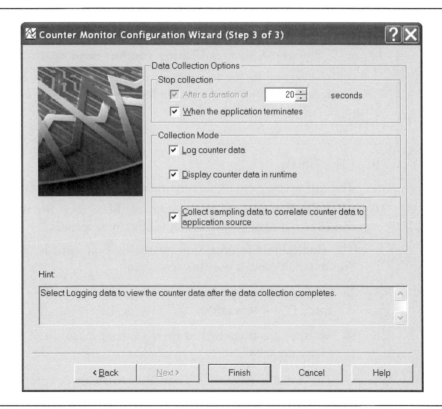

Figure 6.2   Step 3 of the Counter Monitor Wizard

Using these default settings, collection will stop when the application exits; Logging and Runtime data collection modes are both enabled.

Note

Here are a few tips to remember:

Monitor operating system counters over a reasonable period of time to analyze your system performance. Be aware of the available free disk space when specifying the duration time.

For example, monitoring default counters only takes about 10 megabytes when the activity runs for dozens of minutes. On the other hand, monitoring objects with multiple instances, such as the *Thread* performance object, takes about 10 megabytes when the duration is only a few dozens seconds and the default logging interval is 1 second.

Running an application with a very short duration (less than 1 second) with Runtime Data view enabled may cause the VTune analyzer to appear erratic. To prevent this, uncheck **Display counter data at runtime**.

If you specify zero (0) as the duration, data collection continues until you manually halt the activity by clicking the **Stop Activity** icon on the toolbar:

.

9. Click **Finish**.

    The Advanced Activity Configuration window appears.

10. Click **Configure...** in the middle of the screen for the **Counter Monitor** data collector, which is already selected.

    The Configure Counter Monitor dialog box appears as shown in Figure 6.3. You can use this screen to:

    ■ Add or remove performance objects and counters to be monitored (Counters tab).

    ■ Set specific triggers and their values for run time and logging (Triggers tab).

    The default trigger is Time but you can develop your own triggers, register, and launch them. Then, you can pick your triggers from the drop-down menu in the **Triggers** column on the **Triggers** tab.

For logging, you can configure each trigger separately, while you can only configure one trigger for runtime display.

■ Customize when the Counter Monitor starts and stops (General tab).

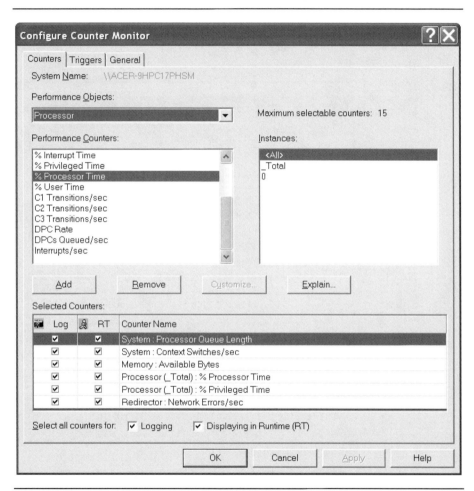

Figure 6.3   The Configure Counter Monitor Dialog Box

11. Notice that the Customize button is grayed out on the Counters tab. This button is only active if you select a counter that you created yourself using the *Performance DLL SDK*. See "Customizing DLLs, Counters, and Triggers" at the end of this chapter.

12. At the bottom of the Counters tab, notice the default counters preselected for Logging and Runtime display. These do not necessarily have to be the same. You can set up totally different objects and counters to monitor in each case.

13. Select **Memory** under Performance Objects, select **<All>** under Performance Counters, and click the **Explain...** button.

    An explanation of the *Memory* performance object appears as shown in Figure 6.4.

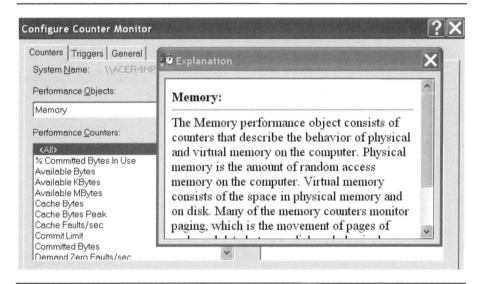

Figure 6.4   Using the Explain… Button for Help with a Performance Object

Had you selected a performance counter other than <All> such as *Available Bytes*, you would have seen an explanation of that counter instead of the object.

14. Click **OK** or **Cancel** to return to the Advanced Activity Configuration window.

15. Click **OK** to launch data collection with the specified setup.

    The VTune analyzer launches the Runtime Data view so you can watch data collection in real-time mode.

Runtime Data View

The Runtime Data view charts the counters selected for runtime display. The VTune analyzer generates a graph that shows the changes to monitored counters as they happen. The Runtime Data view includes the toolbar, chart, data table, and legend, as shown in descending order in Figure 6.5.

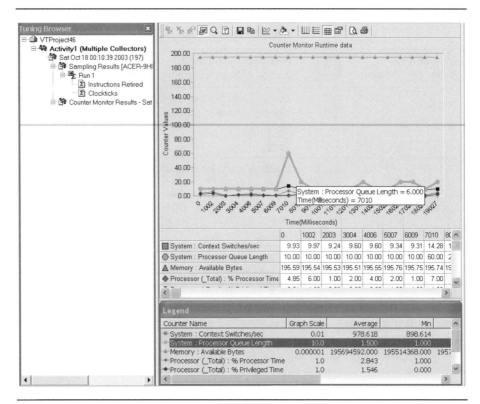

Figure 6.5   Runtime Data View of Real-time Counter Monitor Data Collected

The Runtime toolbar looks like this:

If you do not see this toolbar above the chart, right-click on the chart and select **Toolbar**. Table 6.3 explains some of the icons of special interest on this toolbar.

Table 6.3   Icons of Special Interest on the Runtime Toolbar

Name	Icon	Description
Freeze /Unfreeze Runtime Display		Toggles between freezing and unfreezing the onscreen display of runtime data collection.
		If you want to pause and resume the actual data collection itself, click the **Pause/Resume Activity** icon on the main toolbar during runtime data collection:
Select Range to Zoom, Drill Down		Prepares the cursor so you can select and highlight a portion of the chart before you click the Zoom icon.
Zoom		Zooms in on the selected portion of the chart that was highlighted using the Select Range icon:
View As		Displays a choice of chart types for viewing the collected counter data.
Data Table On/Off		Switches display of the Data Table between On and Off. The Data Table shows the information in the chart in tabular format.
Chart Properties		Displays the Chart FX Properties dialog box that allows you to change the appearance of chart components.

Each line in the chart represents data for a specific performance counter. Data from each counter appears with a separate line and color. Each line includes a distinct symbol—such as square, triangle, or circle—for the corresponding counter, representing the point at which data was taken. The y-axis represents counter values (scaled or actual), while the corresponding time in milliseconds appears on the x-axis.

Hovering over a counter on the chart displays a Tooltip that shows the counter value at that point in data collection, as illustrated in Figure 6.5. A peak in the chart indicates a high counter value. From viewing the chart, you can determine at what point in time the counter values were highest during data collection.

Clicking the **View As** and **Chart Properties** icons lets you customize the chart display in various ways. For example, you can view charts in **3D** using the **Cluster (Z-axis)** option to view counters in different rows along the z-axis. You can then save the chart to the Clipboard by clicking the **Copy** icon and pasting the bitmap image such as the one shown in Figure 6.6 into a graphics package for later inclusion in a document like this one.

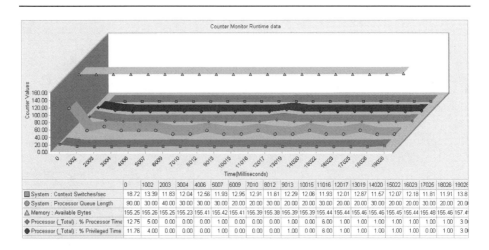

	0	1002	2003	3004	4006	5007	6009	7010	8012	9013	10015	11016	12017	13019	14020	15022	16023	17025	18026	19028
System : Context Switches/sec	18.72	13.39	11.83	12.04	12.56	11.93	12.95	12.91	11.61	12.29	12.06	11.93	12.01	12.87	11.57	12.07	12.18	11.81	11.91	13.8
System : Processor Queue Length	90.00	30.00	40.00	30.00	30.00	30.00	20.00	20.00	30.00	20.00	20.00	30.00	20.00	20.00	30.00	20.00	20.00	30.00	20.00	20.0
Memory : Available Bytes	155.25	155.26	155.25	155.23	155.41	155.42	155.41	155.39	155.38	155.39	155.39	155.44	155.44	155.46	155.45	155.44	155.48	155.46	157.4	
Processor (_Total) : % Processor Time	12.75	5.00	0.00	0.00	0.00	1.00	0.00	0.00	0.00	1.00	0.00	6.00	1.00	1.00	1.00	1.00	1.00	1.00	1.00	3.0
Processor (_Total) : % Privileged Time	11.76	4.00	0.00	0.00	0.00	1.00	0.00	0.00	0.00	1.00	0.00	6.00	1.00	1.00	1.00	1.00	1.00	0.00	1.00	3.0

Figure 6.6   3D Cluster Z-Axis Chart Copied and Pasted from the VTune Analyzer

The *Legend* provides the names and symbols as well as minimum, maximum, average, and last values for each counter in the chart. To make a line in the chart show up better, double-click its counter name in the Legend to turn on highlighting, or right-click the name and select **Highlight**. Thereafter, you can just click once on other counters to move the highlight.

Logged Data View

The Logged Data view charts the counter data that was logged during the activity run. After run time ends, the VTune analyzer prompts you to select a view to open from the Sampling and Counter Monitor results. Double-click the Counter Monitor results in this window or in the Tuning Browser to see the Logged Data view shown in Figure 6.7.

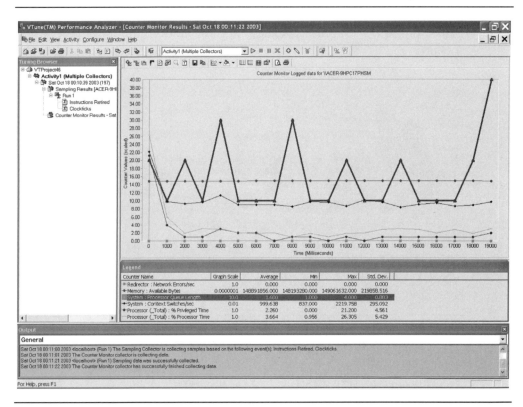

Figure 6.7　Logged Data View of Counter Monitor Data Collected

The Logged Data view is similar to the Runtime Data view, but the Legend shows the standard deviation instead of the last value, and the toolbar capabilities differ. The Logged toolbar looks like this:

Table 6.4 explains some icons of particular importance on this toolbar. The first three items in the table are unique to the Logged toolbar, providing the ability to:

■ Add other counters for performance objects selected for logging when you first configured the activity.

■ Toggle the display between Logged Data view and Summary Data view.

■ Drill down to see correlated data in Sampling Data views or get advice from the Tuning Assistant, as described in Chapter 7.

Table 6.4   Icons of Special Interest on the Logged Toolbar

Name	Icon	Description
Add Counters		Displays the Add Performance Counters dialog box (similar to Figure 6.3) so you can add other counters for the performance objects selected.
Toggle Logged and Summary View		Switches back and forth between Logged Data view (Figure 6.7) and Summary Data view (Figure 6.8).
Drill Down to Correlated Sampling Data View		Drills down to Sampling Data views for the time range highlighted in the chart using the Select Range icon:
Select Range to Zoom, Drill Down		Enables or disables selecting and highlighting a portion of the chart before you click the Zoom, Drill Down, or Tuning Advice icon to investigate the selected time range.
Zoom		Zooms in on the selected portion of the chart that was highlighted using the Select Range icon:
View As		Displays a choice of chart types from which to select for viewing the collected counter data.
Data Table On/Off		Switches display of the Data Table between On and Off.
Chart Properties		Displays the Chart FX Properties dialog box that allows you to change the appearance of chart components.

Summary Data View

To see the Summary Data view, click the **Display Logged Data or Summary View** icon:

The Summary Data view provides statistical information for each counter in the Logged Data view. This summary graph lets you see which values were the most active or interesting, so you can drill down from a Logged Data view of those values. The default Summary Data view is a bar graph of each counter showing maximum, average, and minimum values. Figure 6.8 shows Summary Data viewed as an Area-Curve with Point Labels.

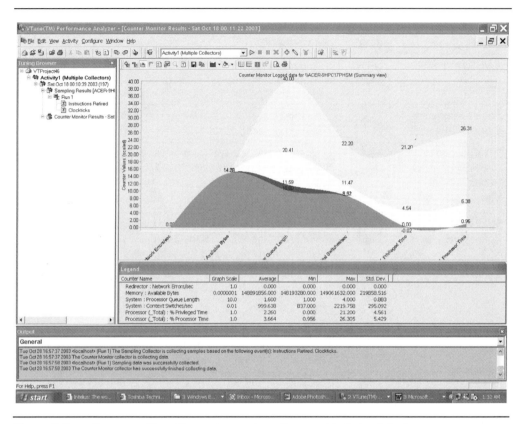

Figure 6.8   Summary Data Viewed as an Area-Curve with Point Labels

Click the **Display Logged Data or Summary View** icon again to switch back to Logged Data view.

Selecting a Chart Range

You can select a portion of the chart to investigate by clicking the **Select Range to Zoom/Drill Down** icon, and then clicking and dragging to highlight the range, as shown in the gray area of Figure 6.9. You can then either zoom in on the chart to magnify the data, get tuning advice for that range, or drill down into correlated Sampling data by clicking the **Drill Down to Correlated Sampling Data View** icon.

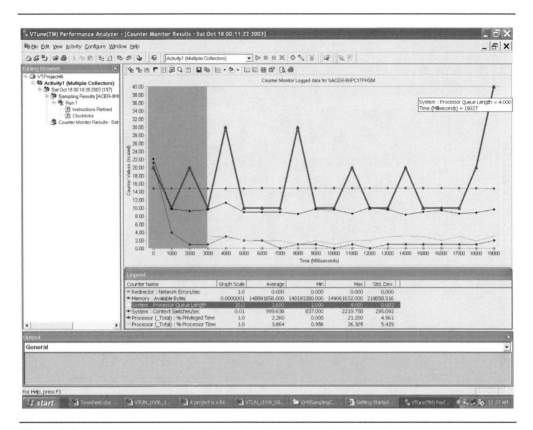

Figure 6.9 Range Selected for Zoom, Drill Down, or Tuning Advice

Zooming In

After selecting a range, click the **Zoom** icon to zoom in on a portion of the chart data. The VTune analyzer expands the selected area so it fills the entire chart as shown in Figure 6.10.

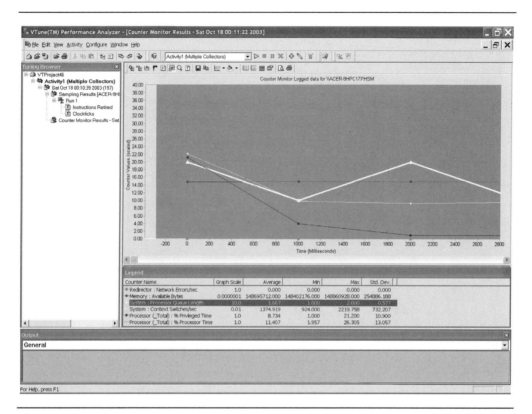

Figure 6.10   Zoomed View of Previously Selected Range of Chart

The highlighted *Processor Queue Length* counter measures how many threads are waiting to execute. The average value is about 1.6, not an unreasonable number for a single processor system. When the value of this counter is less than or equal to 2, you have enough processor power to handle the thread load on the system at that point.

Although the chart shows that the *%Processor Time* counter was erratic, on average it remained low. The average counter value, displayed in the Legend, is about 11 percent. If the processor is not being utilized 100 percent, and the code is reasonably optimized, a system bottleneck likely exists. The exact element in which the bottleneck resides depends on the application. For example, if the application is disk heavy, the bottleneck is likely to be with the disk. If the application is Internet-based, network traffic may be causing the delays.

The next logical step might be to add some appropriate objects, such as *PhysicalDisk* or *Network Interface*, and counters to the activity. You could do this by right-clicking the activity in the Tuning Browser and selecting **Modify Collectors...** Then you would rerun the activity to collect counter data again, and perhaps use the Tuning Assistant, as described in Chapter 7, to get advice about Counter Monitor data.

Once you identify and resolve system-level problems and ensure 100 percent processor utilization, you can continue on to application-specific tuning using other data collectors.

Drilling Down to Sampling View

After correcting any problems with processor utilization, you can select a range in the Logged Data view and drill down to Sampling data to investigate your application's performance. Clicking the **Drill-down to Correlated Sampling Data View** icon opens the Sampling Module view, which reveals Sampling data correlated to the selected time interval, in this case:

🔁 11149_to_16108

Clicking the **Process** icon shows all the processes executing during the selected period of time, including prog040, as shown in Figure 6.11. In Sampling Data views, you can see what processes, threads, and modules were executing when certain counter values were at the highest. For instance, you might select a range in time when the most page faults occurred in Logged Data view, then drill down to Sampling view to see what application, module, or function could potentially have generated these page faults.

In the example shown here, notice that the prog0401.exe application's clocks per instructions (CPI) is only 0.8. The CPI can give you a general indication of optimization opportunities. A value of 0.75 or less is considered good. A high CPI value of 4 or more is considered poor, indicating that instructions are requiring more cycles to execute than they should.

Contrast this value with the System Idle Process, which shows an artificially high CPI of 11, because relatively few statements executed when the processor was not in the halt (idle) state. In the Intel® Pentium® M processor used to create this example, the *Clockticks* event only counted the number of clockticks during which the processor was not in a halt state. Not counting idle task cycles is important in event ratios. CPI makes more sense without diluting the number with time spent in the idle task. For more about CPIs, see "Evaluating the CPI Ratio" in Appendix B.

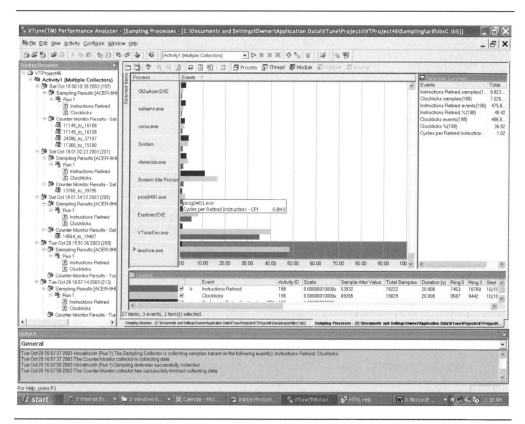

Figure 6.11 Sampling Process View After Drill Down from Logged Data View

Figure 6.11 should look familiar, because Counter Monitor has led to a view seen in the Sampling Chapter. From the Process view, you could, of course, drill down to Hotspot view and then drill down to the Source view of the `Sort` function. In this case, the `Sort` function is found to be the Hotspot function, rather than the `Read` function as was discovered in the Sampling example in Chapter 4. This variance, however, is only true when events are ordered by *Instructions Retired*. In any case, the difference in number of *Instructions Retired* in each function is negligible, as shown by the length of the lowest horizontal bar for each function in Figure 6.12.

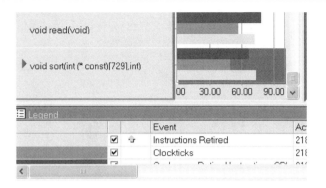

Figure 6.12   Sampling Hotspot View Ordered by *Instructions Retired*

To return to previous Counter Monitor views, click the Previous icon in the Standard toolbar

or select a view from the **Windows** menu. From the Logged Data view, click **Select Range to Zoom/Drill Down** to toggle back to full-chart display.

Collecting Counter Data for a Running Thread/Process

The Counter Monitor collects data on all the counters and instances of a monitored performance object. You can add counters and instances to the Logged Data view, even after the activity result is created. To view the counter data for a running thread or process:

1. Right-click the activity in the Tuning Browser, select **Modify Collectors...**, select the **Counter Monitor** collector, and click **Configure...**

2. From the Counters tab of the Configure Counter Monitor dialog box, add the *Thread* (or *Process*) performance object to log, the *%Processor Time* counter, and a thread such as `Explorer(6)`, as shown in Figure 6.13.

3. Run the activity.

    The VTune analyzer collects data on all the counters and instances of all threads, but shows data only for the counters and instances you selected for logging.

4. In the Logged Data view, click the **Add Counters** icon and the *Thread* (or *Process*) object and add any other required instances and counters.

The Logged Data view updates, displaying the added instances and counters.

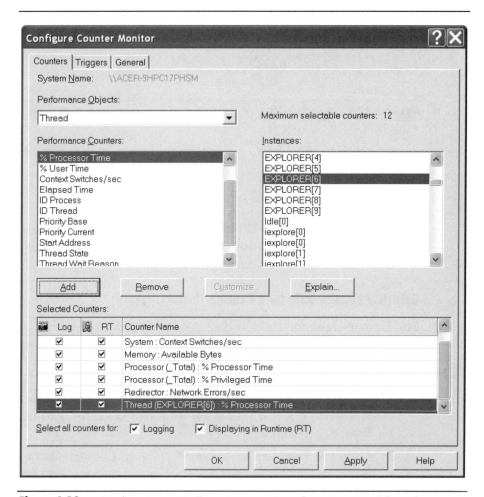

Figure 6.13 Configuring to Collect Counter Data for a Running Thread

Identifying Bottlenecks Using Counters

All systems are subject to performance bottlenecks. The VTune analyzer can help you identify how your application contributes to these bottlenecks. The most common bottlenecks occur with memory, disk, processor, or network.

Bottlenecks are usually the result of insufficient resources such as memory or disk capacity, incorrectly configured resources, uneven sharing of workloads, or malfunctions on the system.

Table 6.5 identifies some good performance counters to target to help locate bottlenecks. Depending on your system configuration, you may not see the exact objects and counters shown here. Regardless of your target platform, the table shows just a fraction of the many performance objects and counters available for monitoring.

Table 6.5   Good Performance Counters to Target to Help Locate Bottlenecks

Type of Bottleneck	Performance Object	Performance Counter	Description
Memory	Memory	Available Bytes	The amount of physical memory in bytes, available to processes running on the computer. A value of 4MB should be considered low, and a value of 10 MB or greater should be considered acceptable.
Memory	Memory	Pages/Sec	The rate at which pages are read from or written to disk to resolve hard page faults. This counter is a primary indicator of the kinds of faults that cause system-wide delays.
Disk	PhysicalDisk	% Disk Time.	Percentage of elapsed time that the selected disk drive was busy servicing read or write requests.
Disk	PhysicalDisk	% Idle Time.	Percentage of time during the sample interval that the disk was idle.
Disk	PhysicalDisk	Disk Reads/sec	Rate of read operations on the disk.
Disk	PhysicalDisk	Disk Writes/sec	Rate of write operations on the disk.
Disk	PhysicalDisk	Avg. Disk Queue Length	Average number of both read and write requests that were queued for the selected disk during the sample interval.

Table 6.5   Good Performance Counters to Target to Help Locate Bottlenecks
(continued)

Type of Bottleneck	Performance Object	Performance Counter	Description
Disk	LogicalDisk	% Free Space	Percentage of total usable space on the selected logical disk drive that was free.
Processor	Processor	Interrupts/sec	Average rate at which the processor received and serviced hardware interrupts. This value is an indirect indicator of the activity of devices that generate interrupts such as the system clock, the mouse, disk drivers, data communication lines, network interface cards, and other peripheral devices.
Processor	Processor	% Processor Time	Percentage of elapsed time that the processor spends to execute a non-Idle thread. This counter is the primary indicator of processor activity, and displays the average percentage of busy time observed during the sample interval.
			Generally, if the processor is not being used 100%, there is a system bottleneck The exact element in which the bottleneck resides depends on the application.
Processor	Process: *process*	% Processor Time	Percentage of elapsed time that a selected process thread (instance) used the processor to execute instructions.
Processor	System	Processor Queue Length	Number of threads in the processor queue. Unlike the disk counters, this counter shows ready threads only, not threads that are running. A sustained processor queue of less than 10 threads per processor is normally acceptable depending on the workload, but a sustained processor queue of greater than two threads can indicate processor congestion and is worth investigating.
Network	Network Interface	Bytes Total/sec	Rate at which bytes are sent and received over each network adapter, including framing characters. This is a sum of Bytes Received/sec and Bytes Sent/sec

Table 6.5 Good Performance Counters to Target to Help Locate Bottlenecks *(continued)*

Type of Bottleneck	Performance Object	Performance Counter	Description
Network	Network Interface	Bytes Sent/sec	Rate at which bytes are sent over each network adapter, including framing characters.
Network	Network Interface	Bytes Received/sec	Rate at which bytes are received over each network adapter, including framing characters.
Network	Server	Bytes Total/sec	Number of bytes the server has sent to and received from the network. This value provides an overall indication of how busy the server is.
Network	Server	Bytes Transmitted/sec	Number of bytes the server has sent on the network. Indicates how busy the server is.
Network	Server	Bytes Received/sec	Number of bytes the server has received from the network. Indicates how busy the server is.

To correctly identify bottlenecks, monitor your entire system rather than just the specific resources you suspect are causing the problem. For example, high counter values related to the disk might be resolved by using a faster disk or controller. However, if the high disk counter values are coupled with high memory counter values caused by excessive system paging—that is, memory areas are being written and read to disk—you may choose to add memory instead of replacing your disk.

Developing Custom DLLs, Counters, and Triggers

The VTune analyzer comes with a *Performance DLL Software Development Kit (SDK)* that allows you to extend the functionality available through the Counter Monitor Analysis. Using this software, you can write DLLs that track performance counters in hardware devices, device drivers, or software applications. The SDK includes online help, a fully referenced class library, and a wizard for creating a working template.

You can configure the Counter Monitor to collect and display counter information for DLLs that you create using this package. If you develop application-specific counters using Performance DLLs, the VTune analyzer monitors and displays these counter values.

You can also create your own triggers using three supplied API functions: `VT_RegisterTrigger`, `VT_UnregisterTrigger`, and `VT_SetTrigger`. Using these functions, you can easily develop triggers to signal the VTune analyzer to collect counter data on events other than a periodic timer at intervals based on criteria that you set. For example, you might add a trigger to collect data after each video frame finishes rendering, or based on the size and rate of packets moving across a network.

Counter Monitor Usage Tips

Be sure not to overlook this analysis. It is an important part of looking for unexpected things. It is most popular with developers who already are using tools to look at the counters present under the Windows operating system. Those users find value as they move to the VTune analyzer in continuing to use the counters. If you liked the counters before using the VTune analyzer, by all means continue; you will like them even better with the VTune analyzer.

Setting up your own counters opens up a fantastic world of possibilities. I've seen only modest examples of this despite great promise. After exploring the counters which already exist on your system, I encourage you to create your own counters to monitor the subsystems in your own application using the *Performance DLL Software Development Kit (SDK)*. This is the way you can leave performance hooks in your own application, to make tuning it far into the future an easier and more productive task. Leaving your own hooks can even make automation of performance tracking easier.

The Counter Monitor is the least used of the three analysis methods. It is relatively unknown among users of the VTune analyzer. Bring this up with the Intel support team for the VTune analyzer and you will find that they think the lack of use is unjust, and a matter of lack of education. "Puzzling" is a word I hear used to describe the small user following for this feature. The feature has its strong fans and is unlikely to disappear. In fact, the absence of the Counter Monitor analysis support under Linux has not gone unnoticed and appears a strong candidate for inclusion in a future version of the VTune analyzer.

How Counter Monitor Analysis Works

Once you have configured Counter Monitor data collection, either through a wizard or through manual setup, you run the configured activity. Running the activity launches the specified application, if any. The analyzer starts monitoring and logging counter values, collecting data for every counter of each performance object you selected, but graphing only those counters you chose.

A trigger event tells the VTune analyzer when to collect the counter data. The VTune program uses the system timer as the default trigger mechanism, collecting data at a default interval of once every second, or 1,000 milliseconds.

If the run-time display option was checked, the analyzer displays the Runtime Data view of real-time counter data in chart form as it is being collected. If Sampling data collection was turned on, the analyzer starts collecting time- or event-based Sampling data. If Call Graph data collection was turned on, the analyzer profiles the instrumented application until it either terminates or you manually stop running it.

At the end of an activity run, if Counter Monitor data was logged, the VTune analyzer creates an activity result for the Counter Monitor data and displays an icon in the Tuning Browser. The analyzer immediately displays the Logged Data view if Counter Monitor data was the only type of data collected, or prompts you to pick a view if multiple types of collectors ran.

Recap

Here are some key points in this chapter:

- Counter Monitor data collection can help you:
  - Obtain an overview of overall performance.
  - Determine system resource usage.
  - Identify system-level bottlenecks.

- A *performance object* is a collection of *performance counters* for a particular hardware or software entity.

- The *Runtime Data view* charts real-time counter data for selected performance objects.

- The *Logged Data view* charts counter data logged after the activity finishes running.

- The *Summary Data view* charts summary information for each counter being monitored.

- The Counter Monitor adds overhead in these ways:
  - Runtime display mode produces some processor overhead.
  - Logging mode writes data to disk, which can affect physical disk performance.

- Unlike Sampling and Call Graph, the Counter Monitor does not associate collected data with any specific application or code.

- You can, however, run Sampling on your application concurrently with the Counter Monitor and then correlate the two kinds of information.

- From Logged Data view, you can drill down to see correlated Sampling views.

- You can monitor counters for running threads and processes.

- You can use the built-in SDK to create your own counters to use with Counter Monitor analysis. This SDK also allows you to develop custom performance DLLs and triggers.

Chapter 7

Automatic Hotspot Analysis

Within the problem lies the solution.

— Milton Katselas

Where to start? This is the most common problem users of the VTune™ analyzer encounter. Even experienced users can get into interesting discussions about this issue when they compare notes about how they use the analyzer. Experts at Intel have constructed their answer to this challenge: it is known as the *Intel® Tuning Assistant.*

Based on Intel expert advice that is built into the tool, the Intel Tuning Assistant automatically analyzes hotspots and offers expert advice on the hardest question of all: "What should I make of all these graphs and information?" The Tuning Assistant guides you through the key steps of performance tuning methodology. Used properly, this automated feature of the VTune Performance Analyzer can give some very useful advice. The trick is to help the Tuning Assistant visit the right data, so that it can draw a conclusion and offer advice for you. Choosing the right data takes careful thought.

You can invoke the Tuning Assistant from the Counter Monitor, Sampling, or Source view by clicking an icon on the main toolbar. The tool offers many possibilities including advice about code, processes, modules, threads, and time ranges that you select. If you furnish symbol information, the Tuning Assistant window provides links from your program's function names directly to the corresponding source code sections in Source view. The Tuning Assistant can help you compare two or three activity results, as described in Chapter 8, and offers tuning advice on performance counter data as well as disassembly code.

After you obtain advice from the Tuning Assistant, you can export the report to a comma separated values (.csv) text file for viewing and editing in a spreadsheet application such as Microsoft Excel. Simply select the **Export** option from the **Files** menu.

Table 7.1 Tuning Assistant at a Glance

Feature:	Tuning Assistant
Benefit at a glance:	Automatically analyzes data, identifies performance issues, and offers tuning advice. Available for Counter Monitor and Sampling data, all views including Source view and Disassembly view.
Versions:	All versions of the VTune™ analyzer from the graphical user interface. Some usage from some command lines is possible, but not likely to be a popular choice.
OS/Environments:	Microsoft Windows
Collectors:	Counter Monitor and Sampling data collectors
Languages:	C, C++, Fortran, or Java† source code
Processors:	Expertise built-in for Intel® Itanium® 2, Pentium® 4, Pentium M, and Pentium III processors, including support for Hyper-Threading Technology.

Types of Tuning Advice

The Tuning Assistant uses multiple knowledge bases to analyze the data collected by the VTune Performance Analyzer, identify performance issues, and provide tuning advice. It can provide advice on:

■ Counter Monitor data measured on systems running Microsoft Windows NT 4.0, Windows 2000, or Windows XP

■ Sampling data measured on Pentium® III and Pentium 4 processors, including support for Hyper-Threading Technology[1]

■ C, C++, Fortran, or Java† source code

■ Disassembled assembly code

---

[1] VTune Analyzer version 7.0 (or later) supports Sampling-based analysis only on Intel Pentium III and Pentium 4 processors, including Pentium 4 processors with Hyper-Threading Technology. If you are using a different processor, explore other types of advice or try sampling on a machine with a supported processor.

Counter Monitor-based Advice

On systems running Microsoft Windows, the Tuning Assistant offers advice about data collected using the Counter Monitor tool described in Chapter 6. The Tuning Assistant bases its analysis on all counters measured as part of the current activity, not just the counters displayed in the current view. The current view does, however, define the context, or range, of data used in the analysis. Select the time range for analysis in the Counter Monitor, and then select the Tuning Assistant, since the Tuning Assistant bases its analysis on the data range that is currently in view.

Sampling-based Advice

The Tuning Assistant can offer performance-related advice about data obtained using the Sampling tool described in Chapter 4. You can invoke the Tuning Assistant for advice on the entire Sampling database or just the processes, threads, modules, or functions you select. In Sampling views, the Tuning Assistant bases its analysis only on the selected code range, if any.

Figure 7.1 shows the three parts of the Tuning Assistant advice delivered for sampling data: *Workload Insights*, *Module Insights*, and *System Info*. You can toggle between the three sections by clicking the purple tab at the top of the screen that corresponds to each.

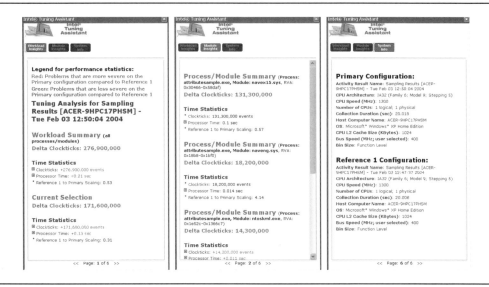

Figure 7.1   The Three Intel® Tuning Assistant Parts: Workload, Module, and System Info

You can obtain tuning advice from any Sampling view including Source view. Getting Sampling advice in Source view, however, is not the same thing as obtaining what VTune analyzer terminology calls *Source-based Tuning Advice*, described next.

Source-based Tuning Advice

You can configure the Tuning Assistant so that it uses compiler technology to suggest possible source code transformations that could speed up your code. Configuring the Tuning Assistant to provide such advice, however, can be complicated and is therefore not recommended for default use. In practice, this feature tends to offer the kind of advice you hope the team that wrote your compiler already knew about, rather than the sort of information you want to use to tune your own application.

Still, if you want to try using the Tuning Assistant's source-based advice functionality, see "Configuring the Intel Tuning Assistant for Source-based Tuning Advice" in the VTune analyzer's online documentation. This Help screen explains how to configure the Tuning Assistant with source-based tuning enabled and the appropriate build environment selected.

The VTune Performance Analyzer provides advice on optimizing C, C++, Fortran, and Java source code. Once the VTune analyzer identifies, analyzes, and displays the source code for hotspots (or static functions) in your application, you can invoke the Tuning Assistant for advice on how to rewrite that portion of code to optimize its performance. The Tuning Assistant examines the entire block of code or function you selected and searches for optimization opportunities. After analyzing your code, it displays the problems and relevant advice items in the Tuning Assistant viewer.

For example, language pointer semantics typically restrict compiler code optimization. The Tuning Assistant suggests source-based modifications to overcome these and other compile-time restrictions. It also recognizes commonly used code patterns in your application and suggests modifications to improve performance.

Static and Disassembly-based Advice

The VTune Performance Analyzer can perform Static Assembly Analysis of your program when no event data are involved. After performing this analysis, the VTune analyzer displays annotated information about any problem areas in the code.

To view static assembly penalties and warnings, open Source view in Mixed or Disassembly only mode. The Penalties and Warnings column lists penalties and warnings for each code line. *Penalties* indicate specific problems and how they affect performance, such as the number of cycles affected. *Warnings* indicate potential problems that may cause performance degradation in specific cases; however, since the analysis is static, the actual impact in run time is unknown. To verify the real impact of penalties and warnings, run event-based Sampling with the relevant events selected.

■ Before You Begin Using the Intel® Tuning Assistant

If you want to obtain source-based tuning advice (disabled by default), you need to enable it and select the appropriate build environment. Select **Configure** → **Options** → **Intel Tuning Assistant** → **Source Information** to see the relevant screen for detailing this information. You must specify a Project file, Make file, or Preprocessed (.i) file as the Build file. In most cases, you will not want to enable this feature, for the reasons already stated.

■ Using the Tuning Assistant

Using the Tuning Assistant is a little like using a fish finder. If you frown on such devices, and they do seem a bit unfair to the fish, then think of the Tuning Assistant as a super-duper rod and reel versus a cane pole. Activities like going fishing and tuning software are hard enough tasks; why struggle when you can take advantage of the latest technology?

Inside the VTune™ Analyzer: The Intel® Tuning Assistant

What exactly happens when you run the Intel Tuning Assistant? When you launch this tool, the VTune analyzer:

1. Analyzes the selected range of data. The Tuning Assistant can base its analysis on all the counters or event data in the current activity result, or just on a subset you select.

2. Identifies performance issues, drawing on a number of knowledge bases for information. Depending on the type of data it is analyzing, the Tuning Assistant uses different technologies to analyze the data and generate the advice.

3. Displays tuning advice in one of two kinds of reports:

   ■ The first type of report pertains only to Sampling-based advice and can contain insights for either: a single activity result (Primary), or two or three activity results (Primary + Reference1 and Reference2).

   ■ The second type of report is displayed:

      – When you are viewing Counter Monitor activity results.

      – When you drill down to Source view or when you do not have debug information and your code is disassembled in Source view, select Disassembly mode, and select a single line of assembly code.

      – When you drill down to Source view and source-based advice is enabled.

      – When you view Static Analysis data and no event data are involved.

Choosing a Program Example

To help you learn about the Tuning Assistant, turn again to the program from the companion Web site called `prog0401`. This example is the same one used in Chapters 4, 5, and 6. If you have your own application complete with source code, feel free to use that instead. If using your own application, be sure to:

■ Compile/link with symbols and line numbers.

■ Make *release* builds with optimizations.

Example 7.1: Getting Advice from the Tuning Assistant

In this example, you collect Counter Monitor performance data for the default set of objects and counters, and also collect event-based Sampling data for a selected event and event ratio. Once you have the activity results, you then zoom in to get advice on a peak in the Counter Monitor data graph, and then drill down to get advice on a hotspot in Sampling View, Mixed View and Source View.

Collecting Counter Monitor and Sampling Data

Follow these steps to collect Counter Monitor and Sampling data using VTune analyzer's graphical interface:

1. Double-click the **VTune Performance Analyzer** icon to start the VTune program.

2. Click **New Project** (or open an existing project and create a new activity in it by clicking **Activity** → **New Activity**).

   The New Project window appears with a list of wizards from which to choose.

3. Choose **Complete Setup Wizard**. This wizard lets you enable multiple kinds of data collection in a single activity.

4. In the **Application To Launch** text box of the Step 1 wizard screen, type this path or browse to its location:

   ```
   C:\examples\ch4\windows\prog0401.exe
   ```

5. In the **Command Line Arguments** text box, type:

   ```
   input0402.txt 1000 3
   ```

   As you may recall from Example 4.3 in Chapter 4, the third parameter causes the program to slow down when it has certain values.

6. Check **Collect sampling with counter monitor data** and click **Next**.

7. On the Step 2 wizard screen, click **Configure...** to configure event-based Sampling.

   The Event-based Sampling Configuration window appears with Event-based sampling selected and the Calibrate Sample After value checkbox checked.

8. Click the **Events** tab and select **All events** from the Event Groups pull-down menu.

9. If you have a Pentium M processor:

    – Highlight **Misaligned Data Memory Reference** from the Available Events scroll-down list and click the **>>** button to select this event for Sampling.

    – Click the **Event Ratios** tab and select **Memory Statistics** from the Ratio Groups pull-down menu.

    – Highlight **Misaligned References Ratio** from the Available Ratios scroll-down list and click the **>>** button to select this event ratio for Sampling.

    – Click **OK**.

Note

> As you may recall from Example 4.3 in Chapter 4, integers are not aligned on 4-byte boundaries in the prog0401 program example. This causes misaligned data memory references on Pentium M processor-based systems.
>
> On other processors, find one or more event(s) that measure a similar memory condition caused by alignment problems. For example, if you have a Pentium 4 processor, highlight and select *Split Stores Retired (TI-E)* and *Split Loads Retired (TI-E)*. These two memory conditions are caused when memory loads and stores are not aligned to natural boundaries, because the loads and stores sometimes have to involve two cache lines.

10. Click **Finish** on the Step 2 wizard screen to launch data collection with the specified setup.

    The VTune analyzer launches the Runtime Data view so you can watch Counter Monitor data collection in real-time mode.

11. Select **Counter Monitor Results** from the Select Activity Results window and click **View**.

    The Counter Monitor's Logged Data view appears.

Getting Counter Monitor-based Advice

1. Pick an area of particular interest to investigate on the Counter Monitor's Logged Data view, such as a place where the graph spikes suddenly. Select that portion of the chart by clicking the **Select Range to Zoom/Drill Down** icon and then click and drag to highlight the range.

2. Click the **Zoom** icon to zoom into the selected range if you need to see the range better.

3. Launch the Tuning Assistant by pressing **F8** or clicking the **Get Advice Using the Intel Tuning Assistant** icon from the main toolbar:

The Tuning Assistant displays four insights into potential performance problems based on the highlighted portion of the Counter Monitor data, as shown in Figure 7.2:

■ *The variation in processor utilization is high.* Chapter 6 on Counter Monitor analysis pointed out that running an application with a very short duration (less than 1 second) with Runtime Data view enabled could cause the VTune analyzer to become unstable. Since the `prog0401` sample program is short, this might account for any erratic results. To prevent this possibility, you could uncheck **Display counter data at runtime** and rerun the program.

■ *There are more threads ready to run than there are processors on which to run them.* In this case, the system used to prepare this example was a single-processor system, so the limitation is hardware-based.

■ *Privileged mode processor activity is high.* This heavy operating system activity could be a clue to I/O blockages or memory problems, as you shall see.

■ *Processor utilization is low.* This processor is capable of much more compute-intensive processing than it is being asked to do in our simple example.

A high percentage next to each insight indicates that the selected data are highly relevant to criteria for that particular insight.

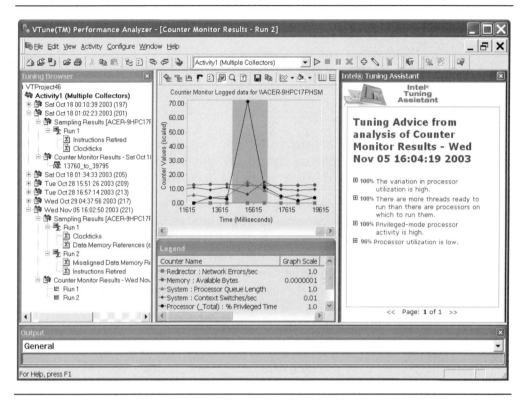

Figure 7.2   Tuning Advice from the Counter Monitor

Each of these insights links to an associated explanation.

4. Click the third insight, which suggests that privileged mode processor activity is high. A window pops up revealing more information.

5. Click the plus sign (+) next to each insight to see more related advice, and click the link associated with each piece of advice to see a detailed explanation.

Figure 7.3 shows a piece of advice that suggests revising the application to do less privileged-mode activity. The advice warns that you should check whether the amount of I/O that is occurring is reasonable for the amount of work being done, and to make sure there are no bugs causing more I/O than necessary.

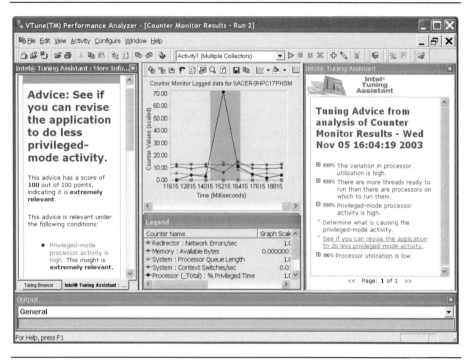

Figure 7.3   More Advice from the Counter Monitor

Getting Sampling Advice in Module View

Armed with these clues from Counter Monitor data, let's take a look at the sampling data collected during the same run.

1. From the Tuning Browser, select the **Sampling Results** that were collected along with the Counter Monitor results when you ran the activity.

    A horizontal bar graph appears showing prog0401.exe selected from among the modules whose sampling results appear in Module view.

2. If necessary, sort the modules so that they appear in ascending order by the event of interest (in this case, by *Misaligned Data Memory References*). Clicking the column heading for this event once or twice should accomplish this task.

3. Launch the Tuning Assistant by pressing **F8** or clicking the **Get Advice Using the Intel Tuning Assistant** icon from the main toolbar:

The Tuning Assistant Options for Sampling dialog box appears, as shown in Figure 7.4. This dialog box pops up whenever you invoke the Tuning Assistant from a Sampling view. It lets you set options that determine which activity result (s) the Tuning Assistant should analyze and provide advice on. You can get advice on all or part of the data in this activity result alone, or compare this activity result with other runs, as described in Chapter 8. You can also filter the types of advice the Tuning Assistant displays.

Note   Make sure you only select activity results that were generated on an Intel Pentium III or Pentium 4 processor, since the Tuning Assistant does not support Sampling data collected on other processors.

4. Specify the **Name** of the Primary activity result you selected in Step 1 (the default name should appear automatically filled in), and select **<none>** for Reference activity results, since no comparisons are being made in this example.

5. Select the front-side **Bus Speed** (in megahertz) of the system you used to collect the result. The Tuning Assistant uses this speed to compute event frequencies. If you are unsure about what to select, you can find out the frequency by using Intel's free frequency ID tool at:

   http://support.intel.com/support/processors/tools/FrequencyID/FreqID.htm

6. Leave **Analyze the current selection** as the **Output option**.

7. To save time and screen space, check the box next to **Only show regions that contain insight information**.

8. Click **OK**.

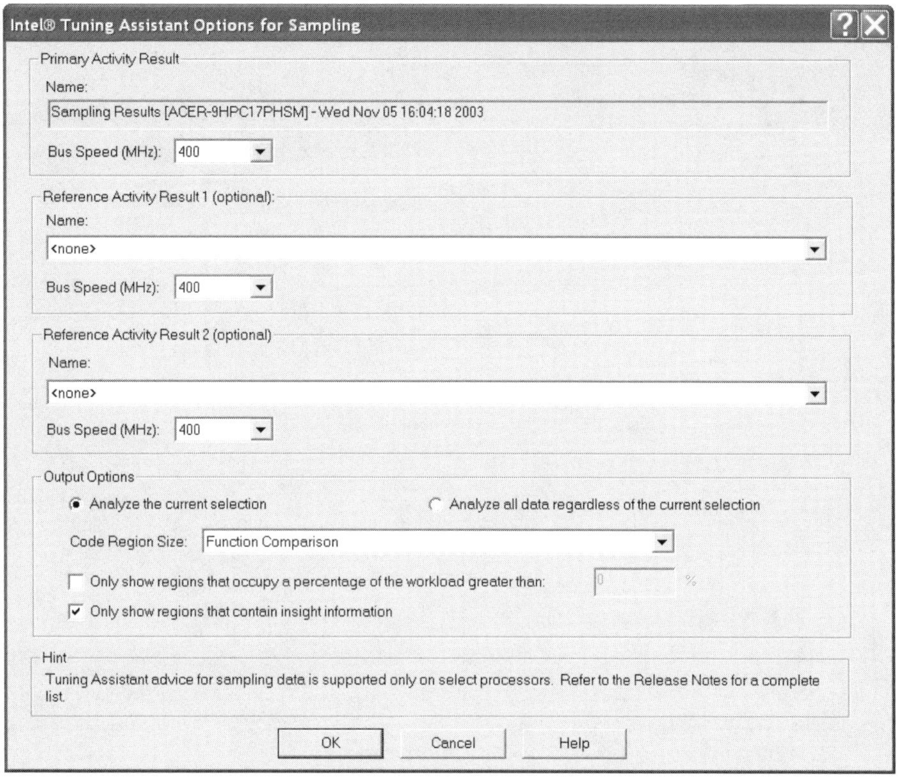

Figure 7.4 The Tuning Assistant Options for Sampling

The Tuning Assistant identifies the Primary configuration and displays insights about possible problems detected for the Process/Module and various functions within it.

Figure 7.5 shows the explanation associated with an insight suggested as a possible problem. Not surprisingly, given the intentional flaw built into the sample program, the Tuning Assistant has found that misaligned memory references are occurring.

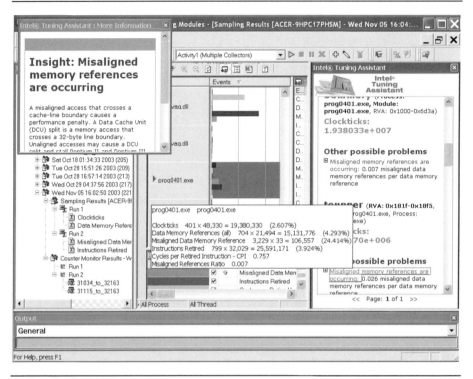

Figure 7.5   Advice from Sampling Module View

9. Click the plus sign (+) next to the identified problem to reveal more advice related to it, and click the link associated with each piece of advice to see the explanations.

Getting Sampling Advice in Hotspot View

From Module view, you can drill down to see any hotspots where the memory problems are occurring in greater numbers.

1. Double-click the `prod0401.exe` module name or select the **Hotspot** icon to drill down to the next level to see which function in the module is experiencing the most misaligned memory references.

   As Figure 7.6 reveals, the `toupper` function has a 26-percent *Misaligned references ratio*, and a whopping 95-percent occurrence of the *Misaligned Data Memory Reference* event. The Tuning Assistant suggests that you make sure the code is efficiently aligned and offers advice on how to accomplish this. The best way to ensure efficient alignment is to use an optimizing compiler that automatically enforces alignment rules.

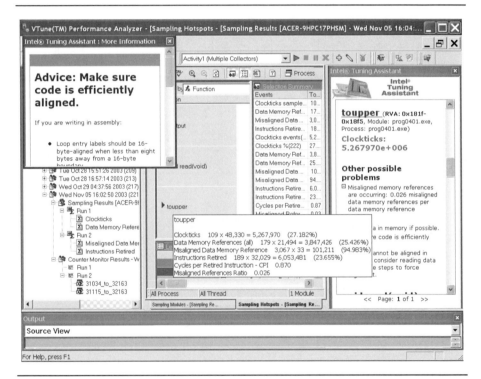

Figure 7.6   Tuning Advice in Sampling Hotspot View

2. Double-click the link to the `toupper` source code in the Tuning Advice window.

   Since the source code for this macro function—defined in the `tchar.h` header file—is unavailable, the program suggests that you try switching to Mixed or Disassembly mode.

Getting Static Analysis Advice in Mixed View

1. Select the **Mixed by Execution** icon and scroll down to look for any Penalties and Warnings in the listing.

2. Double-click the line of code for which a **Partial Stall** warning appears, and click the plus sign (+) to expand the results for the advice that appears in the Static Analysis window.

   A new link appears saying: *To avoid partial stalls, write to the same or larger register than you read.*

3. Click this link.

   The VTune analyzer pops up a help screen as shown in Figure 7.7.

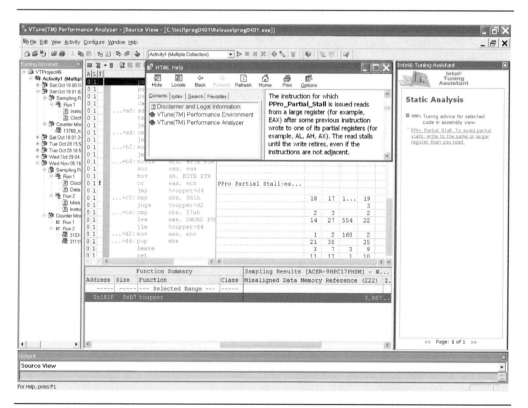

Figure 7.7   Static Analysis Advice in Sampling Mixed Execution View

The message explains that the instruction for which the stall occurred reads from a large register after writing to a partial register. The help message goes on to suggest ways to change the code to avoid a partial stall, as shown in Figure 7.8.

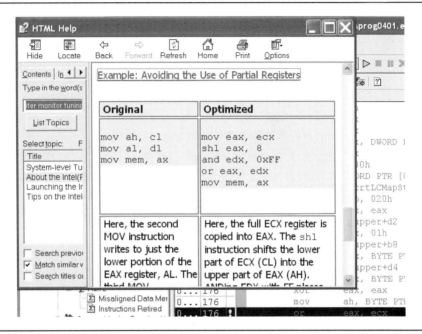

Figure 7.8   More Static Analysis Advice in Sampling Mixed Execution View

Getting Sampling Advice in Source View

To get sampling advice from Source view, you'll have to select a function for which you have the source code.

1. Return to the **Sampling Hotspots** for this activity run by selecting that result from the **Windows** menu.

    A set of horizontal graphs similar to those in Figure 7.6 appears.

2. This time double-click the `Read` function, which is included in the `prog0401.cpp` source code supplied by the Web site.

    The Source view of the `prog0401` program appears with the `Read` function visible onscreen.

3. Right-click on the code and select **Get Tuning Advice → For Entire View**.

As before, the Tuning Assistant Options for Sampling dialog box appears similar to Figure 7.4.

4. Select **<none>** for Reference activity results, since no comparisons are being made in this example, and click **OK**.

The Tuning Advice window displays advice for all the processes that ran during data collection, such as Explorer.exe and the system idle process, as well as the prog0401.exe process. You may see other insights and advice associated with these processes.

5. Scroll down to see the insights associated with **prog0401.exe**, click the plus sign (+) to expand the advice below the *Misaligned memory references are occurring* insight, and select one of the links to see more detailed information.

Figure 7.9 shows the results. Since the read function calls the toupper macro with the partial stalls, it is not surprising that misaligned memory references are taking place in the read function also, although not as frequently as in the toupper macro.

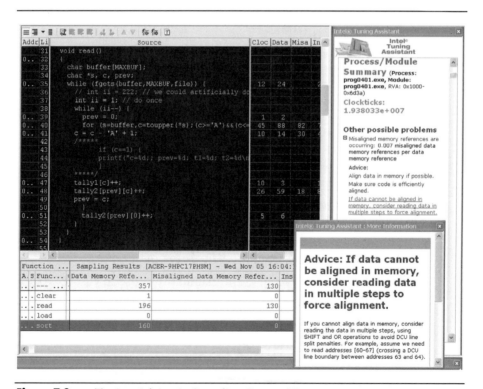

Figure 7.9 Tuning Advice in Sampling Source View

The Function Summary at the bottom of the screen shows that 130 out of 357 memory references were misaligned in the selected range, in this case, the entire `prog0401` program, and 130 out of 196 references were misaligned in the `Read` function. At line 40 of the listing, notice that 82 out of 88 memory references were misaligned when the `for` clause with the `toupper` assignment statement executed. This analysis lends further weight to the conclusion that reading from a large register after writing to a partial register is a definite no-no, as shown in the `toupper` disassembly warning message.

As the *Make sure code is efficiently aligned* advice points out, the best defense against such an error is to use an optimizing compiler (such as Microsoft or Intel's C++ compiler) that avoid such errors in the first place by following the rules of data alignment.

Getting Source-based Tuning Advice

If Source-based tuning advice had been enabled, you would have seen this type of advice in Source view. This level of advice is geared more to software engineers who specialize in writing compilers rather than to writers of more typical applications. To enable this feature, select **Configure** → **Options** → **Intel Tuning Assistant** → **Source Information** and uncheck **Disable source-based tuning advice**.

Selecting Events for Which Advice Is Available

Following best tuning practice means tuning for specific goals. One goal might be to collect Sampling data for all Pentium M processor events for which Tuning Assistant Advice is available. To collect the data for this event group:

1. On a Pentium M system, use the **Complete Setup Wizard** to create an activity with the Sampling data collector (see Chapter 4). Check the **Modify default configuration when done with wizard** option and uncheck the **Run Activity when done with wizard** option.

2. By default, this wizard configures the Sampling collector to conduct event-based sampling (EBS) using the *Cycles per Instruction Retired (CPI)* event ratio. Since you need to collect more events than the two involved in this ratio, click **Configure...** on Step 2 of the wizard and from the **Events tab** of the Event-based Sampling Configuration dialog box (see Figure 7.10), select the Event Group named **Events for Tuning Assistant Advice**, highlight all the available events for that group (see Figure 7.11), and click **>>**.

3. Run the activity to collect the data.

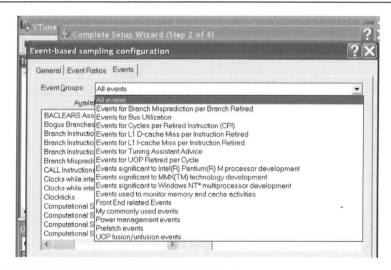

Figure 7.10   Event Groups Available on Pentium® M Processor

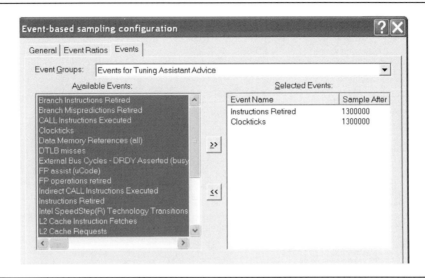

Figure 7.11   Events for Tuning Assistant Advice (Pentium® M Processor)

Recap

Here are some key points in this chapter:

- ■ The Tuning Assistant is a powerful automated tool that offers insights about software performance issues with detailed suggestions for dealing with them.

- ■ Tuning Assistant advice is available from:
    - – Counter Monitor views
    - – All sampling views including the Source view
    - – Static Assembly Analysis and Disassembly views

- ■ If you configure the VTune analyzer to enable something called *source-based tuning advice*, you receive Source view advice geared to compiler writers rather than application programmers.

- ■ Choosing the right data to investigate is key to getting the best automated advice.

Part III
Usage Models

Chapter 8

Comparing Multiple Activities

History doesn't repeat itself; it rhymes.

—Mark Twain

Comparing different activities can reveal interesting information about your application or the system configurations on which you depend. For example, you can compare various runs under different network conditions or data workloads. As you develop various versions of a program, you can cross-reference Call Graph and Sampling results, including correlated Sampling data collected during a Counter Monitor run. This chapter looks at some reasons for comparing, some methods of comparing, and the details of how the VTune™ analyzer handles comparisons and extends tuning advice. A sample script for automating the handling of multiple activities appears towards the end of the chapter.

Table 8.1   Comparing Activities at a Glance

Feature:	Support for Comparing Activities
Benefit at a glance:	Allows you to compare items of data side by side that were gathered using different data collectors. Intel® Tuning Assistant provides insights into comparative information. VTune™ analyzer's command line permits automated scripts for QA regression testing and comparative runs across target systems.
Versions:	All versions.
OS/Environments:	Microsoft Windows and Linux operating systems.
Collectors:	Remote and local data collection. Sampling, Call Graph, and correlated Sampling collected during Counter Monitor data collection.
Languages:	As supported by the collectors.
Processors:	As supported by the collectors.

Comparing Performance Across Target Systems

Some software teams use the VTune analyzer to compare program sessions on different target systems. For example, you might compare how your program runs on machines that differ only by the type of disk drive or the amount of main memory they contain. Some users build graphs of their application's performance across problem sizes and use these charts to discover areas of code that do not scale well as the program size grows.

You can compare the performance of a single binary across multiple systems—such as a single-processor system, a multiprocessor system, and a processor system using Hyper-Threading Technology. The Tuning Assistant can help you see and evaluate the differences. What is more, as you make these comparisons, a VTune analyzer feature called *Pack and Go* makes it easy for you to transport an entire project to different systems using a single file.

Transporting Projects to Different Systems

The VTune Performance Environment lets you bundle all the different files related to a project in one step. Later, you can unpack and view the bundled files on any machine that has the VTune environment installed. This process is called *Pack and Go*.

The Pack and Go feature packages the items selected in the Tuning Browser, bundles all the different files related to the selection, and saves this combination of files and information in the .vxp format. If you select a single activity result rather than an entire project or activity, the VTune analyzer packs the parent activity along with it, but does not pack any other activity results under that activity. You can then unpack and view the .vxp file on a different computer.

To pack and unpack an item from the Tuning Browser:

1. In the Tuning Browser, right-click the project, activity, or activity result you want to pack and select **Pack and Go**.

   The Pack and Go dialog box appears.

2. Type a name for the file and click **Save**.

3. Figure 8.1 shows the Nov5 activity results and its parent activity being saved in .vxp format.

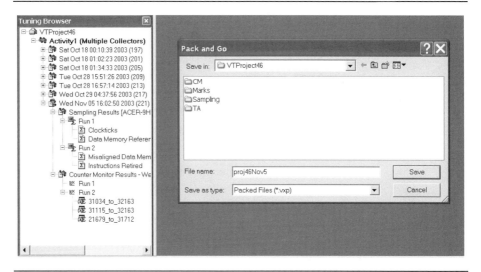

Figure 8.1   Packing an Activity Result for Transport to Another System

4. Copy the file to a location accessible to the computer where you want to view it.

5. From the Tuning Browser of the new computer, select a project, right-click, and choose **Unpack**.

   The Unpack dialog box appears.

6. If you select **Unpack into a new project** and click **OK**, the VTune analyzer unpacks the file into its own project as shown in Figure 8.2.

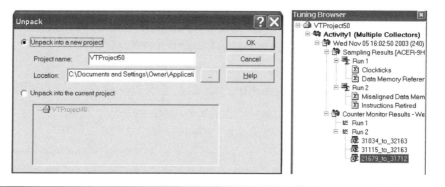

Figure 8.2   Unpacking into a New Project

7. If you select **Unpack into the current project**, the VTune analyzer shows a folder hierarchy of the elements in the current project.

8. Select the location in the hierarchy where you want to place the contents of the packed file and click **OK**.

   The VTune analyzer unpacks the file contents into the current project. Figure 8.3 shows the Nov5 activity results with multiple collectors being added to the VTProject31 project, which already includes several activities of its own.

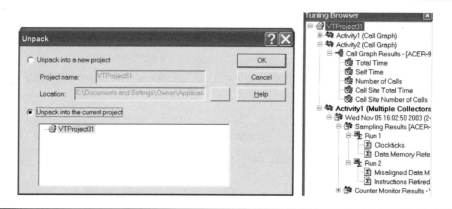

Figure 8.3   Unpacking into an Existing Project

Note

> Pack and Go is different from Export. Pack and Go packages the selected item into a .vxp file for viewing and editing using the VTune analyzer. The Export command exports the currently available table data into a .csv file for viewing and editing in a different application such as Microsoft Excel.

Statically Analyzing Your Code for Specific Processors

For comparison purposes, you can statically analyze the performance of your application on your host system such as a Pentium® 4 processor-based system as well as on other Intel® processors such as Pentium Pro, Pentium II, and Pentium III processors. The Source view shows analysis results and penalty information for the processors you choose. To change the default processor for each type of architecture you want to analyze:

1. Select the **Options** icon from the main toolbar:

    The Options dialog box appears.

2. On the left side of the dialog box, select **Source View → Data Presentation**.

    The Data Presentation panel appears, as shown in Figure 8.4.

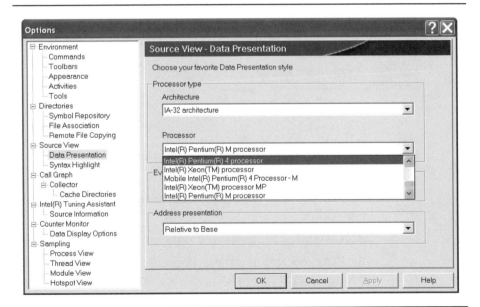

Figure 8.4   Changing the Default Processor to Analyze

3. Choose the default processor for each family of Intel architecture you intend to analyze: IA-32, Itanium®, and Intel XScale® architectures.

Later, if you want to statically analyze other processors in the same family, you can switch to another processor in Source view. To select a different processor to analyze:

1. While in Source view, right-click the source pane and select **Change Processor**.

   A list of possible processors in the same architectural family appears, as shown in Figure 8.5.

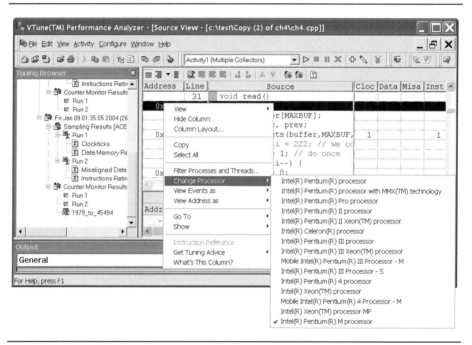

Figure 8.5   Changing the Processor for Static Analysis

2. Choose the new processor for which you want static analysis information.

3. Select **Mixed** or **Disassembly only** mode from the Sampling toolbar.

   The Penalties and Warnings column lists any static penalties and warnings based on assembly code corresponding to the processor you selected.

Comparing Versions of a Developing Program

Another reason for comparing results might be to evaluate successive versions of the same binary after modifying the code. To compare Sampling results during program development, for example, you would run an activity that monitors the performance of your application, then make changes to your code and re-run the activity. Compare the two activity results—before and after the change—in a single window and determine if the changes you made to your code improved its performance. The change in the number of samples collected for an event, before and after the change in code, can tell you if any performance improvements took place.

Comparing Activity Results

The VTune analyzer uses the familiar Windows paradigm, so that you can view multiple activity results in separate windows by selecting the **Cascade**, **Tile Horizontally**, or **Tile Vertically** command as described in Chapter 3. To allow closer scrutiny, the VTune analyzer also provides a drag-and-drop feature that allows you to compare individual items from different activity results side by side in the same window.

Comparing Sampling Results

You can embed two or more activity results in any of the Sampling views. After opening a Sampling view, drag and drop one or more of the other activity results from the Tuning Browser onto it, rearrange the columns if necessary, and examine the results side by side.

Bar Chart Format

When you drag and drop activity results into a Sampling view in horizontal bar chart format, the VTune analyzer creates an additional stack of colored bars against each item for each result, as shown in Figure 8.6. Each bar represents a specific event in a particular activity result.

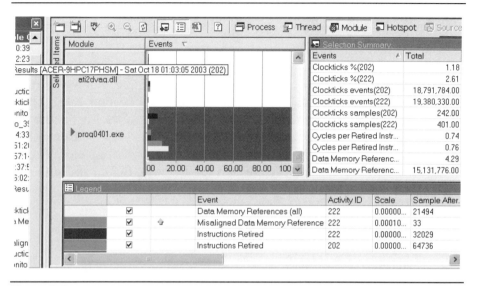

Figure 8.6   Comparing Results in a Bar Chart

Use the legend colors and activity IDs, 202 and 222 in the example, to associate a specific color-coded bar with a particular event and activity result. By comparing the lengths of the bars for all items in all results, you can identify the events with the highest number of samples or event totals. A high number of samples or events might indicate a potential performance bottleneck.

Table Format

Instead of just one row, two header rows ordinarily appear if you drag and drop multiple activity results onto the Sampling view in table format. For example, Figure 8.7 shows sample counts of the October 18 results for activity ID 202 and November 5 results for activity ID 222 side by side under the top heading *Clockticks samples*.

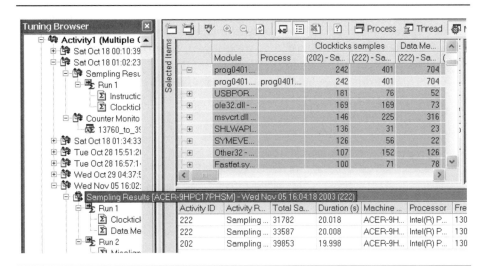

Figure 8.7   Comparing Results in Table Format

Note

Full activity result names appear in column headers in Sampling view. If you right-click the activity results in the Tuning Browser and select **Rename**, you can assign shorter names such as Results1 and Results2.

Another option is to narrow the column width and use the activity result numbers displayed in parentheses () to associate the table data with the activity results shown in the Tuning Browser.

Viewing Multiprocessor and Hyper-Threading Information

If you want to see how the workload is distributed across multiple processors—whether a physical or a logical processor—one strategy is to use the Sampling data collector and to profile your application on a multiprocessor system, with or without Hyper-Threading Technology. Click **Show/Hide CPU Information**

on the Sampling toolbar to see a breakdown of the number of events sampled on each logical processor. You can display this processor breakdown in Process, Thread, Module, and Hotspot Sampling views in either horizontal bar chart or table format.

Multiprocessor information in horizontal bar chart format. In this format, use the legend to associate the color with the event and logical processor on which it was monitored. If you click **Show/Hide CPU Information**, the legend includes an additional column, *Processor Number*. This column lists all the logical processors in your system on which samples were collected. Figure 8.8 shows Sampling Process view of a system with multiple logical processors.

ProcessName	Events △			
VTUNDEMO.EXE		VTUNDEMO.EXE Bus Not Ready of The Processor (TI) - Processor0		
Explorer.EXE		VTUNDEMO.EXE		
VTUNDEMO.EXE Instructions Retired - Processor0	169,728,696	Instructions Retired - Processor1 40.00 50.00 60.00 70.00 80.00 90.00 100	791,140,203	

			Event	Proces... ▽	Package	Hardware Thread
	✔		Instructions Retired	Processor1	0	1
	✔		Bus Not Ready of The Processor (TI)	Processor1	0	1
	✔	↵	Instructions Retired	Processor0	0	0
	✔		Bus Not Ready of The Processor (TI)	Processor0	0	0

Figure 8.8   Bar Chart of Multiple Logical Processors in Process View

For processors using Hyper-Threading Technology, two more columns, *Package* and *Hardware Thread*, appear in the legend. The Package column lists all the physical processors in your system. The Hardware Thread column lists the two hardware threads per package. In the example shown in Figure 8.8, the 0s under Package indicate that the system has only one physical processor. This processor has two hardware threads, 0 and 1.

The VTune analyzer records sampling events and displays bar charts differently for *Thread-Specific (TS)* and *Thread-Independent (TI or TI-E) events.*

For Thread-Specific (TS) events, depending on the number of processors on your system, a horizontal bar contains that number of uniquely colored sections, where each section represents a logical processor. If you place your cursor over a section of the bar, you can see the number of events sampled for that processor, as shown on the second bar in Figure 8.8. All the sections that make up one bar should add up to the total number of samples collected for an event.

Because Thread-Independent (TI or TI-E) events are logical-processor independent, each TI or TI-E event appears as a single horizontal bar unbroken into sections, as in the top bar of Figure 8.8. In this case, the horizontal bar represents the total number of samples collected for an event.[1] See "Hyper-Threading Technology" in Appendix B for more about Thread-Specific and Thread-Independent events.

Multiprocessor information in table format. If you are running the VTune analyzer on a multiprocessor system and want to compare results in table format with a breakdown by processor, first select **Show/Hide CPU Info** from the Sampling toolbar, then drag and drop multiple activity results onto a view. The Sampling view in table format displays three rows of headers, as shown in Figure 8.9.

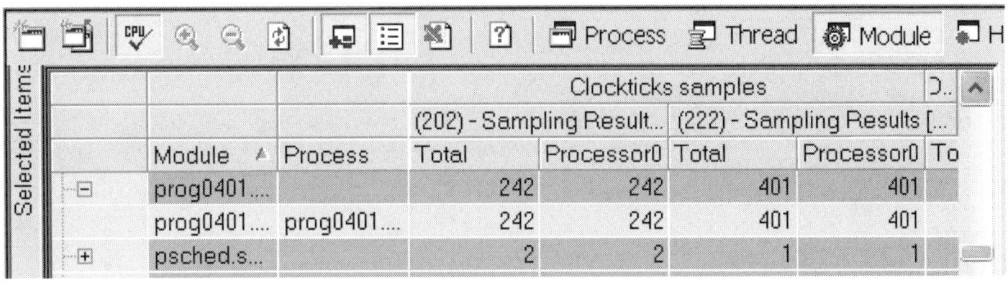

			Clockticks samples				
			(202) - Sampling Result...		(222) - Sampling Results [...		
	Module ▲	Process	Total	Processor0	Total	Processor0	To
⊟	prog0401....		242	242	401	401	
	prog0401....	prog0401....	242	242	401	401	
⊞	psched.s...		2	2	1	1	

Figure 8.9   Comparing Sampling Results with a Breakdown by Processor

You can see the number of samples collected per processor for each event. For processors with Hyper-Threading Technology, the breakdown of collected samples by logical processor is only accurate for TS events. The information on TI and TI-E events is accurate only for data collected at the system level.[1]

---

[1] For microarchitectural reasons, TI or TI-E events cannot attribute collected samples to specific logical processors and all samples display as collected on logical processor 0. Because of this limitation, drill-down data for TI and TI-E events are not accurate and your application analysis should not rely on those results.

Comparing Event Ratios Across Several Runs

Event ratios enable you to understand and compare results across several runs of an activity. Consider the activity results shown in Table 8.2. In this example, the difference between the two runs is much clearer when you compare the two ratios. As mentioned in Chapter 4, when looking at events alone, you would need to check all four results in order to understand the difference between the two runs. The difference in the data is much more apparent when you have event ratios displayed in addition to the events themselves.

Table 8.2   Comparing Event Ratios Is Easier Than Comparing Events

Activity Result	Run 1	Run 2
Events	50 Instructions Retired 100 Clockticks	100 Instructions Retired 100 Clockticks
Event Ratio	0.5 Instructions/Clocktick	1 Instruction/Clocktick

Comparing Source View Results

To compare columns of activity results side by side in Source view:

1. From Sampling, Call Graph, or Static Analysis view, drill down to open the Source view of one activity result.

2. From the Tuning Browser window, drag another activity result onto the open Source view.

3. Repeat for any additional activity result you would like to compare.

   New columns appear for each activity result dragged onto Source view, with each column name marked by the number in parentheses that corresponds to its activity results number in the Tuning Browser, as shown in Figure 8.10. In this particular example, the activity result ID numbers are 82 and 84.

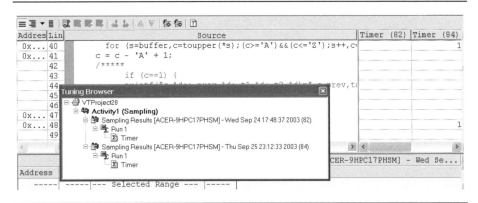

Figure 8.10   Comparing Sampling Results in Source View

Comparing Call Graph Results

You can compare the data for Call Graph results collected during different runs of an activity or for different activities. Use the drag-and-drop functionality to compare Call Graph data for various activity results or sub-results. To compare Call Graph results:

1. In the Tuning Browser, double-click a Call Graph result, such as the one under **Activity1**.

2. Select the desired module and function, such as the **read** function in module **prog0401.exe**, right-click and select **View Source** to drill down to Source view, as shown in Figure 8.11.

3. Drag and drop some other Call Graph results into Source view.

    New columns appear with data specific to the Call Graph results that you dragged onto Source view. In Figure 8.12, for example, dragging the Total Time sub-result from the Activity2 result updates the Source view of the read function selected from the Activity1 result. The identifying activity result IDs, 130 for Activity1 and 245 for Activity2, appear in the column headers.

    The first activity took half as long as the second activity, 7989 versus 15,103; not surprising since the second activity ran prog0401.exe using the added output argument 3. Using that argument resulted in Split Stores Retired (TI-E) and Split Loads Retired (TI-E) on a Pentium 4 processor in Example 4.3, and Misaligned Data Memory References on a Pentium M processor in Example 7.1.

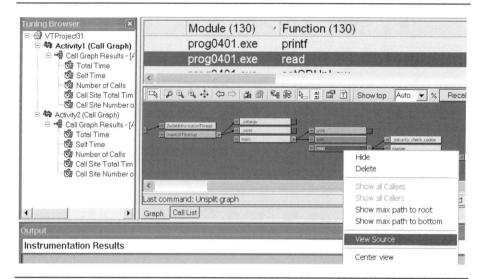

Figure 8.11   Selecting the Function of Interest in Call Graph

4. If necessary, drag and drop the headers of columns of interest to rearrange them so they are side by side; or right-click, select **Column Layout**, and uncheck any columns you are not interested in seeing. You could also select the headers of unwanted columns, and then right-click and use the **Hide Column** feature to accomplish the same goal.

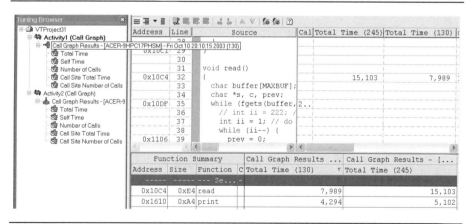

Figure 8.12   Comparing Call Graph Results in Source View

Comparing Call Graph and Sampling Results

You can do more than compare like-to-like results in the VTune environment. You can also drag and drop a sampling result onto the Call Graph Function Summary view, or drag and drop the Call Graph result onto the Sampling view. With this capability, you can compare function call information and sampling information for each function of your application.

To view Sampling data in the Call Graph Function Summary view:

1. Right-click and deselect the **View by thread** mode.

2. Click the **Call List** tab.

3. Select the Sampling Result in the Tuning Browser window and drag and drop it onto the Function Summary view.

   New Sampling view columns, such as *Misaligned Data Memory Reference* and *Cycles per Retired Instruction*, appear in the Function Summary view alongside Call Graph columns such as *Calls* and *Self Time*.

   In this example, the Call Graph results (ID 245) corroborate the Sampling results (ID 247), since both activities ran prog0401.exe with the added output argument 3 that triggered memory problems. The Self Time of the read function in Figure 8.13 (9710) is nearly twice that shown in Figure 5.7 (5801), where the activity ran without the extra output argument.

| Call Graph Results - [ACER-9HPC17PHSM... | | | Sampling Results [ACER-9HPC17PHS... | Sampling Results [A... |
Function (245)	Calls (245)	Self Time (245)	Misaligned Data Memory Reference (247)	Cycles per Retired In...
toupper	323160	1608	3067.00	0.870
fgets	49669	3219	1.00	0.867
sort	1	3672	0.00	0.668
read	1	9710	130.00	0.685
Focus function				
read	1	9710	130.00	0.685

Caller Function	Contributi...	Edge Time	Edge Calls	
main	100.0%	15,103		1

Figure 8.13   Comparing Sampling and Call Graph Results in Call Graph View

To view Call Graph data in Sampling view:

1. Open the results of Sampling data collection.

2. Select the Call Graph result in the Tuning Browser window and drag and drop it onto the default Module view.

   The Module view is updated with the Call Graph data.

3. Toggle to Hotspot view to compare Sampling Results and Call Graph data for each function.

   The Call Graph results (activity ID 251) appear commingled with the Sampling Results (activity ID 241) as shown in Figure 8.14 for the read function.

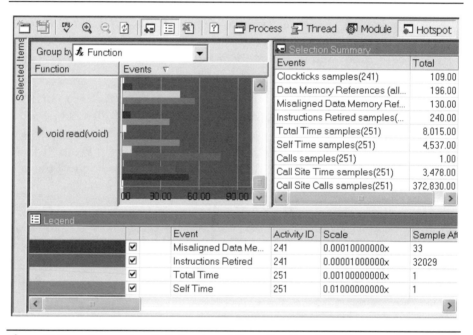

Figure 8.14　Comparing Call Graph and Sampling Results in Hotspot View

Merging Activity Results of Different Workloads

You can merge the results of multiple Call Graph or Sampling activities to get an integrated picture of all performance data collected during multiple runs. Run the application and the activity several times with different workloads, collect several sets of results, and then use the **Merge** command to merge the results.

Note | Comparing and merging results are two different operations. *Comparing* simply displays two or more results side by side so you can compare individual items. *Merging* combines the data from multiple results to form a new result. In merging, you lose the original values of the results because the data are combined to form a new result with more generalized information about application performance.

To merge activity results:

1. Press and hold **Ctrl** and select two or more activity results in the Tuning Browser window, as shown on the left side of Figure 8.15.

2. Click the **Merge Activity Results** icon in the toolbar:

The Merge Activity Results dialog box appears as shown on the right side of Figure 8.15.

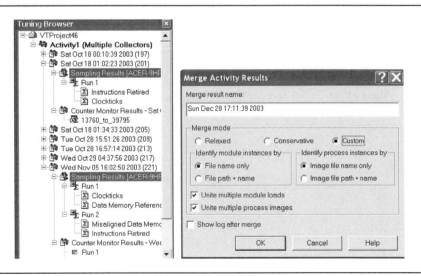

Figure 8.15   Selecting Activity Results to Merge

3. Select a Merge mode:

   Relaxed mode merges module and process files with the same names, irrespective of directories.

   Conservative mode only merges process and module files with the same names and full paths.

   Custom mode allows you to customize the merge process.

4. Click **OK**.

   The VTune analyzer adds the new merged activity result in the Merge Results folder of the current project and automatically saves it.

5. Double-click the merged result to display the data view.

   The merged results appear in all Sampling views, including Source view. Figure 8.16 shows the merged results in Hotspot view.

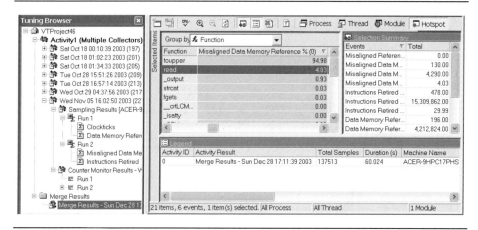

Figure 8.16　Merged Activity Results in Hotspot View

Getting Help from the Intel® Tuning Assistant

On Intel Pentium III or Pentium 4 processors, the Tuning Assistant can help you compare up to three different binaries, one for each activity result. This comparison can help you figure out where and why a particular change in the binary caused an overall slowdown or speedup. Typically, you would use this feature after finding a performance problem and changing the binary—either by using a different compiler or compiler switch, or by changing the source code itself.

Comparing Up to Three Binaries on the Same System

To get tuning advice when comparing up to three different binaries on a Pentium III or Pentium 4 processor:

1. Change the binary so that you have at least one old and new binary to compare.

2. Collect the same events for the new binary that you did for the old one.

3. After Sampling, select all the processes and/or modules that you are interested in tuning on the new binary.

4. Press the **F8** key to launch the Tuning Assistant.

5. In the Tuning Assistant Options for Sampling dialog box, set the Primary activity result to the main workload run you want to analyze.

   In this case, set the result from the new binary as Primary. By default, the VTune analyzer automatically inserts the name of the most recent result in the Primary field.

6. Set the Reference activity results to one or more runs that use older binaries. These will be compared with the Primary Activity.

7. Be sure to specify the bus speed in megahertz of the system(s) used to collect each binary, especially if you want the Tuning Assistant to compare binaries that ran on different systems,

8. Choose how much of the current activity result to analyze (all or just the current selection) and select the size of the code regions you want to compare.

   You can define code regions at the function level or by lines of source code, as shown in Figure 8.17.

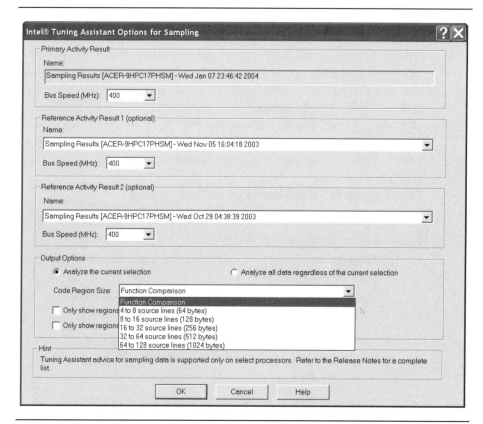

Figure 8.17   Choosing Reference Runs to Compare to the Primary Result

If you want to compare two different compilations of the same executable, use Function Comparison, since RVA values might be different across versions. If you are comparing the same compilation of the same executable, even on different processors, you can compare at the code region level by specifying the number of source lines/bytes). If you have a number of large functions that you want to analyze, using this technique provides a way of breaking your function up into smaller parts.

If you do not have any symbol information for part or all of the modules that you are analyzing, set a code region size; otherwise, you will only get a summary at the process/module level for those modules that lack symbol information.

The example shown in Figure 8.17 selects two activities that ran on October 29 and November 5 for comparison to a run on January 7. All three runs took place on a system with the same bus speed. The previous two activities used the third output argument with the `prog0401.exe` file; the most recent one did not.

9. Press **OK** and study the Tuning Assistant report from the top down.

The Tuning Assistant first lists code regions that slowed down most using the new binary. Code regions that speeded up the most appear at the bottom of the report. In each code region, the Tuning Assistant lists any problems it found with the microarchitecture. Figure 8.18 shows some sections from the Tuning Assistant report.

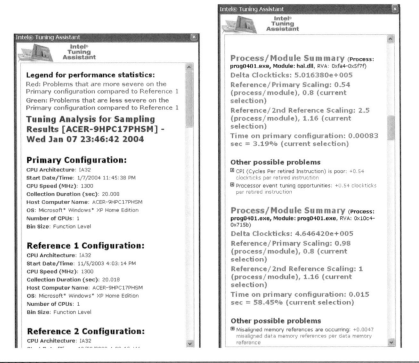

Figure 8.18   Intel® Tuning Assistant Feedback Comparing Three Configurations

As the legend explains, problems that are more severe on the Primary configuration than on the Reference configuration appear in red; problems that are less severe on the Primary than on the Reference configuration appear in green. In this case, all the problems appear in red, indicating more severity on the Primary configuration. For example, in the `prog0401.exe` binaries, the difference between the Primary and Reference 1 insight scores for *Misaligned Memory References* appears in red as `+0.0047`.

10. To see the advice on fixing a problem, expand the insight by clicking on the + sign.

    The right side of Figure 8.19 shows individual insight scores for *Misaligned Memory References* and *CPI* event ratios for the Primary, Reference 1, and Reference 2 results for the `hal.dll` module.

11. If you are not sure what the problem is, click on the insight link in the Tuning Assistant report to learn more about the indicated problem.

    A message box with more information appears, as shown on the left side of Figure 8.19 for the **Measure events required to compute advanced event ratios** insight link.

12. If the Tuning Assistant advice tells you to collect more events to get to the root cause the problem, collect those additional events and launch the Tuning Assistant again.

Comparing Binaries Across Two or Three Systems

To compare binaries across two or three systems:

1. Before data collection, select all modules of interest that you want analyzed by the Tuning Assistant.

2. After collection is complete on the Reference system, pack the reference project(s) using the **Pack and Go** command.

3. Copy the packed project to the Primary system.

4. On the Primary system, unpack the project into an existing project that contains the Primary activity result.

5. Make sure the binaries (modules of interest) are present on the Primary system.

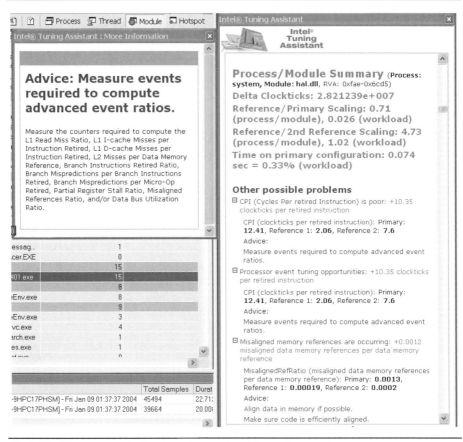

Figure 8.19 Expanded Advice Regarding Three Comparisons

6. Use the Module Associations dialog box to resolve paths for the modules of interest of the unpacked project.

Steps 5 and 6 are required if you want to drill down to Source view using symbol information (function names) and in order for the Tuning Assistant to make a one-to-one comparison between activity results from the different systems.

Note

If the binary for each activity result is different (for example, if they have slightly different code, come from different compilers, or are compiled with different flags), you can only make function-level comparisons, because the RVA values of the binaries will probably not match up correctly.

Function names must remain the same in order to do an accurate comparison.

Computer Architecture-level Tuning

Chapter 1 introduced a top-to-bottom methodology involving three levels of tuning to be performed in order. That discussion stopped short of diving into the details of the last stage of tuning. Now that you have become familiar with concepts such as Sampling, automatic hotspot analysis using the Tuning Assistant, and Pack and Go, consider this third and final stage: computer architecture-level tuning.

General Methodology

Just to review, the goal of computer architecture-level tuning is to speed up performance by improving how the application runs on the processor. This type of tuning is especially relevant for processor-intensive applications. If you know that your application is very I/O-intensive—for example, disk-intensive or network-intensive—and not very processor-intensive, be especially sure you have used system-level and application-level tuning to improve processor utilization before trying computer architecture-level tuning.

The general methodology for computer architecture-level tuning is to:

1. Find the most time-consuming code regions that have a high impact on application performance.

2. Analyze the execution of those code regions on the target Intel architecture.

3. Identify computer architecture-level performance problems.

4. Determine how to avoid them to improve performance.

Using Sampling

Here are some suggested steps for using sampling to identify code regions that have a high impact on application performance:

1. Use the Sampling wizard to create an activity with the Sampling data collector (see Chapter 4). See the next section, "Tuning for Specific Goals," to understand which processor events to collect on which systems first.

2. Press the **F8** key to launch the Intel Tuning Assistant.

3. In the dialog box, select the activity result you want to analyze and specify the size of the code regions, as shown in Figure 8.17. You can choose up to three activity results for the Tuning Assistant to compare. The Tuning Assistant divides your selected functions or modules into the code sizes you specify and prioritizes them according to regions that have the most impact on performance, that is, the highest number of Clockticks.

4. Click on the insight links in the Tuning Assistant report to learn more about the indicated problem. To see the advice on fixing a problem, expand the insight by clicking on the + sign. In some cases, the Tuning Assistant will suggest additional processor event groups for you to investigate. In this case, repeat this process from Step 1, substituting the appropriate processor event group.

Note

> The Tuning Assistant can quickly sort through data for your entire application to provide you with a prioritized summary of performance issues. You may also wish to view sampling data and event ratios directly in the Sampling views at a lower level of abstraction and a higher level of detail.
>
> Many times, the Tuning Assistant advice references the Optimization Manual for your Intel processor, which can be a valuable source of information on computer architecture-level tuning.

Tuning for Specific Goals

When you are tuning software, your goals should be specific. One plan, for example, might be to tune for multiple configurations on the same base architecture. For example, you might collect Sampling data for all primary events on Pentium 4 processor-based platforms with or without Hyper-Threading Technology. To see the impact of various configurations, you could simultaneously compare results from runs on:

■ a single processor with Hyper-Threading Technology enabled

■ a single processor without Hyper-Threading Technology enabled

■ a multi-processor system

This goal would require you to collect sampling data for all primary events on multiple systems before you began tuning. To collect the data for multiple configurations of the same base architecture:

1. If necessary, install the VTune analyzer on the system(s) on which you need to collect data.

2. On each system, use the **Complete Setup Wizard** to create an activity with the Sampling data collector (see Chapter 4). Check the **Modify default configuration when done with wizard** option and uncheck the **Run Activity when done with wizard** option.

3. By default, this wizard configures the Sampling collector to conduct event-based sampling (EBS) using the *Cycles per Instruction Retired (CPI)* event ratio. Since you need to collect different events than this, click **Configure...** on Step 2 of the wizard and from the **Events tab** of the Event-based Sampling Configuration dialog box, select all events in the event group(s) of interest.

4. Run the activity to collect the data.

Tuning Single-Processor Systems

To perform computer architecture-level tuning on a single-processor system such as the Pentium 4 processor:

1. Choose one of the options in Table 8.3 and Table 8.4; then collect Sampling data using the specified systems, binaries, and event groups. If you collect activity results on multiple systems, use the **Pack and Go** command to move these all onto the same system.

Note

> If you compare different types of processors, the report will only show the Primary system insight scores, because the performance events between the two processors do not match. For example, if you capture the Primary result on a Pentium 4 processor-based system and the first Reference result on a Pentium III processor-based system, the Pentium III processor-based result is only used to show the difference in time (in *Clockticks*) between the Primary and Reference system for each code region.

Table 8.3   Comparing Systems with Single Processors

Activity Result	System	Binary	Event Group	Benefit
Primary	Single Pentium® 4 processor	Current	Performance Tuning Events - Primary	(required step)
Reference (optional)	Single Pentium® III processor	Current	The *Clockticks* event is the only one required.	May help highlight coding pitfalls by bringing them to the top of the list.

Table 8.4   Comparing Multiple Binaries on a Pentium® 4 Processor

Activity Result	System	Binary	Event Group	Benefit
Primary	Single Pentium® 4 processor	Current	Performance Tuning Events - Primary	(required step)
Reference (optional)	Single Pentium® 4 processor	Previous	Performance Tuning Events - Primary	Reveals detailed information about the location and nature of performance changes caused by the last round of code changes.
Reference 2 (optional)	Single Pentium® 4 processor	A third version	Performance Tuning Events - Primary	Same as above, for a third version of the binaries.

2. After collecting Sampling data and double-clicking on the Primary Activity result in the Tuning Browser, start at a high level by selecting all processes and/or modules that you are interested in tuning.

3. Launch the Intel Tuning Assistant by pressing **F8** to help you find high-impact code regions within the processes and modules that you selected.

4. In the Tuning Assistant Options for Sampling dialog box, choose the **Primary Activity result, Reference Activity result**, and/or **Reference Activity result 2** corresponding to the data you collected in Step 1.

5. Try changing the code as indicated in the Tuning Assistant's advice, and rebuild the application binary. If you make significant code changes, go back to Step 1 to collect a new set of activity results using the new application binaries.

6. If the Tuning Assistant advice tells you to collect more events to further identify the problem, go back to Step 1 and collect a new set of activity results on all of the systems. Make sure that you collect *Clockticks* data with the new events to avoid having to recollect the original event data from Step 1.

Tuning Dual and Multiprocessor Systems

To use the VTune Performance Analyzer for computer architecture-level tuning on multiple Pentium 4 processors:

1. Follow the steps in *Tuning Single-Processor Systems* to find general Pentium 4 processor optimizations. You could still get some benefit from not tuning on this platform first, but it would be more difficult, time-consuming, and probably not yield the same speedup results.

   Even if the processor is being fully utilized and you get good scaling on a dual-processor system, several coding pitfalls may be unnecessarily using up processor cycles. For example, you could see a large impact from stores that are not forwarding or from denormalized number assists. Once you have tuned the application for Pentium 4 processor microarchitecture, find out how well the application scales on two physical processors. In general, if the speedup increases less than 1.5× on a dual-processor system, significant opportunities probably exist to increase that speedup to 1.8 or even 1.9×.

2. Choose one of the options in Tables 8.5, 8.6, and 8.7; then collect Sampling data using the specified systems, binaries, and event groups. If you collect activity results on multiple systems, use **Pack and Go** to move these all onto the same system.

3. Perform Steps 2 through 6 of *Tuning Single-Processor Systems.*

Table 8.5 Comparing Dual- to Single-Processor Systems

Activity Result	System	Binary	Event Group	Benefit
Primary Activity result	Dual Pentium® 4 processor	Current	Performance Tuning Events - Primary	(required step)
Reference Activity Result (optional)	Single Pentium® 4 processor	Current	Performance Tuning Events - Primary	Allows you to see the scaling from one to two processors.

Table 8.6   Comparing 4-Processor to Dual- and Single-Processor Systems

Activity Result	System Type	Application Binary Type	Event Group	Benefit
Primary	Four Pentium® 4 processors	Current	Performance Tuning Events - Primary	(required step)
Reference (optional)	Dual Pentium® 4 processors	Current	Performance Tuning Events - Primary	Allows you to see the scaling from two to four processors.
Reference 2 (optional)	Single Pentium® 4 processors	Current	Performance Tuning Events - Primary	Allows you to see the full range of scaling from one to two to four processors.

Table 8.7   Comparing Multiple Binaries on a Dual-Processor or 4-Processor System

Activity Result	System	Binary	Event Group	Benefit
Primary	Dual or Four Pentium® 4 processors (whatever is the target)	Current (last round of changes)	Performance Tuning Events - Primary	(required step)
Reference (optional)	(same as Primary)	Previous	Performance Tuning Events - Primary	Reveals detailed information about the location and nature of performance changes caused by the last round of code changes.
Reference 2 (optional)	(same as Primary)	A third version	Performance Tuning Events - Primary	Same as above, for a third version of the binaries.

Tuning Systems with Hyper-Threading Technology

The typical tuning methodology recommended for multiple Pentium 4 processors with Hyper-Threading Technology is as follows:

1. Follow the steps in *Tuning Single-Processor Systems* to find general Intel Pentium 4 processor optimizations.

2. Follow the steps in *Tuning Dual and Multiprocessor Systems* to find dual-processor/multiprocessor optimizations.

   If you do not have access to the above systems in the order listed above, you could tune in a random order and still get some benefit, but it will be more difficult, more time-consuming, and probably not yield as much speedup results.

3. Choose one of the options in Tables 8.8 and 8.9, then collect Sampling data using the specified systems, binaries, and event groups. If you collect Activity results on multiple systems, use Pack and Go to move these all onto the same system.

4. Perform Steps 2 through 6 of *Tuning Single-Processor Systems.*

Table 8.8 Comparing Systems with HT Technology to Systems without HT Technology

Activity Result	System	Binary	Event Group	Benefit
Primary	Single Pentium® 4 processor with HT Technology	Current	Performance Tuning Events for HT Technology	(required step)
Reference	Single Pentium® 4 processor	Current	Performance Tuning Events for HT Technology	Reveals opportunities to speed up the application for HT Technology.
Reference 2	Dual Pentium® 4 processor	Current	Performance Tuning Events for HT Technology	Reveals upper-bound on performance for the system with HT Technology.

Table 8.9   Comparing Multiple Binaries on Single-Processor Systems with HT Technology

Activity Result	System	Binary	Event Group	Benefit
Primary	Single Pentium® 4 processor with HT Technology	Current (last round of changes)	Performance Tuning Events for HT Technology	(required step)
Reference (optional)	Single Pentium® 4 processor with HT Technology	Previous	Performance Tuning Events - Primary	Reveals detailed information about the location and nature of performance changes caused by last round of code changes.
Reference 2 (optional)	Single Pentium® 4 processor with HT Technology	A third version	Performance Tuning Events - Primary	Same as above, for a third version of the binaries.

Automating Multiple Tasks

Chapters 3 and 4 introduced you to the use of the VTune analyzer's command line, which lets you collect performance data without the need for direct participation. The VTune analyzer's batch mode API expands this capability by allowing you to build Windows-based programs or scripts that control the VTune analyzer automatically. Such automated tools are especially powerful when performing multiple or repetitive tasks that are best handled in batch mode.

Collecting Performance Data in Batch Mode

You can create a control program using programming tools that support COM objects (such as Microsoft Visual C++ or Borland Delphi), or scripting languages such as Visual Basic or Perl. By using a control program written in one of these languages, you can automatically create a batch file, run it, and collect overnight data about your application's performance. Later, you can launch the graphical interface to view and analyze the collected data using tools like Merge and the Tuning Assistant.

To collect application performance data in batch mode:

1. Create a batch file using either of the following:

   ■ Any Windows scripting language that supports the Microsoft ActiveX scripting interface such as Jscript, VBScript, PerlScript, Pscript or Python.

   ■ Programming tools that support COM such as Microsoft Visual C++ or Borland Delphi. (See the sample .vbs file in Example 8.1.)

2. Launch the VTune analyzer.

3. Use a wizard to create a project. For example, if you want to collect function call information for your application, use the Call Graph Wizard to create a Call Graph project.

4. Close the VTune analyzer.

5. Launch the batch file, specifying the project. You can use Microsoft `CScript.exe` to launch the batch file. The VTune analyzer launches the activity and the specified application, collects data, and creates the activity result.

6. After the data is collected, launch the VTune analyzer and open the project to view the results.

Using the VTune™ Analyzer's Batch Mode API

Use the objects and methods in Table 8.10 to create a batch file that automates various VTune analyzer functions.

Table 8.10   VTune™ Analyzer Objects and Methods for Creating a Batch File

Object/Method	Explanation/Example

VTuneBatch object	The main VTune Performance Analyzer object. Use the following statement to create an instance of this object:
	
	`Set VTune =`
	`CreateObject("VTuneBatch.VTune")`

LoadProject method	Loads the project you created using the VTune analyzer user interface. Returns a list of activity names that this project contains as a string array. The *object* is always the name of the VTune analyzer object variable.
	
	Input parameter: project name
	
	Result: activity names string array
	
	`VARIANT saActivityNames =`
	`object.LoadProject(BSTR projectName)`

RunActivitySynchronous method	Runs an activity synchronously; waiting until the activity completes execution.
	
	Input parameters: activity name, duration time (in sec)[2]
	
	Result: activity result object
	
	`VARIANT ActivityResult =`
	`RunActivitySynchronous(BSTR`
	`activityName, long nDuration)`

RunActivity method	Runs an activity asynchronously; that is, it returns before the activity is finished.
	
	Input parameters: activity name, duration time (in sec)[3]
	
	Result: none
	
	`RunActivity(BSTR activityName, long`
	`nDuration)`

WaitActivity method	Waits until the activity stops running and returns the result. Input parameters: none Result: activity result object `VARIANT ActivityResult = WaitActivity`

(continued)

---

[2] Duration values are not supported for Call Graph projects.

Table 8.10 VTune Objects and Methods for Creating a Batch File *(continued)*

Object/Method	Explanation/Example
ExportProject method	Uses the Pack and Go command to package all the files related to the project in one file. Input parameter: filename Result: none `ExportProject(BSTR fileName)`

ReplaceProject method	Replaces the current project with another project. Returns a list of activity names that this project contains.
	
	Input parameter: project name to replace
	
	Result: activity names string array
	
	`VARIANT saActivityNames =`
	`ReplaceProject(BSTR projectName)`

Log method	Provides a .log file. Input parameter: filename Result: none `Log(VARIANT_BOOL log, BSTR fileName)`

Merge method	Merges Activity results. You must specify a merge mode.
	
	Input parameters: activity results to merge, merge mode
	
	Result: merged result
	
	`VARIANT MergeResult = Merge(VARIANT`
	`saActivityResults, VARIANT saOptions)`

SaveProject method	Saves results. Parameters: none Result: none `SaveProject`

Example 8.1: A Sample Batch Merge Program

This example contains a listing of a sample program called VTune-Batch.vbs written in VBScript. This program uses Microsoft cscript.exe to run the batch file and expects you to type command line arguments in the form:

cscript VTuneBatch.vbs *VTuneprojectfilename.vpj*

The program creates a batch file that loads the specified project, runs each of its activities synchronously, merges the activity results, and exports the project.

File from companion Web site: examples\ch8\VTuneBatch.vbs

```
1     'VTuneBatch.vbs
2     '--------------
3     ' Declare variables.
4     Dim Fso
5     Dim errCount
6     Dim VTune
7     Dim activityNames
8     Dim activityResult
9     Dim mergeResult
10    Dim mergeOptions
11    ' Provide the procedure to handle errors.
12    Sub ErrHandle(Err, ErrMsg)
13      newString = ErrMsg
14      If Err.Number <> 0 Then
15        newString = newString & " Failed. Error #" &
               Err.Number
16        errCount = errCount + 1
17      Else
18        newString = newString & " OK"
19      End If
20      Wscript.Echo newString
21    End Sub
22    '--------------------
23    'Start the script.
24    ' Turn error handling on.
25    On Error Resume Next
26    ' Clear error counter.
27    errCount = 0
28    ' Obtain all command-line parameters.
29    Set objArgs = Wscript.Arguments
30
31    If objArgs.Count = 0 Then
32      Wscript.Echo "Command Line: cscript VTuneBatch.vbs
            <VTune-project-filename.vpj>"
33    Else
```

```
34       ' Create the object to access the file system.
35       Set Fso = CreateObject("Scripting.FileSystemObject")
36       ' Run the main script procedure.
37       Run()
38       ' Perform cleanup before exit.
39       mergeOptions = Nothing
40       activityNames = Nothing
41       activityResult = Nothing
42       WScript.DisconnectObject VTune
43     End If
44   '--------------------
45   'Provide the main procedure.
46   Sub Run
47   ' Create an object.
48   Wscript.Echo "VTune object creating..."
49   Set VTune = CreateObject("VTuneBatch.VTune")
50   ' Check errors.
51   Call ErrHandle(Err, "Create VTune object:")
52   If errCount > 0 Then Exit Sub
53   ' Obtain the full path and name of the project file
     ' passed as an argument.
54   fullPath = Fso.GetAbsolutePathName(objArgs(0))
55   ' Load the specified project.
56   Wscript.Echo "Loading the project..." & fullPath
57   activityNames = VTune.LoadProject( fullPath )
58   ' Check errors.
59   Call ErrHandle(Err, "Load the Project:" & fullPath)
60   If errCount > 0 Then Exit Sub
61   ' Obtain the number of Activities.
62   activitySize = UBound(activityNames)
63   ' Check if there are Activities to run.
64   If (activitySize + 1 > 0 And Err.Number = 0) Then
65     ' Prepare an array to store Activity results.
66     Redim activityResult(activitySize)
67     For I = 0 To activitySize
68       Wscript.Echo "Running the activity [ " &
             activityNames(I) & " ] synchronously..."
69       ' Run the Activity with duration equal to 40 sec.
         ' Store the result in the array.
70       Set activityResult(I) =
             VTune.RunActivitySynchronous(activityNames(I), 40)
71       ' Check errors.
72       errString = "Run the activity [ " & activityNames(I)
             & " ] synchronously"
73       Call ErrHandle(Err, errString)
74       If errCount > 0 Then Exit For
75     Next
76     If errCount > 0 Then Exit Sub
77     ' Make sure there are at least two Activities to merge
       ' results.
```

```
78      If (activitySize + 1 > 1) Then
79         ' Prepare merge options array.
80         ReDim mergeOptions(3,1)
81         mergeOptions( 0, 0 ) = "MA_ModuleCheck"
82         mergeOptions( 0, 1 ) = 0
83         mergeOptions( 1, 0 ) = "MA_ProcessCheck"
84         mergeOptions( 1, 1 ) = 1
85         mergeOptions( 2, 0 ) = "MA_MergeModuleInstances"
86         mergeOptions( 2, 1 ) = True
87         mergeOptions( 3, 0 ) = "MA_MergeProcessInstances"
88         mergeOptions( 3, 1 ) = False
89         ' Merge collected results (works with Call Graph or
           ' Sampling).
90         Wscript.Echo "Running the merge of activities..."
91         Set mergeResult =
             VTune.Merge(activityResult,mergeOptions)
92         ' Check errors.
93         Call ErrHandle(Err, "Run the merge of activities:")
94         If errCount > 0 Then Exit Sub
95      End If
96   End If
97   Wscript.Echo "Exporting the project..."
98   ' Create the exported project name: change filename.vpj
     ' to filename_1.vxp.
99   expString = Left(fullPath, Len(fullPath) - 4) & "_1.vxp"
100  ' Export project.
101  Call VTune.ExportProject(expString)
102  ' Check errors.
103  Call ErrHandle(Err, "Export the Project:")
104  End Sub
```

Let's look at what is going on in this code:

Lines 1 through 10

These lines declare a set of array variables. These include a variable called fso for the project name (file system object), one for error handling, one for the VTune analyzer's batch object to be created, ones for the project's activity names and results, and ones for the merge results and options.

Lines 11 through 22:

This subroutine provides error handling for exception conditions encountered when loading, running, merging, or exporting the project. This routine displays an error message that includes the error number.

Line 23 through 27

The script begins here by initializing error handling.

Lines 28 through 32:

These lines obtain the command line arguments that invoke the specified batch file on the specified project. If none are provided, the program prints out an explanation and exits.

Lines 33 through 44:

Assuming you entered the right command line arguments, this logic creates a file system object to store the project name, runs the main script procedure and performs cleanup on variables before exiting.

Lines 45 through 54:

The main procedure begins here. It first creates a VTune analyzer batch file (by creating an instance of the `VTuneBatch` object) and gets the full pathname of the project file that was passed as an argument.

Lines 55 through 66:

This logic uses the `LoadProject` method to load the specified VTune analyzer project file. This method returns a list of activity names that the project contains. Based on this information, the program checks to see if there are any activities to run, gets the number of activities, and prepares an array to store the activity results.

Lines 67 through 76:

Next, the program sets up a loop to run each activity synchronously for 40 seconds using the `RunActivitySynchronous` method.

Lines 77 through 96:

This logic makes sure there are at least two activities to merge, prepares the merge options array containing the fields shown in the Merge Activity Results dialog box in Figure 8.15, and uses the `Merge` method to merge the Call Graph or Sampling activity results.

Lines 97 through 104:

Finally, the subroutine uses the project name as a basis for creating an export project filename with the correct file extension, and uses the `ExportProject` method to export the project under that filename.

Preparing Linux-based Scripts

You can use one of several Windows-based third-party automation and scripting tools to simulate user inputs to the VTune analyzer and perform scripting of these runs. Examples of such tools include:

- AutoIt
  http://www.hiddensoft.com/AutoIt/index.html

- AutoMate
  http://www.unisyn.com/automate/

- QuickMacros
  http://www.google.com/search?hl=en&q=quick+macros

Try using one of these tools in conjunction with Windows-based SSH clients, such as PuTTY, to perform automation remotely on the Linux side. The PuTTY tool is available at
http://www.chiark.greenend.org.uk/~sgtatham/putty

The VTune™ Analyzer as a Tool for Quality Assurance Groups

Automated scripts are particularly handy for performing repetitive tasks that are part of the Quality Assurance function. These programs can be run in batch mode on multiple activities without the need to monitor them live.

Automated comparisons can be especially useful to Quality Assurance groups. Using the objects and methods in Table 8.10 and techniques similar to those employed in Example 8.1, your QA organization can write scripts to perform comparisons of the same program run on the same or different platforms. You can build automated scripts for such tasks as:

- *Regression testing that compares versions of a developing program.* Try out a new compiler switch, a new compiler altogether, or a source code change. Here you are interested in finding out where performance got better or worse and why.

- *Platform variation testing that compares performance across target systems.* In such cases, use the Pack and Go feature to prepare a project file that includes activities results from multiple platforms. Then run an automated script overnight to compare the results using the Tuning Assistant and to export the Tuning Assistant advice for viewing on the following day.

Recap

Here are some key points in this chapter:

- You can use the Pack and Go feature to transport projects to different systems.

- On your own host system, you can statically analyze the performance of your application on other Intel processors.

- The VTune analyzer provides a drag-and-drop feature that allows you to compare items from different activity results side by side in the same window in Sampling, Call Graph, and Source views.

- You can compare Sampling View results to Call Graph results and vice versa.

- You can merge the results of multiple Call Graph or Sampling View activities to get an integrated picture of all the performance data collected during multiple runs.

- The Tuning Assistant is a powerful automated tool that offers insights about software performance issues with detailed suggestions for dealing with them. It can help you compare up to three different binaries on the same system, or compare binaries across two or three different systems.

- When tuning the same base architecture, a recommended methodology exists for comparing configurations and getting the best results.

- The *VTune batch mode API* allows you to build Windows-based programs or scripts that control the VTune analyzer automatically.

- Automated scripts are particularly handy for performing repetitive tasks that are part of the Quality Assurance function.

Chapter **9**

Analyzing Interpreted Languages

There are no facts, only interpretations.

— Friedrich Nietzsche

Interpreted languages that compile at run time are changing the software landscape, promising to increase code portability and accelerate software development. To deal with special issues such as Just-In-Time Compiling and special launching requirements, the VTune™ analyzer includes tailored Sampling and Call Graph wizard paths for applications running under Java and .NET runtime environments.

When working in an environment that includes Java or C#, be sure to make the VTune analyzer aware that you are working with managed code as you set up the session. The VTune analyzer shows managed code alongside unmanaged code, but to do so, the analyzer has to listen differently, so to speak, when dealing with unmanaged code in the mix.

Table 9.1   Interpreted Language Support at a Glance

Feature:	Support for Interpreted Languages
Benefit at a glance:	Provides Sampling and Call Graph profiling support for interpreted languages. This support includes Java in the Java Runtime Environment and a variety of .NET languages in the .NET Managed Runtime Environment.
Versions:	All versions of the VTune™ analyzer.
OS/Environments:	Windows and Linux operating systems.
Collectors:	Local data collection, plus remote for Java on Pentium® processors running under Linux.
Languages:	All languages when compiled, interpreted code supported for C# and Java. Display of source code for compiled code requires symbol information in the executable. Java source code display requires use of JITs with support for Java performance tuning, based on Java SDK 1.3 or later.
Processors:	Pentium processors and Itanium® processors.

The VTune analyzer version supports:

■ Java and .NET wizards tailored to different profiling scenarios such as using scripts to launch applications and launching applications outside of the VTune analyzer.

■ The wizards allow entry of a JAR file or a package name of a Java application and allow specifying the Java application CLASSPATH.

■ Java applet profiling when Microsoft Jview serves as the underlying JVM.

■ Java/Win64 mixed mode Call Graph: mixed mode Call Graph of Java calls and native module calls on Microsoft Windows operating systems running on Itanium® and Itanium 2 processor-based systems.

■ 32-bit Linux Java: remote Java profiling on IA-32 systems on Linux for both Sampling and Java classes only Call Graph.

■ Profiling of managed C++ applications, including mixed DLLs, and Call Graph and Sampling profiling of COM+ .NET applications.

■ ASP.NET mixed mode Call Graph profiling for managed and unmanaged calls.

■ .NET/Win64 Call Graph support.

Analysis of Java Code

The VTune analyzer provides support for Java. In a compatible Java development environment, the VTune analyzer communicates with the Virtual Machine to monitor and sample your JIT-compiled Java code. The VTune analyzer obtains the required information to analyze your Java application or applet from the Virtual Machine and Just-in-Time (JIT) compiler, using an industry-standard Java Virtual Machine Profiling Interface (JVMPI).

When your Java application executes, the JIT compiler converts your VM bytecode to native machine code. Depending on your Java environment, either the VM or the JIT provides the VTune analyzer with information about active Java classes and methods, such as their memory addresses, sizes, and symbol information. The VTune analyzer uses this information to keep track of all the classes and methods loaded into memory and the processes that are executed. It also uses this information for final analysis.

You can collect sampling data about a Java application running on a remote machine by configuring for remote sampling data collection. See Chapter 10, "Remote Analysis" for details.

When creating your Java bytecode, use the /g option to generate symbol and line number information on the Microsoft Java SDK 1.3 and above. Use the –g option to generate symbol and line number information on the Sun and IBM compilers. For instance, the command-line on the Microsoft Java SDK 1.3 compiler to generate a .class file called myClass.class that contains symbol and line number information is:

```
jvc /g myClass.java
```

As a Java .class file executes, the Just-In-Time (JIT) compiler supported by your Java environment translates the interpreted Virtual Machine (VM) *bytecode* into native machine code. The term *JIT-compiled Java code* refers to this JIT compiler output. A JIT-compiled Java application generally executes much faster than interpreted bytecode.

Supported Java Environments

The VTune analyzer supports these Java development environments for Sampling and Call Graph on IA-32 systems:

■ IBM JDK 1.3.1 for both Windows and Linux, 1.4.0 for Linux only

■ Sun JDK 1.4.1 / 1.4.2 for both Windows and Linux

■ BEA WebLogic JRockit[†] 8.0 for Linux and Windows, 8.1 for Windows only, and 8.1 SP1 for Linux and Windows (on Linux, these are supported on Red Hat Advanced Server 2.1 only)

■ Microsoft Jview

The VTune analyzer supports these Java development environments for the Itanium processor family:

■ BEA WebLogic JRockit 8.0 and 8.1

■ IBM JDK 1.3.1

The VTune analyzer for Linux supports these Java Development Kits (JDKs):

■ BEA WebLogic JRockit 7.0 SP2, 8.0, and 8.1 SP1 (BEA/JRockit is formally supported on Red Hat Linux AS 2.1 and EL3.0 only)

■ IBM JDK 1.3.1, 1.4.0

■ Sun JDK 1.4.1 and 1.4

Additional support is added from time to time, so you should consult information about the latest versions of the VTune analyzer for up-to-date information.

Call Graph profiling tracks Java calls only; at the time of this writing, no support exists for mixed Java and native calls. Additionally, the VTune analyzer currently does not support profiling of Java applications on versions of Linux for the Itanium processor.

Configuring Java Sampling: Command Line

When sampling from the command line, you use one of these options: java, applet, or jitprofiling. To create and run an Activity for a Java application, type:

```
vtl activity <name> -c sampling -o "<java_options> <sampling_options>"
-app <jvm_name>,"[JVM_options] <java_class/JAR_filename>" run
```

where:

- ■ *<java_options>* is is one of the following:
    - – java if your application is a Java application
    - – applet if your application is a Java applet
    - – JIT-profiling if your application uses the JITProfiling API
- ■ *<sampling_options>* are sampling collector configuration options (see Chapter 4)
- ■ *<JVM_name>* is the full path to the JVM executable
- ■ *[JVM_options]* are any JVM options, such as `-cp <class_path>`, `-Xms`
- ■ *<java_class/JAR_filename>* is the name of the main class or `.jar` file, for example: `MyAppClass`, `MyPackage.MyAppClass`, or

    `MyJarFile.jar`

The following are some examples for the Microsoft Windows Operating System.

```
vtl activity –d 120 –c sampling –o "java"
-app D:\SunJVM\bin\java,"-jar C:\jarfiles\Java2Demo.jar" run
```

In this example, the VTune analyzer samples the `Java2Demo.jar` application for 120 seconds.

```
vtl activity -d 180 -c sampling -o "java -cal no"
-app D:\IBMJava\bin\java,"-cp C:\Joe\roots roots" run
```

In this example, the VTune analyzer runs the `java` launcher to sample the `roots` application located in the `~\roots` directory. The Activity duration is 180 seconds.

The following are some examples for the Linux Operating System.

```
vtl activity –d 120 –c sampling –o "java"
-app /opt/SunJVM/bin/java,"-jar ~/jarfiles/Java2Demo.jar" run
```

In this example, the VTune analyzer samples the `Java2Demo.jar` application for 120 seconds.

```
vtl activity -d 180 -c sampling -o "java -cal no"
-app /usr/java/j2sdk1.4.1/bin/java,"-cp ~/java Xform" run
```

In this example, the VTune analyzer runs the `java` launcher to sample the `Xform` application located in the `~/java` directory supplied with the VTune analyzer. The Activity duration is 180 seconds.

Viewing of any of these results is the same as seen in Chapter 4 with other sampling with the addition of the `-hc` option. To display the hot-spot view of active C++ classes or Java classes within the `Jitcode.bin` module, use the `-hotspot-class` (or `-hc`) option and specify module name(s) with the `-module-name` (or `-mn`) option.

Configuring Java Sampling: GUI

To configure an activity for a Java application using the Sampling Wizard under VTune Performance Analyzer 7.1 or later:

1. Click **Create New Project** to open the New Project dialog box.

2. Select **Sampling Wizard** and click **OK** to open the Sampling Configuration Wizard screen, as shown in Figure 9.1.

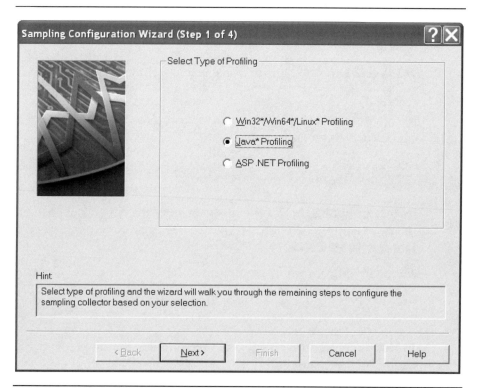

Figure 9.1   Selecting Java Profiling in the 7.1 Sampling Wizard

3. Select **Java Profiling** and click **OK** to move to the next screen.

4. From the screen shown in Figure 9.2, select one of the three launching modes:

   ■ **Application** to specify a Java launcher and application

   ■ **Script** to specify a script that launches a Java application

   ■ **Applet** to specify a Java viewer and applet to launch

Optional steps:

5. Select **Modify default configuration when done with wizard** to launch **Advanced Activity Configuration** from the wizard and continue configuring your activity manually after you click **Finish**:

   a. In the Data Collectors box, click **Sampling**, click the **Events** tab, choose the events you want to monitor, and click **OK**.

   b. If you have specific modules you want to sample, click the application name in the Application/Module Profiles box, click the **Configure** button, and browse to the source files for the modules you want to add. Click **OK** when finished.

   c. Click **OK** to close the Sampling wizard.

6. Select **Run Activity when done with wizard** to run the activity immediately after configuring the Sampling collector. If you decide not to select this option, click **Run Activity** after Step 9 to start data collection.

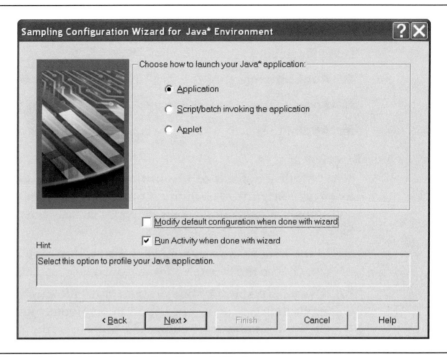

Figure 9.2   Selecting the Java Launch Mode

To continue configuring the Sampling Wizard:

7. Click **Next** to move to the next screen, which varies depending on your previous selection.

    –   If you selected **Application**, your next steps are:

        a. Enter the name or browse for your Java launcher in the **Java Launcher** field in the Step 1 of 4 screen:

            jview.exe if you use the Microsoft Java launcher

            java.exe if you use the IBM or Sun Java launcher

        b. Enter the name, such as Appmain.class, or browse for your Java application in the **main class (package.class) or JAR file** field in the Step 2 of 4 screen. The **Package root or working directory** field automatically fills with the location of the file.

        c. If necessary, edit the command line that invokes the Java application in the Step 3 of 4 screen.

For Microsoft Java launchers:

To launch a Java applet, add /a before the .html file-name.

To launch a Java application (.class file), no command line argument is needed.

For IBM and Sun Java launchers:

To launch a Java applet, add -J "-Xrunjavaperf" before the .html filename.

To launch a Java application, add -Xrunjavaperf. No "" is required in the case of a .class file.

When working with the Intel Itanium processor, use Xrunjavaperf64. instead of -Xrunjavaperf, the default setting for IA-32).

- If you selected **Script/batch invoking the application**, enter the name or browse for the script, .cmd or .bat file, in the **Launching script** field in the Step 1 of 2 screen. The **Working directory** field automatically fills with the location of the file.

- If you selected **Applet**:

   a. Enter the name or browse for your Java applet viewer in the **Applet Viewer** field in the Step 1 of 3 screen:

      jview.exe if you use the Microsoft Java applet-viewer.

      appletviewer.exe if you use the IBM or Sun Java applet viewer.

   b. Enter the name, such as index.html, or browse for the .html applet file in the **Java applet starting page** field in the Step 1 of 3 screen. The **Working directory** field automatically fills with the location of the file.

   c. If necessary, edit the command line that invokes the Java applet in the Step 2 of 3 screen.

8. Click **Next** to move to the last step of the Sampling Wizard and select the Sampling mechanism and the condition for stopping data collection.

9. Click **Finish** to close the Sampling Wizard.

10. If necessary, click **Run Activity** to start data collection.

   The VTune analyzer executes and profiles your Java application together with other active Win32/Win64 modules in your application. At the end of the profiling and data collection, the VTune analyzer creates an activity result with the collected data.

11. Double-click the activity result in the Tuning Browser to open the Sampling view and analyze the performance of your Java application or applet.

Example 9.1: Analyzing a Sampled Java Application

The companion Web site for this book contains a Java example called Mandelbrot including the necessary source and executable files. The Java source file is called Appmain.java, and has five classes, as shown in Figure 9.3. You might have to give the pathname to the source file the first time you view results.

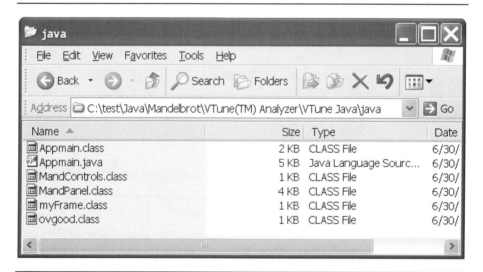

Figure 9.3   Source and Class files in the Appmain Example

To run the `Appmain` application, start the Sampling session as you normally do. When the application window appears, click the **Run** button. You can do this a few times to refresh the colorful graphic shown in Figure 9.4. Try to keep the application painting while it runs to minimize idle time during Sampling. To stop the application, click the application window's **Close** button in the upper right hand corner.

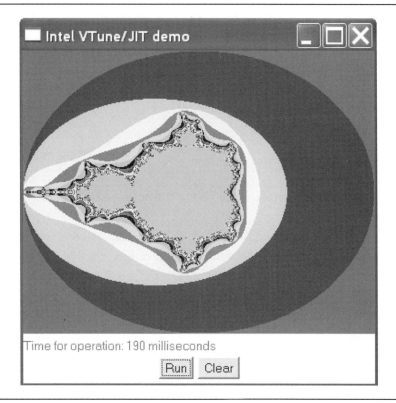

Figure 9.4   Mandelbrot Java Application

Microsoft Java Example

Figure 9.5 shows the Process view of Sampling data collected for the `Appmain` Java application. At this point, the process of interest is the Microsoft `jview.exe` launcher.

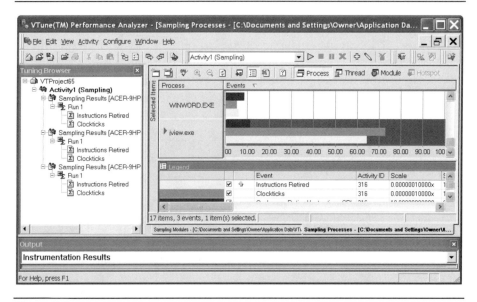

Figure 9.5   Microsoft Java Launcher Application in Process View

After drilling down to Module view, Figure 9.6 shows the Java module of interest at this point, which contains JIT-compiled application code.

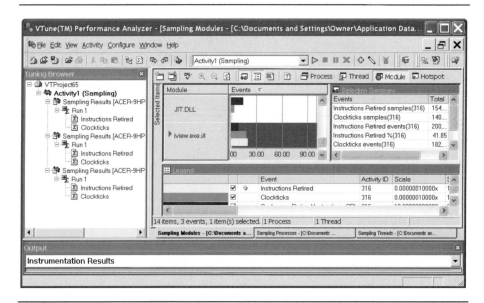

Figure 9.6   Microsoft Java Module of Interest in Module View

In Module view, the VTune analyzer groups together all JIT-compiled Java methods into a single category represented by a single horizontal bar.

■ For Java applications running on a system with the Windows operating system, the horizontal bar is named `jview.exe.jit`, as shown in this example.

■ For Java applications running on Sun or IBM JVMs, the horizontal bar is named `java.exe.jit`.

You can have multiple bars representing multiple `.jit` files, depending on the number of VMs running in your system. A module is assigned the name Java, plus the ID, the last two hexadecimal digits of the process ID, and a `.jit` extension; for example, `Java1299.jit`.

You can drill down to Hotspot view by double-clicking the horizontal bar to view individual methods. Figure 9.7 shows the `java.exe.jit` Java application code in Hotspot view, where a function breakdown lists all the individual Java functions, including a function of interest called `MandPanel.Point`.

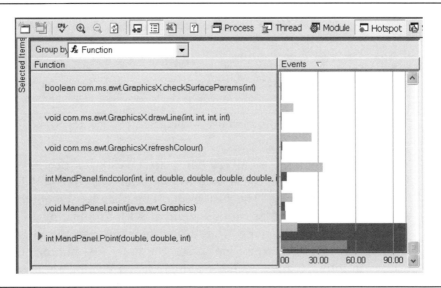

Figure 9.7   Java Function of Interest in Hotspot View

Figure 9.8 shows the `Point` method of the `MandPanel` class in Source view, where the hotspot with the highest *Clockticks* event (293) appears to be an `If` statement.

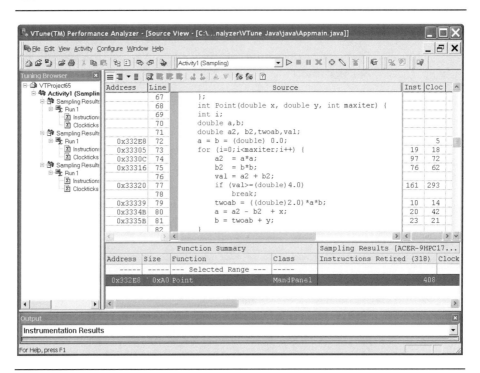

Figure 9.8   Java Application in Sampling Source View (Microsoft JVM)

After switching to Mixed view to investigate the assembly code shown in Figure 9.9, the reason for the seeming "hotspot" looks apparent, but is deceiving. The Just-in-time compiler has combined the floating-point add for the previous statement with the floating-point compare and the conditional jump. Watch out for cases like this, where the JIT compiler generates equivalent assembly code for multiple Java instructions in lines 76 and 77 under a single listed Java instruction in line 77. Such cases are not true hotspots and are not necessarily candidates for tuning.

Address	Line	?	Source	Pena	Inst	Cloc
0x33312	74		fstp QWORD PTR [esp+010h]		53	24
0x33316	75		b2 = b*b;		76	62
0x33316	75		fld QWORD PTR [esp+08h]		21	18
0x3331A	75		fmul st(0), st(0)		1	25
0x3331C	75		fstp QWORD PTR [esp+018h]		54	19
	76		val = a2 + b2;			
0x33320	77		if (val>=(double)4.0)		161	293
0x33320	77		fld QWORD PTR [esp+010h]		22	15
0x33324	77		fadd QWORD PTR [esp+018h]		42	45
0x33328	77		fst QWORD PTR [esp+028h]		34	71
0x3332C	77		fcomp QWORD PTR [043d6650h]		5	38
0x33332	77		fnstsw ax		19	23
0x33334	77		sahf		15	42
0x33335	77		jp Point+51		11	18
0x33337	77	Point+4f:	jae Point+84		13	41
	78		break;			

Function Summary				Sampling Results [ACER-9HPC17...	
Address	Size	Function	Class	Instructions Retired (318)	Clock
-----	-----	--- Selected Range ---	-----		
0x332E8	0xA0	Point	MandPanel	408	

Figure 9.9   Two Java Lines Combined in Sampling Mixed View

Sun Java Example

The companion Web site to this book provides another version of this Java example called AppmainDbl.java, with a loop added to the Paint method to obtain a larger number of samples and to avoid having to push the **Run** button. If you run this example under Sun Java, further investigation uncovers another hotspot in the Point method, as shown in Figure 9.10.

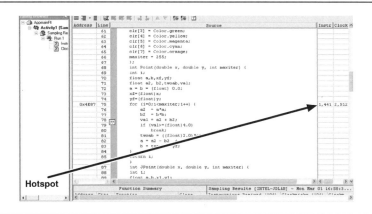

Figure 9.10   Java Hotspot in Sampling Source View (Sun JVM)

The mixed source and disassembly view in Figure 9.11 reveals the area where the hotspot occurs. The `fstp` instruction is the problem. Since some events are not precise, you may only find the general area where the hotspot occurs, as is the case here.

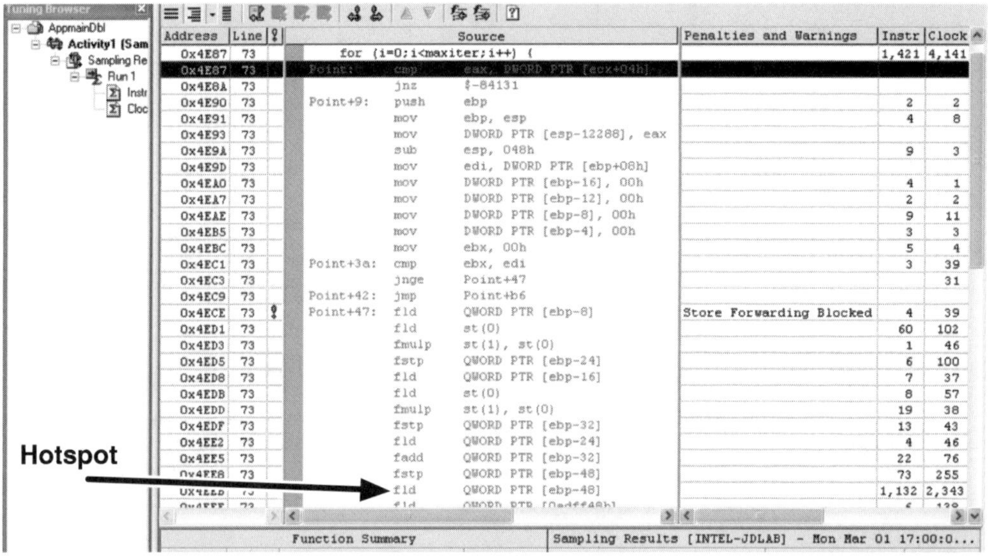

Figure 9.11 Hotspot Discovered in Mixed View (Sun JVM)

At this point, you might decide that speed is more important than precision for the application, change the `double` data types to `float`, and rerun the analysis. Figure 9.12 shows this improved version of the Java code in source view, from the file provided on the companion Web site named `AppmainFit.java`.

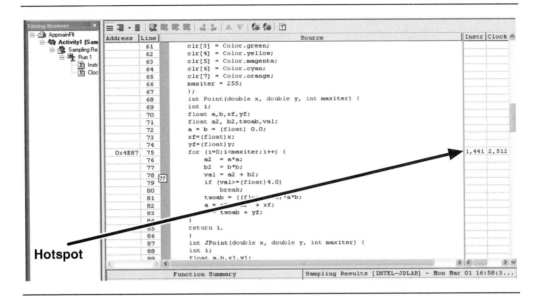

Figure 9.12 Java Code Improved for Speed (Sun JVM)

Figure 9.13 shows the resulting improvement in mixed view, with a significant reduction in the hotspot for the `fstp` instruction.

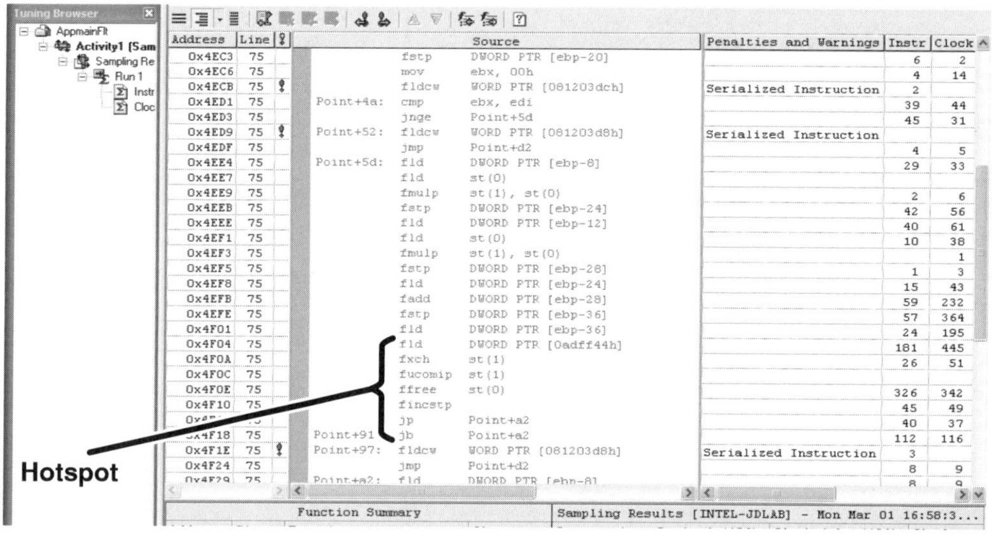

Figure 9.13   Improved Java Code in Mixed View (Sun JVM)

Call Graph Profiling for Java Applications

In a compatible Java development environment, you can use the VTune analyzer to generate a Call Graph profile of your Java code. During profiling, depending on the Java environment, either the Java Virtual Machine or the Just-In-Time compiler provides the VTune analyzer with information about active Java classes and methods such as their memory addresses, sizes, and symbol information. The VTune analyzer uses the information to keep track of the executed processes and the classes and methods loaded into memory. At the end of profiling and data collection, the VTune analyzer creates an activity result with the collected data.

The VTune analyzer supports Call Graph analysis exclusively via the GUI on Windows, while on Linux the command offers the ability to collect Call Graph data while still using the viewer or GUI to view the data graphically. Call Graph analysis for Java programs is examined here using the GUI on Windows.

Configuring Java Call Graph Profiling

To configure an activity for a Java application using the Call Graph Wizard under VTune Performance Analyzer 7.1 or later:

1. Click **Create New Project** to open the New Project dialog box.

2. Select **Call Graph Wizard** and click **OK** to open the Call Graph Configuration Wizard screen, shown in Figure 9.14.

3. Select **Java Profiling** and click **Next** to move to the next screen.

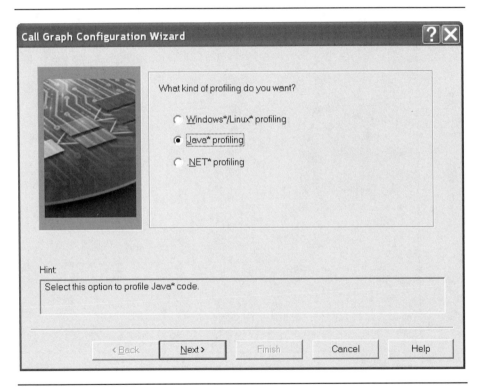

Figure 9.14 Selecting Java Profiling in the 7.1 Call Graph Wizard

4. From the screen shown in Figure 9.15, select one of the three launching modes:

   ■ **Application** to specify a Java launcher and application

   ■ **Script** to specify a script that launches a Java application

   ■ **Applet** to specify a Java viewer and applet to launch

Optional steps:

5. Select **Modify default configuration when done with wizard** to launch **Advanced Activity Configuration** from the wizard and continue configuring your activity manually after you click Finish.

6. Select **Run Activity when done with wizard** to run the activity immediately after configuring the Call Graph collector. If you decide not to select this option, click **Run Activity** after Step 9 to start data collection.

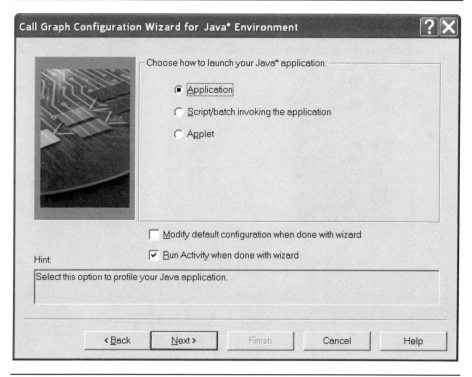

Figure 9.15   Selecting the Java Launch Mode

To continue configuring the Call Graph Wizard:

7. Click **Next** to move to the next screen, which will vary depending on your previous selection.

    – If you selected **Application**:

        a. Enter the name or browse for your Java launcher in the **Java Launcher** field in the Step 1 of 4 screen:

            `jview.exe` if you use the Microsoft Java launcher

            `java.exe` if you use the IBM or Sun Java launcher

        b. Enter the name, such as `Appmain.class`, or browse for your Java application in the **main class (package.class) or JAR file** field in the Step 2 of 4 screen. The **Package root or working directory** field automatically fills with the location of the file.

            If necessary, edit the command line that will invoke the Java application in the Step 3 of 4 screen.

            For Microsoft Java launchers:

                To launch a Java applet, add `/a` before the `.html` filename.

                To launch a Java application `.class` file, no command line argument is needed.

            For IBM and Sun Java launchers:

                To launch a Java applet, add `-J "-Xrunjavaperf"` before the `.html` filename.

                To launch a Java application, add `-Xrunjavaperf`. No `""` is required in the case of a `.class` file.

When working with the Intel Itanium processor, use `Xrunjavaperf64` instead of `-Xrunjavaperf`, which is the default setting for IA-32.

– If you selected **Script/batch invoking the application**, enter the name or browse for the `.cmd` or `.bat` script file in the **Launching script** field in the Step 1 of 2 screen. The **Working directory** field automatically fills with the location of the file.

– If you selected **Applet**:

    a. Enter the name or browse for your Java applet viewer in the **Applet Viewer** field in the Step 1 of 3 screen:

        `jview.exe` if you use the Microsoft Java appletviewer

        `appletviewer.exe` if you use the IBM or Sun Java applet viewer

    b. Enter the name, such as `index.html`, or browse for the `.html` applet file in the **Java applet starting page** field in the Step 1 of 3 screen. The **Working directory** field automatically fills with the location of the file.

If necessary, edit the command line that will invoke the Java applet in the Step 2 of 3 screen.

8. Click **Next** to move to the last step of the Call Graph Wizard in Figure 9.16 and select the data collection mode:

– Select **Java classes only** to get a Call Graph of your Java program only *without* all the native DLLs that execute under the profiled process.

– Select **All Java classes and all native modules** if you have calls from Java functions to Windows functions or vice versa. You will get a Call Graph of your Java program *including* all the native DLLs that execute under the profiled process.

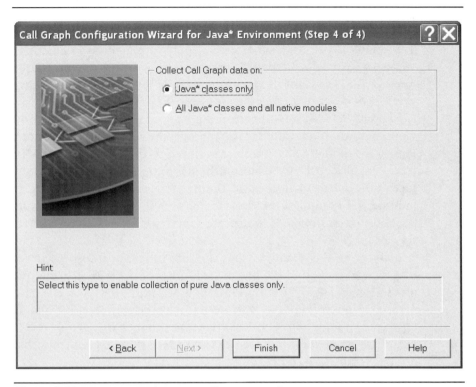

Figure 9.16   Selecting the Java Collection Mode

9.   Click **Finish** to close the Call Graph Wizard.

10.   If necessary, click **Run Activity** to start data collection.

The VTune analyzer executes and profiles your Java application together with other active Win32 modules in your application.

11.   Double-click the activity result in the Tuning Browser to open the Call Graph views and analyze the performance of your Java application or applet.

The VTune analyzer automatically displays Java functions and Windows functions in the same Call Graph view. You can view Java function calls to Win32 function calls and vice versa together in the same Call Graph.

Example 9.2: Analyzing a Java Call Graph

This example uses the same `Appmain` Java application as Example 9.1. To view these results firsthand, create a Call Graph activity that profiles `Appmain.class`, and then run the sample Java application shown in Figure 9.4, as described earlier in Example 9.1.

Figure 9.17 shows the resulting Call Graph data collected in Graph view, with the JIT-compiled version of `MandPanel.Point` selected in the Function Summary and graph. As shown in the example, the VTune analyzer enables you to distinguish JIT-compiled from interpreted Java methods, and to examine the timing differences between each type of method. JIT-compiled methods are grouped together into modules with the `.jit` extension, and interpreted methods into modules with the postfix `_interpreted`.

Notice in this example that the less efficient, interpreted version of the `jview.exe` module has a Self-Time of 54,946,301 microseconds, much longer than the JIT-compiled version that has a Self-Time of 3,153,527 microseconds. Also notice that the number of Calls in the interpreted module is much less than the number of Calls in the JIT module. Since these methods are seldom called, this may indicate that it may not be worthwhile trying to optimize them.

By clicking on the Self-Time column heading in the JIT module to arrange functions in descending Self-Time order, you can see that about a third, or 1,215,413, of the total JIT-compiled time was spent executing the `Point` function, which was called 1,794,690 times. The next most time-consuming function was `findcolor`, with a Self-Time of 658,946. The graph reveals that the `Paint` function calls `findcolor`, which in turn calls `Point`. All three functions belong to the `MandPanel` class.

Figure 9.18 shows the thread breakdown of both interpreted and compiled Java modules. The `Point`, `findcolor`, and `paint` functions all belong to `Thread_2`, which accounts for most of the calls, execution time, and wait time in the JIT-compiled version of the code. The `Point` function accomplished 64 percent of the work of `findcolor`, the focus function that called it.

Notice that most of the Self-Wait time of the JIT-compiled code was spent in the `convertToOld` function of the `java.awt.AWTEvent` class. This is the time spent inside a function while its thread was suspended, and does not include any inactive time spent in its callees. Fortunately, this Self-Wait time is not persistent. Running the program a second time reveals that, in this case, the wait was probably caused by the user waiting to press the **Run** button.

Module (320)	Function (320)	Class (320)	Calls (320)	Self Time (3...	Total Time (320)	Self \
⊟ Total			4,516,501	58,099,828		
⊞ jview.exe.interprete...			221,038	54,946,301		
⊟ jview.exe.jit - Total			4,295,463	3,153,527		
jview.exe.jit	Point	MandPanel	1,794,690	1,215,413	1,215,413	
jview.exe.jit	findcolor	MandPanel	1,794,690	658,946	1,874,359	
jview.exe.jit	paint	MandPanel	18	524,695	2,963,029	
jview.exe.jit	convertToOld	java.awt.AW...	180	396,531	396,876	
jview.exe.jit	refreshColour	com.ms.awt....	106,513	116,079	182,859	
jview.exe.jit	drawLine	com.ms.awt....	110,550	98,329	544,030	
jview.exe.jit	checkSurfacePara...	com.ms.awt....	110,783	38,323	223,666	
jview.exe.jit	getColorType	com.ms.awt....	106,513	21,525	21,525	
jview.exe.jit	setColor	com.ms.awt....	110,841	18,672	18,672	
jview.exe.jit	getRGB	java.awt.Color	106,368	14,766	14,766	

Figure 9.17   A Java Call Graph in Self-Time Order

Similarly, most of the time in `Thread_2` and `Thread_3` of the interpreted Java module was spent waiting while its thread was suspended. Global observations such as these help provide a context for a particular function of interest, and provide clues to its importance in the big picture.

Module (320)	Thread (...	Function (320)	Class (320)	Calls (320)	Self Time (3...	Self Wait Time...	T
⊟ Total				4,516,501.	58,099,828.	55,090,937.	
⊟ jview.exe.interp...				221,038.	54,946,301.	54,676,850.	
⊞ jview.exe.interp...	Thread_0(...			321.	10,861.	5,307.	
⊞ jview.exe.interp...	Thread_2(...			220,030.	16,053,714.	15,792,400.	
⊞ jview.exe.interp...	Thread_3(...			687.	38,881,726.	38,879,143.	
⊟ jview.exe.jit - T...				4,295,463.	3,153,527.	414,087.	
⊞ jview.exe.jit	Thread_0(...			2,173.	4,286.	1,373.	
⊞ jview.exe.jit	Thread_1(...			192.	59.	0.	
⊟ jview.exe.jit	Thread_2(...			4,287,395.	3,134,153.	401,575.	
jview.exe.jit	Thread_2(...	Point	MandPanel	1,794,690.	1,215,413.	261.	
jview.exe.jit	Thread_2(...	findcolor	MandPanel	1,794,690.	658,946.	0.	
jview.exe.jit	Thread_2(...	paint	MandPanel	18.	524,695.	0.	
jview.exe.jit	Thread_2(...	convertToOld	java.awt.AW...	180.	396,531.	396,034.	

Focus function							
jview.exe.jit	Thread_2(B£	findcolor	MandPanel	1,794,690.	658,946.	0.	

Caller Functi...	Contribution	Edge Calls	Module	Full Name	Source File	Thread
paint	100.0%	1,794,690.	jview.exe.jit	void MandPanel.paint(jav...	Appmain.java	Thread_2(B...

Callee Funct...	Contribution	Edge Calls	Module	Full Name	Source File	Thread
Point	64.8%	1,794,690.	jview.exe.jit	int MandPanel.Point(doub...	Appmain.java	Thread_2(B...

Figure 9.18   Interpreted and JIT-Compiled Java Threads in Call List View

Right-click the `findcolor` method name and select **View Source** to bring up the Source view. Figure 9.19 shows the `findcolor` function of interest in Source view, where a call to the `Point` function is made. The Total Time shown for `findcolor` is 1,874,359 and includes the time spent executing the `Point` function. Self-Time is 658,946 and *excludes* the time spent executing the `Point` function.

Address	Line	Source	Total Tim	Self Tim	Calls (32
	100	return i;			
	101	}			
	102	int findcolor(int ri, int rj			
	103	double ydelta, int maxi)			
	104	{			
	105				
0x31674	106	double x = xmin + ((double)rj	1,874,359	658,946	1,794,690
0x3168B	107	double y = ymax - ((double)ri			
	108				
	109	// int j = JPoint(x, y, maxi);			
0x3169D	110	int i = Point(x, y, maxi);			
0x316BC	111	return i&7;			
	112	}			
	113				
	114	public void paint(Graphics g)			
	115	Rectangle r = bounds();			

Function Summary				Call Graph Results - [ACER-9H...	
Address	Size	Function	Class	Total Time (320)	Self Time (320)
-----	-----	--- Selected Range ---	-----		
0x31674	0x58	findcolor	MandPanel	1,874,359	658,94

Figure 9.19   Java Application in Call Graph Source View

A switch to Mixed view, shown in Figure 9.20, reveals a warning message from the static assembly-level analyzer for the `Point` function call instruction. The warning indicates that transfers between implicit and explicit use of the ESP register are incurring a penalty. The advice suggests trying to separate the implicit ESP register usage from the explicit ESP register usage and trying to minimize the transfers between them.

Since this assembly code is the work of the Java JIT compiler, you would probably not want to perform this type of computer architecture-level tuning. Any gain from hand-tuning the assembly code would be offset by losing the portability of a Just-In-Time compiler.

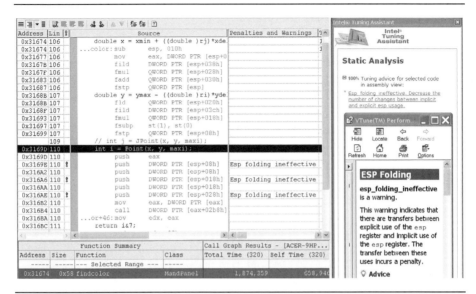

Figure 9.20   Java Application in Call Graph Mixed View

Analysis of .NET Code (Including C#)

The VTune analyzer provides Managed Runtime Environment support for Microsoft's object-based *.NET Framework*. This infrastructure of unified tools and libraries provides a *Common Language Runtime* engine for distributed computing and software development productivity. Within this framework, an application written in multiple languages can share data with other applications across multiple platforms using just-in-time compilation. New enabling technologies like .NET Web Services and ASP.NET, as well as .NET programming languages such as Microsoft C#, Visual Basic .NET, Visual C++.NET, and Jscript, help make all this possible.

To benefit from the Common Language Runtime (CLR) managed execution environment, you must use a language compiler that targets this runtime environment. Code that you develop with a language compiler that targets the CLR is called *managed code*. During execution, managed code receives services such as garbage collection, security, interoperability with unmanaged code, cross-language debugging support, a simplified model for component interaction, and enhanced deployment and versioning support.

JIT-Compiled Versus Interpreted MSIL

One concept that Java and .NET share is the use of expressive file syntax to deliver executable code: bytecode in the case of Java, Microsoft Intermediate Language (MSIL) for .NET. Being much higher-level than binary machine code, these CPU-independent intermediate files are translated into more efficient code by a Just-In-Time compiler before execution.

As a .NET file executes, the Just-In-Time (JIT) compiler supported by your .NET environment translates the interpreted Microsoft Intermediate Language into native machine code. The term *JIT-compiled .NET code* refers to this JIT compiler output. A JIT-compiled .NET application executes much faster than interpreted MSIL code.

Before You Begin

Before using the VTune analyzer to do Sampling or Call Graph profiling of a .NET application or Web service, make sure you have installed these components on your system:[1]

- ■ Microsoft .NET Framework

- ■ Internet Information Server (IIS); required for ASP.NET services only

Common Language Runtime Considerations

When you select **NET Profiling** in the Sampling or Call Graph Wizard, the VTune analyzer automatically enables Common Language Runtime profiling, which permits profiling of the Internet Information Server. To enable CLR profiling, the VTune analyzer sets these environment variables:

```
Cor_Enable_Profiling to 1
COR_PROFILER to {91663010-0D1E-4ABD-8F0C-0B4B84CCA809}
BISTRO_COLLECTORS_DO_CALLGRAPH to 1
```

---

[1] For remote Sampling or Call Graph profiling, install these components on the remote system. You do not have to install them on the controlling system.

Note

One caveat: If you cannot see specific functions in Sampling or Call Graph view even though you are sure these functions consume a lot of CPU cycles in your application, the compiler may be the culprit. The .NET JIT compiler sometimes inlines functions into their calling functions. As a result, the CPU cycles consumed by the callees are associated with the callers, and the callees are not explicitly mentioned.

ASP.NET Considerations

Here are some points to keep in mind when tuning an ASP.NET application:

■ Before ASP.NET data collection, the VTune analyzer sets environment variables and restarts IIS and related Web services. After ASP.NET data collection, the VTune analyzer deletes environment variables and restarts IIS and related Web services again.

■ When profiling in event-based Sampling mode with calibration, all ASP.NET worker processes are terminated between calibration and actual Sampling.

■ Since the data are collected within the context of the ASP.NET worker process, you must grant access to the VTune analyzer project directory, so that the data can be written. The easiest way to do this is to follow these steps:

1. Create the project, or if you have one existing already, use Windows Explorer to locate the project directory.

2. Right-click on the directory and select **Properties**.

3. Select the **Security** tab and add **Everyone** to the list.

4. Grant **Full Control** by checking the appropriate box.

Server-Side DLL-level Call Graph Profiling

The VTune analyzer enables you to collect data not only on applications but on user DLLs as well. You can instrument and collect data on a DLL and its dependent functions, even if the application itself cannot be instrumented. This mode is especially useful when you want to instrument and collect data on:

■ Web-server server-side applications that are loaded inside a server process

■ DLLs inside applications that cannot be restarted and/or stopped

■ MTS objects

The VTune analyzer replaces the original DLL with the instrumented DLL before running the Activity and collects data. After saving runtime information, the VTune analyzer restores the original DLL. Note that DLL-level profiling is possible only for user DLLs with debug information. You cannot select a system DLL, an executable, or a .NET DLL as an application/module profile.

Note

> When running DLL-level Activities, the VTune analyzer replaces the original DLL with the instrumented DLL. If the server stops running for any reason such as a power failure, the VTune analyzer may not be able to restore the original DLL. To restore the original DLLs, run the batch file. The name and location of that batch file are displayed when DLL-level data collection starts running.

Configuring .NET Sampling

To configure an activity for a .NET application using the Sampling Wizard under VTune Performance Analyzer 7.1 or later:

1. Click **Create New Project** to open the New Project dialog box.

2. Select **Sampling Wizard** and click **OK** to open the Sampling Configuration Wizard screen, as shown in Figure 9.21.

3. Select **.NET Profiling** to profile .NET applications and Web services and click **OK** to move to the next screen.

4. From the screen shown in Figure 9.22, you can choose to profile an executable, an executable launched by a script, an ASP.NET application, or an executable that interacts with a COM+ service you want to profile. Select one of the four application types for Sampling:

   Executable to specify a .NET application. The VTune analyzer launches the application.

   Script/batch invoking the application to specify a script that launches a .NET application.

   ASP .NET to specify an Active Server Page (ASP) .NET application. The application will be executed under a system-launched process so the VTune analyzer will not launch the application.

   COM+ Enterprise Services to specify an application that interacts with the COM+ services that you want to profile.

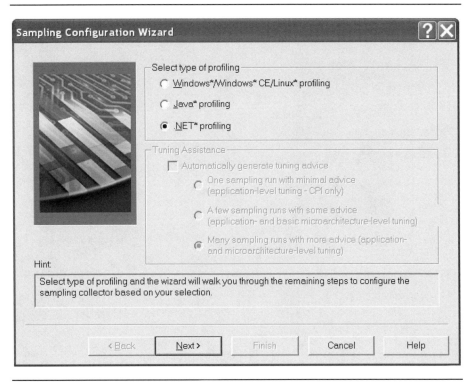

Figure 9.21   Selecting .NET Profiling in the 7.1 Sampling Wizard

Optional steps:

5. Select **Modify default configuration when done with wizard** to launch **Advanced Activity Configuration** from the wizard and continue configuring your activity manually after you click **Finish**.

6. Select **Run Activity when done with wizard** to run the activity immediately after configuring the Sampling collector. If you decide not to select this option, click **Run Activity** after Step 9 to start data collection.

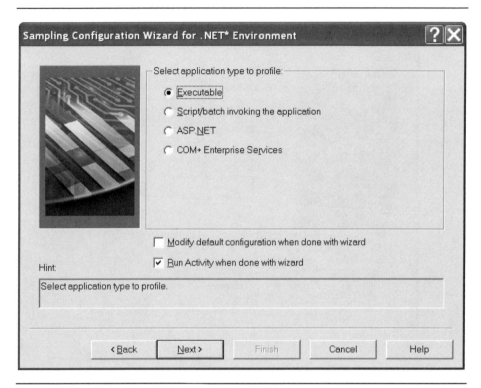

Figure 9.22   Selecting the .NET Application Type for Sampling

To continue configuring the Sampling Wizard:

7. Click **Next** to move to the next screen, which will vary depending on your previous selection.

   – If you selected **Executable** or **COM+ Enterprise Services**, enter the name, such as `HelloWorld.exe`, or browse for your .NET application in the **Application to Launch** field in the Step 1 of 2 screen.

   – If you selected **Script/batch invoking the application**, enter the name or browse for the `.cmd` or `.bat` script file in the **Launching script** field in the Step 1 of 2 screen.

- If you selected **ASP .NET**, a message appears on the Step 1 screen warning that all IIS and IIS-dependent services will be restarted before the collection starts. Enter the application name, such as `program.asp` or `index.html`, or the process name, such as `aspnet_wp.exe`, to profile a .NET Web service within the IIS server process or browse for your ASP.NET worker process in the **Application to Launch** field in the Step 2 of 3 screen.

   The **Working directory** field automatically fills with the location of the file.

8. Click **Next** to move to the last step of the Sampling Wizard and select the Sampling mechanism and the condition for stopping data collection.

9. Click **Finish** to close the Sampling Wizard.

10. If necessary, click **Run Activity** to start data collection.

   The VTune analyzer executes and profiles your .NET application, taking advantage of the Common Language Runtime environment. At the end of the profiling and data collection, the VTune analyzer creates an activity result with the collected data.

11. Double-click the activity result in the Tuning Browser to open the Sampling view and analyze the performance of your .NET application.

Example 9.3: Analyzing a Sampled Visual C# .NET Application

The companion Web site to this book contains a C# example named `Plasma`, including the necessary source and executable files and symbol file. The C# source file is called `Plasma.cs`. The first time you view results, you might have to give the pathname to the source files in order to drill down to the source code.

Note

> When preparing this example, I first tried using a much simpler example called `LocalizedHelloWorld` that comes with Visual Studio .NET. No Hotspot or Source View appeared (other than Disassembly View), because the program was not running long enough to collect any samples! After adding a loop that executed 100,000 times, I eventually was able to see a few samples and drill down to Source View. The moral of this story: Make sure your program runs long enough to generate some samples.

Resolving Symbol Information

If you cannot drill down to the source code, do the following to resolve the symbol information provided:

1. Right-click the Sampling Activity result that contains one or more runs in the **Tuning Browser** window.

2. Choose **Module Association**.

3. In the dialog box that appears, locate the module of interest and edit the path to the symbol file. If symbol information is embedded in the executable, then just point to the executable.

For an unpacked Pack and Go file, you need to perform module association on each unpacked activity result. Remember to save your project after making module associations; otherwise, you will have to perform module association on each activity result again the next time you load the project.

Create your own VTune analyzer project with a Sampling activity using the executable named `plasma.exe`. To run the `Plasma.exe` application, just start a Sampling or Call Graph activity and the program begins running, displaying a moving Plasma-like display in a small window, as shown in Figure 9.23. To stop the application, click the application window's **Close** button in the upper right-hand corner.

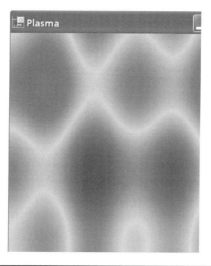

Figure 9.23   Plasma .NET Application

Figure 9.24 shows the Process view of sampling data collected for the `Plasma` C# application. At this point, the process of interest is the `Plasma.exe` process.

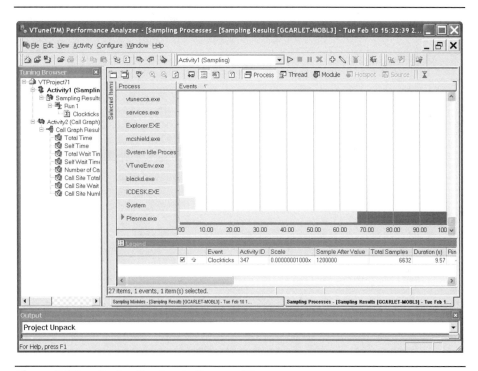

Figure 9.24　C# Application in Process View

After drilling down to Module view, Figure 9.25 shows the .NET module of interest at this point, which contains JIT-compiled application code.

In Module view, the VTune analyzer groups together all JIT-compiled .NET functions into a single category represented by a single horizontal bar.

■ For .NET applications running on a system with the Windows operating system, the horizontal bar is named *application*.exe.jit. For example, here the application is named `Plasma.exe.jit`.

■ Modules other than JIT-suffixed modules contain native (unmanaged) code. You can drill down to Hotspot view by double-clicking the horizontal bar to view individual functions. Figure 9.26 shows the `Plasma.exe.jit` .NET application code in Hotspot view, where a function breakdown lists all the individual .NET functions, including a function called `Plasma.Form1.Run`.

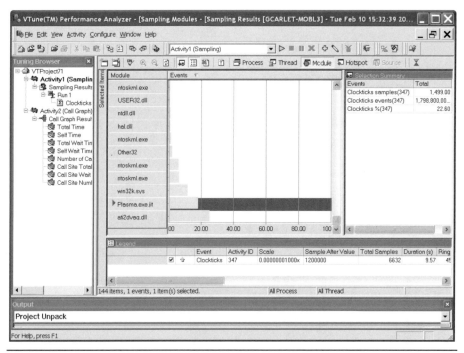

Figure 9.25 C# Application in Module View

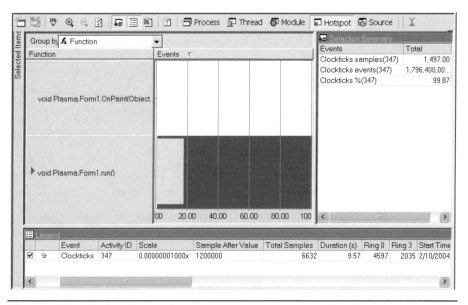

Figure 9.26 C# Application in Hotspot View

Figure 9.27 shows the `Run` method in Source view. Notice that Sampling information—*Clockticks* data, in this case—appears for each source code instruction. The hotspot with the highest *Clockticks* events, 385, 580, and 221, appears to be the inner `for` loop at lines 310 to 312. Since this loop is the hotspot, the algorithm here bears more investigation to see whether the code could be written in a more efficient way.

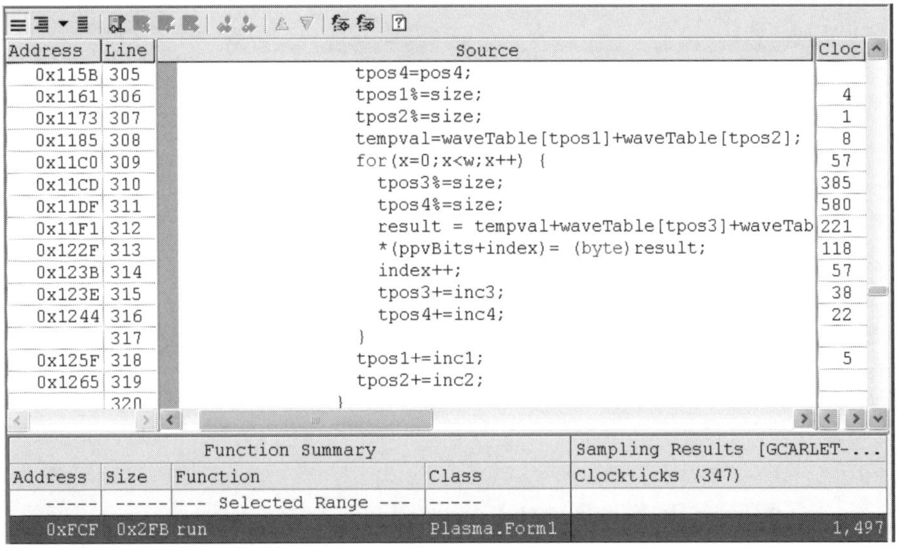

Address	Line	Source	Cloc
0x115B	305	tpos4=pos4;	
0x1161	306	tpos1%=size;	4
0x1173	307	tpos2%=size;	1
0x1185	308	tempval=waveTable[tpos1]+waveTable[tpos2];	8
0x11C0	309	for(x=0;x<w;x++) {	57
0x11CD	310	tpos3%=size;	385
0x11DF	311	tpos4%=size;	580
0x11F1	312	result = tempval+waveTable[tpos3]+waveTab	221
0x122F	313	*(ppvBits+index)= (byte)result;	118
0x123B	314	index++;	57
0x123E	315	tpos3+=inc3;	38
0x1244	316	tpos4+=inc4;	22
	317	}	
0x125F	318	tpos1+=inc1;	5
0x1265	319	tpos2+=inc2;	
	320	}	

Function Summary				Sampling Results [GCARLET-...
Address	Size	Function	Class	Clockticks (347)
-----	-----	--- Selected Range ---	-----	
0xFCF	0x2FB	run	Plasma.Form1	1,497

Figure 9.27   C# Application in Sampling Source View

After switching to Disassembly view to investigate the assembly code shown in Figure 9.28, notice that Sampling information appears for each assembly instruction. A series of long latency penalties found by Static Analysis point to areas where the assembly code generated by the C# compiler could be more efficient.

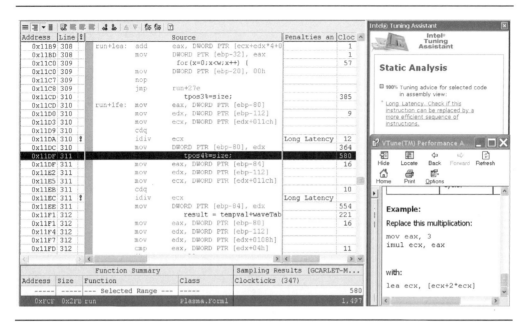

Figure 9.28 C# .NET Application in Sampling Mixed View

Call Graph Profiling for .NET Applications

In the .NET Framework development environment, you can use the VTune analyzer to generate a Call Graph profile of your .NET code. During profiling, the Just-In-Time compiler provides the VTune analyzer with information about active .NET classes and methods such as their memory addresses, sizes, and symbol information. The VTune analyzer uses the information to keep track of the executed processes and the classes and methods loaded into memory. At the end of profiling and data collection, the VTune analyzer creates an activity result with the collected data.

For Java and .NET applications, Call Graph uses the Java Virtual Machine Profiling Interface (JVMPI) and the .NET Profiling API, respectively, to collect performance data for managed code. By using instrumentation and the profiling APIs together, Call Graph can provide mixed mode performance data for both Java and .NET. Mixed mode profiling allows you to see how your managed code calls result in unmanaged code calls. However if you are only interested in Java and .NET method calls, you can use pure mode profiling.

Configuring .NET Call Graph Profiling

To configure an activity for a .NET application using the Call Graph Wizard under VTune Performance Analyzer 7.1 or later:

1. Click **Create New Project** to open the New Project dialog box.

2. Select **Call Graph Wizard** and click **OK** to open the Call Graph Configuration Wizard screen, shown in Figure 9.29.

3. Select **.NET Profiling** and click **OK** to move to the next screen.

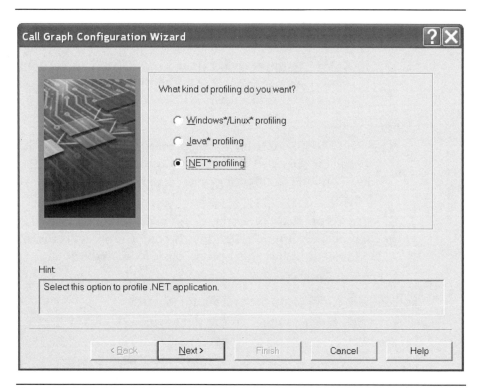

Figure 9.29   Selecting .NET Profiling in the 7.1 Call Graph Wizard

4. From the screen shown in Figure 9.30, you can choose to profile an executable, an executable launched by a script, an ASP.NET application, or an executable that interacts with a COM+ service you want to profile. Select one of the four application types for call profiling:

   – **Executable** to specify a .NET application. The VTune analyzer will launch the application.

   – **Script/batch invoking the application** to specify a script that launches a .NET application.

   – **ASP .NET** to specify an Active Server Page (ASP) .NET application executed under a system launched process.[2]

   – **COM+ Enterprise Services** to specify an application that interacts with the COM+ services that you want to profile, such as a COM+ service with .NET portions.

Optional steps:

5. Select **Modify default configuration when done with wizard** to launch **Advanced Activity Configuration** from the wizard and continue configuring your activity manually after you click **Finish**.

6. Select **Run Activity when done with wizard** to run the activity immediately after configuring the Call Graph collector. If you decide not to select this option, click **Run Activity** after Step 9 to start data collection.

To continue configuring the Call Graph Wizard:

7. Click **Next** to move to the next screen, which will vary depending on your previous selection.

   – If you selected **Executable** or **COM+ Enterprise Services**, enter the name (such as `HelloWorld.exe`) or browse for your .NET application in the **Application to Launch** field in the Step 1 of 2 screen.

   – If you selected **Script/batch invoking the** application, enter the name or browse for the script (`.cmd` or `.bat`) file in the **Launching script** field in the Step 1 of 2 screen.

---

[2] This is the only method of creating an activity for an ASP.NET application. You cannot create an activity for ASP.NET Web services using the Advanced Activity Configuration option.

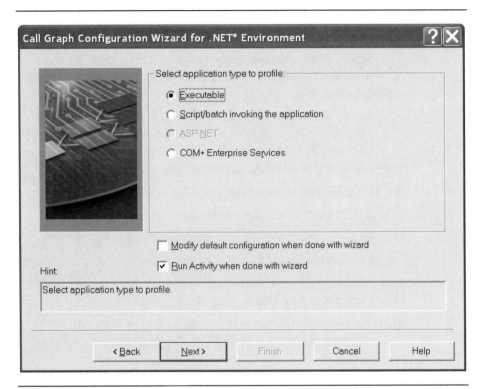

Figure 9.30   Selecting the .NET Launch Mode

If you selected **ASP .NET**, a message appears on the Step 1 screen warning that all IIS and IIS-dependent services will be restarted before the collection starts. Enter the name, such as `program.asp`, or browse for your ASP.NET worker process in the **Application to Launch** field in the Step 2 of 3 screen. If you want to collect Sampling data for ASP .NET Web Services remotely on a Windows system, click the **Remote** button on the Step 2 screen and specify the remote system as described in Chapter 10, "Remote Analysis."

The **Working directory** field automatically fills with the location of the file.

8. Click **Next** to move to the last step of the Call Graph Wizard, shown in Figure 9.31, and select the data collection mode:

   Select **.NET classes only** to get a Call Graph of your .NET program only *without* all the native DLLs that execute under the profiled process.

   Select **All .NET classes and all native modules** if you have calls from .NET functions to Windows functions, or vice versa. You will get a Call Graph of your .NET program *including* all the native DLLs that execute under the profiled process.[3]

9. Click **Finish** to close the Call Graph Wizard.

10. If necessary, click **Run Activity** to start data collection.

11. Launch your application if prompted.

    The VTune analyzer executes and profiles your .NET application together with other active Win32 modules in your application.

12. Click **Stop Activity** to stop data collection.

13. Double-click the activity result in the Tuning Browser to open the Call Graph views and analyze the performance of your .NET application.

    The VTune analyzer automatically displays .NET functions and Windows functions in the same Call Graph view. You can view .NET function calls to Win32 function calls and vice versa together in the same Call Graph.[3]

---

[3] For ASP.NET applications, you can only get pure .NET call graphs. Mixed mode of managed and unmanaged (native) code is not available.

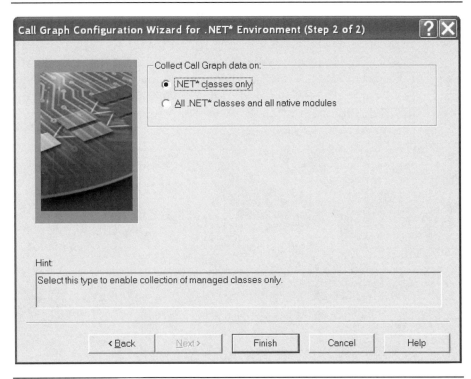

Figure 9.31   Selecting the .NET Collection Mode

Example 9.4: Analyzing a Visual C# .NET Call Graph

This example uses the same `Plasma` C# application as Example 9.3. To view these results firsthand, create your own Call Graph activity that profiles `plasma.exe`, and then run the sample C# application shown in Figure 9.23 as described earlier for Example 9.3.

Figure 9.32 shows the resulting Call Graph data collected in Graph view, with the JIT-compiled version of `Plasma.Form1.Run` selected in the Function Summary and graph. As shown in the example, the VTune analyzer enables you to see how your profiled JIT-compiled .NET code interacts with the C# runtime system code contained in the `mscorlib.dll.jit` module (the Microsoft C Runtime Library module). The Call Graph also allows you to view the call sequence to any non-managed, native DLLs that execute under your code.

By clicking on the Self-Time column heading to arrange functions in descending Self-Time order, you can see that most of the `Plasma.exe.jit` module's time of 8,482,980 was spent executing the `Plasma.Form1.Run` and `Plasma.Form1.OnPaint` methods. The `Plasma.Form1.Run` method spent more than half of its total time in its children, which are included in the Total Time of 10,269,428, but not in the Self Time of 4,279,832. Wait Time was not a factor, since it only amounted to 22,023 milliseconds.

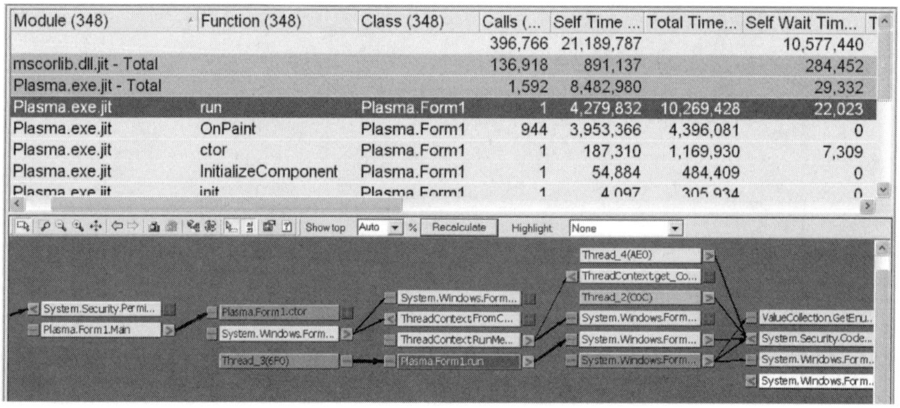

Module (348)	Function (348)	Class (348)	Calls (...	Self Time ...	Total Time...	Self Wait Tim...	T
			396,766	21,189,787		10,577,440	
mscorlib.dll.jit - Total			136,918	891,137		284,452	
Plasma.exe.jit - Total			1,592	8,482,980		29,332	
Plasma.exe.jit	run	Plasma.Form1	1	4,279,832	10,269,428	22,023	
Plasma.exe.jit	OnPaint	Plasma.Form1	944	3,953,366	4,396,081	0	
Plasma.exe.jit	ctor	Plasma.Form1	1	187,310	1,169,930	7,309	
Plasma.exe.jit	InitializeComponent	Plasma.Form1	1	54,884	484,409	0	
Plasma.exe.jit	init	Plasma.Form1	1	4,097	305,934	0	

Figure 9.32 A C# .NET Call Graph in Self-Time Order

Figure 9.33 shows the Call List view with `Plasma.Form1.Run` selected as the focus function. The `Refresh` function of the `System.Windows.Form.Controls` class and its chain of callees accomplished 55.9 percent of the work of `Run`, the focus function that called it.

You could then select `Refresh` as the focus function to investigate more about its callees, and discover that the `Invalidate` method contributed 99.9 percent of its time. As an alternative, you could switch to Call Graph view, find the `System.Windows.Form.Controls.Refresh` function after first clicking the Class column head to arrange classes in alphabetical order, and view the chain of callees graphically.

Function (348)	Class (348)	Calls (...	Self Time ...	Total Time...	Self Wait Tim...	Total Wait Tim...	Callers (..
		1,592	8,482,980			29,332	
run	Plasma.Form1	1	4,279,832	10,269,428	22,023	5,994,358	
OnPaint	Plasma.Form1	944	3,953,366	4,396,081	0	0	
ctor	Plasma.Form1	1	187,310	1,169,930	7,309	57,599	
InitializeComponent	Plasma.Form1	1	54,884	484,409	0	46,706	
init	Plasma.Form1	1	4,097	305,934	0	3,584	

Focus function							
	Plasma.exe.iit	run		Plasma.Form1	3	4,279,832	10,269,428	22

Caller Fun...	Contrib...	Edge Time	Edge Wait Time	Edge Calls	Class		Module	Full Name
Thread_3(...	100.0%	10,269,4...	5,994,358	1				

Callee Fun...	Contrib...	Edge Time	Edge Wait Time	Edge Calls	Class	Module	Full Name
Refresh	55.9%	5,736,765	5,719,504	943	System.Windows.Forms.Control	system.w...	virtual void
set_Priority	2.5%	252,831	252,831	1	System.Threading.Thread	mscorlib....	void Syster

Figure 9.33   C# .NET Call List View of Callers and Callees

Then you might select **Top 10 Self-Time** for highlighting with orange boxes, and click the graph to see the results. Another way to view key functions would be to select **Show Top 5%**, and click **Recalculate** to recalculate the graph as shown in Figure 9.34. Based on the Total-Wait Time of the `Invalidate` function, most of its execution time (and that of its children) was spent waiting while the thread was blocked.

If this information were important to you, you could right-click and select **Save Graph State**, so that later you could click **Restore Graph State** to retrieve it.

Class (348)	Calls (...	Self Time ...	Total Tim...	Self Wait Tim...	Total Wait Tim...	Callers
System.Windows.Forms.NativeWindow	5,727	22,247	4,782,610	0	0	
System.Windows.Forms.Control	945	5,721,557	5,733,501	5,719,504	5,719,504	
System.Windows.Forms.Control	943	2,055	5,736,765	0	5,719,504	
System.Windows.Forms.UnsafeNative...	1	4,573,377	9,133,643	4,498,712	4,498,712	
ThreadContext	1	7,506	9,286,892	0	4,498,712	
System.Windows.Forms.Application	1	3,279	9,292,138	0	4,498,712	
	136,918	891,137		284,452		
	29,656	59,940		23,708		

Show top 5 % Recalculate Highlight Top 10 Self Time

Plasma.Form1.run → System.Windows.For... → System.Windows.For...

Figure 9.34   Alternate Call Graph Views Showing Critical Paths

Figure 9.35 shows the `Plasma.Form1.Run` method in Source view. Notice that the Total Time, Self-Time, Calls, and similar columns appear in this view along with the source code.

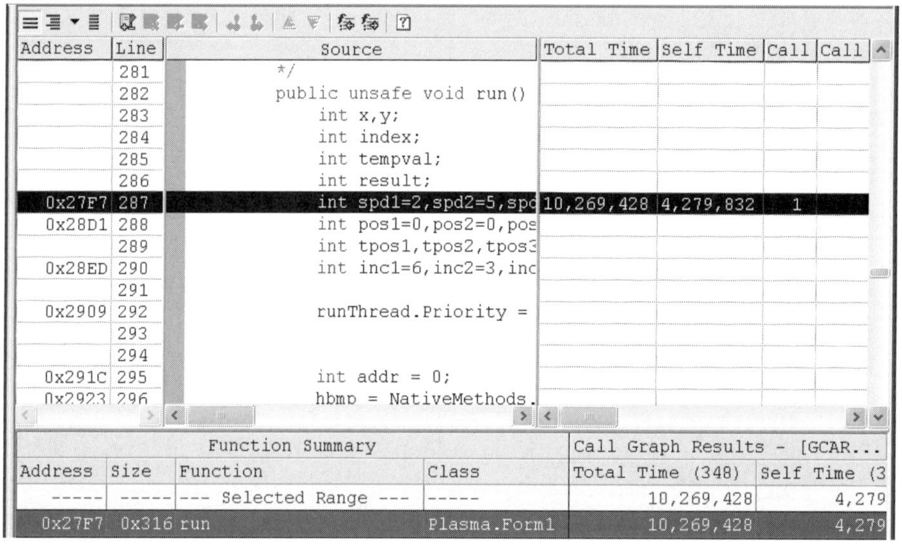

Figure 9.35 C# Application in Call Graph Source View

Analysis of Visual Basic Code

To analyze Visual Basic code, you need to avail yourself of the option to completely compile your VB code because Visual Basic does not support the correlation of interpreted code to source code. This is not a feature that the VB interpreter supports, so the VTune analyzer cannot provide the details it can when the code is compiled. Compile your code (not interpreted), and you will find it operates just like the C/C++ code examples. To generate base relocations for Visual Basic before Call Graph data collection, see Chapter 5. To generate symbol information for Microsoft Visual Basic .NET (VB.NET) technology projects, see Appendix A.

Recap

Here are some key points in this chapter:

- The VTune analyzer includes tailored Sampling and Call Graph wizard paths for applications running under Java and .NET runtime environments.

- In Sampling Module view, the VTune analyzer groups together all JIT-compiled Java or .NET methods into a single category represented by a single horizontal bar. You can drill down to Hotspot view to see individual methods.

- You can get a Call Graph that only shows pure Java or .NET code, or one that *includes* all the native DLLs that execute under the profiled process.

- VTune analyzer Call Graphs enable you to distinguish JIT-compiled from interpreted Java methods, and to examine the timing differences between each type of method.

- Code that you develop with a language compiler that targets the Common Language Runtime is called *managed code*. The VTune analyzer provides Managed Runtime Environment support for Microsoft's object-based *.NET Framework*.

- Before collecting Sampling or Call Graph data for a .NET application, make sure you have installed the Microsoft .NET Framework on your system.

Part IV
Advanced Topics

Chapter 10

Remote Analysis

Space isn't remote at all. It's only an hour's drive away if your car could go straight upwards.

— Fred Hoyle

The ability to conduct remote performance analysis is a clear advantage in shortening a product's time-to-market. Remote analysis permits you to launch and test program performance on a range of platforms from a single workstation. If you are running a Windows-based version of the Intel® VTune™ analyzer, you can collect performance data remotely from networked systems running under Windows, Linux, or WinCE. Not only can you profile other computers with Pentium® and Itanium® processors from your Windows-based workstation, you can also remotely profile and analyze smart handheld devices.

Next-generation mobile handheld devices are accelerating the delivery of wireless Internet applications and becoming an important new software development platform. Intel XScale® technology powers many of these new consumer devices, ranging from smart cellular phones to wireless personal digital assistants (PDAs). The programs running on these WinCE-based devices must be tuned and optimized just like any other, all the more so given their compact storage space. Even if you have no network connection, you can still collect data locally on a handheld device and then manually transfer the files to a Windows-based system running the VTune analyzer.

Table 10.1   Remote Analysis at a Glance

Feature	Support for Remote Analysis
Benefit at a glance	You can use the VTune™ analyzer to remotely collect and analyze performance data from networked Windows or Linux systems, as well as from many handheld PDAs and smart cell phones.
Versions	All current and recent versions of the VTune analyzer support remote analysis.
OS/Environments	Controlling systems: manual control is possible under Windows or Linux, but only the Windows versions support control from the GUI in a simple and easy to use interface Remote agent systems: Linux, Windows or Windows CE / CE .NET. For Sampling on a PDA device to take place, its WinCE image must have the PMU enabled.
Collectors	Remote Sampling and Call Graph profiling on Windows- and Linux-based systems. Remote Sampling on WinCE-based systems with Intel XScale® technology using one of three collection modes: Integrated (IRDC), Target (TLDC), or Standalone (SRDC).
Languages	All languages. Remote Java Sampling on IA-32 systems running Linux. Remote Java Call Graph for Java classes only.
Processors	Pentium® processors, Itanium® processors, and Intel processors with Intel XScale technology.

How Remote Data Collection Works

For remote data collection, you use a *controlling system* running under Microsoft Windows to collect data remotely from one or more *remote agent systems*. Each remote agent system can run on a different supported operating system. Currently supported operating systems are Windows, Linux, and WinCE. The controlling and remote agent systems must be networked so they can communicate with each other.

The controlling system and remote agent approach make this easy, but the same results can be managed manually by running the command line for data collection on a system and doing a pack-and-go, and then moving the data to another system to do analysis. The control/remote-agent does make this much easier and faster. Since previous chapters have already covered command line usage, it will not be reviewed here. Please keep them in mind if the limitations in support for control/remote-agent do not suit your system configurations.

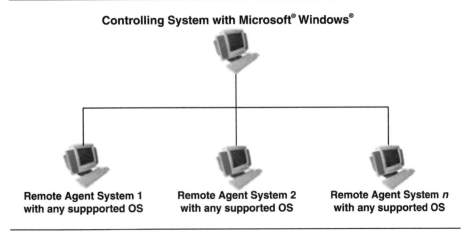

Controlling System with Microsoft® Windows®

Remote Agent System 1
with any suppported OS

Remote Agent System 2
with any supported OS

Remote Agent System *n*
with any supported OS

Figure 10.1 Controlling and Remote Agent Systems

Linux-based Remote Agents

You can remotely collect Sampling and Call Graph data from systems running Linux. Linux-based remote agents use a server program called vtserver to communicate with the VTune analyzer running on a Windows-based controlling system, as shown in Figure 10.2.

The vtserver program initializes the collectors on the remote agent system and listens on port 50000 by default for requests from the VTune analyzer on the controlling system. After data collection completes, vtserver sends any requested activity results back to the VTune analyzer.

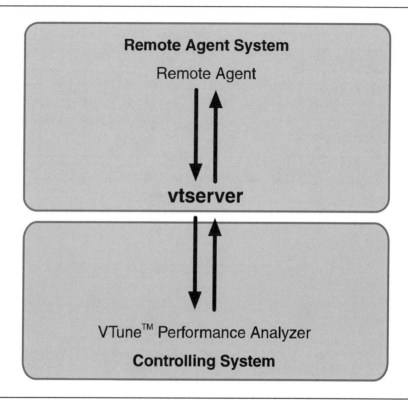

Figure 10.2   Linux-based Remote Agents Use `vtserver`

Windows-based Remote Agents

You can also remotely collect Sampling and Call Graph data from remote systems running Windows. Windows-based remote agents create the `VTRemote user` account, which is used to launch applications on the server side.

WinCE-based Devices with Intel XScale® Technology

The world of handheld devices changes daily. For you to perform VTune analyzer Sampling on Intel XScale technology-based devices such as PDAs and smart cell phones running WinCE, the device must have the Performance Monitoring Unit (PMU) enabled in the OS image. Currently, only certain PDA models, such as the Viewsonic V35, ship with the OS configured this way. As other vendors release new models with the PMU enabled, this restriction should go away. For the latest information, visit the Intel VTune analyzer Web site.

Another option is to use an Intel XScale development board. These boards typically provide multiple OS images with the PMU enabled. The boards usually come with all connection types on them to support creating any kind of device before the delivery of real hardware.

To help you tune your Intel XScale technology-based device, the VTune analyzer software offers a choice of two remote and one local method of configuring a Sampling activity:

- *Integrated Remote Data Collection (IRDC)* uses the Sampling wizard built into the VTune analyzer GUI that runs on your host/analysis system.

- The *Target Local Data Collection (TLDC)* utility (`VTuneTDC.exe`) runs on the target system.

- The *Standalone Remote Data Collection (SRDC)* utility (`XScVTuneHostDC.exe`) runs on the host system.

Integrated Remote Data Collection (IRDC)

With the integrated (IRDC) mode shown in Figure 10.3, you use the familiar VTune analyzer GUI on the Windows host to collect data remotely from an Intel XScale technology-based target. The remote agent server (`VTRemoteSvr.exe`) runs on the target. This method is similar to that used to collect remote data on Windows- and Linux-based systems, which makes for an easy learning curve. No serious data limitations exist with this method, since the collected data ultimately resides on the host. You can pack and unpack activities generated this way, unlike other modes.

A possible disadvantage is the increase in overhead, because data copy over to the host periodically during data collection. You can minimize this overhead by reducing the duration of the activity.

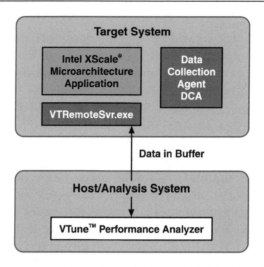

Figure 10.3   Integrated Remote Data Collection on an Intel XScale®
Technology-based System

Target Local Data Collection (TLDC)

With the target (TLDC) mode shown in Figure 10.4, you use the
VTuneTDC.exe data collection utility to create, configure, and run a Sampling activity locally on the Intel XScale technology-based target. You
transfer the data collected in two raw files, .rsf and .rmf files, to the
host/analysis system, and then use another utility to convert it into a single result file that you can open with the VTune analyzer.

An obvious disadvantage to this method is the time consumed by
manual transfers and conversions. The data collected cannot exceed the
FlashFile memory storage space, and you need an adequate display and
input method such as a keyboard or touch screen to configure the TLDC
utility on the target handheld system.

On the plus side, this method carries a lower overhead, since data
collection suspends while data copy to the local file. As a result, only
minimal invasion to target processor usage takes place during collection.
Obviously, no network connection is necessary for local data collection—making this solution a logical choice when no high-speed LAN or
USB connection exists.

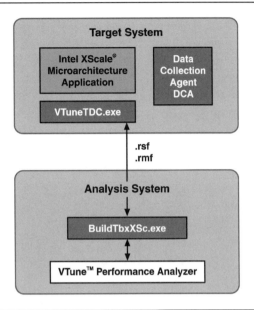

Figure 10.4 Target Local Data Collection (TLDC)

Stand-alone Remote Data Collection (SRDC)

With the stand-alone (SRDC) mode shown in Figure 10.5, you use the `XScVTuneHostDC.exe` data collection utility to create and configure the Sampling activity on the host system. The user interface for this utility resembles the one used for target mode but runs on the host instead. Consequently, you can use the host to start remote collection on the Intel XScale technology-based target. If necessary, you transfer this activity result to an *analysis system*, if different from the host, and then launch the VTune analyzer to view the data. This mode requires some type of *transport media* between the host and target for data collection. Possible choices are LAN, USB, or Batch File.

Like the integrated mode, the remote agent server `VTRemoteSvr.exe` runs on the target. Unlike the integrated mode, however, the host you use to start data collection need not have the VTune analyzer installed. No serious data limitations exist with this method, since the collected data ultimately reside on the host via LAN transfers.

A potential disadvantage to this method is the increase in overhead, because data copy over to the host system periodically during data collection if you have a LAN connection. You can minimize this overhead by adjusting the remote data collector's memory buffer size on the target.

Using the USB or Batch File option is similar to using the target mode. However, in this case, you use the host to create/open/configure an activity for the target, then transfer the configuration file to the target, run Sampling there, and move the results back to the host/analysis system for VTune analysis.

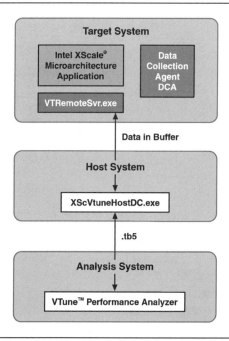

Figure 10.5   Stand-alone Remote Data Collection (SRDC)

Configuring Remote Agents for Data Collection

This section describes how to configure remote agents on target Linux-, Windows-, or WinCE-based systems to work with the VTune analyzer's integrated remote capability on the host. Later sections discuss target and standalone types of remote analysis on WinCE-based devices with Intel XScale technology.

Installing VTune™ Analyzer Software

Before performing remote analysis, make sure you have installed the right software on each system:

■ Install the full version of the VTune Performance Analyzer on a Windows-based *controlling system*. On this system, you can initiate remote data collection and use the VTune analyzer GUI to view the results collected from the remote agent systems.

■ Install the *remote agent*, a small set of files that includes a subset of the collectors, on the target system where the application you want to profile resides. Different operating systems require different files. To install the remote agent:

1. Log into your controlling system as the `root` user.

2. Insert the VTune Performance Analyzer installation CD in your CD-ROM drive.

   The Autorun page launches automatically.

3. Choose an option on the left panel based on the operating system on the remote system.

   When you install the remote agent, it copies to your hard drive.

4. Transfer these file(s) to the target system, uncompress the files, and run the installer.

5. Prepare the remote agent and possibly your application for remote data collection.

Preparing Remote Agents

The following section shows how to prepare and enable remote agents on target Linux-, Windows-, or WinCE-based systems.

Preparing Windows-based Remote Agents

To enable a Windows-based remote agent:

1. Insert the VTune Performance Analyzer CD into your CD-ROM drive.

2. Select the **Windows Agents** option.

   The Remote Agent Configuration - Password dialog box opens.

3. Type a password for the remote agent system and click **OK**. The remote and controlling systems must share the same password.

   The Accounts dialog box opens.

4. Select the account(s) to be used when logging into the controlling system(s) to collect data on the remote agent system. You can choose a group of users in addition to individual accounts. If you choose a local user account, it must have the same username and password as an account on the controlling system(s).

5. Reboot the remote agent system.

After enabling the remote agent, enable the Windows-based controlling system:

1. Log in as a user belonging to the account or group you specified when enabling the remote agent system.

2. Install the VTune analyzer and reboot the system.

3. Select the **Remote Agent Configuration Utility** option from the installation CD.

   The Remote Agent Configuration - Password dialog box opens.

4. Type the same password that you specified for the remote agent system.

5. Launch the VTune analyzer and use the Sampling or Call Graph wizard to configure remote data collection for the Windows-based target system:

Preparing Linux-based Remote Agents

Before starting data collection on a Linux-based remote agent, enable the remote agent:

1. Log in as the `root` user.

2. If the remote Linux agent has not been installed, obtain the setup `.tar` file from the VTune analyzer installation CD, copy it to the Linux system, unpack the file, and run the installer.

3. If you want to perform remote Linux Sampling, load the Sampling driver in the kernel (`vtune_drv-*.o`) before starting the remote agent.

4. Start the remote agent

    `/opt/intel/vtune/bin/vtserver -d /path/to/data/directory`

    where `-d` `/path/to/data/directory` specifies the location where you want to store transient, but potentially large, performance data. If this option is not given, the current working directory is used.

5. If necessary, run a remote file service. For example, if the Linux-based system is configured to export its file system through Samba (`http://www.samba.org`), start that service so the VTune analyzer can access source files from that file system. Otherwise, you transfer source files manually from the remote agent to the controlling system.

After enabling the remote agent, install and launch the VTune analyzer on the Windows-based controlling system and use the Sampling or Call Graph wizard to configure remote data collection for the Linux-based target system.

Preparing Intel XScale® Technology-based Remote Agents for IRDC

To enable the XScale technology-based remote agent using the integrated (IRDC) method:

1. Copy the Remote Agent for Intel XScale technology software from the controlling system to the target.

2. Start the `VTRemoteSvr.exe` remote server on the target:

    From the **Start** menu on the target system, select **Remote Agent** to launch the remote agent.

    A splash window displaying copyright information appears.

    The remote agent starts listening to the connection from the host, as shown in Figure 10.6.

Figure 10.6 Intel XScale® Technology-based Remote Agents Use
`VTRemoteSvr.exe`

After enabling the remote agent system, install and launch the VTune analyzer on the Windows-based controlling system. Use the Sampling wizard to configure remote data collection for the WinCE-based target system with Intel XScale technology.

Preparing to Run Java or ASP .NET Programs Interactively

By default, the remote system is set up to launch applications non-interactively, so that the VTune analyzer can collect data or invoke an executable without anyone logged into the remote system. This flexibility does, however, prevent interaction with an application's user interface, if one exists.

For situations that require interaction with an application remotely invoked through the VTune analyzer, you can manually configure the remote system to launch applications interactively. If you are using either the Microsoft Java launcher or ASP .NET Web services to launch your applications manually on the remote agent, set your application to launch interactively before configuring for remote data collection; otherwise, no `.jit` file entries will appear in Module view. See the Help files for details on launching programs interactively, either through DCOM on Windows-based systems (after setting up `dcomcnfg`), or using other methods on Linux-based systems.

Before You Begin Remote Data Collection

Here are some points to keep in mind when preparing to do remote data collection from a Linux system.

Run vtserver as a non-root user. If your files are located on a networked filesystem, such as through NFS, AFS, or Samba, restrictions may exist on root access to those files or directories containing those files. For this reason, it is a good idea to run vtserver as a *non-root* user. If multiple users need to use vtserver, add those users to a special group and make sure members of that group can access the relevant files and directories—then run vtserver as one of the non-root members of that group.

A firewall can block communication. Windows-to-Linux remote data collection uses TCP/IP communication over ports 50000 and 50001. A firewall between the two machines will probably block communication. If this happens, do one of the following:

■ Contact the firewall administrator to have communication on ports 50000 and 50001 turned on.

■ Remove the firewall between the machines.

Specifying Environment Variables. You can pass environment variables to your application using any of these approaches:

■ Set the environment variable in the shell where vtserver starts from, and then start vtserver. All environment variables known to vtserver will be passed to the launched application.

■ When configuring the application to launch in the VTune analyzer, select **New Project** → **Advanced Activity Configuration**. Under Application/Module Profile, select the application, select **Configure...**, click the **Advanced...** button, uncheck the **Use default environment** option, and then type lines in the form *variable=value*. Variables specified here will override matching ones inherited by the application from the vtserver program's environment.

■ Create a shell script that sets the variables and then runs the application. In the VTune analyzer, specify that shell script as the application to launch and specify the executable (not the shell script) as the module of interest. Make sure the directory where the executable resides is writable.

Configuring a Wizard on the Controlling System

Use a configuration wizard on the host system to create and configure an activity to collect data remotely:

1. From the VTune analyzer **File** menu, select **New Project** and select the wizard of your choice.

2. Select the type of profiling you want to do and click **Next**.

3. On the first step of the wizard, select the name or IP address of the remote agent system from the Machine Name pull-down list.

4. If you do not see the remote agent machine name or IP address in the Machine Name pull-down list, click the **Remote...** button to define the properties of the new machine.

   The Remote Target Configuration dialog box appears, as shown in Figure 10.7.

5. Enter the remote agent machine name such as `localhost` as shown in Figure 10.7, or the IP address such as `132.365.23.98` as shown in Figure 10.8.

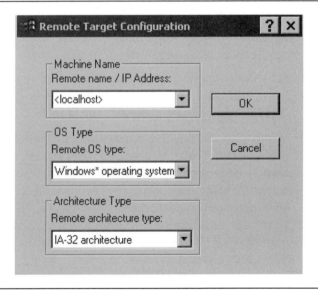

Figure 10.7   A Remote Agent Specified by Name

6. Select the operating system type and architecture type of the remote agent system, and click **OK** to return to the Step 1 screen of the wizard.

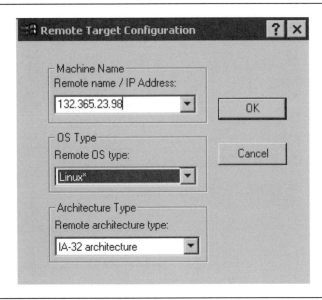

Figure 10.8   A Remote Agent Specified by IP Address

7. Enter the path and name of the application that you want to launch on the remote agent system, as in the following examples.

   – On a Windows-based remote agent:

   `C:\`*path*`\`*to*`\app.exe`

   – On a Linux-based remote agent:

   `/`*path*`/`*to*`/app.exe`

   `\\`*remote.machine.name*`\`*path*`\`*to*`\app.exe`

   – On a Windows CE-based remote agent with Intel XScale technology:

   `\path\to\app.exe`

   – For Java applications:

   `jview.exe` if using the Microsoft Java launcher

   `java.exe` if using the IBM or Sun Java launcher

   `appletviewer.exe` if using the IBM or Sun Java launcher to launch Java applets

   The VTune analyzer automatically populates the Working Directory field, as shown in Figure 10.9.

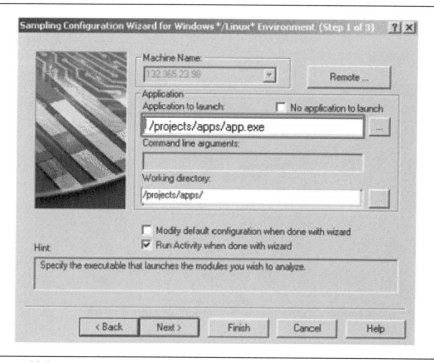

Figure 10.9 Specifying the Application to Launch

8. If necessary, add any additional modules of interest on a subsequent wizard screen.

9. Click **Finish** to start remote data collection.

Viewing Remotely Collected Data

During data collection, the VTune analyzer software automatically transfers performance data from the remote agent system to the controlling system, where you can use the VTune analyzer GUI to analyze the data. This view should look and feel just like local analysis has in prior chapters. One challenge arises from the issue of where the source code resides. Since the transferred data do not include binary or source files, you may be prompted for the location of binaries of modules or source files that that the VTune analyzer cannot automatically find. Use one of these techniques to retrieve the binary file from a Linux system:

- Through `vtserver`: the file location must be of the form `/path/to/the/binary` and must be accessible by the `vtserver` process

- Manually copy it from Linux to Windows using Windows file-name syntax:

  `DRIVE:\path\to\source`

- Export a remote Linux file system through a network using Windows filename syntax:

  `\\linuxMachineName\path\to\source`, if not mapped to a `DRIVE:` letter), or

  `DRIVE:\path\to\source`.

Similarly, use one of these techniques to retrieve the source file:

- Manually copy it from Linux to Windows using Windows file-name syntax.

- Export a remote Linux file system through a network using Windows filename syntax.

More About Sampling on Handheld Devices

Due to limitation of embedded devices, sampling of Intel XScale technology-based devices differs from other Intel platforms in a number of ways:

- Time-based sampling (TBS) is based on processor counters rather than the OS timer.

- The default buffer size is 500 Kb rather than 2,000 Kb.

- The default sampling interval is 1,000 microseconds instead of 1 millisecond.

- The default event selected for event-based sampling (EBS) is *Icache Miss* rather than *Clockticks* and *Instructions Retired*.

- Calibration is not enabled by default.

- Event ratios, Sampling Over Time, thread creation, the Tuning Assistant, and Call Graph profiling are not supported.

Table 10.2 summarizes the various ways to perform data collection on Intel XScale technology-based devices. Notice which stages take place on the host and which on the target using the various collection techniques.

Table 10.2 Different Types of Data Collection on Intel XScale® Technology-based Systems

Integrated Remote (IRDC)	Target Local (TLDC)	Standalone Remote (SRDC) with LAN	Standalone Remote (SRDC) with USB or Batch File
LAN Ethernet connection	No physical connection; use storage card for transfers	Select LAN transport media	Select USB or Batch File transport media Use USB or storage card for transfers
Configure using VTune™ analyzer GUI wizard on host `VTRemoteSvr.exe` on the target	Configure using `VTuneTDC.exe` utility on the target	Configure using `XscVTuneHostDC.exe` utility on the host `VTRemoteSvr.exe` on the target	Configure using `XscVTuneHostDC.exe` utility on the host
Activity results stored on host	Activity results stored on target	Activity results stored on host	Transfer the `.saf` file to the target via USB or storage card
Start Sampling from the Activity menu or taskbar icon	Use a batch utility (`VTBatchDC.exe`/ `VTBatchDCGUI.exe`) to launch the `.saf` file and start Sampling	Start Sampling from the Sampling menu of host	Batch: Use a batch utility to launch the `.saf` file and start Sampling USB: Use Remote Launcher on the host to launch the file (or batch utility that launches the `.saf` file) and start Sampling
Sampling results stored on host	Sampling results stored on target	Sampling results stored on host	Sampling results stored on target
	Transfer the two raw result files to host/analysis system via storage card	Raw result files automatically transferred to host	Transfer the two raw result files to host /analysis system via USB or storage card
	Use `BuildTbxXSC.exe` utility on host to convert raw files to `.tb5` format	Raw files automatically converted to `.tb5` format	Use `BuildTbxXSC.exe` utility on host to convert raw files to `.tb5` format
The VTune analyzer creates the `.tb5` Sampling result file automatically	Import the `.tb5` file into a VTune analyzer project to view and analyze the data	Import the `.tb5` file into a VTune analyzer project to view and analyze the data	Import the `.tb5` file into a VTune analyzer project to view and analyze the data

Example 10.1 Analyzing a PDA Using Target or Standalone Mode

Earlier you saw how to collect remote data from an Intel XScale technology-based handheld device using the integrated (IRDC) mode that is built into the VTune analyzer. This example walks you through the other two modes.

Starting Up the Data Collector

Although they run on different platforms, the target (TLDC) and standalone (SRDC) data collection utilities share a similar user interface and functionality. A few exceptions include differences in the menu orientation, the additional screen space present on the host system, and some additional steps specific to the SRDC utility.

To start up the Target Local Data Collection user interface `VTuneTDC.exe` on the target device, select **Start → Data Collector**.

To use the Standalone Remote Data Collection user interface `XScVTuneHostDC.exe` instead, do both/one of the following:

■ On the target device, select **Start → Remote Agent** to launch the remote agent as you would for the IRDC method. Refer to Figure 10.6.

A splash window displaying copyright information appears.

The remote agent `VTRemoteSvr.exe` starts listening to the connection from the host SRDC utility.

■ On the host/analysis system, launch the `XScVTuneHostDC.exe` data collector utility and configure the Transport Media Settings.

Figure 10.10 shows the Data Collector program icon that appears on a mobile handheld device if you use TLDC, or on a host that remotely controls the device if you use SRDC.

Figure 10.10 TLDC or SRDC Data Collector Program Icon

Configuring Transport Media Settings (SRDC Only)

The SRDC usage model requires some kind of connection to communicate between the target and the host. To configure this connection, follow these steps:

1. From the Data Collector dialog box, select **Settings → Transport Media Settings**.

   The Transport Media Settings dialog box opens as shown in Figure 10.11.

2. Select one of the three options and click **Next**.

   ■ **TCP/IP.** To use this option (the most typical), an Ethernet LAN connection (typically wireless) must exist from the target to the host. Type the IP address of the target (for example, `192.168.80.5`). The address on the host and target must match. After you click **OK**, a connection is attempted.

   ■ **Microsoft Platform Manager.** To use this option, the Microsoft Platform Manager software must be installed on the host and a USB connection with the target should exist via Microsoft ActiveSync.

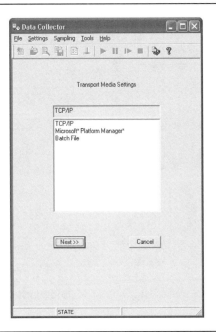

Figure 10.11 Transport Media Settings Dialog Box

■ **Batch File.** Use this option if you have no LAN or USB connection, and your target does not have enough real estate for data entry or does not support a data collector with a user interface.

Based on your selection, the appropriate Data Collector dialog box appears. Figure 10.12 shows the three possibilities. Choose values suitable to your facility and network environment.

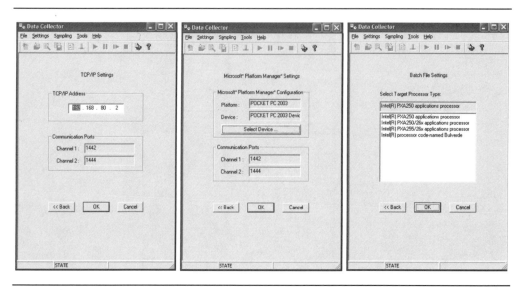

Figure 10.12 Transport Media Data Collector Configuration Choices

Creating an Activity

To create an activity using either the TLDC or SRDC user interface, follow these steps:

1. From the Data Collector dialog box, select **File → New Activity**.

    The New Activity Step 1 dialog box appears as shown in Figure 10.13.

2. Type the activity name and folder or use the defaults.

3. For the TLDC user interface, select the Location for the results: **Main Memory** or **Storage Card**.

4. Click **Next**.

    The New Activity Step 2 dialog box appears as shown in Figure 10.14.

5. Type the name of the program and any command parameters you want to use.

6. Click **Next**.

    The New Activity Step 3 dialog box appears as shown in Figure 10.15.

Figure 10.13 New Activity Step 1 Dialog Box

Figure 10.14 New Activity Step 2 Dialog Box

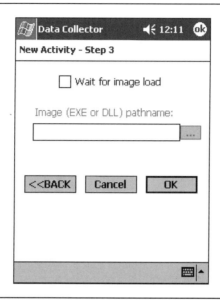

Figure 10.15 New Activity Step 3 Dialog Box

7. If you want to closely examine a .dll or .exe file, check the **Wait for Image Load** box and type its path and name. Use this feature to tune a specific binary image at a precise start time, especially one that cannot be executed directly such as a .dll file.

8. Click **OK** to create an activity.

9. Select **File** → **Save Activity** to save the activity result in an .saf file.

Configuring Other Sampling Settings

Using either the TLDC or SRDC user interface, you can configure other Sampling settings for the activity or just use the defaults:

1. From the Data Collector dialog box, select **Settings** → **Configuration Settings**.

   The Configure Settings dialog box appears with options displayed on various tabs.

2. From the **General Settings** tab shown in Figure 10.16, specify the sampling method: time-based (**TBS**, the default), event-based (**EBS**), or **Both**.

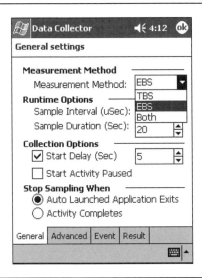

Figure 10.16 Selecting the Measurement Method

3. On the **Advanced** tab shown in Figure 10.17, use the Max. Memory size as a reference for adjusting the size of the **Sample Buffer** and the **Module Buffer**, if necessary. Small buffer sizes can cause the data collector to frequently flush the buffer to file, which can negatively impact system performance.

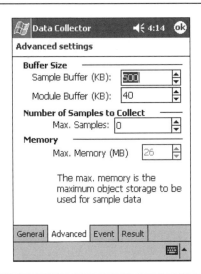

Figure 10.17 Adjusting the Buffer Size

4. From the **Event** tab shown in Figure 10.18, select the events you want to monitor, or use the default: *ICache miss*.

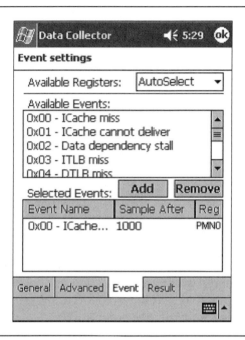

Figure 10.18 Selecting Events to Monitor

5. Click **OK** in the top right corner to close the dialog box.

The data collector utility configures the Sampling collector and creates (or modifies) the activity result in an .saf file.

Starting Sampling

Depending on your collection method and host/target interface, you can start Sampling using one of three ways:

■ If you are using the SRDC user interface and have a LAN connection:

From the Data Collection dialog box on the host, select **Sampling** → **Start** to start collecting data on your remote target system.

Stop, **Pause**, and **Resume** options are also available from this menu.

■ If you are using the TLDC user interface, or if you are using the SRDC user interface and manually transferred the .saf file from the host to the target:

Use one of the batch utilities to launch the .saf file and start Sampling:

– Use the non-interactive **VTBatchDC.exe** utility on a target device that does not support a GUI. It collects data using the .saf file without displaying any status messages, but does create a .log file that you can later review.

– Use the **VTBatchDCGUI.exe** utility on a target device that supports a GUI. When you launch this utility from the **Start** menu, it prompts you for the .saf file. Use the **Up** and **Down** buttons on a device such as the one shown in Figure 10.19 to highlight the directory and file, and use the **OK** button to make selections.

Figure 10.19   An Intel XScale® Technology-based Smart Cell Phone with a GUI

A splash window pops up, as shown in Figure 10.20, with status messages about the starting and stopping of calibration or sampling.

The activity executes, launches the program and Sampling data collector, and starts collecting the data, saving it in system memory or on a storage card. The batch utilities do not support any start or stop options from the Sampling menu or any predefined start and stop conditions.

Figure 10.20 Batch Data Collector Splash Screen

■ If you are using the SRDC user interface, you can launch target files remotely from your host via a USB host-to-target ActiveSync connection:

– Transfer the activity (.saf) file from the host to the target using ActiveSync or a storage card.

– From the Data Collection dialog box on the host, select **Tools → Remote Launcher**.

The Remote Launcher dialog box appears.

– In the Executable Image Path field, type the name of the file that you want to launch on the target. If you specified Batch File as your transport media, specify the path and name of one of the batch utilities, **VTBatchDC.exe** or **VTBatchDCGUI.exe**.

- In the Arguments field, specify the required command line arguments. For a batch file, specify the configuration file name (-saf) and the (-log) options as shown in Figure 10.21.
- Click the **Launch** button.

  The remote launcher launches the specified application on the target system.

A successful Sampling run creates these files in the working directory:

■ *ResultName*.rsf (raw sample file)

■ *ResultName*.rmf (raw module file)

■ *ActivityName*.log (log file)

■ *ActivityName*.saf (contains changes that occurred during calibration or sampling)

■ *ActivityName*.old.saf (backup of the original .saf file)

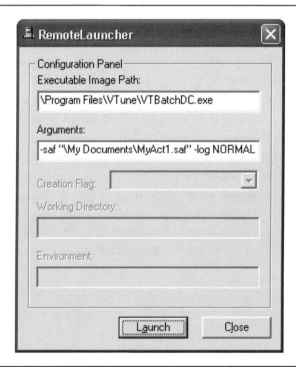

Figure 10.21 SRDC Remote Launcher Screen

Locating, Converting, and Viewing Result Files

An SRDC activity run generates Sampling results on the host. A TLDC activity run generates Sampling results on the target.

To locate activity result files:

1. From the Data Collection dialog box on the host or target, select **Settings** → **Configure** to open the Configure Settings dialog box.

2. Select the **Result** tab shown in Figure 10.22 to view the location and name of the result files.

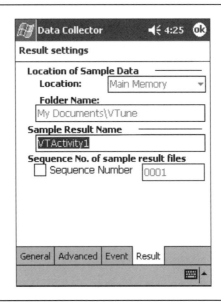

Figure 10.22 The Results Tab Shows the Location of the Result Files

If you have a LAN connection, the data collector automatically transfers the raw result files, `.rsf` and `.rmf`, to the host and generates a viewable `.tb5` file in the result folder, whose default location is `C:\VTune`.

If you have a USB connection, transfer the raw result files from the target to the analysis/host system using ActiveSync or a storage card.

3. If necessary, use the `BuildTbxXSC.exe` console utility to combine the raw results and convert them to a `.tb5` file. By default, this utility is located in:

`\program files\Intel\VTune\RDC for XSC\Host`

At the command line prompt, in the directory that contains the result files, type:

BuildTbxXSC *ResultName*.rsf *ResultName*.rmf *ResultTBxName*.tb5

substituting the actual names for your result files. You can omit the file extensions.

To view the activity results on the analysis system:

1. Launch the VTune analyzer and select **File → Open File**.

2. In the Files of Type field, select **Sampling Result Files**.

3. Select the `.tb5` file you want to open and click **Open**.

   The **Import** dialog box opens.

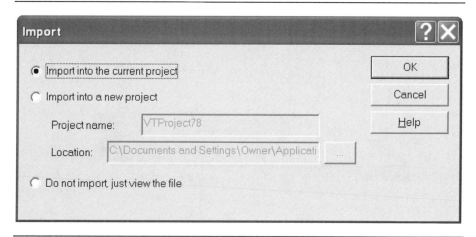

Figure 10.23 Selecting a Sampling Result File to Import

4. Choose whether to just view the `.tb5` file or import it into a new or existing project and click **OK**.

   The results open in Sampling view.

Recap

To recap, here are some key points in this chapter:

■ The Windows version of the VTune analyzer allows you to remotely collect performance data from a networked computer by using your Windows machine to control the activity of a remote agent.

■ You can collect Sampling or Call Graph data from a remote Linux- or Windows-based computer using remote control or manually with command line capabilities.

■ You can use integrated, target, or standalone mode to collect Sampling data from a WinCE-based handheld device such as a PDA.

Chapter 11

Handling Some Special Needs

The cause is hidden. The effect is visible to all.

—Ovid

This chapter looks at two special situations you may encounter. The first is the very common situation in which you want to analyze only part of your application, in order to focus your work with the VTune™ analyzer. The second is when you need to analyze code in a device driver or operating system.

Table 11.1 Partial Analysis at a Glance

Feature	Support for Partial Analysis of an Application or OS
Benefit at a glance	You can use the VTune™ analyzer to analyze part of an application or operating system that you are interested in, thereby allowing you to focus on areas of concern to you.
Versions	Pause/Resume API: All versions of VTune analyzer for local analysis. Windows Version 7.1 or later required for remote sampling on Linux.
OS/Environments	Windows and Linux operating systems
Collectors	Remote and local data collection.
Languages	Not language dependent, although the interfaces supplies require C language access.
Processors	Pentium® and Itanium® processors, not currently supported on processors with Intel XScale® technology.

Analyzing Only Parts of Your Application

At times, you may find it useful to restrict your analysis to specific regions of code or specific phases of execution that are of particular interest. For example, you may want to:

■ Avoid generating an excessive amount of profiling data. Unnecessarily large amounts of data take longer to process and can make isolating a performance issue more difficult.

■ Avoid unnecessary overhead. Collecting data over the entire life cycle of a server application, for example, would contribute to overhead by repeatedly causing writes to the hard disk to store results.

■ Overlook how your application performs during a particular time such as startup, because that activity does not represent typical operation or significant processing.

■ Focus on certain predictable areas of interest, such as inside an algorithm, during I/O to disk, or when accessing the network.

The VTune analyzer gives you multiple ways to achieve partial analysis. One method is to use checkboxes and buttons built into the VTune analyzer graphical user interface. Another method is to embed program calls into your source code. You can use these techniques separately or together.

Start Delays

In some cases, you may want to control the starting and stopping of analysis. The VTune analyzer user interface includes options to delay data collection for so many seconds or to stop it under certain circumstances. Figure 11.1 shows some configuration options that appear on the General tab for delaying data collection or stopping it under given conditions. In addition, when configuring an activity, you have the opportunity to specify the exact duration of data collection in seconds.

Configure Sampling

General | Event Ratios | Events |

Sampling Mechanism

  ○ Time-based sampling (TBS)

   TBS based on: OS Services

  ● Event-based sampling (EBS)

   ● Calibrate Sample After Value based on the selected

   ○ Calibrate Sample After Value for all the selected ever

   ○ Don't Calibrate Sample After Value

Sampling Collection Options

  Sampling interval: 1   millisecond(s)

  Sampling buffer size: 2000   KB

  ☑ Delay sampling: 30   second(s)
  ☑ Track thread creation
  ☑ Terminate application when Activity ends
  ☑ Display sampling results over time

Stop Collection

  ☐ When application terminates (before duration completes)
  ☐ Maximum samples collected: 0

Configure Counter Monitor

Counters | Triggers | General |

Stop Collection:

  ☐ When application terminates (before duration completes)

  ☑ Terminate application when Activity ends

Collection Options

  ☑ Delay monitoring 30   second(s)

Figure 11.1   Options on the General Tab for Delaying or Stopping Data Collection

Pause/Resume Buttons

You can also interactively disable and enable data collection while running an activity by using the **Pause/Resume Activity** button on the main taskbar, which acts as a toggle.

Typically, if you plan on using this button, you would check **Start with data collection paused** on the Advanced Activity Configuration dialog box, and then click the **Pause/Resume Activity** button when the section of your program that you want to profile begins to run.

The command line equivalent to this is the **ActivityController** command, which supports -pause and -resume options. For the Linux command line, this support has so far been limited to call graph data collection.

Program Control: Pause/Resume API

From within a C/C++ program, the Pause and Resume API gives you control over when the VTune analyzer performs data collection. You can use these API calls to pause and resume data collection during sampling, Call Graph, or Call Monitor.

For example, if during sampling you wish to focus analysis on the measured portion of your application, you can incorporate Pause and Resume calls into your application to save samples during normal operation but avoiding the startup and shutdown portions of your application. A very crude but effective alternative is to use the option in sampling set up to delay the start of sampling and to have sampling end before the application. If you want to do anything more precise or complex, it becomes obvious why the Pause and Resume API is so useful.

Example 11.1 Pausing and Resuming Data Collection

To see how the Pause and Resume API works, create an activity and configure a data collector (Sampling, Call Graph, or Counter Monitor) using the Advanced Activity Configuration wizard.

To use the Pause and Resume API, you must include the `VTuneApi.h` header file in your application and link to the `vtuneapi.lib` before compiling and executing your application to collect data. You can find the `VTuneApi.h` file in the `...\analyzer\include` folder and the `vtuneapi.lib` file in the `...\analyzer\lib` folder. For applications running on Itanium® processor-based systems, use `VtuneAPI64.lib` instead of `vtuneapi.lib`.

The Pause and Resume API is clearly designed and supported for C and C++ programmers, but the API can be used by any program that can call these C language interfaces.

Change the Source File

You can target specific sections in your application that you would like to profile by inserting the `VTPause()` and `VTResume()` API calls in your code. Make these changes to your C/C++ source code to incorporate the Pause and Resume API.

1. Include a VTune analyzer header file:

    ```
    #include "vtuneapi.h"
    ```

2. Insert calls to `VTResume()` to resume recording data:

```
// Resume VTune analyzer data collection - focus on
// the following code
VTResume();
```

3. Insert calls to `VTPause()` to pause recording data:

```
// Pause VTune analyzer data collection - focus on
// the above code
VTPause();
```

Build Your Project

Once you have included references to the APIs in your source code, resolve these references by building your project with the location of the header and library files.

In a Windows development environment such as Microsoft Visual Studio, the steps are:

1. Use the `/I` option to specify *VTune-installation-directory*`Analyzer\Include` as an additional include directory for the compile phase. For a default installation, use:

```
/I "C:\Program Files\Intel\VTune\Analyzer\Include"
```

2. Likewise, use the `/libpath` option to specify *VTune-installation-directory*`\Analyzer\Lib` as an additional library path for the link phase. For a default installation, use:

```
/libpath:"C:\Program Files\Intel\VTune\Analyzer\Lib"
```

3. Finally, add the `VTuneAPI.lib` library to the list of linker input modules. For applications running on Itanium processor-based systems, use `VtuneAPI64.lib` instead.

The Linux environment expects similar information, so you specify the path to the include file with `-I`, the path to the library file with `-L` and add the linkage to the library with `-lVtuneApi -ldl`.

Since the API library requires the `DL` library, refer to this library as well. For a default VTune analyzer installation, for example, you would include the switches in this example:

```
gcc -O2 -g -I/opt/intel/vtune/analyzer/include
-o gzip gzip.o zip.o deflate.o trees.o bits.o unzip.o
inflate.o util.o crypt.o lzw.o unlzw.o unpack.o
unlzh.o getopt.o match.o
-L/opt/intel/vtune/analyzer/bin -lVtuneApi -ldl
```

Start with Data Collection Paused

To avoid recording data collected during your application's initialization code, start the activity with data collection paused. To do so, check the **Start with data collection paused** option on the Advanced Activity Configuration dialog box when configuring or modifying an activity, as shown in Figure 11.2.

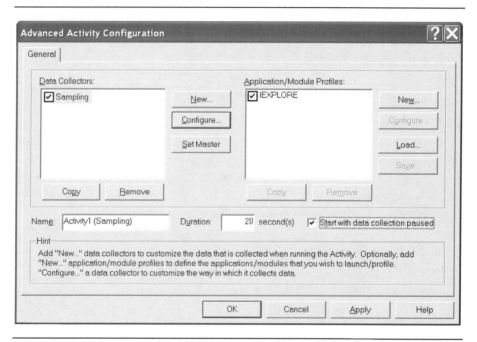

Figure 11.2   Check the Start with Data Collection Paused Checkbox

Run Your Program

After compiling and executing your application, click **Run Activity** to start data collection. When your program runs, data collection only begins after the Resume API call in your code executes (or you press the **Pause/Resume Activity** button). Calls to the Pause and Resume API change the value of a program flag. The appearance of the **Pause/Resume Activity** button updates onscreen after this program flag changes. The onscreen update in appearance may occur with a noticeable delay, nevertheless, data collection pauses or resumes exactly as directed by the embedded calls in your program.

Calibration and Pause and Resume

Calling the Pause and Resume API affects the recording of data but does not impact automatic calibration. During automatic calibration, the VTune analyzer counts events and then modifies the Sample After Value to collect about the same number of samples as *Clockticks* samples—roughly 1000 samples per processor per second.

Since calibration ignores the Pause and Resume API, the VTune analyzer may collect too many or too few samples in the unpaused portion of the code. With too many samples, the code to handle event interrupts and collect sample data may noticeably slow application or system performance, thereby affecting the results. With too few samples, the VTune analyzer may not have enough data to identify hotspots.

Figure 11.3 shows the total samples for a sample run before adding calls to `VTPause()` and `VTResume()`. Notice that the total samples for *64k Aliasing Conflicts* (19,711) is close to the total samples for *Clockticks* (20,863). In this example, the test system has a Pentium® 4 processor supporting Hyper-Threading Technology and thus two logical processors. You can see that the VTune analyzer captured approximately 2,000 samples per second, or 1,000 samples per logical processor per second.

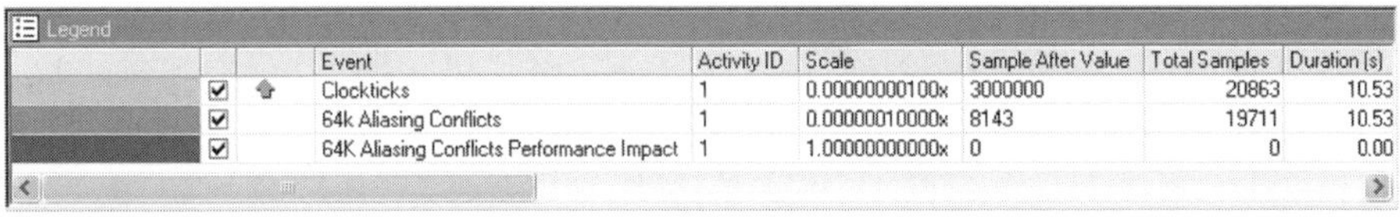

		Event	Activity ID	Scale	Sample After Value	Total Samples	Duration (s)
☑	⬆	Clockticks	1	0.0000000100x	3000000	20863	10.53
☑		64k Aliasing Conflicts	1	0.0000010000x	8143	19711	10.53
☑		64K Aliasing Conflicts Performance Impact	1	1.0000000000x	0	0	0.00

Figure 11.3   Example with Automatic Calibration

When using the Pause and Resume API and automatic calibration, check the total samples for other events to make sure they are close to the total number of samples for *Clockticks*. Figure 11.4 shows the results for this example after adding Pause and Resume to limit Sampling. Notice that the Sample After Values are similar to those in Figure 11.3 because calibration ignores Pause and Resume.

		Event	Activity ID	Scale	Sample After Value	Total Samples	Duration (s)
☑	⬆	Clockticks	2	0.00000001000x	3000000	3299	10.61
☑		64k Aliasing Conflicts	2	0.00000010000x	7860	17041	10.61
☑		64K Aliasing Conflicts Performance Impact	2	1.00000000000x	0	0	0.00

Figure 11.4   Example with Pause and Resume Calls

The total samples for *64k Aliasing Conflicts*, however, are far from the total samples for *Clockticks*. This is a case where you need to use manual calibration by specifying the Sample After Value yourself.

Manual Calibration

To determine a new Sample After Value for the *64k Aliasing Conflicts* event:

1. First, determine the total number of *64k Aliasing Conflicts* events. You can find out the total number of events by multiplying the Sample After Value by the Total Samples. For *64k Aliasing Conflicts*, the total number of events is $7,860 \times 17,041 = 133,942,260$.

2. Determine the new Sample After Value by dividing this result by the number of *Clockticks* samples. Therefore, the new Sample After Value for *64k Aliasing Conflicts* should be $133,942,260 \div 3,299 = 40,600$.

To manually change the Sample After Value for an event:

1. Right-click the activity in the Tuning Browser, select **Modify Collectors...**, and click **OK**.

2. If necessary, select **Sampling** as the data collector, and click **Configure**.

3. Select the **Don't Calibrate Sample After Value** option on the **General** tab, as shown in Figure 11.5.

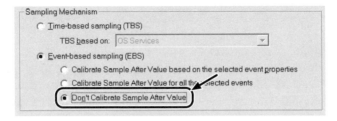

Figure 11.5   Turning Off Automatic Calibration

4. After turning off automatic calibration, select the **Events** tab and click inside the **Sample After Value** field for the event you wish to change. Figure 11.6 shows the field selected before changing its value.

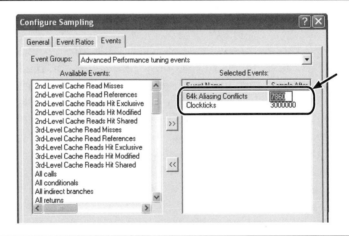

Figure 11.6   Modifying the Sample After Value

5. Type the new calculated value.

6. Run the activity and your program again.

    Figure 11.7 shows the results collected after manually modifying the Sample After Value to 40,600.

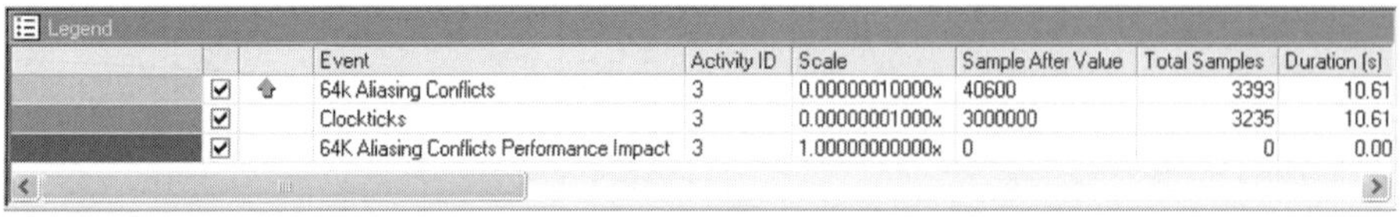

Legend

			Event	Activity ID	Scale	Sample After Value	Total Samples	Duration (s)
	☑	⇧	64k Aliasing Conflicts	3	0.00000010000x	40600	3393	10.61
	☑		Clockticks	3	0.00000001000x	3000000	3235	10.61
	☑		64K Aliasing Conflicts Performance Impact	3	1.00000000000x	0	0	0.00

Figure 11.7 Results After Manually Modifying the Sample After Value

Notice that the total samples for *Clockticks* and *64k Aliasing Conflicts* are close. On a system with two logical processors, the approximate 3,200 *Clockticks* samples indicate that data collection was unpaused for approximately 1.6 seconds or 1,600 milliseconds. So, even though the duration is reported as 10.61 seconds, data was only collected for 1.6 seconds, during the time period when data collection was unpaused.

Analyzing Code Incorporated in the OS

During Sampling, the VTune analyzer tracks the number of samples taken at two privilege levels of execution. *Ring 0* is the highest privilege level and is the level at which the operating system kernel runs (kernel mode). *Ring 3* is the lowest privilege level and is the level at which user applications run. Some device drivers run at Ring 0; others at Ring 3.

Figure 11.8 illustrates how you can drill down to see hotspots in operating system code just as you would any application. The figure shows `memmove` to be the hotspot function in the NT-OS kernel `ntoskrnl.exe`, running under the Windows Client/Server Runtime Server Subsystem `csrss.exe`.

The additional window pane came from the Selected Items feature. When moving between various views such as Process, Thread, Module, Hotspot, and Source view, you can see a hierarchy of items already viewed in previous screens by clicking on the vertical column labeled Selected Items on the left side of the data pane. This sub-pane toggles open or closed each time you select it. In this case, the user selected `csrss.exe` in Process view and `ntoskrnl.exe` in Module view before arriving at the Hotspot view shown here.

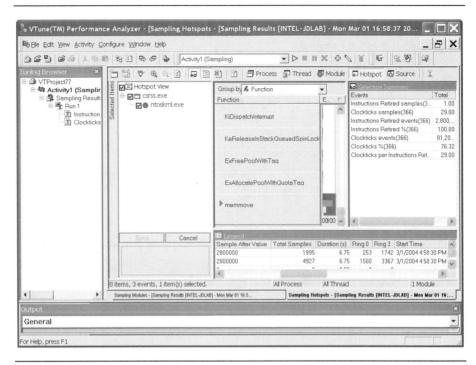

Figure 11.8   Hotspot View of Some Operating System Functions

Issues with Ring 0, Device Drivers, and Kernels

For the most part, analyzing and tuning the performance of Ring 0 code is no different from analyzing any other type of code. The VTune analyzer is a tool to identify bottlenecks and improve performance in all software—not just in applications, but also in kernel mode device drivers.

The Sampling data collector collects system-wide performance data non-intrusively. Time-based sampling uses interrupt-based, instruction-pointer techniques to monitor all active software on your system, including the operating system, device drivers, and application software. As a natural result of this system-wide sampling, the VTune analyzer gathers samples in Ring 0 drivers just as it does in applications. Sample interrupts do occur in Ring 0; in particular, Microsoft Windows XP, NT and 2000 use very high priority interrupts.

Not only can the VTune analyzer find execution bottlenecks for device drivers, it can also track all of the performance sensitive CPU events available in Event-Based Sampling such as cache misses and misaligned data access. You can drill all the way down to source code and assembly language code for device drivers just as for applications. In addition, Counter Monitor operating system counters and Static Assembly Analysis also work with drivers.

Limiting Event Sampling to Ring 0 or Ring 3 Only

A very useful feature is the ability for the sampling driver to look at events only when the occur in Ring 0 or only in Ring 3. If you monitor events from Ring 0 only, as shown in Figure 11.9, you can focus on events happening exclusively inside the device driver or operating system.

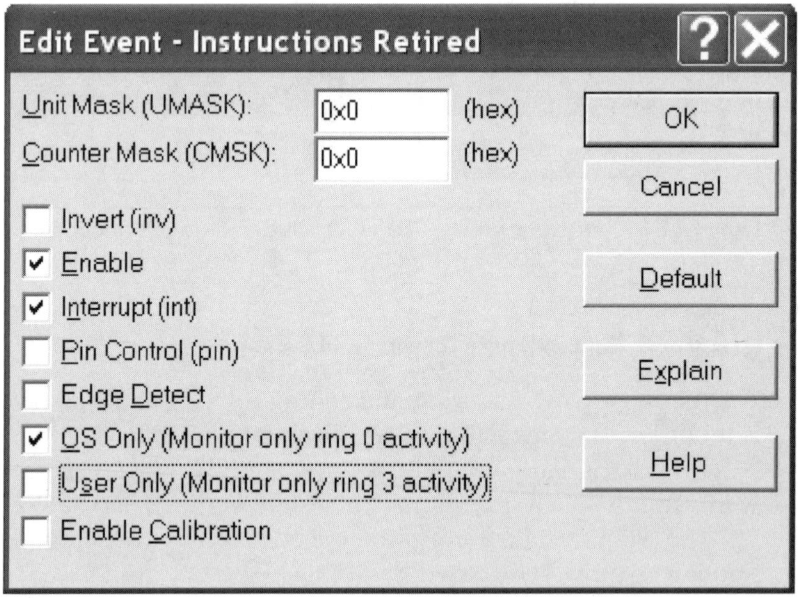

Figure 11.9   Ignoring Ring 3 Monitoring for a Specific Event

A Few Caveats

Despite these similarities, a few caveats arise when tuning parts of an operating system such as device drivers:

- You cannot use the Call Graph collector to profile Windows device drivers. Call Graph runs at Ring 3 and communication between Ring 0 and Ring 3 is very costly in terms of performance. Consequently, at run time when doing Call Graph analysis, the VTune analyzer only instruments and collects data about Ring 3 applications.

- You cannot directly invoke the binary file of a device driver, DLL, or OCX. To analyze such a binary file, specify the name of an executable that will invoke the file you are interested in. In other words, use the VTune analyzer to run an application that uses the driver. Do one of the following when configuring the Sampling collector:

  – Choose an application that launches the binary file so that the VTune analyzer automatically invokes that application.

  – Select **No application to launch** and invoke the application manually.

- You should not try to access the Pause and Resume APIs except from Ring 3 code.

- As with any application, the VTune analyzer needs a symbol file and access to a Ring 0 file's source code in order to display source code. If you are unable to compile the code in this manner, you will be treated to the disassembly view instead of source code when you drill down in your analysis.

Recap

To recap, here are some key points in this chapter:

- You can pause and resume a program's execution during data collection to capture performance data in a focused manner.

- You can collect for operating system code, such as device drivers, just as you would any application.

- You can limit event sampling to Ring 0 only code.

Chapter **12**

Threaded Programs: Correctness

The future is a hundred thousand threads, but the past is a fabric that can never be rewoven.

— Orson Scott Card

In 2003, Intel introduced a very interesting new tool called Intel® Thread Checker that combines the VTune™ analyzer technology with some new technologies for finding threading errors. The first version focused on Windows threads, but more recent additions to this product family include support for Linux and pthreads. While not a performance analysis tool, because of its strong ties to the technologies in the analyzers and the fact that current versions share GUI controls, it is important to devote a chapter to introducing this tool. An entire book could be written about threading and Intel Thread Checker, so this chapter must only whet your appetite for more.

Threaded applications have become more common in recent years as Hyper-Threading Technology hardware and software has evolved. Testing these applications, each of which executes as a collection of threads, has proven to be a challenge. Fortunately, Intel Thread Checker is an automated tool that is now available to simplify the task.

Intel Thread Checker automatically locates software threading correctness issues such as race conditions, stalls, and deadlocks. In the first field trials of Intel Thread Checker, the tool accurately detected real threading bugs in more than half of the commercially available applications on which it was tested. In each instance, the companies that designed the applications found the error when they tried the tool, and they each chose to change their program to correct the error in their next shipment.

Intel introduced Intel Thread Checker in 2003, based on an earlier tool from Kuck and Associates, Inc. (KAI) called Assure. Intel acquired KAI in part for this technology, which instruments a program and determines where it *could* fail due to coding errors. The fact that Intel Thread Checker can find potential failures, even when they do not cause actual failures in testing, makes it a very exciting tool.

It is not possible to successfully catch every problem by trying to provide all the hardware and software configurations that set up the proper timing conditions to induce a threaded-program failure. Many threaded programs ship having passed all tests, only to discover intermittent failures on customer machines, which then prove very difficult to reproduce and trace back to the source.

Table 12.1   Intel® Thread Checker at a Glance

Feature	Thread Checking
Benefit at a glance	Automatically locate thread synchronization errors in a program
Versions	An extra cost add-on for some versions of Linux
OS	All versions: Windows[†] operating system Starting version 3.0: Linux[†] operating systems
Collectors	Remote and local data collection on Windows Remote only for Linux
Languages	All compiled languages, dependent on threading models instead Win32 threads for Windows, pthreads for Linux
Processors	Pentium® processors No support (yet) for Itanium® processors, or Intel® processors with Intel XScale® technology

About Intel® Thread Checker

Use Intel Thread Checker in the VTune Performance Environment to locate errors in your multithreaded programs that employ Microsoft[†] Windows[†] 32-bit threading or OpenMP[†] threading. Thread Checker identifies errors induced by the nondeterministic scheduling of thread execution.

Multiple threads can create a situation where more than one thread simultaneously accesses the same memory location (variable). This type of race condition is known as a storage conflict or a *data race*. Data races can cause erratic program behavior and lead to indeterminate results.

Deadlock is another type of race condition in which a thread waits for a resource that it can never acquire or an event that will never happen. Bad locking hierarchies—where two threads hold separate locks and need to obtain the lock held by the other—can also deadlock threads. Thread Checker identifies the following types of errors and potential issues:

- *Data race.* A situation where two threads can potentially access the same memory location in an unpredictable order.

- *Deadlocks.* A thread is deadlocked when it is waiting for a critical section, mutex, or handle of a thread that can never be acquired. For example, if two threads each hold a different mutex and need the mutex held by the other thread in order to proceed, the threads are deadlocked. Neither thread can give up the mutex it already holds and neither thread will be able to acquire the second mutex.

- *Abandoned locks.* If a thread terminates while holding a lock, such as a Win32[†] CRITICAL_SECTION or mutex HANDLE, the lock is in an abandoned state. Attempting to acquire abandoned locks can lead to unexpected results. For example, threads that attempt to acquire an abandoned CRITICAL_SECTION are deadlocked.

- *Stalled thread.* A stalled thread is an active thread that, due to a synchronization object or some other external force, is not making progress on a workload but is expected to be doing so. Stalled threads are usually caused by incorrect parallel program logic and are different from threads that are in the sleep state.

■ *API usage errors.* For example, the Win32 Threading function `WaitForMultipleObjects` accepts an array of thread `HANDLE`s to be waited on by some other thread. Another argument to the function is the number of objects being waited on in the array. A limit of 64 objects can appear in a single call to `WaitForMultipleObjects`. If the number of objects is 65 or greater, Thread Checker identifies an error.

Because Thread Checker keeps track of *all* memory accesses, it causes significant overhead; however, you can drastically reduce this overhead by reducing your overall workload. Selecting a small workload is an essential part of using this product.

Note
> Reduction of workload is a critical, required step before running Thread Checker. The workload reduction is similar to what might be done to reduce the data set when setting up an interactive debugging session.

Terminology

Activities are at the core of the data-collection process in the VTune analyzer. Intel Thread Checker enables you to create Activities in the VTune Performance Environment. Within an Activity, you can specify the types of performance data you wish to collect. For each type of performance data, you need to configure the appropriate data collector and define the application/module profiles. These profiles contain information about the application to execute and the modules to analyze.

Running an Activity is analogous to running an experiment. When you run an Activity, the data collectors collect performance data and save it in the Activity results. You can view the results later without having to rerun the Activity. You can also drag and drop different Activity results into a view to compare data from different experiments.

Building Code for Use with Intel Thread Checker

Depending on the needs of your program, you can choose from among three ways to prepare your application for data collection with Intel Thread Checker:

- binary instrumentation mode
- source instrumentation mode
- a mix of both

Binary Instrumentation Mode

You can use binary instrumentation with software built with the Intel Compilers or the Microsoft Visual C++ Compiler. Because of limitations on what binary instrumentation can do, fewer details about any found errors are available with this mode than when using source instrumentation.

Use binary instrumentation in the following situations:

- To quickly get started using Intel Thread Checker.
- When you do not have access to an appropriate Intel compiler.[1]
- When you do not want to completely rebuild your application, for example, because it might take several hours to do so.
- When you do not have source code.

Use the following options to control binary instrumentation for Intel Thread Checker:

- Build with thread-safe libraries using one of the −MD −MDd −MT −MTd compilers options. These options apply whether you are using the Intel Compiler or you are using Microsoft Visual C++. In Microsoft Visual C++ version 6, you can find these options under the menu **Project** → **Settings** → **C/C++** → **Code Generation** by selecting one of the Multithreaded DLL options.

- Build with symbols and line numbers, using one of the -Zi -ZI -Z7 options. These options enable the Thread Checker to show you the source code corresponding to threading errors.

---

[1]   Even if your software is built with the Intel Compilers, you may want to use binary instrumentation to quickly get started with only a re-link, and not a whole re-compile.

■ Disable optimization with –Od. Turning on optimization does not speed Thread Checker and may actually slow it down.

■ Link so that the executable can be re-located with the /fixed:no option. Most .DLL files default to linking /fixed:no, but most .EXE files need to have this option specified.

Source Instrumentation Mode

Source instrumentation provides more information than binary instrumentation. It is also required if you want to analyze OpenMP-threaded programs.

To perform source instrumentation:

■ Use the –Qtcheck compiler option and the /fixed:no linker option when building your application.

■ Additionally, you should use the binary instrumentation options.

Mixed Mode

You can operate with a mixed mode, using source instrumentation on some files and binary instrumentation on others. This mode may be useful in order to get more detailed information on specific critical files, while minimizing the amount of output generated from other files and saving the time that would otherwise be needed to recompile everything.

Example 12.1: Checking an Application Using the Intel Thread Checker

This example walks you through the creation of an Activity using the Intel Thread Checker. Follow these instructions to use Thread Checker to check your multithreaded code for errors and potential problems.

Step 1: Verify That Your Fortran Program Does Not Rely on Static Allocation

If you are not using Fortran, skip to Step 2.

If you are using Fortran, verify that your program does not rely on static allocation of local variables for correct execution. Most Fortran compilers provide an option to make all local variables static, using the –Qsave option of the Intel Fortran compiler. This option is equivalent to declaring variables with the SAVE attribute on variables, placing them in a

SAVE statement, or initializing them with a DATA statement. Subprograms with static variables are not thread-safe for two reasons:

■ Static variables are shared among threads.

■ Static variables maintain state between invocations.

To test whether your program relies on static allocation:

1. Compile your program with the -Qauto option of the Intel Fortran compiler to place local variables on the stack.

2. If your program gives correct results, proceed to "Step 2: Instrument Your Application." If your program gives incorrect results, this generally indicates that your code has subprograms that maintain state across invocations.

3. Find the subprograms that maintain state. Identify the variables in these functions whose values must be saved across invocations. For example, the seed value of a random number generator is often saved across invocations.

4. Give these variables the SAVE attribute or place them in a SAVE statement. For example, use one of the following statements:

   ```
   INTEGER, SAVE :: static_variable
   ```

   or

   ```
   INTEGER static_variable
   ```

   ```
   SAVE static_variable
   ```

5. Recompile with the -Qauto option and verify that the program gives correct results. Proceed to Step 2, knowing that static variables are shared among threads. Intel Thread Checker may report data races on these variables that you will have to fix.

Step 2: Instrument Your Application

Collecting data with Thread Checker requires instrumentation. Instrumentation inserts calls to Thread Checker library into your code to record memory accesses, and calls to threading and synchronization routines.

You can use either source or binary instrumentation methods, or a combination of both, depending on the needs of your program. Source instrumentation provides more information than binary instrumentation. If you are using OpenMP threading, you must use source instrumentation. Otherwise, you can use binary instrumentation to get started.

Note

> When using source or binary instrumentation, operation of Thread Checker causes additional debugging information to be embedded into your object (.obj) files. That information is merged from there into the .exe and .dll files, causing file size to grow. If this causes problems in your debugger, contact Intel's technical support for assistance.

To perform source instrumentation, use the -Qtcheck compiler option and the /fixed:no linker option when building your application. Additionally, you should use the binary instrumentation options.

To perform binary instrumentation, use a debug build that includes symbols (-Zi or /ZI) and disables optimization (-Od) of your software and link it with the /fixed:no option. Also, be sure to build with thread-safe run-time libraries by using the -MDd or -MTd option. For example, to build test.exe with the Microsoft Compiler, use the following:

```
cl -MDd -Od -Zi test.cpp /link /fixed:no
```

Step 3: Select a Small but Representative Data Set

Because Thread Checker keeps track of all memory accesses, using it has significant overhead. However, you can drastically reduce the overhead by reducing your overall workload.

Note

> Since Thread Checker instrumentation can drastically increase the runtime and memory requirements of your application, choose a small but representative data set rather than a large, production-scale data set. Data sets with runtimes of a few seconds are ideal.

To reduce your workload, use one or more of the following strategies:

- ■ *Reduce input data sets sizes.* For example, if you are analyzing an image, use a 10×10 pixel image, not a 2000×1000 pixel image.

- ■ *Reduce loop iterations.* Usually, a few iterations uncover all the problems in a loop.

- ■ *Reduce update rates.* For example, limit the number of display updates from 30 to 3 per second.

The workloads do not have to be realistic. They just have to exercise the relevant sections of the multithreaded program. This approach is similar to the smaller workloads typically used in serial debugging.

Step 4: Use the Thread Checker Wizard

The wizard enables you to create a new project and a new Intel Thread Checker Activity that gathers and analyzes information on multithreading correctness. The wizard prompts you to enter values only for the basic parameters and uses default values for others. To launch the Intel Thread Checker wizard, follow these steps:

1. Start the VTune Performance Analyzer.

2. Click **New Project** in the main toolbar to open the New Project dialog box.

3. In the Category drop-down box, choose **Threading Wizards**.

4. Select **Intel Thread Checker Wizard**.

5. Click **OK**.

6. Use the Intel Thread Checker Wizard to configure the Activity with the application to run, the working directory, and the command-line arguments to use, if any. For all other options, you can use default values.

7. Click **Finish** to run your application and collect results.

Thread Checker instruments your application before execution. Remember that instrumentation expands run-time and memory requirements, so be sure to select a small but representative data set as described in Step 3.

Step 5: Investigate Errors and Compare Results

If you have successfully run the Thread Checker Wizard, you should see Activity results in the Project Navigator pane, and messages about errors or warnings in the Diagnostics List and Graphical Summary panes. Congratulations! You are now ready to analyze errors, if any, in your threaded application.

Thread Checker is particularly good at finding data races, in which multiple threads access a shared variable without synchronization, and at least one thread is attempting to update the variable. To understand the errors reported by Thread Checker better, do the following:

1. Click the **Severity** column heading to sort errors according to severity, placing the most serious errors at the top of your list

2. Double-click an error to drill down to source views to see where errors occur in your code. Look for the variables accessed in these lines of the program. At least one of these accesses is a write to the variable. This access can give you insight into the error.

3. Tab through Context, Definition, 1st Access and 2nd Access views to gain different perspectives on the source of the issues.

Context View. For OpenMP code, the Context view takes you to the parallel region where the current error exists in the source code, to provide the *context* of the error. For code that does not use OpenMP, the Context view shows the function where the error is located.

Definition View. Typically an error results when two different threads are trying to access the same piece of memory at once. The *Definition view* attempts to take you to the place where the variable was declared or allocated.

1st Access and 2nd Access Views. The *1st Access* location is the line that the first thread was executing when the conflict occurred. The *2nd Access* location is the line that the second thread was executing when the conflict occurred.

4. Click the **Stack Traces** tab at the bottom of the view to understand the execution path each thread took to arrive at the point of the specific error.

Note

> If the counts in the error view are large (100s or greater), you could reduce your workload and get the same results from Thread Checker.
>
> To see more details about the error, use source instrumentation to create an additional Activity. Refer to "Source Instrumentation Mode" for instructions.

As you develop solutions to the errors found by Intel Thread Checker, you can recompile the modified code and run it through Thread Checker again. If you find many errors, you may wish to address a few at a time before passing the code through the tool again to see if your solutions were correct and did not introduce any new errors. Depending on your work, this technique may require several iterations of fixing and checking to eliminate all errors.

The online help included with Thread Checker includes more complete details on advanced Thread Checker configuration options and Thread Checker views.

Recap

Here are the major points covered in this chapter:

- Use Intel Thread Checker in the VTune Performance Environment to locate errors in your multithreaded programs that employ Microsoft[†] Windows[†] 32-bit threading or OpenMP[†] threading. Thread Checker identifies errors induced by the nondeterministic scheduling of thread execution.

- Reduction of workload is a critical, required step before running Thread Checker. The workload reduction is similar to what might be done to reduce the data set when setting up an interactive debugging session.

Appendix A

Types of Line Number and Symbol File Information

To drill down to the source-code level using the VTune™ analyzer, you must generate *line number and symbol file information* when you compile your code. Your compiler generates this information, also referred to as *debug information*, either in a separate file or as part of the binary file. The VTune analyzer recognizes many types of line information/symbol files:

- Internal COFF symbol tables residing in the object files (.obj).

- Integrated debug information for Microsoft (NB09, NB11 debugging file format), Borland[†] (FB09, FB0A format), IBM[†] VisualAge[†] C++ (NB04 format), Watcom[†] (DWARF 2 format), and Novell[†] (NB05 format) compilers.

- W3 and W4 formats for virtual device driver files (.VxD) distributed by Microsoft.

- Program database files (.pdb) generated within Microsoft[†] Visual Studio[†] or Visual Studio .NET by the Intel® or Microsoft compilers (in Microsoft NB10 format).

- DBG files (.dbg) distributed by Microsoft with their software development kits (SDKs) and driver development kits (DDKs).

You can also generate a .dbg file using the Microsoft Visual Studio rebase.exe utility tool. See the Visual Studio documentation for more information.

■ Symbol files (.sym) distributed by Microsoft or Novell with their software development kits (SDKs) and driver development kits (DDKs). Symbol files are usually installed in the Microsoft Windows\System directory.

■ Linker map file (.map). Refer to your linker documentation for details on how to create a linker map file.

Note

> Try to avoid using the .map file format because it provides less complete symbol information, does not enable code level tuning assistance, and restricts some source view display options.

■ With the /EXPORTS option, you can export a function from your program so that other programs can call that function.

The following sections explain how to generate symbol and line number information using several popular compilers. You can often produce supported types of line information/symbol files as well from other compilers not discussed here.

Borland[†] C++ Builder[†] Compiler

To generate symbol and line number information in the executable, do *one* of the following:

- In the **Options** → **Project** → **Compiler** tab, under the **Debugging** panel check:
  - – Line number information
  - – Debug information
  - – Disable Inline Expansions
- Use the /v flag with bcc32 on the command line.

To generate a map file instead, do *one* of the following:

- Check **Publics** in the **Options** → **Project** → **Linker** tab **/Map** panel.
- Use the /M flag with bcc32 on the command line.

Use similar options to generate symbol information for Borland Windows Pascal compilers.

Note | Order of preference for symbol information is in a .tds file (FB0A) or in the executable (FB09) first, then in a .map file.

The 3.x and 5.0 versions of the compiler do not generate a .tds file. The symbol information (FB09 format) is included in the binary file.

GNU Project C/C++ Compiler for Linux[†]

These steps generate code with symbol and line number information from the command line using the `gcc 2.96` and `g++` compiler on Red Hat[†] 7.1 Linux systems:

- Use the `-gstabs` option for files in the STABS format, or the `-gdwarf-2` option for files in the DWARF format.

- Use the `-g` option to specify the debug information level (levels 2 and 3 are recommended), as in the example:

```
gcc -o test -gdwarf-2 -g3 test.7
```

> **Note**
> For compilations targeted to IA-32 processor systems, the compiler uses `-gstabs` as the default.
>
> For compilations targeted to Itanium® architecture systems, the compiler uses the default `-gdwarf` option.

Java[†] Compilers

To generate code with symbol and line number information from the command line using Java compilers, do *one* of the following:

- Use the `/g` options on the Microsoft[†] Java compiler.
- Use the `-g` option on Sun[†] and IBM[†] compilers.

For example, you could type:

```
jvc /g myClass.java
```

This Microsoft Java compiler command generates a `.class` file called `myClass.class` that contains symbol and line number information.

Intel® and Microsoft† Compilers

Note | The order of preference for symbol information is in a .pdb file first, then in the executable, then in a .map file.

Specify whether you want to run the Intel compiler or the Microsoft C++ compiler when you install the Intel compiler plug-in.

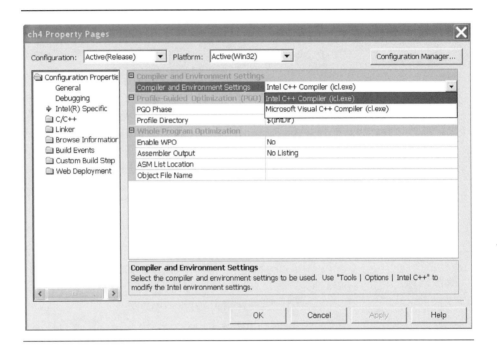

Intel or Microsoft Compilers with Visual Studio†

These methods generate symbol and line number information using Microsoft Visual Studio† with these compilers:

- Microsoft Visual C++† (or Visual Basic†)
- Intel compiler plug-in (C++ or Fortran)

Intel or Microsoft Visual C++[t] Projects (PDB, MAP, EXE, DLL)

You can generate a program database (`.pdb`) file or `.map` file, or you can include the symbol information in the executable or `.dll` file:

■ Under the **Project** → **Settings** → **C/C++** tab:

    – Set **Category** to **General**.

    – Set **Debug Info** to **Program Database** or **Program Database for Edit and Continue**.

■ Click the **Link** tab.

    – Add **/fixed:no** to the switches listed in the **Project Options** box to enable base relocations for Call Graph profiling.

    – Set **Category** to **General**.

    Check the **Generate debug info** option (default).

    Another option is to uncheck the **Generate debug info** option and check the **Generate mapfile** option instead to generate a `.map` file. However, this option does not enable code-level tuning assistance and restricts some source view display options.

■ If you checked the **Generate debug info** option:

    – Set **Category** to **Debug**.

    Check the **Debug info** option, choose **Microsoft format** (default).

    Uncheck the **Separate Types** option.

    – Set **Category** to **Customize** and do one of the following:

    Check the **Use Program Database** option to generate a `.pdb` file, or clear the **Use Program Database** option if you want to include the symbol information in the executable or `.dll` file (instead of in a `.pdb` file).

Intel or Microsoft Compilers with Visual Studio .NET

These methods generate symbol and line number information using Microsoft Visual Studio .NET with these compilers:

■ Microsoft Visual C++ or Visual Basic .NET or Visual C#

■ Intel C++ compiler plug-in

Intel or Microsoft Visual C++ Projects (PDB File)

To create a program database (.pdb) file, follow these directions:

■ In the Solution Explorer window, right-click the **Project** and select **Properties**.

■ Click the **C++** tab.

   – Select **General**.

   – Set **Debug Information Format** to **Program Database** or **Program Database for Edit and Continue**.

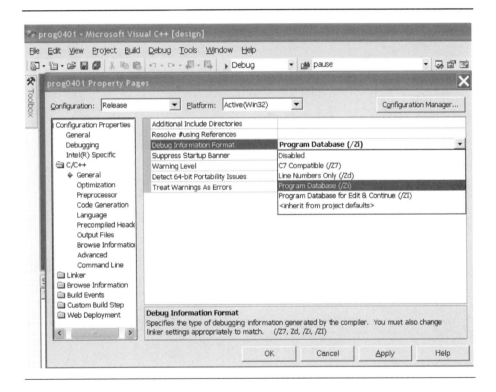

■ Click the **Linker** tab.

- Select **Command Line**.
- Add /fixed:no to the **Additional Options** to enable base relocations for Call Graph profiling.
- Select **Debugging**.
- Set **Generate Debug Info** to **Yes (/DEBUG)**.
- Leave **Generate Program Database File** set to $(OutDir)/$(ProjectName).pdb

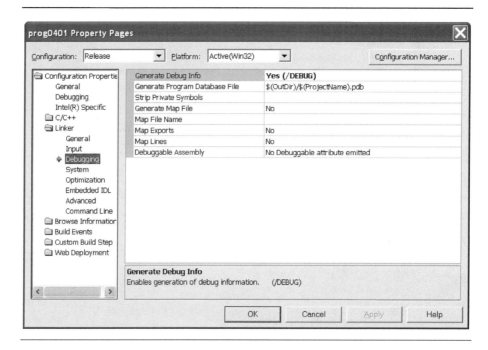

Microsoft VB.NET Projects:

To work with Microsoft VB.NET Projects:

■ In the Solution Explorer window, right-click the **Project** and select **Properties.**

■ Choose **Configuration Properties → Build.**

■ Check the **Generate Debugging Information** option.

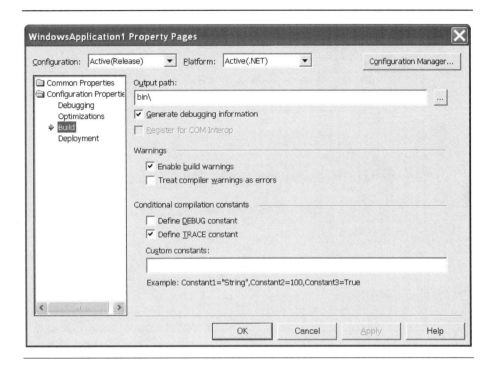

Microsoft Visual C#[†] Projects:

To work with Microsoft Visual C# Projects:

- ■ In the Solutions Explorer window, right-click the **Project** and select **Properties**.
- ■ Choose **Configuration Properties** → **Build** → **Outputs**.
- ■ Set **Generate Debugging Information** to **True**.

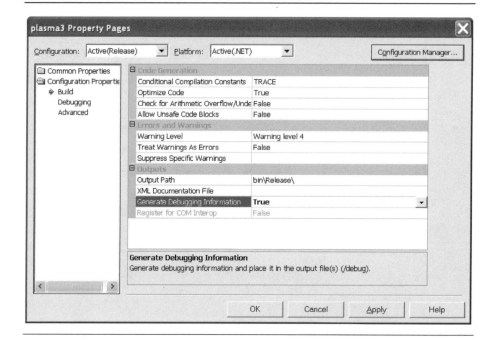

Microsoft Compilers from the Windows Command Line

These methods generate symbol and line number information in the executable file using the command line interface of these compilers:

■ Microsoft Visual Studio

- Microsoft Visual C++[†] Compiler (6.0 or later)
- Microsoft Visual Basic[†] 6.0/.NET Compiler

■ Microsoft .NET Framework SDK Compiler

PDB File

To generate a program database (.pdb) file in NB10 debug format, use one of the following methods:

■ Single command example:

```
cl -GR -ZI program.cpp -link -fixed:no
```

■ Separate commands example:

```
cl -GR -c -ZI program.cpp

link -fixed:no -debug program.obj
```

Executable or DLL File

To generate symbol information in the executable or `.dll` file in NB09/NB11 debug format, use one of the following methods:

- A single-command example is:

```
cl -GR -ZI program.cpp -link -pdb:none
    -fixed:no -debugtype:cv
```

- A separate-commands example is:

```
cl -GR -c -ZI program.cpp

link -pdb:none -fixed:no -debug -debugtype:cv
    program.obj
```

MAP File

To generate a map file, add `-map` to the linker command.

Intel Compilers from the Command Line

To generate symbol and line-number information in a program database (.pdb) file using the command-line interface of the Intel C++ or Fortran compilers:

- Use the `icl` (or `ecl`) command instead of `cl` to invoke the Intel compiler plug-in from the command line.

- Use the `-ZI` option to direct the compiler to generate code with symbol and line number information.

An example for the IA-32 architecture is:

```
icl -ZI prog1.cpp
```

An example for the Itanium architecture is:

```
ecl -ZI prog1.cpp
```

Note

> For compilations targeted to IA-32 processor systems, the compiler uses -Od as the default when you specify -ZI. Specifying the -ZI or -Od option automatically disables the -Oy option.
>
> For compilations targeted to Itanium architecture systems, the -Oy option is not used.
>
> The compiler lets you generate code to support symbolic debugging while the -O1 or -O2 optimization options are specified on the command line along with -ZI.

Table C.1 summarizes the command-line options you can use and the symbol and line-number information and optimizations they enable.

Table C.1   Intel® Compiler Command Line Options

Command Line Options	Description
-ZI	Produces symbol and line-number information, -Od enabled, -Oy disabled for IA-32-targeted compilations.
-ZI -O1 -ZI -O2	Produces symbol and line-number information, -O1 or -O2 optimizations are enabled. Note: These combinations of command-line options may cause inaccuracies in the generated symbol and line number information.
-ZI -O3 -Oy	Produces symbol and line-number information, -O3d optimizations enabled, -Oy disabled for IA-32-targeted compilations.
-ZI -Qip	Produces limited symbol and line-number information, -Qip option enabled.

Watcom[†] Compiler

To generate symbol and line-number information using the Watcom[†] V11.0 compiler, specify the linker option in *one* of the following ways:

■ From the IDE:

- Select **Full Debugging Info** from **Options** → **C++ Compiler Switches** → **6. Debugging Switches**.

- Uncheck **Produce Symbol File** from **Options** → **Windows Linking Switches** → **3. Advanced Switches**.

■ From the command line:

- Specify -d2 for full symbol information;

- Do *not* specify op symf.

Use the default compiler options.

Note

> The order of preference for symbol information is in the executable (DWARF or Codeview) first, then in a .map file, then in a .sym file.
>
> If you are using cvpack, try to avoid symbol information that exceeds 64KB. See Microsoft PSS ID Number: Q112335 for more information. Using the -d1 line number information compiler option instead of -d2 usually produces less symbol information.

DBG Files

The VTune analyzer recognizes .dbg files as sources of line number information.

On the Microsoft Windows NT[†] operating system, .dbg files distributed by Microsoft with their software development kits (SDKs) and driver development kits (DDKs) are installed under the %System-Root%\symbols directory. For example, the .dbg file for CRTDLL.DLL is in:

```
SystemRoot%\symbols\DLL\CRTDLL.DBG
```

To use an alternate symbol path for .dbg files, define the _NT_ALT_SYMBOL_PATH environment variable. For example, if your .dbg files are under c:\sdk\debug\symbols\dll*.dbg, set:

```
_NT_ALT_SYMBOL_PATH = c:\sdk\debug
```

You can also generate a .dbg file using the Microsoft Visual Studio rebase.exe tool. See the Visual Studio documentation for more information.

W3/W4 Files

A W3 file is a Windows archive of virtual device drivers (.VxD) packed together into one file. A W4 file is a packed W3 file that Windows opens at runtime. Usually only one W3 and one W4 file exists in a Windows system.

When you double-click a file that uses the W3/W4 format in Hotspot view, or disassemble a W3/W4 format file using the Static Assembly Analysis, the VTune analyzer prompts you to select the device driver associated with that file. If you double-click a device driver, the program tries to associate that driver with the files in the path, and searches inside the system's W3/W4 files. If no match is found, the program prompts you for the full name and path of the driver such as:

```
C:\Win\System\MyW4File.vxdMyDriver
```

Once the association of files is complete, the VTune analyzer uncompresses, disassembles, and saves a temporary W3 file in your temporary directory in this format:

```
TEMP\filexxxxxx.vxd
```

where *xxxxxx* is the current date and time in hexadecimal format. If you disassemble a W3/W4 file, a `LipsW3.$$$` file is also created.

Exports

Exports are usually defined in a `.dll` file. Three methods exist for exporting a definition, listed in recommended order of use:

- The `_declspec(dllexport)` keyword in the source code
- An `EXPORTS` statement in a `.DEF` file
- An `/EXPORT` specification in a `LINK` command

In case some functions are exported, a special EXPORTS table is created in the executable (or `.dll`) file. The VTune analyzer recognizes symbols represented in this table if it cannot find a more preferable format in the file.

> **Note**
>
> Information provided by this format is limited. In particular, symbol sizes are not stored, so they are prolonged to the next symbol start address. Since the EXPORTS format contains just a part of the symbol information (only exported procedures), some symbols might be missed, and the size of the visible symbol may contain the size of the adjacent symbol which is not included in the EXPORTS data. To get correct results, take care to use the appropriate compiler option to generate full debug information.

Appendix **B**

Sampling Events and Event Ratios

Great events make me quiet and calm; it is only trifles that irritate my nerves.

—Queen Victoria

Chapter 4 introduced time- and event-based sampling techniques without dwelling on the events themselves. This appendix explores the categorization of events themselves and covers the variety of events available for sampling a little more deeply. Many *event counters* are on hand for use with the VTune™ Performance Analyzer; the exact counters differ based on the processor used to run your program. Some counters make more sense, or at least a different sense, when combined to create *event ratios*. The VTune analyzer offers a large selection of such ratios.

Events are dependent on the processor you are using because they are actual counters of activities deep within the microprocessor. Processors have many similarities because of common architectural features such as those discussed in Chapter 2. Generic tuning, which will benefit all platforms, focuses on events that are common to all processors. Even an event such as a cache miss, which is common to all processors, will vary from processor to processor based on the cache size. Your program may generate very few cache misses on a system with a large cache and need no adjustment, while on a processor with a small cache you may have an opportunity to optimize for cache size and improve performance. Less generic tuning that is specific to only a certain class of processors may become important based on your target machine. Certain events can point to very real performance problems for your application that are present only on the most modern and high-speed processors.

This overview of major processor events provides a bridge between the concepts of Chapter 4 and the details available in the processor and VTune analyzer documentation sets on every event available. The VTune analyzer online documentation has hundreds of pages of details and is frequently updated for new processors and new processor features. Be sure to explore the full range covered in the online help for the VTune Performance Analyzer.

Event Counters and Event Ratios

Every processor that Intel manufactures includes many event counters that you can sample using the VTune analyzer. This appendix explains these counters in terms of the tasks a processor performs—such as memory operations or computational activity.

The VTune analyzer also makes some commonly requested comparisons available as predefined ratios between counters. When you select an event ratio, the VTune analyzer automatically uses two event counters, does the division necessary to obtain the ratios, and displays information in terms of the ratios.

One example of a ratio is clocks per instruction (CPI), which measures the effectiveness of a program segment in using the processor's computational power. Other event ratios commonly have the term *effectiveness* in the name to emphasize their usage as gauges in finding inefficiencies.

Each processor is sufficiently unique for the VTune analyzer to offer counters specific to that processor. Specific event registers are not part of the basic functionality of every Intel® processor. Instead, they are part of what Intel calls the *model-specific* part of the processors. In other words, event registers differ from design to design. While a Pentium® 4 processor running at 1 GHz has mostly the same event registers as a Pentium 4 processor running at 3 GHz, it shares less event registers with the Pentium III and even less with the Itanium® 2 processors. Nevertheless, the most important and commonly used counters have similar names and functions across all of Intel's processors.

When tuning your application, treat processor performance-monitoring events only as guides neither designed for nor guaranteed by Intel to be perfectly accurate. Use the counter values reported by the processor only as relative indicators for tuning purposes.

This appendix provides an overview of the performance measurement capabilities for Intel's current processors: Pentium M, Pentium 4, Intel® Xeon™, Itanium 2, and processors based on Intel XScale® technology. Depending on the version of VTune Performance Analyzer you have, the help system documents the performance counters of earlier chips that it supports. From time to time, newer versions of the analyzer will drop support for older processors.

Advice for All Processors

Regardless of the type of processor you are using, here are some tips for sampling processor events and event ratios.

Evaluating the CPI Ratio

Looking at the clocks per instruction (CPI) ratio (also called the cycles per instruction ratio) should be your first step in optimizing for micro-architecture. The CPI is the quotient of the Clickticks counter divided by the Instructions Retired counter. When using event ratios to locate optimization opportunities:

■ Check the CPI for a general indication of optimization opportunities. A high CPI value of 4 or more is considered poor, indicating that instructions are requiring more cycles to execute than they should. A value of 0.75 or less is considered good.

■ If the CPI ratio is high, check the micro-ops per instructions ratio (Micro-ops/Instructions Retired). If the latter ratio is also high and you are using STRING instructions, poor CPI is expected and should not be considered a problem.

■ If the CPI ratio is high and the micro-ops per instructions ratio is low, this indicates that optimization opportunities exist in the code. Investigate ways to modify your code to improve the efficiency of instruction execution. Check the ratios relevant to your code: floating-point ratio for floating-point code, MMX™ technology ratios for MMX technology code, and so forth.

■ For every area where the CPI is poor, check memory-related events and branch-related events to understand why the CPI is poor.

Compilation Tips

When compiling your program let the compiler optimize as much as possible for you before you drive into tuning with the VTune analyzer. Consult the tuning guides for your favorite compiler. Here are some tips to consider:

■ Use a highly optimizing compiler such as one of the Intel compilers. Consider making your builds with the appropriate processor tuning flag (such as –G6 or –G7).

■ Use the Interprocedural Optimizations (IPO) switch to increase the scope of optimizations your compiler is performing. This can lead to reductions in many critical events. For Intel compilers, use /Qipo. For Microsoft compilers, use /BL.

■ Use profile-guided feedback. This is particularly good at reducing branch and instruction cache events.

Disabling Power Management

In general, you will want to disable power management to get more accurate and consistent measurements from run to run. Power management transitions are designed to save battery and affect your machine by reducing its frequency. As a result, some frequency-dependent event ratios and time calculations are inaccurate under battery power. If you leave power management active you may find yourself confused by variations in execution from run to run. To avoid this, connect your machine to an A/C power source (not battery), change the power option of the system to a performance setting such as high system performance, and then run the sampling Activity and request advice using the Intel Tuning Assistant.

Optimizing Branch Predictability

Mispredicted branches cause reduced performance in your application because the processor starts executing instructions along the path it predicts. When the misprediction is discovered, all the work done on those instructions must be discarded, and the processor must start again on the right path.

In general, compilers do much of the work to optimize branching for you. However, some of this optimization may occur only at the highest optimization levels (-O3) and when using advanced optimization techniques (like /Qipo and *profile guided* feedback). You can optimize your code for branch predictability in these ways:

- Arrange code to be consistent with the branch prediction guidelines provided in the optimizations manual for your processor type. Following these guidelines optimizes instruction prefetching.

- Avoid mixing near and far calls and returns.

- Avoid implementing a call by pushing the return address and jumping to the target. Instead, allow the hardware to pair up call and return instructions to enhance predictability.

- Use the pause instruction in spin-wait loops.

- Use inline functions according to coding recommendations.

- Eliminate branches.

To reduce branch mispredicts and improve performance:

- Use the Intel compiler Profile Guided Optimization (PGO) option to rearrange basic blocks so they result in fewer branches.

- Use the Intel compiler option -Qxi (or higher) to replace branch instructions with cmov and fcmov instructions.

- Design your code to improve branch predictability:

  - Ensure that each CALL instruction has a matching RETURN.

  - Avoid intermingling data and instructions.

  - Unroll very short loops.

  - When a branch is based on randomly predicted data, consider modifying your code to avoid a branch, by using conditional MOV instructions or Streaming SIMD Extensions (SSE) or MMX technology instructions. For example, change the following code:

Before	After

`if (a>0)`
`    c=x`
`else`
`    c=y`
	`int val[2]={x,y};`
	`c=val[a>0];`

■ In assembly language, consider eliminating branch instructions by replacing them with `cmov`, `fcmov`, and `setcc` instructions. Also, in some cases you might be able to use the SIMD compare (create mask) and logical instructions (`and/or/not`) to perform the operation as a Boolean operation.

Branch mispredictions incur a large penalty on deeply pipelined microprocessors. In general, branches can be predicted accurately. However, in the event of a misprediction, instructions that were scheduled to execute along the mispredicted path must be canceled. Such canceled instructions are referred to as *bogus*.

To determine the branch misprediction ratio, divide the number of Mispredicted Branches Retired events by the number of Branches Retired events. To determine the number of mispredicted branches per instruction, divide the number of Mispredicted Branches Retired events by the number of Instructions Retired events.

Reducing the Working Data Set to Avoid Cache Misses

While cache misses are inevitable, reducing their numbers can improve performance since a cache miss represents a request for the contents of memory that cannot be satisfied by a cache and requires a fetch from a higher level of cache or memory. Regardless of the type of cache, when you encounter frequent cache misses:

■ If possible, reduce the working data set. Try to revise the algorithm so that the working data set fits in the cache. Techniques like *loop blocking* transform the memory domain of a given problem into smaller chunks, rather than sequentially traversing through the entire memory domain. Each chunk is small enough to fit all the data for a given computation into the cache, thereby maximizing data reuse. Optimizing compilers can help with loop blocking, as can optimized libraries such as Intel's Math Kernel Library.

■ If you cannot reduce the working data set, consider using prefetch instructions to fetch data into cache before it is needed. Unless programming in assembly language, you can generally accomplish prefetching by using an optimizing compiler or optimized libraries.

General Coding Tips

When coding your application, follow these tips:

■ Avoid using C++ constructs that compile into indirect calls because they are very difficult for the processor to predict and result in a performance penalty. For this reason, you should:

– Reduce the usage of function pointers.

– Avoid using abstract classes and virtual and pure-virtual methods as much as possible.

– Avoid calling a method from the base class when using inheritance in C++. If you can, replace these calls with explicit calls to the actual object class. Use explicit function-calling whenever possible.

■ Sort or group objects by type before processing a large set of objects derived from a base class. This technique enables the branch prediction mechanism to correctly predict the indirect calls generated.

■ Try to eliminate branches as much as possible.

■ Finish coding the algorithm itself before optimizing for architecture. After all, no amount of tuning can turn a bubble sort into a quicksort.

Common Event Concepts

Three types of events occur on every processor and have very special significance related to:

■ Passage of time

■ Program control flow change

■ Instruction mix

■ Memory accesses

Clockticks, branching, new instruction counting and cache/TLB events are discussed here because they are very important and relatively standard across all processors. These event counters are also the most important and commonly encountered.

Clockticks: Does Time Exist If You Are Not Moving?

A processor runs by doing work to the beat of a clock. Also referred to as a *clock* or a *CPU cycle*, a *clocktick* is the smallest unit of time recognized by the processor. The term is also sometimes used to indicate the time required by the processor to execute the simplest instruction or micro-op. Clockticks are a component in many key event ratios offered by the VTune analyzer.

In most processors, the *Clockticks* event counts the number of clock-ticks during which the processor was *not* in a halt state. Consult the documentation for your processor to see if time is counted during a halt state.

Many operating systems implement the idle task using the HLT instruction. In these operating systems, clockticks for the idle task are not counted. If you perform event-based sampling with this event, you may see an unexpectedly low clockticks count that may not seem to correlate to the sampling time and the processor frequency. Not counting the idle task cycles is very important for use in event ratios. For instance, CPI (clocks per instructions) makes more sense without diluting the number with time spent in the idle task. Therefore, users generally find performance issues to be easier to debug on systems where clockticks do not count idle time.

If you want to perform sampling based on a timeframe that includes halted time, use the VTune analyzer's time-based sampling feature instead of event-based sampling on clockticks.

Many Branches

Even though you can *count* the number of branches, frequent branching is not likely to indicate a significant performance issue unless frequent branch mispredictions are occurring. Therefore, event counters for mis-predicted branches or calls are much more useful for determining performance issues.

Call Overhead (High CALL Event Counts)

Using compiler optimizations that increase inlining can reduce large numbers of calls. To complement the information provided by event-based sampling, try using the VTune analyzer's call graph feature to help pinpoint the source of such calls.

Misprediction, Speculation, Retired, and Executed

Misprediction is simply a speculation that did not pay off. Speculation is a guess, before it is certain, that an operation will be needed. Increasing the accuracy of such guesses can result in performance gains, so they are of interest when tuning performance.

Modern processors execute many instructions at once. On Intel processors featuring dynamic execution, such as the Pentium 4, Pentium M, and Intel Xeon processors, instructions will be decoded or executed before prior instructions are completed. This occasionally means the processor is decoding or executing an instruction without being certain that it should be completed. To maintain correct behavior, these processors have the concept of retirement. Many events have "executed" and "retired" versions. In general, software developers have more interest in retired events because these represent work they have essentially requested in their programs. However, it is very important to look for instances with a high degree of executed instructions with a low count of retired. The solution to such issues is generally more likely to be in the choice of compilers or compiler optimization choices than it is in the structure of the program.

Many events count misprediction, such as Mispredicted CALL Instructions Executed. Events that count mispredicted things may come in detailed forms to tell at what stage the misprediction occurred. For example, the misprediction of a branch for a Pentium M processor may occur at decode time or at execution time, giving rise to events called Mispredicted Branch Instructions (Mispredicted at decoding) and Mispredicted Branch Instructions (Mispredicted at execution). The subtle differences here are of intense interest to processor designers and compiler engineers, but to those not designing processors or writing compilers these can all safely be lumped together as mispredicted. The solution is still almost certainly in the choice of compilers or compiler optimization choices. In the rare case when, even after careful compilation choices, mispredictions occur in a high number in a concentrated part of your application, you may find changes in your source code to be productive. Examples of such almost always involve some form of dispatching code often using indirect branches or calls. For such cases, careful consideration of how to create a series of predictable branches to accomplish the same work can yield significant performance gains.

The Intel Itanium processors utilize explicit parallelism techniques instead of dynamic execution. For these processors, the "speculated" operations are the equivalent of "executed" in that they may or may not actually be needed. On these processors, the issue of whether the speculated operation was indeed needed is not known to the hardware, and therefore no computation is performed based on event counts to determine the number of unused speculative operations. Such a count would not be useful because the design of the EPIC architecture, for Itanium processors, is to be highly parallel and use lots of speculation; it would therefore be a mistake to eliminate speculations that were not always used. Compiler writers try different algorithms and look to minimize time, not the number of speculations.

It is worth noting that Pentium and Intel Xeon processors do have two types of speculation. The first, under software control, is actually called prefetching. Hardware controlled speculations also exist, including instruction prefetching past a branch operations, execution past a branch operation, and some types of load operations. Hardware speculation is only effective when branches are correctly predicted. When a branch is mispredicted, hardware speculation is wasted. Therefore, minimizing the number of event mispredicts is essential to optimizing hardware speculation.

For the software speculation known as prefetching, programmers generally do not think of it as speculation even though that is what it is. Prefetching is an action to request that data be loaded into data cache before an actual usage of the data is requested. A prefetch instruction is a memory request that doesn't require the processor to actually wait for and then use the data.

MMX™ Instructions and Streaming SIMD Extensions (SSE) Events

Since MMX, SSE, SSE2 and SSE3 instructions are not available on all processors, a very common error is to have conditional code to use them on a certain processor actually fail to activate. This might be code you have written in your application, or might be the correct linkage and activation of a key library. The counter events involving streaming Single-Instruction Multiple-Data (SIMD) extensions tell you how many of these types of instructions are executed. These are most helpful in verifying that any processor specific optimizations that you hope to have active on processors supporting these instructions are actually working.

Cache and Memory Events

Most programs yield important performance gains from effective cache usage. All Intel processors provide events that monitor the caches built into the processors, which may be one to three levels of caches depending on the processor. In general, the L1 caches are separated into data and instruction caches while the L2 cache is unified (cache and data). In some processors, the L1 instruction cache may be complicated by having a decoded cache of micro-operations.

Not all cache misses stall the processor, and the processor does not necessarily stall from a cache miss. More than a trivial number of cache misses in a given time-span, however, almost certainly means that the processor will run out of work to do while data is being fetched.

L2 cache misses have a much greater impact on performance than L1 cache misses, and L2 cache problems are often easier to solve than L1 cache problems. Many L2 events are defined as *highly correlated*. Highly correlated event locations are accurate, but the event totals are not always accurate. Therefore, for highly correlated events, focus on the location where the event occurs, not the number of times it occurs. For more information about avoiding cache misses, see "Reducing the Working Data Set to Avoid Cache Misses" in the "Advice for All Processors" section of this appendix.

The DTLB Misses event indicates the number of *data translation look-aside buffer (DTLB)* misses. Typically, a high count for this event indicates that your program accesses a large number of data pages. If your program randomly accesses a great deal of sparse data, techniques to condense the data or access it in a more ordered fashion might improve performance. When you cannot improve the randomness and sparse nature of accesses in large database programs, use large page sizes to avoid DTBL misses.

Intel® Pentium® M Processors

The Intel Pentium M processor is most often found in laptop computers, and therefore has some additional event counters for power management. In conjunction with the Intel 855 Chipset Family and the Intel PRO/Wireless 2100 network connection, this processor is a key component of Intel Centrino™ mobile technology. The Intel Pentium M processor includes performance enhancements such as a power-optimized system bus, Micro-Ops Fusion, and Dedicated Stack Manager for faster execution of instructions at lower power.

With Pentium M processors, Intel modified and enhanced the performance monitoring counter mechanism. This new mechanism permits a wider variety of events and greater control over the selection of events to be monitored than was possible with earlier processors.

Pentium M Processor Events

Clockticks Event

In the Intel Pentium M processor, the Clockticks event counts the number of clockticks during which the processor was not in a halt state.

Branch and Call Events

The processor can count branches that were executed but not necessarily retired. Although *calls* are essentially branch instructions, the processor counts them separately. Since the Pentium M processor hardware can speculate a limited amount, the numbers for branch and call events could exceed the number of branches and calls that the program would logically seem to execute in a traditional sense.

Decoder Event

High numbers of this event reassure you that your compiler is doing a good job. The Decoder event (Decode ESP Additions Executed) counts the number of stack pointer (ESP) additions performed automatically by the decoder. High numbers of this event are good, since each automatic addition performed by the decoder saves a micro-op from the execution units.

If you are a compiler writer or assembly language programmer, select instructions whenever possible that implicitly use the ESP such as PUSH, POP, CALL, and RET. Doing so maximizes the number of ESP additions performed automatically by the decoder.

Fused Micro-Ops Event

High numbers of this event reassure you that your compiler is doing a good job. The Fused Micro-Ops event (Fused Micro-Ops Retired) counts the total number of fused micro-ops retired. *Fused micro-ops* are two micro-ops that are fused together and counted as one micro-op, but executed in parallel by two separate execution units. Fused micro-ops improve performance by reducing the number of overall micro-ops. This event is a component of the event ratio MicroOps Fusion Effectiveness, which can help compiler writers or assembly programmers measure the effectiveness of the code they generate.

Power Management Events

Intel SpeedStep® Technology events. The Pentium M processor has some special power consumption features, most of which are involved in conserving energy. Using these events allows you to understand the tradeoffs in battery conservation or power consumption versus performance.

Thermal Trips. One exception is thermal tripping, which enables the processor to escape self-destruction from overheating. Typical causes for overheating include a hardware failure such as a failed cooling fan or an environmental condition such as an out-of-range operating environment. The performance impact of thermal tripping is nontrivial. You should not expect to encounter systems that trip thermal protection, but if you are concerned this may be occurring then you can use the VTune analyzer to check.

Stall Events

Your program could fall into two traps, both with very severe performance penalties caused by the stalls they induce.

Floating-Point Assist (Micro-Code). Some floating-point operations implemented in hardware cannot complete without the use of *floating-point assist* microcode. Mathematical operations involving denormalized numbers generally invoke floating-point assist, which in turn causes delays. Heavy use of denormalized floating-point numbers can invoke lengthy delays in processing. Often the extra precision offered by denormalized numbers is not needed, and the use of *flush to zero mode* can result in significant performance gains. The Intel compiler offers a switch to enable flush to zero mode automatically for your application.

You can also set up this mode manually by using assembly code to rewrite the floating-point controls.

Self-Modifying Code Detected. If your application modifies instructions on-the-fly, processor optimizations to run standard code do not apply and many stalls due to self-modifying code can occur. If you are triggering such events, try redesigning your code to avoid these stalls if at all possible.

Pentium M Processor Event Ratios

Ratios have the advantage of being relative instead of absolute; the raw number of events occurring during application execution is not meaningful without checking its ratio in relation to other events. Event ratios enable more understanding about the performance of your application. The number of instructions retired alone tells you nothing unless you know how much time has elapsed. Combining time and instructions to create clocks per instructions (CPI) yields a very meaningful event ratio. This section details the most important event ratios for the Pentium M processor, summarized in Table B.1.

Table B.1   Key Pentium® M Processor Event Ratios

Event Ratio Name/Equation	Event Ratio Explanation
Clocks per Instructions (CPI) *Clockticks* (Non-sleep) / *Instructions Retired*	Quotient of the *Clickticks* counter divided by the *Instructions Retired* counter. General indication of optimization opportunities.
Branch Mispredictions Performance Impact (%) *(6*[Mispredicted Branch Instructions (Mispredicted at decoding)] + 20*[Mispredicted Branch Instructions (Mispredicted at execution)])*100/Clockticks*	Cost incurred for all types of mispredicted branch instructions. Represents a weighted combination of branches mispredicted at decoding and branches mispredicted at execution.
Micro-ops Fusion Effectiveness *Fused Micro-ops* Retired / *Micro-ops Retired*	Measures the gain incurred from micro-ops fusion.

Clocks Per Instruction (CPI) Event Ratio

The CPI is the quotient of the *Clockticks* counter divided by the *Instructions Retired* counter. For more information about interpreting this important event ratio, see "Evaluating the CPI Ratio" in the "Advice For All Processors" section of this appendix.

Branch Mispredictions Performance Impact (%)

This event ratio shows the cost incurred for all types of mispredicted branch instructions. It represents a weighted combination of branches mispredicted at decoding and branches mispredicted at execution.

(6*[Mispredicted Branch Instructions (Mispredicted at decoding)] +
20*[Mispredicted Branch Instructions (Mispredicted at execution)])*100/Clockticks

For more information about eliminating branch mispredictions, see "Optimizing Branch Predictability" in the "Advice for All Processors" section of this appendix.

Micro-ops Fusion Effectiveness: Fused Micro-ops Retired / Micro-ops Retired

This event ratio measures the gain incurred from micro-ops fusion. *Fused micro-ops* are two micro-ops that are fused together and counted as one micro-op, but executed in parallel by two separate execution units. Fused micro-ops improve performance by reducing the number of overall micro-ops. This event ratio can guide compiler writers or assembly programmers on the effectiveness of the code they generate.

Intel Pentium 4 and Intel Xeon™ Processors

The Intel Pentium 4 processor is found at work and at home. Intel introduced the Intel NetBurst® microarchitecture with the very first Pentium 4 processors, and later extended this microarchitecture with Hyper-Threading Technology (HT Technology) and then Intel Extended Memory 64 Technology (Intel EM64T). Both the unique microarchitecture and the new technologies offer a rich set of event counters to allow you to examine and tune the performance of your code on these systems.

The Intel Xeon processor is found in servers as well as workstations. The Intel Xeon processor and Intel Xeon processor MP both share core features and designs with Pentium 4 processors. All three processors are sufficiently alike for event registers to be generally the same, and all three offer Intel NetBurst microarchitecture, HT Technology, and Intel EM64T. These features involve the registers that are most unique to these processors.

The VTune analyzer hides the complexity of programming the event counting while providing access to the details if you wish to dig in at that level. The performance counters for these product families are programmed around three types of model-specific registers (MSR), 45 event selection control registers (ESCR), 18 counter configuration control registers (CCCR) and 18 counters. ESCRs describe a particular set of events that are to be recorded, and CCCRs bind ESCRs to counters and configure their operation. The relationship between these registers is quite complex, as are the rules for when they can be used together and when they cannot be used together.

When you specify more than one event to sample at a time, the VTune analyzer uses built-in algorithms to try to run your program as few times as possible to collect all the information you have requested, but an optimal solution is not easy. The VTune analyzer takes this complexity on itself, and each version of the program seems to get a little better at using more of the hardware efficiently.

The VTune analyzer also supports the new precise events capabilities of these processors and the advanced event counters for Hyper-Threading Technology.

Hyper-Threading Technology

Hyper-Threading Technology enables a processor to execute two parts of a software program in parallel so that your software can run more efficiently. With this technology, a single physical processor appears to be multiple logical processors. Each logical processor executes more than one *thread* or part of a program at a time.

Each Pentium 4 or Intel Xeon processor event has a Hyper-Threading Technology classification known as *thread specificity*. In most events, sampling is *thread-specific,* meaning that it can occur on a logical processor basis.

Thread-specific (TS) events are logical-processor-specific. A TS sample count measures the events that occurred on each logical processor. All logical processors are collected simultaneously, with the event interrupting on each logical processor to gather the IP address. Sample counts at a particular IP address are accurate at the process, module, function, or source-code level.

Thread-independent (TI) events are logical-processor-independent. A TI sample count measures the total events that occurred on the physical processor package. The event interrupt for thread-independent events is set on logical processor 0. Sample counts for the total system are accurate by physical processor package; however, sample counts at a particular IP address may not be accurate at the process, module, function, or source-code level. This is because sample counts on logical processor 1 at a particular IP address are counted on logical processor 0, which is very likely to be at a different IP address. The IP address on logical processor 0 is recorded as the location of the event. If you use TI events, be aware of this shortcoming when reviewing data below the system level.

Thread-Independent due to ESCR restriction (TI-E) events. Thread-independent-E (TI-E) events are logical-processor-specific; however, because an ESCR restriction prevents both logical processors from being sampled in the same run, these events are programmed to behave just like thread-independent events. If you use TI-E events, be aware of possible inaccuracies (as noted earlier for TI events) when reviewing data below the system level.

Pentium 4 and Intel Xeon Processor Events

Intel Xeon and Pentium 4 processor performance-monitoring events include the following categories:

- Key CPI-limiting Events
- Events That Indicate Coding Pitfalls
- Instruction Mix Events
- Bus Events
- Front-end Events
- Memory Events
- Stall Events

Key CPI Limiting Events

Table B.2 summarizes events that are involved in or result in clocks per instruction (CPI) ratios. A high CPI value (4 or more) indicates that instructions are requiring more cycles to execute than they should. CPI limiting events include:

■ Non-sleep and non-halted clockticks.

■ Instructions, loads, branches, and mispredicted branches retired.

■ 2nd-level cache load misses retired.

All events are *non-bogus*, meaning they do not include any instructions cancelled as part of a mispredicted branch path.

Table B.2   Pentium® 4 and Intel® Xeon™ Processor CPI-Limiting Events

Event Name	Thread Specificity	Event Explanation
Clockticks (Non-sleep Clockticks)	TS	The basic unit, recognized by each physical processor package in the Intel NetBurst® microarchitecture family of processors, to indicate the time spent by each physical processor package to execute a stream of instructions.
Non-halted Clockticks	TS	Clockticks during which a logical processor is neither in sleep nor halted.
Instructions Retired	TS	Instructions retired.
Loads Retired	TS	Retired load operations that were tagged at the front end.
Branches Retired	TS	Retired branch instructions.
Mispredicted Branches Retired	TS	Retired branch instructions that were mispredicted by the processor.
2nd-level Cache Load Misses Retired	TS	Retired instructions that attempted to load data from the 2nd-level cache, but did not find the data in that cache.

Counting clock cycles. The count of *cycles*, also known as clockticks, forms the basis for measuring how long a program takes to execute, and serves as part of efficiency ratios like cycles per instruction (CPI). On Pentium 4 and Intel Xeon processors, some processor clocks may stop "ticking" under certain circumstances:

The processor is *halted*, for example, during I/O. There may be nothing for the CPU to do while servicing a disk read request, and the processor may halt to save power.

The processor is *asleep*, either as a result of being halted for a while or as part of a power management scheme. Sleep has different levels. In deeper sleep levels, the processor's time-stamp counter stops counting.

The three event mechanisms for counting clock cycles to monitor performance are:

- *Non-halted clockticks*: cycles during which the specified logical processor is not halted.

- *Non-sleep clockticks*: cycles during which the physical processor is not in any of the sleep modes.

- *Time-stamp counter*: cycles during which the physical processor is not in deep sleep.

The first two metrics use performance counters. The time-stamp counter is accessed via the RDTSC instruction.

CPI event ratios of interest. For applications with a significant amount of I/O, these event ratios may be of interest:

- Non-halted CPI: *Non-halted clockticks/instructions retired* measures the CPI for the phases during which that CPU was being used.

- Non-sleep CPI: *Non-sleep clockticks/instructions retired* measures the CPI for the phases during which the physical package is not in any sleep mode.

- Nominal CPI: *Time-stamp counter ticks/instructions retired* measures the CPI over the entire duration of the program, including those periods during which the machine is halted while waiting for I/O.

Non-sleep Clockticks versus Non-halted Clockticks. The counts produced by the non-halted and non-sleep clockticks are equivalent, in most cases, if each physical package supports one logical processor. On processors that support Hyper-Threading Technology, each physical package can support two or more logical processors. Hyper-Threading Technology only provides two logical processors for each physical processor. While both logical processors can execute two threads simultaneously, one logical processor may be halted to allow the other logical processor to execute without sharing execution resources.

Non-halted clockticks can be qualified to count the number of processor clock cycles for each logical processor whenever that logical processor is not halted (it may include some portion of the clock cycles for that logical processor to complete a transition into a halted state).

Non-sleep clockticks are based on the filtering mechanism in the CCCR. They continue to increment as long as one logical processor is not halted.

The time stamp counter increments whenever the sleep pin is not asserted or when the clock signal on the system bus is active. It can be read with the RDTSC instruction. The difference in values between two reads (modulo $2^{**}64$) gives the number of clock cycles between those reads.

The time-stamp counter and non-sleep clockticks count should agree in practically all cases. However, if both logical processors in a physical package halt, most of the chip, including the performance monitoring hardware, powers down. In this situation, the time-stamp counter can continue incrementing because the clock signal on the system bus is still active, but non-sleep clockticks no longer increment because the performance monitoring hardware is powered down.

Clockticks (non-sleep Clockticks). The clockticks event, also referred to as *non-sleep clockticks*, counts the basic unit of time recognized by each physical processor package in the processors with Intel NetBurst microarchitecture. Non-sleep clockticks are used to indicate the time spent by each physical processor package to execute a stream of instructions. You can use this raw data collected by the VTune analyzer to compute various indicators. For example:

■ High ratios of Non-sleep Clockticks to Instructions Retired can indicate that the application code may be stalled in a physical processor package and needs recoding.

■ Non-sleep clockticks can be used to calculate the non-sleep CPI, which computes the inverse of the average throughput of a physical processor package while executing instructions.

If a physical processor package contains only one logical processor, non-sleep clockticks are essentially the same as non-halted clockticks.

Non-halted Clockticks. The non-halted clockticks event represents the number of clockticks during which a logical processor is neither in sleep nor halted. If a physical processor package contains more than one logical processor, the non-halted clockticks event enables the VTune analyzer to count the cycles during which a logical processor is actively executing instructions.

You can use non-halted clockticks to calculate the non-halted CPI, which computes the inverse of the average throughput of a logical processor while executing instructions.

Instructions Retired. This event counts the number of instructions retired. By default, the count does not include *bogus* instructions, where bogus refers to instructions canceled for being on a path that should not have been taken due to a mispredicted branch. This event is used in all per-instruction ratios.

By default, for this event, the mask bits are set to count instructions that are retired during a clock cycle. You can also use the VTune analyzer's Edit Event dialog box to alter the bit mask to change what this event measures. Set the mask bits as indicated in Table B.3 to count bogus or non-bogus instructions, and whether they are tagged via the front-end tagging mechanism.

Table B.3   Instructions Retired Event Mask

Event Mask Bits	Name	Description
Bit 0	NBOGUSNTAG	Non-bogus instructions that are not tagged
Bit 1	NBOGUSTAG	Non-bogus instructions that are tagged
Bit 2	BOGUSNTAG	Bogus instructions that are not tagged
Bit 3	BOGUSTAG	Bogus instructions that are tagged

Loads Retired. This event counts the number of retired load operations that were tagged at the front end. A Streaming SIMD Extensions (SSE) instruction or x87 instruction whose source operand is a memory address is counted once as a load and once as an SSE or x87 instruction, respectively.

Branches Retired. This event counts the number of retired branch instructions. This event is commonly used as part of a ratio, or to characterize your code. Branches do not necessarily reduce performance in your application, but mispredicted branches do.

By default, all the mask bits are turned on for this event. You can use the VTune analyzer's Edit Event dialog box to alter the bit mask to change what this event measures, as shown in Figure B.1.

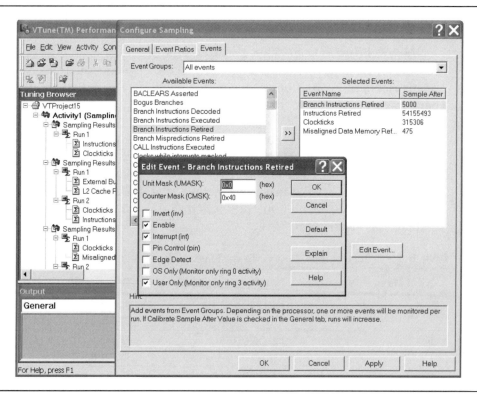

Figure B.1   Editing the Branches Retired Event Mask in the Edit Event Dialog Box

Specify one or more mask bits to count any combination of taken, not-taken, predicted, and mispredicted retired branches, as indicated in Table B.4.

Table B.4   Branches Retired Event Mask

Event Mask Bits	Name	Description
Bit 0	MMNP	Branch Not-Taken Predicted
Bit 1	MMNM	Branch Not-Taken Mispredicted
Bit 2	MMTP	Branch Taken Predicted
Bit 3	MMTM	Branch Taken Mispredicted

Mispredicted Branches Retired. This event counts the number of retired branch instructions that were mispredicted by the processor. In other words, the processor predicted that the branch would be taken, but it was not, or vice-versa. For more information about eliminating branch mispredictions, see *Optimizing Branch Predictability* in the *Advice for All Processors* section of this appendix.

2nd-level Cache Load Misses Retired. This event counts the number of retired instructions that attempted to load data from the second-level cache, but found that the data was not in that cache. The second-level cache on the Intel Pentium 4 processor contains both instructions and data. If the data is not found in the second-level cache, the processor looks in the third-level cache if one exists, or in main memory if one does not.

Second-level cache read misses reduce performance in your application because the processor must then access main memory, or third-level cache if it exists, both of which are many times slower than the second-level cache.

Since this event does not record all causes for second-level cache load misses, it should not be interpreted as a complete count. Therefore, use caution when dividing the number of events by the number of Loads Retired to obtain a miss ratio. You should also not divide it by 2nd-Level Cache Read References, because that event is a measure of bus activity.

To determine the number of second-level cache load misses per instruction, divide the number of these events by the number of Instructions Retired or Non-sleep Clockticks events.

Events That Indicate Coding Pitfalls

Table B.5 shows Pentium 4 and Intel Xeon processor events that indicate coding pitfalls.

Table B.5   Pentium® 4 and Intel® Xeon™ Processor Events that Indicate Coding Pitfalls

Event Name	Thread Specificity	Event Explanation
Split Loads Retired	TI-E SAAT_CR_ESCR1	Retired instructions that caused split loads
MOB Load Replays Retired (Blocked Store-to-Load Forwards Retired)	TS	Retired load instructions that experienced memory order buffer (MOB) replays because store-to-load forwarding restrictions were not observed
Streaming SIMD Extensions (SSE) Input Assists	TI	Streaming SIMD Extensions or Streaming SIMD Extensions 2 (SSE2) floating-point operations needing assistance to handle an exception condition
x87 Input Assists	TS	x87 input operands needing assistance to handle an exception condition
x87 Output Assists	TS	x87 operations needing assistance to handle an exception condition
64k Aliasing Conflicts	TS	64K-aliasing conflicts

Split Loads Retired. This event counts the number of retired instructions that caused split loads. A split load occurs when part of a data value that is read is located in one cache line and part in another.

Split loads reduce performance because they force the processor to read two cache lines separately and then paste the two parts of data back together. Reading data from two cache lines is several times slower than reading data from a single cache line, even if the data is not otherwise properly aligned.

Generally, the compiler aligns data to avoid placing values across cache-line boundaries. However, if you cast a C or C++ pointer (for example, when using SIMD intrinsics) to one of a larger data size or otherwise manipulate a pointer's address, your chance of crossing a boundary increases. You can reduce the likelihood of such splits by using the `__declspec(align(n))` attribute to align arrays or structures of small data values that you plan to access later as larger values via type casting.

MOB Load Replays Retired (Blocked Store-to-Load Forwards Retired). Intel Pentium 4 processors use a store-to-load forwarding technique to enable certain memory load operations to complete without waiting for the data to be written to the cache. In this case, the load operations are from an address whose data has just been modified by a preceding store operation.

This event counts the number of retired load instructions that experienced memory order buffer (MOB) replays because store-to-load forwarding restrictions were not observed. A MOB replay may occur for several reasons. This event is programmed to count those MOB replays caused by loads in which store-to-load forwarding is blocked.

To enable store-to-load forwarding, a dependent load *must* load data of the same size or smaller than the preceding store, and the starting address of the load and store *must* be the same.

Improving memory access patterns to observe these store-to-load forwarding restrictions significantly improves application performance on Pentium 4 and Intel Xeon processors. Using the Intel Compilers or the Microsoft Visual C++ compiler will eliminate the majority of cases of store-to-load forwarding violations.

Streaming SIMD Extensions (SSE) Input Assists. This event counts the number of Streaming SIMD Extensions (SSE) or Streaming SIMD extensions 2 (SSE2) floating-point operations needing assistance to handle an exception condition. This metric is often used in a per-instruction ratio. The VTune analyzer counts increments if one of the following conditions that require assistance occurs while executing either SSE or SSE2 operations:

■ The invalid, divide by zero, or denormal flags are not already set.

■ The hardware cannot handle the input data (mainly because of denormalized operands).

x87 Input Assists and x87 Output Assists. The x87 Input Assists event counts the number of occurrences of x87 input operands needing assistance to handle an exception condition. The x87 Output Assists event counts the number of x87 operations needing assistance to handle an exception condition. These metrics are often used in a per-instruction ratio.

The VTune analyzer counts the retirement of x87 instructions that required special handling. You can use this raw data to compute various indicators. For example, ratios of *Non-sleep Clockticks*, *Instructions Retired*, and *x87 Assists* can give you a good indication that the floating-point computation code in your application is stalled and in need of recoding.

64k Aliasing Conflicts. This event counts the number of 64K aliasing conflicts. A 64K aliasing conflict occurs when a virtual address memory location references a cache line that is modulo 64 kilobytes apart from another cache line that already resides in first-level cache. This is not a precise event, since 64K aliasing events are counted more than once per conflict.

Instruction Mix Events

It is possible to count the number of instructions executed in a particular program by the type of instruction thereby providing an idea of the mix of instruction types you are running. Table B.6 summarizes Pentium 4 and Intel Xeon instruction mix events. The instruction types that can be counted include:

- Floating-point SIMD instructions in single-precision extensions (SSE) and double-precision extensions (SSE2), operating on either packed (SIMD) or scalar data

- 64- and 128-bit integer SIMD instructions (also known as MMX instructions)

- x87 floating-point-unit (FPU) register instructions

All events are *non-bogus*, meaning they do not include any instructions cancelled as part of a mispredicted branch path.

Table B.6   Pentium® 4 and Intel® Xeon™ Instruction Mix Events

Event Name	Thread Specificity	Event Explanation
Packed Single-precision Floating-point Streaming SIMD Extension Instructions Retired	TS	Packed single-precision micro-ops retired. A packed Streaming SIMD Extensions (SSE) instruction consisting of multiple micro-ops may be counted more than once.
Packed Double-precision Floating-point Streaming SIMD Extension 2 (SSE2) Instructions Retired	TS	Packed double-precision micro-ops retired. A packed Streaming SIMD Extensions 2 (SSE2) instruction consisting of multiple micro-ops may be counted more than once.
Scalar Single-precision Floating-point Streaming SIMD Extension (SSE) Instructions Retired	TS	Scalar single-precision micro-ops retired. A packed Streaming SIMD Extensions (SSE) instruction consisting of multiple micro-ops may be counted more than once.
Scalar Double-Precision Floating-Point Streaming SIMD Extensions (SSE) Instructions Retired	TS	Scalar double-precision micro-ops retired. A packed Streaming SIMD Extensions (SSE) instruction consisting of multiple micro-ops may be counted more than once.
128-bit SIMD Integer Instructions Retired (128-bit MMX™ Instructions Retired)	TS	128-bit integer SIMD micro-ops retired. This does not include 128-bit SIMD data movement instructions.
64-bit MMX Instructions Retired (64-bit SIMD Integer Instructions Retired)	TS	64-bit integer SIMD micro-ops retired. This does not include 64-bit SIMD data movement instructions
x87 Instructions Retired	TS	x87 micro-ops retired. Fxch or floating-point load or store or register moves are not included. An x87 instruction consisting of multiple micro-ops may be counted more than once.
x87 and SIMD Register and Memory Moves Retired	TS	This event increments for each x87, MMX Instruction, streaming SIMD extensions (SSE or SSE2) micro-op related to load data, store data, or register-to-register moves, and is specified through the event mask for detection.

Bus Events

The connection between the processor and main memory requires transactions on the memory bus. The number and type of accesses can be counted not only for one processor, but for all agents on the bus. Buffers for optimizing accesses to the bus on the processor, called write-combining buffers, have counters as well. Refer to the VTune analyzer documentation for more information.

Front-End Events

Prior to the execution of instructions by the processor, the *front-end* of the processor must fetch and decode instructions. The decoder turns instructions into micro-operations (micro-ops). Simple instructions turn into single micro-operations, whereas complex ones can translate into many operations or even require a microcode assist. Compilers can optimize their output to maximize the performance of the decoders on the processor by avoiding a few pitfalls. Counters exist to help determine whether pitfalls are being encountered. Generally, these counters are of most interest to compiler writers but they can give guidance on compiler selection or tuning as well. The counting of micro-ops retired is explained below. For other front-end events, you may refer to information documented within the VTune analyzer for more information.

Micro-ops Retired. This event counts the number of micro-ops retired. An instruction is made up of one or more micro-ops. This event is often used in a per clock ratio.

By default, the mask bits for this event are set to count *non-bogus* micro-ops retired during a clock cycle (that is, executed to completion). *Bogus* refers to micro-ops canceled for being on a path that should not have been taken due to a mispredicted branch. You can use the VTune analyzer's Edit Event dialog box to alter the bit mask if you wish. Set the mask bits as indicated in Table B.7, to count bogus or non-bogus micro-ops.

Table B.7   Micro-Ops Retired Event Mask

Event Mask Bits	Name	Description
Bit 0	NBOGUS	Retired micro-ops that are non-bogus
Bit 1	BOGUS	Retired micro-ops that are bogus

Speculative Micro-ops events. These categories of events represent the percentage of speculative micro-ops being put in the micro-ops queue under various conditions. The *micro-ops queue* is the queue from which execution units get their work. *Speculative micro-ops* are micro-ops that might get executed. For example, micro-ops might be loaded into the queue for all execution paths, but only one path will be taken.

Memory Events

Interaction with memory is one of the most significant areas for tuning a program. The most important is cache activity, and the second area that can be very significant is translation look-aside buffers. A few of the key events are explained below. For other front-end events, you may refer to information documented within the VTune analyzer for more information.

DTLB Page Walks and DTLB Misses. These categories of events count occurrences related to *data translation look-aside buffer (DTLB)* misses. DTLB size and organization are processor design-specific. When the processor submits a 32-bit linear data address for cache lookup, the TLB first translates this address produced by the load or store unit into a 36-bit physical memory address.

A *DTLB miss* requires memory accesses to the OS page directory and tables in order to translate the 32-bit linear address. A DTLB miss does not necessarily indicate a cache miss.

To minimize DTLB misses, try to minimize the size of the data and locality so that:

■ Data spans a minimum number of pages.

■ The number of pages that the data spans is less than the number of DTLB entries.

ITLB Page Walks and ITLB Misses. These events count the number of page walk requests due to *instruction translation look-aside buffer (ITLB)* misses. ITLB size and organization are processor design-specific. When the processor submits a 32-bit linear instruction address for cache lookup, it is first submitted to the linear addressed instruction cache, also known as the *trace cache*. Upon a trace cache miss, the address is submitted to the ITLB, where the translation look-aside buffer (TLB) translates the resulting 32-bit linear address into a 36-bit physical memory address.

An *ITLB miss* requires memory accesses to the OS page directory and tables in order to translate the 32-bit linear address. An ITLB miss does not necessarily indicate a cache miss.

To minimize ITLB misses:

■ Make sure your application has good code locality.

■ Try to minimize the size of the source code and locality so that:

    – Instructions span a minimum number of pages.

    – The instruction span is less then the number of ITLB entries.

1st-Level Cache Load Misses Retired. This event counts the number of retired instructions that attempted to load data from the first-level cache, but did not find the data in that cache. The first-level cache on the Intel Pentium 4 processor contains data only, not instructions. If the data is not found in the first-level cache, the processor looks in the second-level cache. If the data is not found in the second-level cache, the processor looks in the third-level cache if one exists, or in main memory if one does not.

First-level cache misses usually reduce performance in your application because the processor must then access the second-level cache. Misses from the second-level cache are more severe than misses from the first-level cache. For more information about avoiding cache misses, see "Reducing the Working Data Set to Avoid Cache Misses" in the "Advice for All Processors" section of this appendix.

Stall Events

Stall events occur when the processor is forced to wait or even backtrack (machine clear). These events can be caused by synchronization methods that can be avoided. Refer to the next section under "Stall Event Ratios" for more information.

Pentium® 4 and Intel® Xeon™ Processor Event Ratios

Ratios have the advantage of being relative instead of absolute. A million conflicts may be very significant for an application that runs a short time while being insignificant for an application that takes an hour to run. Listed here, by category, are event ratios of interest for Pentium 4 and Intel Xeon processors. Notice that, for performance impact ratios, a value of 0.2 is usually considered low and a value of 2 is usually high.

Key CPI-Limiting Event Ratios

Table B.8 shows CPI-limiting event ratios on Pentium 4 and Intel Xeon processors. Using the latest Intel or Microsoft compilers can significantly improve CPI performance on Pentium 4 and Intel Xeon processors.

Table B.8   Pentium® 4 and Intel® Xeon™ Processor CPI-Limiting Event Ratios

Event Ratio Name/Equation	Event Ratio Explanation
Clockticks per Instructions Retired (CPI) *Clockticks (Non-sleep) / Instructions Retired*	High value indicates instructions are taking a high number of processor clocks to execute.
Non-Halted Clockticks per Instructions Retired (Non-Halted CPI) *Non-Halted Clockticks / Instructions Retired*	High value (1 is low, 5 is high) indicates that, over the current code region, instructions are taking a high number of processor clocks to execute.
Cycles per Retired Micro-ops *Clockticks (Non-sleep) / Micro-Ops Retired*	Non-sleep clockticks per micro-ops retired. An instruction is made up of one or more micro-ops.
2nd-Level Cache Load Misses per Instructions Retired *(2nd Cache Load Misses Retired / Instructions Retired)*	2nd-level cache load misses per instruction.
2nd-Level Cache Load Hit Rate *(100-((2nd Cache Load Misses Retired / Loads Retired)*100))*	Low value (89 is low, 99 is high), along with a high value for *2nd-Level Cache Load Miss Performance Impact*, indicates that second-level cache load misses are significantly decreasing performance[1].
Branch Prediction Rate *(100-((Mispredicted Branches Retired / Branches Retired)*100))*	Low value (75 is low, 95 is high), combined with a high value for the *Branch Mispredict Performance Impact* ratio, indicates that branch prediction misses are significantly decreasing performance or the branch misprediction rate is low.
Branch Mispredict Performance Impact *((Mispredicted Branches Retired * 20) / Clockticks)*100*	High value (0.2 is low, 2 is high), combined with a low value for the *Branch Prediction Rate* ratio, indicates that branch prediction misses are significantly decreasing performance or the branch misprediction rate is low[2].
Mispredicted Branches per Instructions Retired *Mispredicted Branches Retired / Instructions Retired)*	Mispredicted branches per instruction. High branch prediction misses can significantly decreased performance or indicate that the branch misprediction rate is low[2].

1   For systems without Hyper-Threading Technology enabled, the working data set should be targeted to fit into half of the first-level cache. When Hyper-Threading Technology is turned on, first-level cache is shared among the two threads. Therefore, the working data set should be targeted to fit into one-quarter to half of the first-level cache. The penalty for a second-level cache miss is much larger than for a first-level cache miss.

2   If the Branch Mispredict Performance Impact metric is low, this issue may not be worth further investigation.

Clockticks per Instructions Retired (CPI). A high value for this ratio indicates that, over the current code region, instructions are taking a high number of processor clocks to execute.

Clockticks (Non-sleep) / Instructions Retired

This could indicate a problem that requires further investigation (unless most instructions are predominately high-latency or coming from microcode ROM). For processors with Hyper-Threading Technology, this ratio measures the CPI for non-sleep phases where at least one logical processor in the physical package is in use. Clockticks are continuously counted on logical processors even if the logical processor is in a halted state (not executing instructions). This can impact the logical processors CPI ratio, because the Clockticks event continues to be accumulated while the Instructions Retired event remains unchanged. A high CPI value still indicates a performance problem; however a high CPI value on a specific logical processor could indicate poor CPU usage and not an execution problem. You can detect an execution problem better by using Non-Halted CPI. If your application is threaded, both CPI and Non-Halted CPI at all code levels are affected. To measure the CPI for phases where a specific logical processor is being used, see "Non-Halted CPI". For more information about interpreting this ratio, see "Evaluating the CPI Ratio" in the "Advice for All Processors" section of this appendix.

Non-Halted Clockticks per Instructions Retired (Non-Halted CPI). A high value for this ratio (1 is low, 5 is high) indicates that, over the current code region, instructions are taking a high number of processor clocks to execute.

Non-Halted Clockticks / Instructions Retired

This ratio could indicate a problem that requires further investigation, unless most instructions are predominately high-latency or coming from microcode ROM.

For processors with Hyper-Threading Technology, this ratio measures the CPI for code regions where logical processors are executing instructions. For the impact of parallel execution on CPI, see "Clockticks per Instructions Retired (Non-Sleep CPI)".

2nd-Level Cache Load Hit Rate. A low value for this ratio (89 is low, 99 is high), along with a high value for *2nd-Level Cache Load Miss Performance Impact*, indicates that second-level cache load misses are significantly decreasing performance. The working data set is too large to fit into the second-level cache.

(100-((2nd Cache Load Misses Retired / Loads Retired)*100))

Event Ratios that Indicate Coding Pitfalls

Table B.9 shows event ratios on Pentium 4 and Intel Xeon processors that indicate coding pitfalls. Using the latest Intel or Microsoft optimizing compilers can decrease or eliminate most of these coding pitfalls.

Table B.9   Pentium® 4 and Intel® Xeon™ Processor Event Ratios That Indicate Coding Pitfalls

Event Ratio Name	Event Ratio Explanation
64K Aliasing Conflicts *((64k Aliasing Conflicts*12) / Clockticks*100*	High value (0.2 is low, 2 is high) indicates that data could not be put in 1st-level cache because data already existed in the cache with the same values for bits 0–15 of the linear address.
x87 Input Assists Performance Impact *((x87 Input Assists*650) / Clockticks) *100*	Assists require micro-code assistance, which can cause a significant performance penalty. A value of 0.2 is low, 2 is high.
x87 Output Assists Performance Impact *((x87 Output Assists*650) / Clockticks) *100*	Assists require micro-code assistance, which can cause a significant performance penalty. A value of 0.2 is low, 2 is high.
Split Loads Performance Impact *((Split Loads Retired*30) / Clockticks) * 100*	High value (0.2 is low, 2 is high) indicates that data is being loaded across cache line boundaries, causing instructions to run 2x to 4x slower.
Store Forward Performance Impact *((MOB Loads Replays Retired*50) / Clockticks) *100*	High value (0.2 is low, 2 is high) indicates that store(s) could not be forwarded to load(s) because of alignment problems, which can cause stalls the length of the pipeline.

(continued)

Table B.9 Pentium® 4 and Intel® Xeon™ Processor Event Ratios That Indicate Coding Pitfalls *(continued)*

Event Ratio Name	Event Ratio Explanation
Streaming SIMD Extensions (SSE) Input Assists per Instructions Retired *(SSE Input Assists) / (Instructions Retired)*	Input assists require micro-code assistance, which causes a significant performance penalty.
Streaming SIMD Extensions (SSE) Input Assists Performance Impact *((SSE Input Assists*1300) / Clockticks) *100*	Input assists require micro-code assistance, which causes a significant performance penalty. A value of 0.2 is low, 2 is high.
Branch Misprediction per Branch Retired Instructions *Mispredicted Branches Retired/Branches Retired*	Rate of mispredicted branches.

64K Aliasing Conflicts. A high value for this ratio (0.2 is low, 2 is high) indicates that data could not be put in first-level cache because data already existed in the cache with the same values for bits 0–15 of the linear address.

((64k Aliasing Conflicts*12) / Clockticks)*100

The performance impact varies greatly depending on the scenario. The following cases give you some illustrative examples.

Case 1

No Hyper-Threading Technology.

64K aliasing caused by code mostly made up of loads.

Loads can compete with other loads for a load request buffer. If most of the 64K aliasing events derive almost entirely from loads (as opposed to loads intertwined with stores), the performance impact is rather insignificant. Move on to other performance issues.

Case 2

No Hyper-Threading Technology.

64K aliasing caused by code with loads mixed with stores.

Loads that need a request buffer can get "stuck" behind a store. The store has to retire and be removed from the cache before the load can proceed. If most of the 64K aliasing events are caused by code that has intertwined loads and stores, the performance impact is significant. Eliminate or reduce the impact of 64K aliasing.

Case 3 **Single processor with Hyper-Threading Technology enabled and turned ON**	Systems with Hyper-Threading enabled and turned ON may experience a significant increase in the number of 64K aliasing events. If the increase is in the 2x–4x range, fixing these cases does not achieve a meaningful speedup. However, fixing cases that experienced 5x or greater increase in 64K aliasing events does achieve a meaningful speedup. Cases 4 and 5 are two such cases.
Case 4 **Hyper-Threading Technology turned ON** **64K aliasing caused by thread stack conflicts in first-level cache**	Operating systems create thread stack spaces aligned on 1- or 2-Mb boundaries (which is modulo 64K). The processor encounters a 64K aliasing event when thread 1 has stack data in first-level cache and thread 2 accesses its stack data; that is, when the processor tries to put data from thread 2 into first-level cache. Eliminate or reduce the impact of 64K aliasing.
Case 5 **Hyper-Threading Technology turned ON** **64K aliasing caused by threads accessing data structures 64K apart**	Each thread is accessing data structures that happen to be 64K apart. Each time the two threads access data structures that are 64K apart, the processor incurs a 64K aliasing penalty. Eliminate or reduce the impact of 64K aliasing.

Instruction Mix Event Ratios

You can use instruction mix event ratios to help understand the instruction mix of your application. In each case, the integer instruction percentage is simply 100 minus the percentage of all other instruction types. Refer to the VTune analyzer documentation for more information on the available ratios.

Bus Event Ratios

Among bus events for Pentium 4 and Intel Xeon processors, *Percentage Prefetches* are of special interest to tuning an application that uses memory a great deal. Since prefetching is the most effective way to deal with hiding latency on unavoidable memory accesses, this ratio is used to measure the effectiveness of prefetching in your application. This ratio compares the number of bus transactions (excluding prefetched sectors) to the total number of all bus accesses (including prefetched sectors) for a processor.

Front-End Event Ratios

Table B.10 shows Pentium 4 and Intel Xeon processor front-end event ratios of interest.

Table B.10   Pentium® 4 and Intel® Xeon™ Processor Front-End Event Ratios

Event Ratio Name	Event Ratio Formula
TC Delivery Rate *(Trace Cache Deliver Mode*100) / Clockticks*	Low value (70 is low, 90 is high) indicates that the front end may not be delivering enough work for the execution units.
Trace Cache (TC) Miss Performance Impact *((Trace Cache Misses*20) / Clockticks) *100*	High value (0.2 is low, 2 is high) indicates that trace cache (TC) misses occurred because the working instruction set is too large to fit into the trace cache.

TC Delivery Rate. A low value for this ratio (70 is low, 90 is high) indicates that the trace cache (TC) is delivering micro-ops to the execution units, meaning that the front end may not be delivering enough work for the execution units.

(Trace Cache Deliver Mode*100) / Clockticks

You may be able to increase performance if no bigger bottleneck in the system exists such as bus bandwidth constraints. Collect data on additional events to characterize the trace cache delivery performance.

Trace Cache (TC) Miss Performance Impact. A high value for this ratio (0.2 is low, 2 is high) indicates that trace cache (TC) misses occurred while in deliver mode. This result means that the working instruction set is too large to fit into the trace cache, which can significantly decrease performance.

((Trace Cache Misses*20) / Clockticks)*100

For more information about avoiding cache misses, see "Reducing the Working Data Set to Avoid Cache Misses" in this appendix.

Memory Event Ratios

Table B.11 shows Pentium 4 and Intel Xeon processor memory event ratios. Using the latest Intel or Microsoft optimizing compilers can decrease or eliminate most of these problems. For more information about avoiding cache misses, see "Reducing the Working Data Set to Avoid Cache Misses" in this appendix.

Table B.11   Pentium® 4 and Intel® Xeon™ Processor Memory Event Ratios

Event Ratio Name	Event Ratio Formula
1st Level Cache Load Hit Rate (100-((1st-Level Cache Load Misses Retired / Loads Retired)*100))	Low value (85 is low, 95 is high), along with a high value for *1st-Level Cache Load Miss Performance Impact*, indicates that first-level cache load misses are significantly decreasing performance. The working data set is too large to fit into first-level cache.
1st Level Cache Load Miss Performance Impact ((1st-Level Cache Load Misses Retired*10) / Clockticks) *100	High value (0.2 is low, 2 is high), combined with a low value for *1st Level Cache Load Hit Rate*, indicates that first-level cache load misses are significantly decreasing performance. The working data set is too large to fit into first-level cache.
Split Stores Performance Impact ((Split Stores Retired*50) / Clockticks) * 100	High value (0.2 is low, 2 is high) indicates that data is being stored across cache line boundaries, causing instructions to run 2 to 4x slower.

Stall Event Ratios

Table B.12 lists Pentium 4 and Intel Xeon processor stall event ratios.

Table B.12   Pentium® 4 and Intel® Xeon™ Processor Stall Event Ratios

Event Ratio Name	Event Ratio Formula
Memory Order Machine Clear Performance Impact *((Memory Order Machine Clear*500) / Clockticks) *100*	High value (0.2 is low, 2 is high) indicates that the pipeline was cleared due to memory ordering issues.
Self-Modifying Code Clear Performance Impact *((Self-Modifying Code Clear*1000) / Clockticks) *100*	High value (0.2 is low, 2 is high) indicates that the pipeline was cleared due to self-modifying code issues.

Memory Order Machine Clear Performance Impact. A high value for this ratio (0.2 is low, 2 is high) indicates that the internal pipeline within the processor was cleared due to memory ordering issues, causing a negative impact on performance.

((Memory Order Machine Clear*500) / Clockticks)*100

This result usually indicates false sharing. *False sharing* occurs when two threads access distinct or independent data that fall into the same cache line.

Case 1 **False sharing due to synchronization issues.**	A synchronization lock from thread 1 and thread-private data from thread 2 occur on the same cache line. When one thread modifies the synchronization variable, the cache line becomes "dirty" and must be written out to each logical or physical processor. On a system employing Hyper-Threading Technology, this situation causes a cache-line eviction to keep the cache coherent. On a multiprocessor system, this situation causes a memory order machine clear violation. Both actions carry a significant performance penalty.
Case 2 **False sharing due to no synchronization handling.**	True sharing of a cache line takes place between two threads without synchronization. This is a program bug and also causes a significant performance penalty.

Self-Modifying Code Clear Performance Impact. Self modifying code is rarely used today, and modern processors incur a large penalty when encountering such programs. A high value for this ratio (0.2 is low, 2 is high) indicates that the pipeline was cleared due to self-modifying code issues, causing a negative impact on performance.

((Self-Modifying Code Clear*1000) / Clockticks)*100

Intel Itanium® 2 Processors

The Intel Itanium 2 processor is found in demanding enterprise and technical applications where high performance is essential. Often the size of the problems that need to be solved simply will not fit within the memory addressing capabilities of anything less than a 64-bit processor. The Itanium architecture includes 64-bit instruction capabilities as well as support for the IA-32 instruction set. High performance and large memory capabilities mean that the Itanium 2 processor makes use of a large, tightly integrated L3 cache that it tracks with L3 event counters. The Itanium 2 processor also tracks L2 and L1 caches with event counters, as other Intel processors do. Itanium processors also include special event counters to differentiate between the running of CISC and EPIC instructions (32-bit and 64-bit programs).

The Itanium 2 processor's Performance Monitoring Unit (PMU) offers counters in the form of four pairs of performance event monitoring registers. Each pair consists of a Performance Monitoring Configuration (PMC) register and a Performance Monitoring Data (PMD) register. The PMC selects the performance event being monitored and the PMD determines the sampling interval. The Itanium processor's PMU triggers sampling with *maskable* interrupts, unlike Pentium processors, which use *non-maskable* interrupts (NMI). Thus, Itanium processor samples do not occur in sections of the 64-bit kernel where interrupts are disabled.

For each individual event, you can use the VTune analyzer's Edit Events dialog box to access many of the bit settings for the PMU registers and to alter bit masks to reconfigure what the event measures.

Itanium 2 Processor Events

Intel Itanium 2 processor performance-monitoring events include the following categories:

- Basic Events: Clock cycles, retired instructions
- Branch Events: Branch prediction
- Instruction Execution Events: Instruction execution, data and control speculation, and memory operations
- Instruction Dispersal Events: Instruction decode and issue
- Stall Events: Stall and execution cycle breakdowns
- Memory Hierarchy: Instruction and data caches
- TLB Events: Instruction and data TLBs
- System Bus Events
- System Events: Operating system monitors
- RSE Events: Register Stack Engine

The Itanium architecture has an enormous number of counters in part to help compiler writers with the task of rapidly adopting to this new architecture. Because of that, only a fraction of the counters are of interest to application tuners since the compilers have already optimized the application for many of the areas that the VTune analyzer can analyze. You may refer to the documentation in the VTune analyzer for details on the available counters.

Basic Events

Table B.13 shows Itanium 2 processor basic events. These events pertain to the clock cycles and retired instructions that make up the CPI ratio. For more information about interpreting this ratio, see "Evaluating the CPI Ratio" in this appendix.

Table B.13   Itanium® 2 Processor Basic Events

Event Name	Maximum Increments per Cycle	Event Explanation
CPU Cycles	1	Clock cycles during which the CPU is not powered down or in a light HALTed state.
IA-32 Instructions Retired	2	IA-32 instructions retired.
Intel Itanium architecture to/from IA-32 ISA Transitions	1	Times the instruction set transitions from Itanium architecture to IA-32 or from IA-32 to Itanium architecture. Corresponds to the number of times the PSR.is bit toggles between 0 (Itanium architecture) and 1 (IA-32).
Itanium Instructions Retired	6	Retired Itanium architecture instructions, excluding hardware-generated RSE operations and instructions that were predicated off.

CPU Cycles. Counts the number of cycles the CPU is not powered down or in a light halted state. By constraining the PMC and PMD registers based on the currently executing instruction set, the CPU Cycles event can break out separate or combined Itanium processor-based/IA-32 cycle counts.

Itanium Instructions Retired. The Itanium processor (64-bit) retired instruction count, Itanium Instructions Retired, includes predicated `true` and `false` instructions and `nops`, but excludes hardware-generated Register Stack Engine (RSE) operations and instructions that were predicated off. This event includes all non-branch instructions that reached retirement with a `true` predicate and all branches regardless of predicate. MLX bundles are counted as no more than two instructions. This event is a sub-event of Retired Tagged Instructions.

Make sure that corresponding registers are set up so that nothing is constrained by the instruction address breakpoint (IABR) and PMC register combination (the power-up default is to have no constraints).

Branch Events

The Itanium 2 processor branch events can events help you track down various types of branch mispredictions. For branch events, retirement means that a branch was reached and committed regardless of its predicate value (`true` or `false`). Refer to the documentation in the VTune analyzer for details on the available counters. For more information about eliminating branch mispredictions, see "Optimizing Branch Predictability" in this appendix.

Memory Events

The Itanium 2 processor's memory hierarchy events are grouped as follows:

- L1 Instruction Cache and Prefetch Events
- L1 Data Cache Events
- L2 Unified Cache Events
- L3 Cache Events

The instruction and the data stream work through separate L1 caches. The L1 data cache is a write-through cache. A unified L2 cache serves both the L1 instruction and data caches, and is backed by a large unified L3 cache.

Figure B.2 shows key event monitors as they related to the Itanium 2 processor memory hierarchy.

The instruction fetch monitors distinguish between demand fetch (L1 Instruction Cache Reads and L2 Instruction Demand Fetch Requests) and prefetch activity (L1 Instruction Prefetch Requests and L2 Instruction Prefetch Requests). The amount of data returned from the L2 into the L1 instruction cache and the Instruction Streaming Buffer (ISB) is monitored by two events (L1 Instruction Cache Fills, and Bundle Pairs Written from L2 into FE). The *Instruction EAR Events* monitor counts how many instruction cache or ITLB misses are captured by the instruction event address register.

Since instruction cache and prefetch events occur early in the processor pipeline, they include events caused by speculative, wrong-path as well as predicated off instructions. Since the address range check is based on speculative instruction addresses, event counts can be inaccurate when the range checker is confined to address ranges smaller than the length of the processor pipeline. Please refer to the documentation in the VTune analyzer product package for details on the available counters.

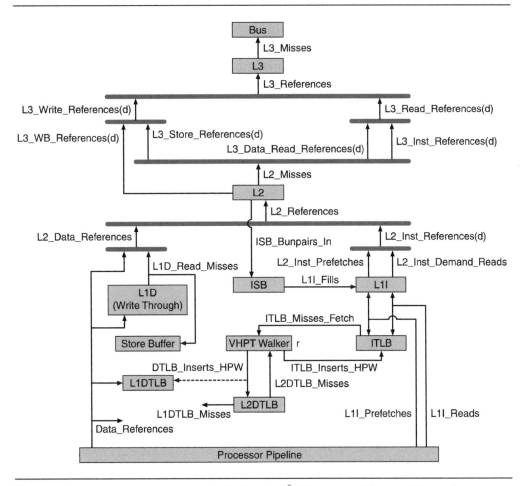

Figure B.2   Key Event Monitors in the Itanium® 2 Processor Memory Hierarchy

TLB Events

In addition to two levels (L1 and L2) of instruction and cache translation look-aside buffers (TLBs), the Hardware Page Walker provides a third-level of address translation; it is an engine that performs page look-ups from the virtual hash page table (VHPT).

The ITLB Misses Demand Fetch event and the L2DTLB Misses event count TLB misses. The *L1ITLB Hardware Page Walker Inserts* event and the Hardware Page Walker Installs to DTLB event count the number of instruction/data TLB inserts performed by the virtual hash page table walker.

Please refer to the documentation in the VTune analyzer for more details on the available counters.

Systems Events

The *Privilege Level Changes* event counts the number of privilege level transitions due to interruptions, system calls (`epc`), returns (demoting branch), and `rfi` instructions. The debug register match events count how often the address of any instruction or data breakpoint register (IBR or DBR) matches the current retired instruction pointer (Code Debug Register Matches derived event) or the current data memory address (Data Debug Register Matches Data Address of Memory Reference event). The *Number of srlz.i Instructions* event counts serialization instructions, which always should be minimized due to their high cost to execute. Please refer to the documentation in the VTune analyzer for more details on the available counters.

Itanium 2 Processor Event Ratios and Other Derived Events

Ratios have the advantage of being relative instead of absolute; the raw number of events occurring during application execution is not meaningful without checking its ratio in relation to other events. Event ratios enable more understanding about the performance of your application. The number of instructions retired alone tells you nothing unless you know how much time has elapsed. Combining time and instructions to create clocks per instructions (CPI) yields a very meaningful event ratio. Itanium 2 processor *derived events* are not measured in hardware directly, but can be *derived* by combining two or more measurable events most often as a ratio or otherwise by restricting a measurable event by its extension.

Basic Event Ratios

Table B.14 *shows* Itanium 2 Processor Basic Event Ratios. Instruction Execution Event Ratios for compiler writers are covered in the VTune analyzer online documentation.

Table B.14   Itanium® 2 Processor Basic Event Ratios

Event Ratio Name/Equation	Event Ratio Explanation
Average Cycles/Transition *CPU Cycles / (ISA Transitions * 2)*	Average cycles per instruction set (ISA) transition between Itanium and IA-32 architectures
Average IA-32 Instructions/Transition *IA-32 Instructions Retired / (ISA Transitions / 2)*	Average IA-32 Instructions per ISA transition between Itanium and IA-32 architectures
Average IA-64 Instructions/Transition *Itanium Instructions Retired / (ISA Transitions / 2)*	Average Itanium architecture instructions per ISA transition between Itanium and IA-32 architectures
IA-32 Instructions Per Cycle *IA-32 Instructions Retired / CPU Cycles*	Average IA-32 instructions per cycle during IA-32 code sequences
IA-64 Instructions Per Cycle *Itanium Instructions Retired / CPU Cycles*	Average Itanium architecture instructions per cycle during Itanium architecture instruction code sequences

Memory Event Ratios

Each level of caching and the translation lookaside buffers all have counters. Table B.15 lists the Itanium 2 processor L1 instruction cache and prefetch event ratios. Table B.16 lists the Itanium 2 processor L2 unified cache event ratios. Table B.17 lists the Itanium 2 processor L3 unified cache event ratios. L3 Unified Cache Event Ratios. Additionally, TLB Event Ratios and Frontside Bus Event Ratios are covered by the online documentation that comes with the VTune analyzer.

Table B.15   Itanium® 2 Processor L1 Instruction Cache and Prefetch Event Ratios

Event Ratio Name/Equation	Event Ratio Explanation
Instruction Streaming Buffer Lines In *Bundle Pairs Written from L2 into FE / 4*	Number of cache lines written from L2 (and beyond) into the front end
L1I Demand Miss Ratio *L2 Instruction Demand Fetch Requests /* *L1 Instruction Cache Reads*	L1 instruction cache demand miss ratio
L1I Miss Ratio *(L2 Instruction Demand Fetch Requests +* *L2 Instruction Prefetch Requests) /* *(L1 Instruction Cache Reads +* *L1 Instruction Prefetch Requests)*	L1 instruction cache miss ratio
L1I Prefetch Miss Ratio *L2 Instruction Prefetch Requests /* *L1 Instruction Prefetch Requests*	L1 instruction cache prefetch miss ratio
L1 Instruction Cache References *L1 Instruction Cache Reads +* *L1 Instruction Prefetch Requests*	L1 instruction cache reads and fills

Table B.16   Itanium® 2 Processor L2 Unified Cache Event Ratios

Event Ratio Name/Equation	Event Ratio Explanation
L2 Data Ratio *Data Read/Write Access to L2 / Requests Made To L2*	Ratio of data requests made to L2 unified cache
L2 Data Reads *Data Read/Write Access to L2* L2_DATA_READS	L2 data read requests
L2 Data Writes *Data Read/Write Access to L2* L2_DATA_WRITES	L2 data write requests
L2 Instruction Fetches *L2 Instruction Demand Fetch Requests+* *L2 Instruction Prefetch Requests*	Requests made to L2 due to demand instruction fetches
L2 Instruction References *L2 Instruction Demand Fetch Requests –* *"Just-In-Time" Instruction Fetch Hitting in* *and Being Bypassed from ISB +* *L2 Instruction Prefetch Requests*	Instruction requests made to L2 unified cache
L2 Miss Ratio *L2 Misses / Requests Made To L2*	Percentage of L2 misses
L2 Recirculate Attempts *Times a Recirculate Issue Was Attempted* *and Not Preempted +* *L2 OZQ Cancels (Set 2)*.DIDNT_RECIRC	Times the L2 issue logic attempted to issue a recirculate

Table B.17   Itanium® 2 Processor L3 Unified Cache Event Ratios

Event Ratio Name/Equation	Event Ratio Explanation
L3 Writeback Hits *L3 Writes*.L2_WB.HIT	L3 writeback hits
L3 Writeback Misses *L3 Writes*.L2_WB.MISS	L3 writeback misses
L3 Writeback References *L3 Writes*.L2_WB.ALL	L3 writeback references
L3 Data Read Hits *L3 Writes*. DATA_READ.HIT	L3 data read hits
L3 Data Miss Ratio (*L3 Reads*.DATA_READ.MISS + *L3 Writes*.DATA_WRITE.MISS) / (*L3 Reads*.DATA_READ.ALL + *L3 Writes*.DATA_WRITE.ALL)	L3 data miss ratio
L3 Data Read Misses *L3 Reads*.DATA_READ.MISS	L3 data read misses
L3 Data Read Ratio *L3 Reads*.DATA_READ.ALL / *L3 References*	Ratio of L3 references that are data read references
L3 Data Read References *L3 Reads*.DATA_READ.ALL	L3 data read references
L3 Instruction Hits *L3 Reads*. INST_FETCH.HIT	L3 instruction hits
L3 Instruction Misses *L3 Reads*.INST_FETCH.MISS	L3 instruction misses
L3 Instruction Miss Ratio *L3 Reads*.INST_FETCH.MISS / *L3 Reads*.INST_FETCH.ALL	Ratio of L3 instruction references that are L3 instruction misses
L3 Instruction Ratio *L3 Reads*.INST_FETCH.ALL / *L3 References*	Ratio of L3 references that are instruction references
L3 Instruction References *L3 Reads*.INST_FETCH.ALL	L3 instruction references

(continued)

Table B.17 Itanium® 2 Processor L3 Unified Cache Event Ratios *(continued)*

Event Ratio Name/Equation	Event Ratio Explanation
L3 Miss Ratio *L3 Misses / L3 References*	Percentage Of L3 misses
L3 Read Hits *L3 Reads*.DATA_READ.HIT	L3 read hits
L3 Read Misses *L3 Reads*.DATA_READ.MISS	L3 read misses
L3 Read References *L3 Reads*.DATA_READ.ALL	L3 read references
L3 Store Hits *L3 Writes*.DATA_WRITE.HIT	L3 store hits
L3 Store Misses *L3 Writes*.DATA_WRITE.MISS	L3 store misses
L3 Store References *L3 Writes*.DATA_WRITE.ALL	L3 store references
L3 Write Hits *L3 Writes* ALL.HIT	L3 write hits
L3 Write Misses *L3 Writes* ALL.MISS	L3 write misses
L3 Write References *L3 Writes* ALL.ALL	L3 write references

Intel XScale® Technology

Intel XScale® technology is commonly found in small power-sensitive devices like cell phones, PDAs, embedded systems and networking devices. Intel XScale technology is designed to optimize low power consumption and high-performance processing for a wide range of wireless and networking applications and a rich array of services. Various processors based on Intel® Personal Internet Client Architecture (Intel® PCA), Intel control plane processors, Intel I/O processors, and Intel network processors use the same processor core design featuring an implementation of the Intel XScale technology. A wide variety of Intel processors, therefore, share the event registers that Intel defined for Intel XScale technology.

Intel XScale Technology Events

For Intel XScale microarchitecture technology, the VTune analyzer supports the monitoring of two independent events. A set of Performance Monitoring Unit (PMU) registers monitor each event. Intel XScale microarchitecture-based processor events fall into these categories:

- Instruction Events: Instruction Cache Miss (0x0), Instruction Executed (0x7), Instruction TLB Miss (0x3), Undeliverable Instruction (0x1)

- Data Events: Data TLB Miss (0x4), Data Cache Access (0xa), Data Cache Miss (0xb), Data Cache Write-back (0xc)

- Branch Events: Branch Instruction Executed (0x5), Branch Misprediction (0x6)

- Stall Events: Data Cache Buffer Full Contiguous Counter (0x9), Data Cache Buffer Full Cycle Counter (0x8), Data Dependency Stall (0x2)

- Software Change Event: PC Software Changes (0xd)

Table B.18 summarizes the Intel XScale technology instruction, data, branch, stall, and software change events.

Table B.18   Intel XScale® Technology Events

Event Name	Number	Event Explanation
Instruction Events		
Instruction Cache Miss	0x0	Instruction cache miss requires fetch from external memory.
Undeliverable Instruction	0x1	Instruction cache cannot deliver an instruction. This can indicate an I-Cache miss or an ITLB miss. This event occurs in every cycle in which the condition is present.
Instruction TLB Miss	0x3	Instruction TLB miss.
Instruction Executed	0x7	Instruction executed.

Event Name	Number	Event Explanation
Data Events		
Data TLB Miss	0x4	Data TLB miss.
Data Cache Access	0xa	Data cache access, including misses and uncached accesses, but not including cache operations.
Data Cache Miss	0xb	Data cache miss, including uncached accesses, but not including cache operations.
Data Cache Write-Back	0xc	Data cache write-back. This event occurs once for each ½ line (four words) written back from the cache.
Branch Events		
Branch Instruction Executed	0x5	Branch instruction executed; branch may or may not have changed program flow. (Counts only B and BL instructions, in both ARM and Thumb mode.)
Branch Misprediction	0x6	Branch mispredicted. (Counts only B and BL instructions, in both ARM and Thumb mode.)
Stall Events		
Data Cache Buffers Full Contiguous Counter	0x9	Stall occurred because the data cache buffers are full. This event occurs once for each contiguous sequence of this type of stall, regardless of the length of the stall.
Data Cache Buffers Full Cycle Counter	0x8	Stall occurred because the data cache buffers are full. This event occurs in every cycle in which the condition is present.
Data Dependency Stall	0x2	Stall due to data dependency. This event occurs in every cycle in which the condition is present.
Software Change Event		
PC Software Changes	0xd	Software changed the PC.

The software change event for Intel XScale technology-based processors, as shown in Table B.18, occurs any time the PC is changed by software and no mode change occurs. For example:

■ A `mov` instruction with PC as the destination triggers this event.

■ Executing a `swi` from user mode does not trigger this event because it incurs a mode change.

The following are counted:

```
b, bl, blx
mov[s] pc, Rm
ldm Rn, {Rx, pc}
ldr pc, [Rm]
pop {pc}
```

The following is not counted:

```
mcr p<cp>, 0,pc, ...,
```

The count also does not increment when an event occurs and the PC changes to the event address. For example:

```
IRQ, FIQ, SWI
```

Index

66 *As the pace of technology introduction increases, it's difficult to keep up. Intel Press has established an impressive portfolio. The breadth of topics is a reflection of both Intel's diversity as well as our commitment to serve a broad technical community.*

I hope you will take advantage of these products to further your technical education. **99**

Patrick Gelsinger
Senior Vice President
Intel Corporation

**Turn the page to learn about titles
from Intel Press for system developers**

Practical Advice for Writing Faster, More Efficient Code

Intel® Integrated Performance Primitives
How to Optimize Software Applications Using Intel® IPP
By Stewart Taylor
ISBN 0-9717861-3-5

Intel® Integrated Performance Primitives (Intel® IPP) is a software library for application developers that increases performance from Intel's latest microprocessors. Incorporating these functions into your code provides time-to-market advantages while reducing the overall cost of development. The lead developer of Intel IPP explains how this library gives you access to advanced processor features without having to write processor-specific code.

Introducing the many uses of Intel IPP, this book explores the range of possible applications, from audio processing to graphics and video. Extensive examples written in C++ show you how to solve common imaging, audio/video, and graphics problems.

You will learn how to:
● Become proficient using the Intel IPP library and application programming interface
● Apply Intel IPP to improve performance and speed up the development of your applications
● Solve common application problems using Intel IPP

❝ *Filled with comprehensive real-world examples. I'm recommending this book to my entire software team.* ❞

*Davis W. Frank,
Software Program Manager,
palmOne, Inc.*

● *The Software Optimization Cookbook*
High-performance Recipes for the Intel® Architecture
By Richard Gerber
ISBN 0-9712887-1-2

Through simple explanations and C/C++ code samples, a former Intel trainer explains the techniques and tools you can use to improve the performance of applications for Intel® Pentium® III and Pentium 4 processors. This book also includes tested food recipes for those long nights of coding and testing.

Use performance tools and tested concepts to improve applications

● *The Software Vectorization Handbook*
Applying Multimedia Extensions for Maximum Performance
By Aart J.C. Bik
ISBN 0-9743649-2-4

The growing popularity of multimedia extensions has renewed an interest in vectorizing compilers. *The Software Vectorization Handbook* provides a detailed overview of compiler optimizations that convert sequential code into a form that exploits multimedia extensions. Compiler engineers and programmers of scientific, engineering, and multimedia applications will learn the latest techniques for improving software performance. The primary focus is on the C programming language and multimedia extensions to the Intel® Architecture, although most conversion methods are easily generalized to other imperative programming languages and multimedia instruction sets.

❝ *Rarely have I seen a book of such a great value to compiler writers and applications developers alike...* **❞**

Robert van Engelen,
Assistant Professor,
Florida State University

● ***Programming with Hyper-Threading Technology***
How to Write Multithreaded Software for Intel® IA-32 Processors
By Richard Gerber and Andrew Binstock
ISBN 0-9717861-4-3

For software developers who are accustomed to single-threaded programs, this book helps you to make a seamless transition to multithreaded code. You will learn how to use Hyper-Threading Technology to maximize processor throughput, efficiency, and parallelism. It is a practical, hands-on volume with immediately usable code examples that enable readers to quickly master the necessary building blocks.

66 *...comprehensive and filled with illustrative examples about parallel programming.* **99**

Oleksiy Danikhno,
Development Director,
A4Vision, Inc.

● ***Programming with Intel® Wireless MMX™ Technology***
A Developer's Guide to Mobile Multimedia Applications
By Nigel C. Paver, Bradley C. Aldrich, and Moinul H. Khan
ISBN 0-9743649-1-6

Learn how to incorporate Intel® Wireless MMX™ technology into mobile and handheld software applications. Intel experts give advice on how to optimize applications, port code from the desktop, and implement algorithmic techniques that yield the best performance. Along with complete information about the instruction set, the book provides an overview of the tools that ease application development.

66 *...the right mix of topics along with step-by-step code examples for real-world applications.* **99**

Eric Hyche,
Software Development
Engineer,
RealNetworks, Inc.

Special Deals, Special Prices!

To ensure you have all the latest books
and enjoy aggressively priced discounts,
please go to this Web site:

www.intel.com/intelpress/bookbundles.htm

Bundles of our books are available,
selected especially to address the needs
of the developer. The bundles place
important complementary topics at
your fingertips, and the price for a
bundle is substantially less than
buying all the books individually.

About Intel Press

Intel Press is the authoritative source of timely, technical books to help software and hardware developers speed up their development process. We collaborate only with leading industry experts to deliver reliable, first-to-market information about the latest technologies, processes, and strategies.

Our products are planned with the help of many people in the developer community and we encourage you to consider becoming a customer advisor. If you would like to help us and gain additional advance insight to the latest technologies, we encourage you to consider the Intel Press Customer Advisor Program. You can **register** here:

www.intel.com/intelpress/register.htm

For information about bulk orders or corporate sales, please send email to
bulkbooksales@intel.com

Other Developer Resources from Intel

At these Web sites you can also find valuable technical information and resources for developers:

developer.intel.com	general information for developers
www.intel.com/IDS	content, tools, training, and the Intel® Early Access Program for software developers
www.intel.com/netcomms	solutions and resources for networking and communications
www.intel.com/software/products	programming tools to help you develop high-performance applications
www.intel.com/technology/itj	Intel Technology Journal
www.intel.com/idf	worldwide technical conference, the Intel Developer Forum

INTEL
PRESS